LINCOLN'S PEACE

LINCOLN'S PEACE

THE STRUGGLE TO END THE AMERICAN CIVIL WAR

Michael Vorenberg

Alfred A. Knopf · New York 2025

A BORZOI BOOK
FIRST HARDCOVER EDITION
PUBLISHED BY ALFRED A. KNOPF 2025

Published by Alfred A. Knopf, a division of Penguin Random House LLC, 1745 Broadway, New York, NY 10019.

Maps by Erin Greb Cartography

Knopf, Borzoi Books, and the colophon are registered trademarks of Penguin Random House LLC.

Library of Congress Cataloging-in-Publication Data
Names: Vorenberg, Michael, [date] author.
Title: Lincoln's peace : the struggle to end the
American Civil War / Michael Vorenberg.
Description: First edition. | New York : Alfred A. Knopf,
2025. | Includes bibliographical references.
Identifiers: LCCN 2024020185 (print) | LCCN 2024020186 (ebook) |
ISBN 9781524733179 (hardcover) | ISBN 9780525434825 (trade paperback) |
ISBN 9781524733186 (ebook)
Subjects: LCSH: Lincoln, Abraham, 1809–1865. | United States—History—
Civil War, 1861–1865—Peace. | United States—History—Civil War, 1861–
1865—Influence. | United States—Politics and government—1861–1865. |
United States—Politics and government—1865–1877.
Classification: LCC E459 .V67 2025 (print) | LCC E459 (ebook) |
DDC 973.7—dc23/eng/20241028
LC record available at https://lccn.loc.gov/2024020185
LC ebook record available at https://lccn.loc.gov/2024020186

penguinrandomhouse.com | aaknopf.com

Printed in the United States of America

2 4 6 8 9 7 5 3 1

The authorized representative in the EU for product safety and compliance is Penguin Random House Ireland, Morrison Chambers, 32 Nassau Street, Dublin D02 YH68, Ireland, https://eu-contact.penguin.ie.

For Katie and Emma

War is an episode, a crisis, a fever the purpose of which is to rid the body of fever. So the purpose of a war is to end the war.

William Faulkner, *A Fable*

CONTENTS

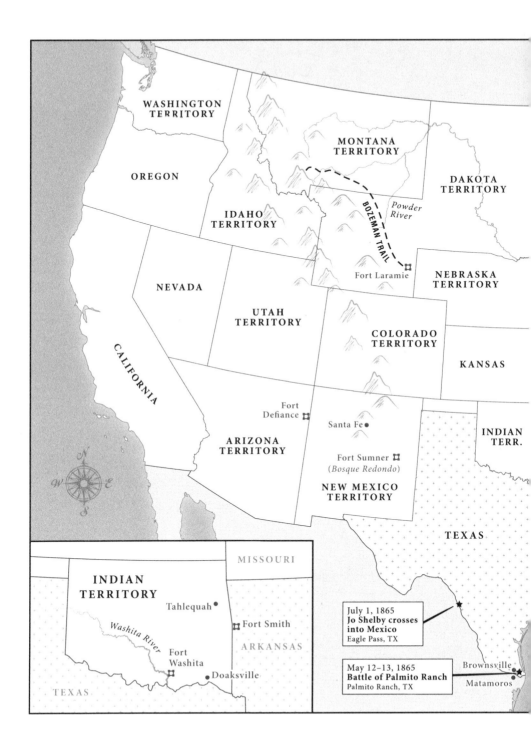

WASHINGTON
TERRITORY

MONTANA
TERRITORY

DAKOTA
TERRITORY

OREGON

IDAHO
TERRITORY

*Powder
River*

BOZEMAN TRAIL

Fort Laramie

NEBRASKA
TERRITORY

NEVADA

UTAH
TERRITORY

COLORADO
TERRITORY

KANSAS

CALIFORNIA

Fort
Defiance

Santa Fe

INDIAN
TERR.

ARIZONA
TERRITORY

Fort Sumner
(Bosque Redondo)

NEW MEXICO
TERRITORY

TEXAS

N
W   E
S

INDIAN
TERRITORY

MISSOURI

Tahlequah

Washita River

Fort Smith

ARKANSAS

Fort
Washita

Doaksville

TEXAS

July 1, 1865
**Jo Shelby crosses
into Mexico**
Eagle Pass, TX

May 12–13, 1865
Battle of Palmito Ranch
Palmito Ranch, TX

Brownsville

Matamoros

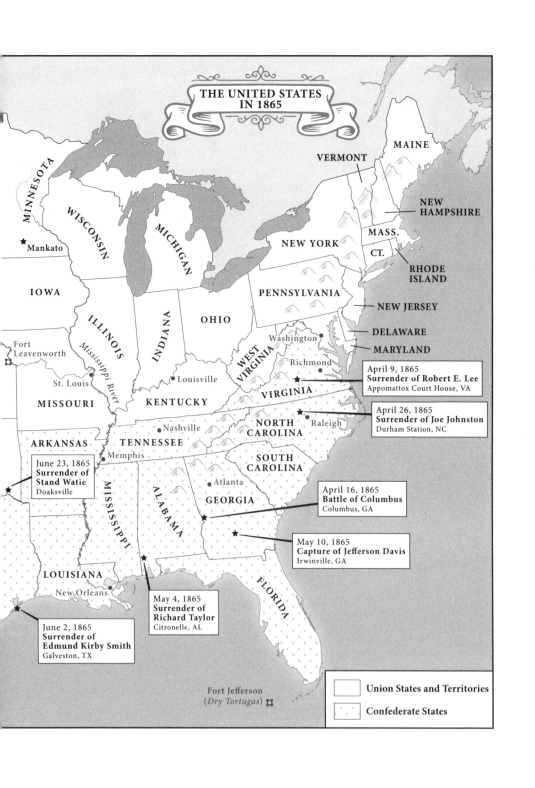

THE UNITED STATES IN 1865

MAINE

VERMONT

NEW HAMPSHIRE

MASS.

CT.

RHODE ISLAND

NEW YORK

NEW JERSEY

DELAWARE

MARYLAND

MINNESOTA

WISCONSIN

MICHIGAN

★ Mankato

IOWA

ILLINOIS

INDIANA

OHIO

PENNSYLVANIA

Washington

Richmond

WEST VIRGINIA

Fort Leavenworth

Mississippi River

• Louisville

St. Louis

MISSOURI

KENTUCKY

VIRGINIA

April 9, 1865
Surrender of Robert E. Lee
Appomattox Court House, VA

• Nashville

NORTH CAROLINA

• Raleigh

April 26, 1865
Surrender of Joe Johnston
Durham Station, NC

ARKANSAS

TENNESSEE

• Memphis

SOUTH CAROLINA

June 23, 1865
Surrender of Stand Watie
Doaksville

★

MISSISSIPPI

ALABAMA

• Atlanta

GEORGIA

April 16, 1865
Battle of Columbus
Columbus, GA

May 10, 1865
Capture of Jefferson Davis
Irwinville, GA

LOUISIANA

New Orleans

FLORIDA

May 4, 1865
Surrender of Richard Taylor
Citronelle, AL

★

June 2, 1865
Surrender of Edmund Kirby Smith
Galveston, TX

Fort Jefferson
(Dry Tortugas) 🏰

Union States and Territories

Confederate States

PROLOGUE

Endings and Beginnings

... to make an end is to make a beginning.
The end is where we start from.

T. S. Eliot, "Little Gidding" (1942), *Four Quartets*[1]

ON APRIL 9, 1865, at Appomattox Court House, Virginia, Ulysses S. Grant, lieutenant general in command of all U.S. armies, accepted the surrender of Confederate General Robert E. Lee and his Army of Northern Virginia. The next day, the *New York Herald*, the most widely circulated newspaper in the United States, blared out on the front page: "The End."[2] The Civil War was over.

One of the U.S. officers there at the end was Lewis Addison Grant. He was not related to Ulysses Grant but served under him and admired him greatly. He also idolized William Tecumseh Sherman, Ulysses Grant's best-known lieutenant. Lewis Grant named one of his sons Ulysses Sherman Grant.

Lewis Grant was a war hero. Of the million U.S. veterans of the Civil War, only about a thousand were awarded a Congressional Medal of Honor. Grant was one of them. He was a lawyer by training, not a soldier. He grew up in Vermont, thought he would be a schoolteacher, but then became a lawyer, joining a practice in southern Vermont just before the Civil War broke out in April 1861. He enlisted in the army right away and quickly rose through the ranks. By 1863, he commanded a brigade. By 1864, he was a major general.

Name a major battle in the eastern theater, and you'll find Lewis Grant there: Fredericksburg, Gettysburg, Cold Harbor, Cedar Creek. He was part of the final assault on Petersburg on April 2, 1865. By the end of the next day, both Petersburg and Richmond, the Confederate capital, had fallen. He joined the pursuit of Lee's army as it headed into the interior of Virginia. He fought at Sailor's Creek, the last major battle against Lee's army. And on April 9, he stood silent and proud outside the home of Wilmer McLean at Appomattox Court House while, inside, Lee surrendered to Ulysses Grant.

As far as Lewis Grant was concerned, the war was over, and he had been there at the end. A few weeks after Appomattox, he mustered out. He moved west, settling in Moline, Illinois, where he established a successful law practice and began investing in land in Iowa and Minnesota. A year after Appomattox, by which point more than 90 percent of the U.S. volunteers had mustered out of the army, he received an offer from his old commander, Ulysses Grant, to lead a regiment in the regular army. If he accepted, he would become a career officer. He said no. He chose law over soldiering.

For two decades after Appomattox, Lewis Grant practiced law, invested in land, and dabbled in politics, becoming a familiar face in Republican meetings across the Midwest. He helped Benjamin Harrison get elected president in 1888. Harrison rewarded the lawyer with an offer of appointment—in the War Department. He was to be the assistant secretary, working under a fellow Vermonter, Redfield Proctor. Grant accepted. Maybe he thought the job would be easy. The nation was not at war, after all. Maybe he could not say no to the president. Whatever his reasons, in 1889 he found himself if not *at* war, employed *by* war.

Legal rather than martial skill was called for now. His adversaries were not armed combatants but paper queries, claims, and applications. His comrades were petty bureaucrats. His weapons were mind-numbing legal manuals—adjutant general reports, army circulars, digests of pension office decisions. He must have longed for the days when an army just tried to kill him directly.

Sometime in 1890, twenty-five years after Appomattox, a case landed on Grant's desk that brought him back to the end of the

Civil War. Or, more precisely, it launched his quest to find the end of the war, the *real* end.

An army veteran named John Barleyoung had lodged a protest after being denied a Civil War pension. The grounds for the rejection seemed straightforward enough: Barleyoung had not served in the Civil War. He had enlisted in the 13th New York Infantry on April 19, 1866, more than a year after Lee's surrender. But Barleyoung contended that the Civil War had not ended by that time. The claim was bizarre. Lewis Grant had been at Appomattox in 1865 and seen the end. The soldier in him was ready to toss the file. The lawyer in him stopped short. When, precisely, *had* the Civil War ended? The question sent him burrowing into the records. He assumed that he would find the answer quickly.

Instead, the search took months. Grant uncovered a history at odds with the end of the war as he and other Americans remembered it. Barleyoung was still not going to get a pension. But that was almost beside the point. The more important thing was this: Barleyoung's claim was not crazy. The Civil War had indeed lasted for at least a year beyond Appomattox. The evidence was everywhere, but the U.S. government, along with most Americans, had stuck with a fiction: the Civil War had ended in the spring of 1865.

Grant set down his findings in a long report to his boss, Secretary of War Proctor. It began: "When did the war of the Rebellion begin, and when did it end?"

As for the beginning of the war, Grant was fine with a start date in mid-April 1861. He did not get bogged down in the quibbling over which day in April the war started. Some said April 12, because that was when the Confederates began shelling Fort Sumter in Charleston Harbor. That date made Confederates responsible for the war: they fired the first shot. But, as Grant knew, a war did not have to ensue at that point; many in the North and South still hoped to arrange some sort of compromise. That hope vanished on April 15, when President Abraham Lincoln responded to the attack on Fort Sumter with a call for 75,000 troops to put down insurrectionaries in the seven states that had seceded and created the "Confederate States of America." For Lewis Grant, April 15 was the clear start date. He then moved on to the end date, no doubt thinking that this, too, would be obvious.

Right away he saw a problem. April 9, 1865, the end date that Grant had assumed—he had been at Appomattox, after all—simply did not work. The first War Department manuals that Grant examined had the end date as May 1, 1865. For example, in an order published in 1890, the department had ruled that promotions were valid only if they had been awarded to those in the regular army (that is, career soldiers) or to volunteers who had served "during the War of the Rebellion." When he investigated what "during the War of the Rebellion" meant, he found that, according to the War Department, the Civil War ended on May 1, 1865.[3] What happened on May 1 to end the war? Grant wondered. He found no answer. He concluded—rightly—that the War Department had been winging it. The claim of May 1 as the end date was completely arbitrary, Grant told Secretary of War Proctor: "I have made a thorough search, and examined all the data and authority (if authority it can be called) . . . and I do not find that the claim is justified in fact." The War Department had simply found May 1 "to be as convenient a date as any, inasmuch as it was about that time that the rebel armies surrendered." Yet, Grant continued, even a cursory glance at events after that date revealed that "as a matter of fact the war did not end May 1, 1865."

As evidence, Grant made a list of some wartime events after May 1: the capture of Jefferson Davis, president of the Confederacy (May 10); a battle on the Texas-Mexico border (May 12–13); the surrender of Confederate General Edmund Kirby Smith's forces west of the Mississippi River (June 2).

Then there were the events far from the battlefields that also indicated a continuation of war beyond May 1. For example, military trials of civilians are supposed to take place only in a time of war. Yet such trials occurred long after the Confederate army surrenders. Most famously, it was a military tribunal in July 1865 that condemned the civilians responsible for the assassination of Abraham Lincoln. Lewis Grant reasoned from the persistence of military trials that the nation must have been at war long after May 1865. Grant also found many instances during the summer and fall of 1865 when the U.S. government had suspended writs of habeas corpus. Here was more evidence of war's continuation, Grant wrote, because the

Constitution declared that the writ could not be suspended "except in case of rebellion or invasion."[4]

At some point in scouring War Department records, Grant discovered that not everyone had used May 1 as the end date. Only ten years earlier, in 1880, a lawyer for the War Department had settled on July 22, 1865. What happened on *that* day? Grant asked himself. Soon he had an answer: Ulysses S. Grant had issued a report with that date in which he said that war operations had concluded. The report was nearly a hundred pages long, but all that really mattered was the last paragraph, which was quoted by every major newspaper. "The supremacy of law over every foot of territory belonging to the United States" had been restored, the general had declared. There was now "hope for perpetual peace and harmony with that enemy whose manhood, however mistaken the cause, drew forth such herculean deeds of valor."[5]

Perhaps Lewis Grant recalled reading these words in 1865; maybe he read them again now, twenty-five years later. Did the words stir fond memories of battlefield glory and a celebratory end of war? If so, it would have taken only a moment for the cold eye of history to cut through his nostalgia. He knew that in July 1865, when Ulysses Grant said farewell to war, the U.S. Army did not control "every foot of territory." Enemies continued to attack U.S. soldiers and civilians. "Perpetual peace"? Hardly. "All through 1865, and late into 1866," Lewis Grant wrote in his report, "armed forces held control of different States and communities."[6] He might have added a fact he surely knew well, that in 1868, when Ulysses Grant first ran for president—and won—the *absence* of peace was the theme of his campaign. "Let Us Have Peace" was his slogan. So how long beyond Ulysses Grant's final report of July 1865 did the Civil War last? Lewis Grant pressed on in his search for the end.

Eventually he found it, or at least an acceptable version of it: August 20, 1866. On that date, President Andrew Johnson had issued a proclamation declaring that "the insurrection is at an end." Johnson had made a similar proclamation back on April 2, 1866, but excepted Texas, where warring continued. The August 20 proclamation covered even Texas. "Peace, order, tranquility, and civil authority now exist in and throughout the whole of the United States of America," read Johnson's declaration. Johnson's opponents didn't buy it. They responded, as one commentator wrote, by asking: "Will the President tell us in what part of the South the war has ceased and in what place peace is really restored?"[7]

Lewis Grant knew about the opposition that Johnson had faced from those who refused to pretend that the war was over. But upon closer examination, he learned that Congress had officially approved the Johnson end date, though it had done so as part of a mundane appropriations bill that few congressmen had actually read. The U.S. Supreme Court used that bill in conjunction with the Johnson proclamation to rule that August 20, 1866, was indeed the end date. The Civil War did not end at Appomattox, Grant concluded. It had ended on August 20, 1866.

Or maybe not.

In the summer of 2003, I came across the report written by Lewis Grant. At the time, I considered myself a Civil War historian, but Grant's research made a mockery of my supposed expertise. I had no idea how complicated the story of the end of the Civil War was. In the courses that I taught, I had treated Lee's surrender at Appomattox as the endpoint, though sometimes I noted that it would take another six weeks or so before the rest of the Confederate armies surrendered. This was the version of history that I had learned as a child. It had been reinforced every time I heard a historian (including myself) use "after Appomattox" to refer to the period after the Civil War. It was the version celebrated in Jay Winik's bestselling book of 2001, *April 1865: The Month That Saved America.* The book centered on events at Appomattox, and though it acknowledged that the Civil War did not end there, it still offered a triumphant tale of enemies opting for peace instead of war, with the rebellion coming to a close within weeks of the legendary meeting between Grant and Lee. I liked the book. I knew that sectional strife and racial violence had continued well beyond Appomattox, but I somehow had no problem holding on to the notion that peace had been made at the McLean house.

Beneath my acceptance of an Appomattox ending hid a deeper assumption, unarticulated and unexamined. I assumed that wars must have endings.

How such a notion could still be rattling around my head in 2003 remains a mystery to me. Didn't I know better? As a child in the 1970s, I had witnessed the multiple endings and restarts of the U.S. war in Vietnam. I knew then and later that the war did not end neatly. Yet somehow I kept that knowledge from disrupting my fundamental faith that every war came to an end. In May 2003, just a month or so before I came upon the report about the end date of the Civil War written by Lewis Grant, I had watched the television clip of President George W. Bush declaring that the U.S. war with Iraq was over. That's what he seemed to be saying, anyway. It became known as his "Mission Accomplished" speech—not because he used the phrase, but because a banner declaring "Mission Accomplished" hung behind him as he announced on the deck of the USS *Abraham Lincoln* that "combat operations" in Iraq were over. Many at the time accepted that this was, indeed, the end of the Iraq war. Even today, a widely used source of modern war data, the Correlates of War Project, uses Bush's speech as the end date of the war. (The same source uses Appomattox as the end date of the U.S. Civil War.)[8] At the time of Bush's speech, I joined many others in mocking the notion that the United States–Iraq war was over simply because the president declared it so. Did anyone really think that this or any war could be ended with a mere piece of political theater?

It turns out that *I* did. A few days after Bush's May 2003 "Mission Accomplished" speech, I tuned in to the History Channel to watch the documentary *April 1865*, based on Jay Winik's book. I was seduced again by the drama of Appomattox. The Civil War ended and peace followed. No drawn-out insurrections. No needless animosities. No broken promises about emancipation. In some part of my brain, I knew that this was all mythology. Yet, in another part, it was genuine history. If the two conflicting accounts were causing discord somewhere in my mind, I did not sense it. Nor did I experience any dissonance when, just days after watching the *April 1865* documentary, I came across Lewis Grant's report in the archives. I dismissed Grant's findings as nothing more than sideshow curiosities. So what if Andrew Johnson had declared an end to the Civil War on August 20, 1866? So what if other authorities, even the U.S. Supreme Court, had accepted this date? These were trivial legalities—nothing more than footnotes to the story of Appomattox.

Yet, over time, the facts reported by Lewis Grant would nag at me more and more. While I was participating in a symposium on presidential war powers in 2005, the memory of Grant's report snuck into my mind, leading me to declare that the greatest war power held by a president was the power to declare a war to be over. People assumed that I was talking about President Bush's "Mission Accomplished" speech of 2003. I told them I was—but only partly. Andrew Johnson had proclaimed the American Civil War over on August 20, 1866, I explained. Both presidential war-ending declarations, the one in 1866 and the one in 2003, had served as official endpoints, and in both instances, war of some sort had gone on beyond the pronouncements. The result in the case of the Civil War was that presidents after Johnson kept making do-over proclamations, either calling for peace or declaring peace attained. James A. Garfield managed to do both in his inaugural of 1881. He declared that liberty and the Union were "restored" but acknowledged that contests continued—"the battlefields of dead issues"—and that the "grander victories of peace" still had to be won.[9] I suspected that similar do-over proclamations would be needed for the American war in Iraq. Sure enough, in 2010, seven years after President Bush had declared "combat operations" concluded in Iraq, President Barack Obama announced that "the American combat mission in Iraq has ended."[10] A low-profile ceremony at a U.S. base in Baghdad on December 15, 2011, was held to mark the end.

Lewis Grant's report stayed on my mind as I watched the very vocabulary of war endings come under scrutiny. By the time that President Obama tried to put an end stamp on the Iraq war, Americans had become increasingly divided over whether it made sense anymore, at least in the current era, to speak of wars as "ending." A 2010 conference of military experts tasked by the U.S. Army to examine "war termination" in American history came to the conclusion that "ending war is . . . a problem more complex than war itself."[11] Obama himself acknowledged the complexity. "Violence will not end with [the end of] our combat mission," he conceded in his 2010 end-of-war speech. "In an age without surrender ceremonies, we must earn victory through the success of our partners and the strength of our own nation."[12] "Victory" was now a process, not an identifiable, celebratory moment. In the new nomenclature, "postwar" was passé, or at best an artificial construct—for the word assumed a discernible break between wartime and peacetime.[13]

As U.S. authorities began drawing down forces in Afghanistan and Iraq, commentators grappled with thorny questions brought on by the new realities of American involvement not only in the Middle East but everywhere else. Who had the authority to end wars? The president? Congress? Were there "peace powers" in the Constitution, just as there were "war powers"?[14] Pundits tried to find a new language for the situation in which the United States found itself. "What we are steaming toward," the journalist Rachel Maddow wrote, "is not so much cold warfare or even peace, but rather a kind of high idle."[15] The phrase "forever war," which once might have been regarded as an oxymoron, has now become commonplace.[16]

Yet, at the same time, somehow, the old assumption about wars having endings has persisted. Maybe holding on to the assumption is the only way to make war fathomable, or at least tolerable. In February 2022, Russia invaded Ukraine. Just over a year later, the journal *Foreign Affairs* hosted a public forum in which diplomatic experts tackled the topic "How Does the War in Ukraine End?" As the journal noted, the question about the war's end had appeared as soon as the war began. No one at the event had the definitive answer—and still no one does—but it was the question, not the answer, that mattered. The question contained a hidden premise that offered solace amid catastrophe: if it's a war, then it must end.[17] At about the same time as *Foreign Affairs* hosted the public forum, it published two articles describing Russia-Ukraine as a forever war. Yet both promised that an end *would* come. The first suggested that the United States would "develop a vision for how the war ends" and then execute this "endgame."[18] The second article, which had the provocative title "How Wars Don't End," managed to conclude that "even prolonged wars eventually end."[19] The unbearable knowledge that some wars cannot end; the undying hope that all wars must end—such is the paradoxical place we inhabit as we stumble into the second quarter of the twenty-first century.

Yet we have been here before. At least Americans have. It is where Lewis Grant found himself when he went looking for the end of the Civil War decades after Appomattox. Well before then, in May 1866, U.S. attorney general James Speed had begun to wonder whether endpoints of war were merely useful fictions. It had been more than a year since the surrender at Appomattox, yet every day Speed read of murderous attacks on U.S. servicemen and defenseless Black civilians. "We are in the habit of saying and thinking that war is the abnormal and peace the normal condition of a nation," Speed wrote to a friend. "Is that true?" he now asked. "Does history so teach?"[20] Ambrose Bierce, the author and satirist—and Civil War veteran—mocked the very idea that time could be divided into war and peace. "Peace," Bierce wrote, was merely "a period of cheating between two periods of fighting."[21]

One might think that Americans in the twenty-first century, like Bierce in the nineteenth, would have resigned themselves to the notion that the line between war and peace is less a reality than a useful fiction. Instead, in the face of today's "forever wars," they have held tighter to an imagined past when wars *did* have discrete endings. Amid such nostalgia, the myth of a Civil War endpoint in the McLean parlor has held strong. The final report of the U.S. Army's 2010 conference on "war termination" acknowledged that recent wars had failed to end cleanly but then looked back to the American Civil War as the ideal—that is, the war with the right kind of ending. It was a war with a final peace agreement, the surrender at Appomattox, followed by a period of "postwar Reconstruction." A year after the "war termination" conference, in 2011, the celebration of the Civil War sesquicentennial began. It ended four years later with a grand finale at Appomattox on April 9, 2015. C-SPAN broadcast a reenactment of the meeting between Grant and Lee. The uniforms were perfect reproductions. The choreography was carefully timed to correspond to each moment of the meeting at the McLean house. The meeting ended. The war was over—again.

There were dissenting voices, to be sure. Historians had begun asking whether the seeming endlessness of twenty-first-century wars had a precedent in the Civil War. Was there really a clean break between war and postwar in 1865? Some contended that the period following Appomattox was not a postwar era but instead, like the U.S.-Iraq war after mid-2003, a new stage of an existing war—a "war of occupation" fought against insurrectionaries who refused to accept defeat.[22] Others suggested that the post-1865 conflict was a new war altogether, perhaps a *Southern* Civil War growing out of the *American* Civil War.[23] Still others said that we should treat the whole period from secession through Reconstruction as one "long Civil War."[24]

At the same time that historians were rethinking *when* the Civil War was, they were asking *where* it was. The where and the when were connected. For example, if the war was as much about the guerrilla fighting in places like Kansas and Missouri as it was about the organized battles in Virginia and Georgia, then the dates of the war needed changing, as guerrilla activity began before 1861 and continued after 1865. What about the skirmishes on the border with Mexico after French troops occupied the country in 1862? Did those count as part of the Civil War? If so, then maybe the end date had to be extended to 1867, when Napoleon III withdrew his armies.[25]

And what about the fighting with Native Americans in the Plains and the Southwest? Were those wars separate from the Civil War? It was hard to believe they were. Consider the pension case that animated Lewis Grant's research in the first place. Grant learned that the U.S. soldier in question had never fought against the Confederacy. He had enlisted in April 1866, a year after Appomattox. He had served not in the South but in the West, fighting Dakota Sioux on the northern Great Plains. Yet he had applied for a *Civil War* pension, which paid out at a higher rate than other army pensions. Were the army conflicts against Native Americans in the 1860s to be counted as part of the Civil War? Grant was unsure how to answer the question. He was able to sidestep it by focusing on the when, not the where, of the pension-seeker's military service. Because the soldier had enlisted in Cincinnati on April 19, 1866, more than two weeks after April 2, 1866, the date affirmed by Grant as the legal end of the Civil War everywhere but Texas (where the end date was August 20, 1866), Grant could deny the pension.[26] The question of whether the Plains Indian Wars and other conflicts of the era between the United States and indigenous peoples were part of the Civil War did not go away, however. It continues to divide historians, with most Civil War scholars taking the position that all of the military conflicts were bound up together in one war.[27]

The idea that the Civil War included U.S. wars against Native

Americans gives yet more reason to rethink the end date of the Civil War. The Plains Indian Wars continued well into the 1870s and did not come to anything like an "end" until the 1890s. Struck by the fact of this commingling of the Confederates' war and the Plains Indian Wars, an increasing number of scholars contended that it no longer made sense to think of a Civil War with clear temporal and geographical boundaries. It was more accurate to posit a "Greater Reconstruction," a set of seismic shifts in U.S. state-building and imperial expansion across the North American continent, punctuated by moments of violence that may or may not be rightly called war.[28]

By 2015, the 150th anniversary of Appomattox, the competing stories I was hearing had stirred me to action. On one side there was a scholarly reconsideration of the temporal scope of the Civil War and a popular outcry against the endlessness of modern wars; on the other, a continued assumption by most Americans, scholars and non-scholars alike, that there *was* an end to the Civil War, and it happened at Appomattox. I returned to the archives, reread Grant's report, retraced the research that he had done, and then did some preliminary investigation of my own, which revealed much that Grant had missed. With an urgent determination to get the story of the Civil War's ending right, I dropped the book project that I had been working on and took up the task of writing what would become *Lincoln's Peace*.

The book's title is an invention. Lincoln did not make peace, and peace had not come by the time that Lincoln was assassinated on April 14, 1865. But Lincoln had hoped to witness peace, and to help orchestrate it. In what turned out to be his final speech, delivered a few days before his death, he spoke of his "hope of a righteous and speedy peace."[29] Had he lived, he would have seen firsthand how difficult it was to make a peace that was both speedy and righteous. Yet he did believe such a peace was possible. So did others among the many warring parties who traveled the roads away from war in the months and years to come. Whether they ever arrived at a place that Lincoln would have called peace remains an open question. Maybe they would have arrived there had Lincoln lived beyond April 1865. Such is the most powerful myth attached to the Lincoln assassination: that with his death, conflict was doomed to last longer than if he had lived. The myth shaped the early histories of Reconstruction, which argued that the absence of Lincoln's moderation and political savvy allowed extremists on all sides to keep the warring spirit, if not the war itself, alive. The history of Reconstruction evolved, but the myth of Lincoln as the fallen peacemaker remained. It was threaded through the 2012 blockbuster film *Lincoln,* directed by Stephen Spielberg.[30] Much would have been better in the country had Lincoln lived, no doubt, but would there have been a peace that was both speedy and righteous? Could Lincoln have orchestrated a discernible end to the Civil War? Perhaps. But it is hard to believe that any such end would have been accepted by all Americans at the time or looked upon as definitive by all Americans today.

An end to the Civil War did not come in Lincoln's lifetime. So when *did* it come?

The answer, as should be clear by now, is this: It's complicated. "It's complicated" is historians' classic response to any question about the past—and the reason why they risk being throttled every time they try to answer a seemingly simple question posed by an impatient audience. But when it comes to finding the end of the Civil War, the answer really *is* complicated. Just enter "When did the American Civil War end?" into an internet search engine and you'll be convinced. April 9, 1865—the date of the Appomattox surrender—will likely top the list of results. But scroll down and you'll come to other dates, including August 20, 1866, the date of Andrew Johnson's end-of-insurrection proclamation. Soon you will know the frustration felt by Lewis Grant when he undertook the same quest—and without the help of Google or Wikipedia.

The way out of this frustration is to embrace the complexity. Anyone who has studied the Civil War should be used to questions that elude simple answers. For example, was it even a civil war? Confederates believed that it was a war between nations. Lincoln insisted that it was a rebellion. The U.S. Supreme Court in the midst of the conflict took both positions at once, declaring in the *Prize Cases* that the Confederates were rebels but for legal purposes could be treated as a single, foreign "belligerent."[31] This duality—the war as a rebellion within one polity *and* a conflict between two polities—added to the unlikelihood that there would be a single, agreed-upon ending.

Alongside the thorny matter of what type of war this was lies an even more contentious question, one with crucial consequences for finding the end of the conflict: What was the Civil War *about*? Was it a contest between organized armies—a military war? Was it a fight to bring seceded states back into the Union—a political war? Was it an armed assault on slavery—an emancipationist war? Was it a clash of ideologies—a cultural war? It was all of these things, of course. But which one mattered most to people at the time? And while we're at it: Which one matters most to people now?

Different responses necessarily lead to different endpoints. The *military* Civil War ended on April 9, 1865, the date of the Appomattox surrender, or perhaps on the date of one of the later surrenders. Seeing as the last of the major surrenders happened in June, an end date around July 1, 1865, works fine for the military war.

The *political* Civil War ended when the U.S. politicians in charge declared the Union restored. But who was in charge? If it was President Andrew Johnson, then the end was August 20, 1866, the date of his war-ending proclamation (and the date accepted by Lewis Grant). If Congress rather than the president was in charge—and it certainly put itself above Johnson—then the end date was February 1, 1871. That was the day when Congress voted to seat a delegation from Georgia, the only remaining seceded state that had been denied representation. After the vote, a number of congressmen declared the Civil War over.[32] (Today we would expect the U.S. Supreme Court to bully its way into the debate and assert itself as the final authority on when the war ended, but the Civil War–era Court was a different animal: it humbly denied having the power to end the war and ultimately accepted the Johnson end date of August 20, 1866.)

What about the *emancipationist* Civil War? Ending slavery was one of the goals of the Union war—indeed its most important goal. So when did slavery end? One candidate for an end date of slavery is June 19, 1865, today known widely as Juneteenth. On that day, U.S. forces in Texas declared slavery abolished in the state. Six months later, in December 1865, the Thirteenth Amendment abolishing slavery was adopted. When legal authorities in the decades after 1865 were tasked with identifying the end date of slavery, some pointed to Juneteenth; others said the adoption of the Thirteenth

Amendment.[33] By 2020, there was still no consensus. On June 19 of that year, the historian Annette Gordon-Reed wrote, "It is staggering that there is no date commemorating the end of slavery in the United States."[34] Exactly a year later, on June 19, 2021, Juneteenth became a federal holiday. Yet even a cursory examination of the historical record reveals that slavery in the United States lasted beyond June 19, 1865, and that, even after the adoption of the Thirteenth Amendment, forms of racialized servitude persisted.[35] Still, Americans today tend to agree that the institution of Black slavery as it had existed in North America since the early 1600s came to an end *sometime* in 1865.

As for the *cultural* Civil War, the end date is . . . to be determined. The United States remains torn between groups whose voices echo those of the combatants during the Civil War. The polarizing positions that prompted and shaped the Civil War—racial justice versus white supremacy; federal authority versus state sovereignty—remain in play today. For this reason, some have contended that the Civil War is still not over. On the 150th anniversary of the Appomattox surrender, as reenactors played out the tableau of national reconciliation, a biting commentary appeared in *The Atlantic* declaring that "not only is the Civil War not over; it can still be lost."[36] The author was the historian David Blight, who happened to be one of the speakers at the 150th anniversary event at Appomattox. But did the conflicts plaguing the nation in 2015 truly amount to a continuation of the Civil War fought in Lincoln's time? Perhaps. The struggles were sometimes violent, to be sure, the opposing sides were deeply entrenched, and the results of the battles were certain to shape the future of the Union. Those who fought in or witnessed the Civil War of the 1860s might well have seen in the current national divisions the ripples of their own war. But they would likely have bristled at the notion that these conflicts represent a *continuation* of their war. Mass armed insurrection, widespread racialized chattel slavery, the destruction of the Union: these were realities for Civil War–era Americans. They are only potentialities today. Maybe they will become realities again—and there are disturbing signs that they will. And maybe as a result there will be a new Civil War, as some have predicted. But if that happens, history will surely record a temporal break between that war and the Civil War that took place in the mid-nineteenth century. For this reason, *Lincoln's Peace* treats the Civil War of the nineteenth century as a distinct, temporally bounded conflict, even as it argues that at least one of its temporal bounds, the endpoint, was not a single fixed, tangible moment.

Why does it matter whether or not the Civil War had a distinct endpoint and when that endpoint was? One reason is that founding myths always need re-examining, and the story of a neat, conciliatory end to the war is one of those myths. It feeds into a larger fiction of American exceptionalism, the tenacious, indulgent belief that Americans are a favored people who do everything better than everyone else. As an example: they win their wars and wrap them up neatly. One might think that the experience of the United States in Vietnam and the Middle East would have put to rest that particular notion.[37] But there are many Americans who regard those conflicts as anomalies and the Civil War as the *true* American war, one with a proper ending. The Appomattox story in particular fixed the war in national memory as "a tragedy with a happy ending," to use a sardonic comment by the writer William Dean Howells.[38] Not everyone was pleased by Appomattox—diehard Confederates were dishonored and enraged by what happened there—but over time, the site came to stand for something that all Americans could believe in: a national greatness strengthened by the repair of reconciliation that followed the strain of war. At the centennial gathering at Appomattox in 1965, Bruce Catton, the foremost Civil War historian of the time, trumpeted that "we have one country now, bought at a terrible price, cemented everlastingly together because at the end of our most terrible war the men who had fought so hard decided that they had had enough of hatred."[39]

The gushing by historians continued long after the centennial. One of Catton's contemporaries, Allan Nevins, used the end of the Civil War—or rather its assumed end at Appomattox—as evidence of the cultural, even racial, superiority of Americans:

> If we can imagine the possibility of the type of civil war known at times in various parts of Europe, where the sinking flames of internal conflict were blown into a more destructive blaze by neighboring countries pursuing malevolent or greedy aims,

and where the victorious as well as the vanquished elements in the population were forced to live in close proximity while their passionate hatreds and increasingly disparate cultural and economic systems generated a succession of angry new collisions, then we can better picture the malign possibilities facing the weary, bewildered people, North and South, in 1865. Fortunately, the background of the conflict was American, not European; and still more fortunately, both Northerners and Southerners had long been committed to the fundamental Anglo-Saxon principle of compromise, and were at last ready to turn to mutual concessions to readjust their differences.[40]

Thirty years after the centennial, another historian expressed his "marvel" at the way that the combatants were able to "put away their guns and . . . pack away their personal rancor forever." It was a testament to "the American character."[41]

More is at stake in the end date of the Civil War than American exceptionalism, a force in American culture that finally may be losing some steam. The choice of an end date also has consequences for how the war is remembered. Wittingly or unwittingly, the choice of an end date makes one complicit in assigning a meaning that matters most to the war. Choose April 9, 1865, and the war is primarily about organized armies. Choose April 11, 1877, the last clash, in South Carolina, between federal troops and states' rights paramilitary forces, and the war is about the general violence of rebellion. (Only on that day, one historian argues, did "the Civil War . . . finally come to a close.")[42] Choose August 2, 1956, when the last Civil War veteran died, and the war is primarily about the combatants, who lived with the glory and trauma of the conflict long after they marched home.[43] The twentieth-century general Douglas MacArthur would have liked that choice. It was in a speech to World War I veterans that he first made the famous quip, "Only the dead have seen the end of war."[44]

Assigning an end date to war—whether done at the time of the conflict or long after—necessarily has an instrumental purpose, or at least an instrumental effect. It is just as likely a "strategy" as a "law or fact," as one scholar has recently argued.[45] When Andrew Johnson declared the war over on August 20, 1866, the end date discovered by Lewis Grant many years later, he had a specific political purpose in mind: to stop the incoming Republican-dominated Congress from claiming that the war still continued and thus that they could continue to use coercive war powers against the South. When Lewis Grant accepted Johnson's date, he, too, was being strategic. He now had a way to determine whether certain pension applications could be summarily dismissed.

Whether by intention or not, the end date of a war defines a war. It signals how the war has been remembered. The most common end dates used for the Civil War—April 9, 1865, and August 20, 1866—tell us that the war is remembered primarily as a military and political affair. The end dates not used for the war—specifically June 19, 1865 (Juneteenth), and December 18, 1865 (the adoption of the Thirteenth Amendment)—tell us that the conflict is not remembered primarily as a war against slavery. It may come as no surprise that emancipation has been sidelined in the national memory of the Civil War. For years historians have been writing about the problem and trying, with much success, to rectify it. Yet, so long as history uses end dates for the Civil War that have no direct connection to emancipation, the struggle to put Black freedom at the center of the memory of the war will remain an uphill battle.

Had Abraham Lincoln had his way, the end date of the war would be tied somehow to the end of slavery. In his Second Inaugural of March 4, 1865, he declared that he was willing to let the war continue for 250 more years "if God wills that it continue" for that long in order to destroy slavery. This was more than moralistic grandstanding. For Lincoln, the end of the war and the end of slavery had to be simultaneous. During his 1864 reelection campaign, he had made sure that his party's platform endorsed the constitutional amendment abolishing slavery. Then he incurred the rancor of a war-weary electorate by announcing that he would not even listen to a proposal for "restoration of peace" unless it included "the abandonment of slavery." These were the preconditions of the "righteous peace" that he had in mind when he gave his last public address on April 11, 1865.[46] By that date, the Confederate surrenders had begun. Lincoln no longer worried about the war lasting another 250 years. But he still did not know how the war—and slavery—would end.

Everyone who tries to understand the past on its own terms faces the conundrum described years ago by the historian C. V. Wedgwood: "We know the end before we consider the beginning."[47] As it turns out, though, when it comes to the Civil War, America's best-known, most transformational event, we *don't* know the end. This book is a journey to find it.

PART I

PEACE WAS NOT MADE

Why is it that we rejoice today with a joy almost too deep for words—a joy that utters itself best in the waving of flags, in bursts of music, and in the roar of artillery? Is it because we have gained a glorious victory? We have had glorious victories before. Is it because peace was made yesterday? No! We rejoice that peace was *not* made. . . .

In such a war as this, peace cannot be MADE: It must COME. It must come, as fair weather comes, after a tempest. It must come, as public health comes, after the plague or the cholera. But whoever heard of public health restored by a compact, to which society was one party and the epidemic the other!

Gen. Grant says to Gen. Lee,—wishing to shift from myself the responsibility for further shedding of blood, I suggest to you the surrender of your army. Gen. Lee asks,—what are to be the terms of peace? In that question was involved the issue of eighty years,—the principle on the right or wrong of which our cause is to be justified or condemned. How nobly Gen. Grant met it! I have nothing to say, replied Gen. Grant, about peace. The subject we are to discuss is the surrender of your army. When Gen. Lee heard that answer, he heard the death-knell of the doctrine of secession. Peace cannot be made. The rebel armies must surrender, the rebel citizens in arms must disperse, and submit to the laws, and then—peace exists.

Richard Henry Dana, Jr., Speech in
Winthrop Square, Boston, April 10, 1865[1]

1

The Peacemaker

THE JAMES RIVER begins as a creek in the hills of northwest Virginia and winds its way to the south and east, picking up speed and breadth until it reaches Richmond, where it slows to still water, bending one way then another. Just below the city, the James enters the Virginia Tidewater. It crests the fall line and drops into boiling rapids. Once at the coastal plain, the river's waters are brackish and gripped by ocean tides. It flows now more than a hundred miles, meandering through oxbow after oxbow, sending off rivulets, sometimes becoming marshland, and finally reaching a small peninsula located only thirty miles south of Richmond by land: City Point. Here the James meets the Appomattox River, which enters from the west. From City Point, the James, now swollen with the waters of the Appomattox, becomes a wide, slow-moving thoroughfare to the Chesapeake Bay. At the meeting of the James and the Chesapeake, the water is still and shallow, forming a delta with the city of Norfolk on the south side and the region known as Hampton Roads on the north. It is impossible to tell the exact point at which one body of water becomes the other.

President Abraham Lincoln arrived at City Point on March 25, 1865. He made the trip aboard the *River Queen*, a comfortable side-wheel-propelled steamboat that had been built the year before. Its original owners had intended it to run excursions for the well-heeled between Providence and Newport, Rhode Island. The U.S. Army had leased it for use by dignitaries and top officers. Lincoln knew the ship well. He was also familiar with City Point, Grant's headquarters. This was not his first visit. But this trip was different. Within days of his arrival, he decided that he would not return to Washington until he had witnessed, or perhaps even orchestrated, the end of the Civil War.[1]

The once-pastoral peninsula of City Point was now a sprawling U.S. Army encampment, the headquarters of Lincoln's top general, Ulysses S. Grant. For nearly four years, U.S. forces had been waging a devastating war with the Confederate States of America. Grant now believed the end was in sight. For weeks the general had been sending messages to Washington suggesting that Lincoln visit City Point, but until now Lincoln had always politely declined.

He had been slow to open his heart to the possibility that the war might soon end. There had been no sign of a weakening of the enemy's resolve—certainly not from the Confederate leadership. Back on February 2, Lincoln had met with three emissaries sent by Jefferson Davis, president of the Confederacy. Any wisp of hope for peace that the president may have clung to dissolved as soon as the discussion began.

The meeting had been held at Hampton Roads. Lincoln was accompanied by his secretary of state, William Henry Seward. The five men had their discussion on board the *River Queen,* the same ship that would take Lincoln to City Point seven weeks later. At Hampton Roads on February 2, the Confederates never mentioned a possible surrender. They instead floated the possibility of an alliance between their country and the United States in order to pursue a war against Mexico. Lincoln said that any plan had to involve the southerners' surrender and their return to "our one common country." That was not going to happen, the Confederates explained. Lincoln played his one card. The constitutional amendment abolishing slavery had just passed Congress and been sent to the states for ratification. Slavery was certain to end. But if the rebels surrendered and the southern states returned to the Union, the South might get a say in *how* slavery ended. Maybe gradual instead of immediate emancipation was a possibility in some places. Maybe some former slaveholders could get compensation from the U.S. government for the loss of their human property. But if the rebellion continued, southern whites would have no say in emancipation. The emissaries, all of them slaveholders, were shaken by the news of the amendment, but

The Waterways of Eastern Virginia

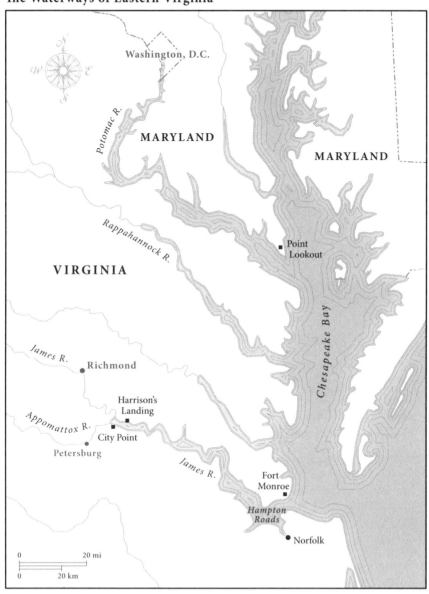

they stuck to the script that Jefferson Davis had written for them: an independent Confederate nation was a nonnegotiable precondition to peace. They headed back to Richmond. Lincoln steeled himself for more war.[2]

Weeks of war lay ahead, Lincoln thought. Maybe months or even years. Late in February, a few weeks after the Hampton Roads meeting, Lincoln brushed off an army supplier angry that he had not yet been paid by telling him that things might be different "if we were nearer the end of the war."[3] On March 2, Grant reported that Robert E. Lee, Grant's counterpart in the Confederacy, wanted to meet the general to discuss a "military convention" that might end hostilities. Lincoln kept hope at bay. He suspected—correctly—that Lee was looking for a ceasefire or some other sort of delaying tactic to allow him to join forces with Confederate General Joseph E. Johnston's army in North Carolina. He had Grant tell Lee that the two generals could meet only if it was about the "capitulation" of Lee's army.[4] Once Lee heard that, he begged off, just as Lincoln knew he would.

Two days later, and about three weeks before his trip down the James, Lincoln delivered his Second Inaugural. The speech contained the most chilling prediction possible of how long the war might last. Slavery, which was "somehow the cause of the war," was the nation's sin. God—or at least justice—might well demand that the country suffer from war for as long as Black people had suffered from slavery. The war could continue, perhaps *should* continue, "until every drop of blood drawn with the lash, shall be paid by another drawn with the sword." These were not the words of a president with optimism—or an exit strategy.[5]

Yet, to keep up his listeners' morale, and perhaps his own, he held out hope of an end that would come soon, and with kindness all around. "With malice toward none," Lincoln urged, the people must "strive on to finish the work we are in" in order to "achieve and cherish a just and lasting peace among ourselves and with all nations."[6] A peace that was "lasting"—the meaning of that was clear enough. A simple ceasefire would not do. But what was a "just" peace? The word allowed for many meanings. "Just" might suggest fairness, as opposed to vengeance, toward one's former enemies. That meaning was suggested by the "malice toward none" phrase. But "just" could also suggest the opposite: retribution in proper measure against those responsible for the war. "Just" also was a synonym for moral, and the moral issue at the heart of the Inaugural was slavery or, more precisely, its abolition. No peace could be just or lasting, Lincoln believed, unless it included the end of slavery.

Within two weeks of the Inaugural, Lincoln was regularly making passing predictions of the coming end of the war. On March 17, he said that the recent decision by the Confederacy to allow states to form regiments of enslaved people was a sign that the South was "near the bottom" and the "end is near."[7] To a Union general in Missouri, on March 19, Lincoln suggested a hands-off approach so that the war might "wind down" there.[8] The next day, he told a Russian diplomat that he expected the war to be over by the end of the year.[9] His secretary of state shared Lincoln's cautious optimism. Seward dropped the phrase "as the war begins to end" into a letter written to his wife.[10]

Like those around him, Lincoln by late March had become hopeful that the end was quite near, probably because reports from Grant had become increasingly optimistic. When Lincoln left for Grant's headquarters at City Point on the *River Queen,* he expected to see the end of the war. "He intended to propose the terms of surrender himself," one of his companions wrote. "He had made up his mind that this fraternal strife should cease in one way or another."[11] So high was Lincoln's confidence that he brought along his wife, Mary, and his young son Tad, no doubt hoping to have them at his side when he toured battlefields and liberated cities. He did not expect to return to Washington until the war was over.

The steamship journey to City Point was rough—a virus or perhaps bad drinking water on the boat made Lincoln feverish and lethargic—but within a day of docking Lincoln was receiving visitors. There was a shine in his eye now, observers remarked, a clear contrast to the melancholy that had deepened the crags of his gaunt face in recent months. He told one of the naval officers that he had "the greatest confidence that the war was drawing to an end."[12] He was eager to steam up the James toward Richmond, the Confederate capital, or down the Appomattox toward Petersburg, the Confederacy's main railroad hub and supply depot. Rear Admiral David Dixon Porter, who was at City Point at the time, offered to be his guide. Porter was the most esteemed Union naval commander next to Vice Admiral David Farragut, Porter's adopted brother, who was currently commanding U.S. naval forces in the Gulf of Mexico. Porter knew that it might be some time before Lincoln could see Richmond or Petersburg. U.S. troops had been laying siege to Petersburg for months and seemed no closer to a breakthrough. Richmond was well defended by Lee's Army of Northern Virginia. Jefferson Davis, the president of the Confederacy (or "so-called president," as Lincoln dubbed him), still resided in the city, only thirty miles away from City Point. He had no plans to leave.

City Point, Virginia. A hub for ships and railcars, as well as the site of General Ulysses S. Grant's headquarters, where President Abraham Lincoln stayed for nearly two weeks beginning in late March 1865.

With General Grant assuring him that Petersburg and Richmond would soon fall, Lincoln began planning for the end of the war. On March 28, he held an impromptu meeting on board the *River*

Queen with Grant, Porter, and Major General William T. Sherman. Sherman's presence at City Point was unexpected. Neither he nor Lincoln knew that the other would be there. Sherman had come from North Carolina, where the army he was commanding was stalking the force under the command of Joseph E. Johnston. He had planned to talk with Grant about coordinating their efforts and keeping Lee and Johnston from joining forces. Sherman and Lincoln had met only once before—a brief encounter four years earlier. They had not been impressed with each other. There was still some distrust there, despite all that each had done to bring the Confederates to heel. When Lincoln first saw Sherman at City Point, he asked in dismay why the general had abandoned his army in North Carolina. It took some soothing from Grant to relieve Lincoln's anxieties. Sherman's men were as firm for a fight as ever. They could make do without their commander for a few days.

The March 28 meeting on board the *River Queen* was the first and only time that Lincoln told his top generals how he wanted the war to end. The one point that he stressed above all was lenience toward the Confederates. He worried that vengeful U.S. commanders would "exact severe terms," as he had recently told his cabinet. In the spirit of "malice toward none," the concluding message of his Second Inaugural, Lincoln told the officers aboard the *River Queen* that he wanted "submission" but "no more bloodshed." The enemy were to be treated "liberally all round." "Get the deluded men of the rebel armies disarmed and back to their homes," Lincoln predicted, and "they won't take up arms again." "We must 'let 'em up easy.'"[13]

The metaphor came from wrestling, a sport Lincoln had mastered as a young man on the frontier. His physical prowess had given him an advantage, but his skill came just as much from knowing when *not* to fight. At twenty-two, he grudgingly accepted the challenge of husky Jack Armstrong, the head of the "Cleary Grove boys" of New Salem, Illinois. People argued for years about who had won the match, but all agreed on how it had ended. One of the men simply let the other "up easy." From that point on, Lincoln, a new arrival to New Salem, was fast friends with Armstrong and his "boys." Like a worn-out wrestler, the Confederacy would soon concede the match. Lincoln would let 'em up with honor. A friendly, lasting peace would ensue.

The commanders understood what Lincoln was asking of them. But were even the leaders of the rebellion to be spared? they wondered. It was one thing to go easy on the ordinary Confederate soldiers, whom Lincoln called the "deluded men," but were they really supposed to be so kind to those who had done the deluding? Was even Jefferson Davis to get a free pass?

What to do with Jeff Davis? That could be tricky, Lincoln conceded. He knew that many in the Union wanted Davis hanged. But executing Davis would only keep animosities aflame and prolong the war, Lincoln worried. The answer was to let Davis escape the country. Eventually, peace would calm tempers, and people would forget about the Confederate leader. Yet Lincoln could not explicitly order his commanders to let Davis go. So he dropped a large hint, in the form of one of his stories. There was a fellow who had taken the pledge against liquor, Lincoln began. When a friend offered him a drink, he asked for lemonade. His host pointed to a brandy bottle and offered to add some to the lemonade to make it more "palatable." The man would not object, he said, so long as the friend could add it "unbeknown" to him. The story was uncharacteristically unfunny for Lincoln. But the message was clear: if possible, the military men should let Davis slip out of the country "unbeknown." Lincoln's story concluded the meeting aboard the *River Queen*.

The president knew that other delicate decisions besides the handling of Davis lay ahead. He preferred to handle them as they came rather than get bogged down in discussions of the "what ifs." This pragmatic side of Lincoln had served him well, but if he really meant to end the war, he had to start tackling some of the thornier problems now. Or so he was told by Secretary of State Seward, who arrived at City Point on March 30, two days after Lincoln's meeting with the military commanders.

No one had invited Seward. He, like Lincoln, was hoping to be part of any end-of-war negotiations that might take place. Also, like Lincoln, he saw the trip to City Point as a bit of adventure. He, too, brought his wife and some family members. But his main reason for coming was to advise Lincoln, even if Lincoln had not asked for any advice. Seward regarded himself as Lincoln's most learned and trusted advisor. Maybe he was. Seward was both an expert in international affairs and a savvy politician. He and Lincoln had gotten off to a rocky start. The onetime New York governor and U.S. senator believed that he, not the inexperienced one-term congressman from Illinois, should have received the Republican presidential nomination in 1860. He took the position as secretary of state assuming that he would do most of the governing of the nation; Lincoln would be the figurehead. The president quickly disabused him of that notion, slapping him down in early April 1861 when he pushed for a solution to the secession crisis that might have entangled the United States in a war with France and Spain.[14] Eventually, the two men came to respect each other; then they became close friends. Only Seward had been with Lincoln when the president met with the southern envoys at Hampton Roads back in February 1865. It was natural that he would assume that he was needed at City Point in case there were to be more such meetings. Also, if Lincoln really was going to try to make some kind of peace, he needed to be briefed about relevant matters of international law.

On March 31, Seward met with Lincoln on the *River Queen*. There is no record of what the two men discussed. Almost certainly, though, international law was part of the conversation. Seward had appointed himself Lincoln's tutor on the reigning theories of war-ending found in dusty tomes by Enlightenment-era European philosophers like Hugo Grotius, Emmerich de Vattel, and Samuel Pufendorf. Lincoln was less than eager for a lecture from Seward. Ever the pragmatist, he had no use for archaic theories about how to end a war. He wanted to settle a peace in whatever way that circumstances of the moment allowed. He had joked with Admiral Porter before Seward's visit that he knew Seward would "talk to me all day about Vattel and Puffendorf [*sic*] . . . , and I don't want to hear any more of that."[15] Lincoln had been right. Seward knew that Lincoln might soon be meeting with Jefferson Davis. If that happened, Seward believed, the president did indeed have to follow the established rules of war-ending. Technicalities mattered—at least to Seward. For example, the president could demand certain military conventions, like disarmament and prisoner release, but he must not arrange anything that suggested an agreement between nations, as that would add legitimacy to Davis's claim—so far rejected by the Lincoln administration—that the Confederacy *was* a nation. Seward had been over this ground with Lincoln before, most recently in preparation for the meeting with Confederate emissaries at Hampton Roads two months earlier. But now the prospects of a meaningful settlement were much brighter, and Seward might not be there to help with the finer points. Lincoln would have listened courteously but impatiently. The end of war need not be a pas de deux, he thought; it could be a manly handshake. The meeting did not last long. Seward then returned to Washington.

Lincoln was thinking of heading back, too. By April 1, he had been away from the capital for a week—his longest presidential sojourn to date. Mary was returning that day, though she was leaving Tad behind. She had had enough of the mud and of Grant's wife, Julia, whose efforts at charm and kindness she found pitiful. Mary's decision to go may have clinched Lincoln's decision to stay. There had been a particularly embarrassing incident during an excursion on horseback a few days earlier when Mary upbraided a general's wife for presumptuously riding beside Lincoln for a few paces. The president welcomed the chance at a separation. He also was still hoping to be in Virginia for the close of the war. He had written to Secretary of War Edwin Stanton, "I begin to feel that I ought to be at home, and yet I dislike to leave without seeing nearer to the end of General Grant's present movement."[16]

At four-thirty in the morning on April 3, Lincoln was awakened by the sounds of far-off explosions coming from up the James. It was the Confederates, someone told him. They were blowing up their own "ironclads," the vessels used for river warfare, to keep them from being seized by U.S. forces. Petersburg had finally fallen, and Lee's army was abandoning Richmond. The moment Lincoln had hoped for had come. "Thank God that I have lived to see this!" Lincoln exclaimed.[17] He believed that the "end of the war was now in sight."[18]

Jefferson Davis did not agree. He had fled Richmond the day before Confederate forces wakened Lincoln by scuttling the ironclads. He had no intention of ending the war—regardless of whether Lincoln let him "up easy" or let him escape the country "unbeknown."

Scrawny and haggard after four years of war, suffering from dyspepsia and nearly blind in one eye, the Confederate president still had his willpower to rely on. Known for his frequent simpering, Davis somehow became more steadfast the more dire the circumstances. During the days before Richmond's inevitable fall, he resolved to stay until the last possible moment. Meanwhile, he arranged for his wife, Varina, and children to travel by train to Charlotte, North Carolina, which was still safely in Confederate hands. Davis would try to join them there. Varina went along with the scheme. She packed her belongings and sold some of the furniture of the Confederate White House for money that she might need while on the run. From her husband she received a tiny handgun that he had ordered specially for her. She was to use it to kill anyone who tried to capture her.

Davis stayed in Richmond until April 2. He was in St. Paul's Church that morning when he heard the news that U.S. troops had taken Petersburg and broken through the Confederate lines protecting Richmond. Calmly he made his way to the train that would carry him and his cabinet safely from the city. Also aboard the train was the entire Confederate treasury, consisting of gold and silver reputed to be of high value, as well as Confederate bonds of no value—unless the Confederacy won. The train was headed west for Danville, in southern Virginia. From there, Davis could use messengers to communicate with his armies, including Johnston's Army of Tennessee, now in North Carolina, and Lee's Army of Northern Virginia, now heading toward the Appalachian Mountains. Davis expected Lee to take his army into the mountains. Once there, Davis imagined, Lee could easily elude Grant's forces and march south to join with Johnston. The Confederates would then have a single massive army that would beleaguer Grant's forces until the Union finally gave up the fight.

When Davis reached Danville on April 4, he issued a printed address "to the People of the Confederate States of America," which soon appeared in newspapers across the South. He grieved the loss of Richmond, "a source of national pride," but he also saw the loss as a blessing. Lee's army was now freed from the arduous task of protecting the capital. It was now "free to move from point to point, and strike in detail the detachments and garrisons of the enemy; operating in the interior of our own country, where supplies are more accessible, and where the foe will be far removed from his own base." The war was not over. It was in "a new phase," and victory was now more certain than ever. "Let us then not despond, my countrymen," Davis concluded. "Let us meet the foe with fresh defiance, with unconquered and unconquerable hearts."[19]

Knowing how things turned out for the Confederacy, it is easy to mock Davis's overconfidence. Maybe the certainty of defeat had made Davis delusional. As one historian has written of Confederates at this late stage of the war, "desperation breeds the most outlandish hopes."[20] Yet the Confederate president was not wrong. He still had tens of thousands of armed soldiers in the field and committed to his cause.

Grant, for one, regarded the war as very much alive so long as Lee's army was on the loose. He decided to leave the coast so he could personally lead his forces in pursuit of the enemy. Lincoln agreed with the move. He had a final talk with the general before Grant headed west. At Grant's suggestion, Lincoln came down to Petersburg on April 3. Grant's army had already begun its march along the Appomattox River, hunting Lee's army. The onetime hub of Petersburg was near empty and desolate. The president and the general sat together in the piazza of a deserted house. "There was not a soul to be seen, not even an animal in the streets," Grant later recalled. Grant reviewed what his strategy had been to date, and Lincoln offered the highest praise, saying that the Army of the Potomac had "every reason to be proud." There was still the task ahead of finishing off Lee's forces, Lincoln acknowledged, but he thought that this might be easier now that the army no longer had Richmond to supply it. He obviously did not share Davis's assessment that Lee was better off now that Richmond had fallen. After the two men talked for a bit longer, Grant rode off to rejoin his army. Lincoln headed back to City Point.[21]

When he arrived there, he learned that Richmond was fully under the control of U.S. troops commanded by Major General Godfrey Weitzel. Weitzel's men had found the Confederate White House vacated. Davis was on his way to Danville. Lincoln did not order any forces to follow—he was letting the Confederate leader escape "unbeknown." Lincoln resolved to go to Richmond the next day. He wanted to see the city that his generals had set their sights on for four years. He wanted to sit in Davis's mansion, even if Davis himself would not be there.

Lincoln started up the James in the *River Queen* on the morning of April 4. He brought Tad along. On the way to Richmond, the presidential party had to transfer ships twice, first to a large navy steamboat and then, just south of the city, to a "Captain's gig," a large rowboat. Standing at the center of the vessel, six sailors rowing behind him and another six in front, Lincoln finally reached the former capital of the Confederacy. He walked the muddy streets and eyed the carnage that Union artillery had wrought on the buildings. The day was hot, the air choked with grit and smoke from the shelling. As Lincoln strode to the Confederate White House, the crowd around him grew huge and unwieldy. People seemed to be pouring out of every street and alley, springing "from the very earth," an observer would recall, to see him. Many in the throng were African Americans. A story would circulate later that an enslaved person bowed down before him and Lincoln told him to rise, that he was free now. This did not happen. Lincoln and African Americans alike knew that the U.S. occupation of the city assured the end of slavery there, but the president did not play the role of liberator, and African Americans did not prostrate themselves before him. Yet all witnesses reported that the loudest cheering came from the freed people.

Not everyone seemed pleased to see Lincoln, though. There were some rough-looking whites in the crowd. Only a handful of soldiers escorted the president, and they began to fear that they could do nothing if Lincoln were attacked by a Confederate sympathizer. Stanton had worried about this very situation when the president sent word of his plan to go to Richmond. "I will take care of myself," Lincoln had promised him.[22] A northern newspaper correspondent in the city was shocked by the "defiant spirit" among some Confederates in the city—not only the "roughs" eyeing Lincoln but also the elites. One woman, clearly a devotee of Jefferson Davis, had adopted Davis's line that the Confederate war effort had been aided, not hurt, by the loss of Richmond. Now the armies of Lee and Johnston could join together, ignore the city, and concentrate their firepower on Grant's forces. "The same God" that saved the Confederacy at other dark moments would "protect and save us now!" she enthused. The reporter found Richmond "full of such people" who were filled with "pluck and confidence." Others he found willing to concede "that their cause is lost." But they did so only because their submission had been "forced," not because they had any genuine desire to rejoin the Union.[23] Lincoln was truly walking through hostile territory.

Finally, after more than thirty minutes of gently elbowing his way through the mass of onlookers, Lincoln arrived at the Confederate White House. The absence of Davis and his cabinet left a vacuum. There was no one to "let up easy." The wrestling phrase was still on Lincoln's mind. Later that day, when General Weitzel asked what he should do with the rebels recently locked up in the city prison by the occupying U.S. troops, the president told him, "If I were in your place, I'd let 'em up easy—let 'em up easy."[24] After Lincoln had entered the White House and looked around a bit, he was directed by some officers to a small drawing room next to the entrance. This became his office. For hours he sat there, but he had little to do. An occasional officer from Weitzel's staff stopped in to introduce himself, and a small reception took place at lunchtime. Lincoln probably spent most of the time wondering how Grant was making out in his pursuit of Lee many miles to the west. In the brief period between Grant's rejoining the army and Lincoln's voyage to Richmond, the president had parked himself by the telegraph at City Point. Every bit of news that arrived from Grant's forces Lincoln had read hungrily and then transmitted to Stanton in Washington. As Lincoln sat in the parlor of Davis's former residence and watched the sun begin to sink, he probably thought about returning to City Point, where he could catch up on Grant's progress. Then one of the officers told him that a delegation of prominent southern gentlemen had arrived, hoping to speak with him. Lincoln agreed to see them.

The spokesman of the group was John A. Campbell. Campbell had been one of the three Confederates who attended the meeting with Seward in Hampton Roads in February. Although he was a southerner and slaveholder, his sympathies with the Confederacy had never run too deep. When Lincoln was elected president in 1860, Campbell was in his eighth year as a U.S. Supreme Court justice. He did not immediately resign. During the secession crisis that followed, Campbell argued for negotiation over separation. For that, strident secessionists ran him out of his home state of Alabama. Eventually settling in Virginia—and resigning from the Court—he was appointed by Jefferson Davis as assistant secretary of war for the Confederacy. He was in Richmond when Davis received word that the city was about to fall. Just before Davis and his cabinet left the city, Campbell resigned his position so he could stay and negotiate with the Yankees for a lenient treatment of Virginia. Two days after Richmond's fall, he had managed to secure an audience with Lincoln.

"There had been much discussion among individuals on the subject of peace," Campbell told the president—"how one could be obtained, and of the condition for a settlement." Lincoln asked which "individuals" Campbell was talking about. He hoped that Jeff Davis might be among them, but he knew that was unlikely. Indeed, Campbell said nothing of Davis. He knew that the Confederate president still believed in victory, a misguided hope in Campbell's opinion. The "individuals" interested in peace, Campbell told Lincoln, were all prominent Virginians. They sought a way for Virginia to be quickly restored to the status of a loyal state of the Union. If Campbell and Lincoln could settle on a way to get Virginia out of the war, the arrangement was sure to meet with their approval. It would also be a model for the other seceded states to follow. Lincoln was dubious that diplomacy would have any effect, especially if Davis was not involved. Grant's success on the battlefield was the only route to peace. But maybe something could come of talking to the Virginians that would make Grant's job easier. Lincoln decided to postpone his return to City Point. He told Campbell to come see him the next morning and to bring along the other peace-seeking "individuals."[25]

When the meeting was over, the president left the Confederate White House. He and Tad traveled by carriage through the city, this time under a much larger military escort. Some who welcomed his presence fired off guns. The noise interrupted the dinner of the Doswells, an elite pro-Confederate family who had remained in the city. They went to the window to see Lincoln "as we would go to look at a wild beast," Frances Doswell later wrote in her diary. Another elite Richmond woman, the wife of a Confederate general, wrote to a friend the next day that she had had "a good look at Mr. Lincoln." "He seemed tired and old," she wrote. "I thought him the ugliest man I had ever seen." Both women were put off by the "huzzaring" of the African Americans who followed the president's party all the way to the James. When Lincoln finally arrived at the river, he went aboard the *Malvern,* Admiral Porter's barge, where he spent the night.[26]

The next morning, Campbell arrived at the *Malvern.* He had found only one friend willing to join him, Gustavus A. Myers, an influential Richmond attorney. The others whom Campbell had invited had begged off, most of them fearing accusations of treachery from their friends if word of their involvement got out. Lincoln began the meeting by presenting a document that outlined the "indispensable" prerequisites "as to peace." The rebels had to accept U.S. authority and all U.S. acts regarding emancipation. There would be "no cessation of hostilities short of an end of the war, and the disbanding of all force hostile to the government." Once those in rebellion had accepted these terms, they could expect a "spirit of sincere liberality" from Lincoln.[27] Campbell was discouraged. These were the same demands that Lincoln had made at the failed peace meeting at Hampton Roads two months earlier. The president then, as now, refused to consider a preliminary ceasefire. Campbell had his own piece of paper, which included such an "armistice." He handed it to Lincoln. As he feared, the president showed no interest. The Confederates had to surrender and submit—only then would the United States suspend hostilities. Campbell knew that further attempts at negotiation were pointless. But then, suddenly, Lincoln went off script.[28]

He turned to Myers and asked whether the Virginia legislature, currently adjourned, might be convened. Myers thought it was possible. Then maybe, Lincoln offered, the legislature should meet and vote for Virginia's "restoration" to the Union. If it did this, he expanded, then the Virginian Robert E. Lee could surrender his Army of Northern Virginia without losing face. Once that happened, the rebellion would begin to collapse. Its leaders would have to accept the peace terms that Lincoln had just shown Campbell and Myers. The Virginians were excited by the plan. This would lead to "perfect peace in the shortest possible time," Campbell predicted.

Lincoln was thinking on his feet, precisely what Seward had feared he might do when he had met with the president a few days earlier. The status of the Virginia state legislature was a sticking point, something that Lincoln and Seward knew but that the president now chose to ignore. As a rebel body, the Virginia legislature that met in Richmond had no legitimacy before U.S. or international law. For this reason, the Lincoln administration had long treated a small, pro-Union assembly that met in Alexandria, just outside Washington, as the true government of Virginia. Its existence had come in handy. In 1862, it had passed the act necessary to create the loyal state of West Virginia. Lincoln knew that most Virginians—and certainly all those who had stood with the Confederacy—regarded only the Richmond body as *their* legislature. If he could get that legislature to declare for the Union, he would bring the nation closer to peace. This was not the first time he had had such a thought. With his oversight and the help of occupying armies, a few states in the Confederacy, like Louisiana, had formed loyal legislatures that had taken the place of the pro-Confederate bodies. But most of the states in the South were still governed by rebel legislatures. At some point in his discussions with Grant and Sherman a week earlier, he had suggested that these legislatures might have to retain their authority during the transition to peace in order to prevent anarchy. But he had wavered over the wisdom of the policy.[29] He was still uncertain, but he had gone ahead and floated the idea to Campbell and Myers that Virginia's legislature might now be considered legitimate. Seward would have been appalled.

Military objectives, not the laws of war and peace, were foremost in Lincoln's mind. The president was using politics to accomplish what Grant was doing with the army: getting the Army of Northern Virginia to surrender. Or, to use the phrase that he had uttered to Grant and Sherman at their meeting on the *River Queen*—getting "the deluded men of the rebel armies disarmed and back to their homes." Considerations of international law could wait. And anyway, his expertise was property law. He told Campbell and Myers that Virginia was in the same position as a tenant of a property claimed by two opposing owners; the state should "attorn" to the party with the best title.

The discussion about the state legislature left a door open to

peace and allowed the meeting aboard the *Malvern* to end with all
in good spirits. Campbell and Myers agreed to sound their allies out
about the idea. Lincoln promised to send a written version of his
proposal once he got back to City Point. Soon after the southerners
left, the president's party steamed downriver.

As soon as he was back at City Point, in the early afternoon of
April 5, Lincoln planted himself again at the telegraph station. He
caught up on news of Grant, who was pursuing Lee ceaselessly. He
wrote out the proposal that he had discussed with Myers and
Campbell in Richmond. This document, along with the paper stating his general peace terms, he sent to Campbell in Richmond. He
also sent General Weitzel a message authorizing him to allow the
Virginia legislature to meet. Then Lincoln pondered how to handle
Seward, whose telegraph asking "shall I go down to you" had been
awaiting him at City Point.[30]

If the secretary of state came down, Lincoln knew, he would question if not quash the scheme the president had hatched with Campbell and Myers. Lincoln himself had little faith in the plan. When
he telegraphed Grant about it, he confessed his doubt that "anything will come of this." Also, the general was making the initiative
unnecessary. By staying so close on Lee's heels, he, not Lincoln, was
"pretty effectually withdrawing the Virginia troops from opposition
to the Government."[31] But the president still wanted his plan for the
Virginia legislature to play out. He told Seward that he expected to
be back in Washington in two days. If Seward could not wait that
long, Lincoln said, he could come down. But privately the president
hoped he would stay put.[32]

The reason that Seward wanted to see Lincoln had nothing to
do with the Virginia legislature. He needed to talk to the president
right away about ending the U.S. naval blockade. Amid the flurry
of events playing out in Virginia, Lincoln would have scoffed at the
idea that lifting the blockade was an urgent matter. Seward, though,
regarded it as a top priority.

Under international law, foreign powers were within their rights
to ally with the Confederacy and attack the United States—if the
Confederacy was a legitimate nation and if the Civil War was still
in progress. Even before the war began, the Confederacy had sought

foreign alliances, especially with France and Great Britain. So far, Seward and his cadre of consuls and ambassadors had successfully parried such efforts. Their main argument had been that the Confederacy was not a real nation and that the war amounted only to a domestic rebellion. International law prohibited a nation from interfering in another nation's internal insurrections. But the U.S. blockade of the South—a crucial tactic to defeat the rebellion—undercut the "domestic insurrection" argument. International law dictated that blockades could be imposed only when *nations* were at war. In the *Prize Cases* of 1863, the Lincoln administration argued before the U.S. Supreme Court that its enemy was something less than a nation—it was a "belligerent"—but it could still be treated like a nation when it came to waging war. The Court approved, but the legal fiction that the war both was and wasn't an international conflict did not sit well with England and France. Southern cotton fueled the textile factories that powered these nations' economies. Were England and France to be denied access to southern ports with no recourse to make an alliance with the Confederacy? Officially, England and France remained neutral, but powerful contingents in both countries argued for siding with the South. Seward and Lincoln had hoped that the Emancipation Proclamation of 1863 would quiet the dissenters. England and France had abolished slavery throughout their empires. Would they really support a polity committed to slavery in a war now explicitly about emancipation? But moral qualms in England and France ran shallow. Advocates of intervention there stood their ground—even when the tide of war seemed to turn against the Confederacy in late 1863.

Faced with this pressure, leaders of England and France were inclined to look the other way when private parties of their nations lent assistance to the Confederacy. In England, for example, wealthy merchants ran into no government interference when they helped outfit and staff two warships, the *Alabama* and the *Shenandoah*. The U.S. Navy had sunk the *Alabama* off the northwest coast of France in June 1864. The *Shenandoah* was still at sea in April 1865. Its mission was to sail to the Pacific and capture or sink as many Yankee vessels as it could. Seward had reliable intelligence that the *Shenandoah* had stopped for repairs and provisions in Melbourne, Australia, in January. British authorities in the port city knew the ship's purpose but let it weigh anchor anyway.[33] On April 1, 1865, a few thousand miles southeast of Japan, the *Shenandoah* captured four vessels flying the U.S. flag, two of which were whaling ships loaded with hundreds of barrels of valuable sperm oil. The crew seized the cargo, transported the hands to a nearby island, then stripped and sank the ships just offshore. The captain of the raider estimated the value of the take to be just under $110,000.[34] With English assistance, the *Shenandoah* had absconded with U.S. treasure that would allow the rebels to keep up the fight.

France had become an even bigger thorn in Seward's side than England. By early 1865, Napoleon III, known familiarly by Americans as Louis Napoleon, controlled most of Mexico. He had installed the Austrian Maximilian as emperor and lent him a French army nearly 40,000 strong. Napoleon's imperial dreams rivaled those of his uncle and namesake. Fawning Confederate visitors to the court in Paris touted the boundless benefits of an alliance. If Napoleon's army would help the Confederacy secure independence, the new nation would lend its military might against the followers of Benito Juárez, the president of the Mexican Republic determined to unseat Maximilian. Napoleon was tempted by the offer, Seward's men reported back. Rumors spread across Europe and North America that French legionnaires might soon be marching across the Rio Grande to revive the Confederate war effort. The threat of intervention by Maximilian was one of the reasons that U.S. troops, beginning in 1863, seized and occupied the northern side of the Rio Grande from the Gulf to Brownsville, about sixty-five miles upriver. By early 1865, though, Confederate troops had retaken Brownsville and pushed the Federals back to the river's mouth. Texans loyal to Jeff Davis and Mexicans loyal to Maximilian were engaged in a bustling trade, the hub of which was Matamoros, across the river from Brownsville. European ships unloaded arms and provisions bound for the Confederate interior and then filled their holds with southern cotton. Matamoros was "to all intents and purposes a rebel port," one of Grant's lieutenants reported to him in February 1865; "there is never a day that there are not from 75 to 150 vessels . . . discharging and receiving cargoes."[35] It was all legal—so long as the Confederacy retained its ambiguous status in foreign affairs as a "belligerent."

Louis Napoleon could officially pledge neutrality while allowing European arms and provisions to be pumped into the Confederacy.

By getting Lincoln to drop the blockade, Seward hoped to take the Civil War out of the gray area between international war and domestic insurrection. An end of the blockade would signal to foreign powers that whatever the conflict had been in the past, it was now solely a rebellion. Maybe England would then take seriously its commitment under international law to refuse assistance to Confederate cruisers like the *Shenandoah*. And maybe Napoleon would halt the Matamoros trade.

When Richmond fell on April 3, 1865, Seward saw his opportunity. The fall of the Confederate capital was not the end of the war, but the Lincoln administration could treat it like it was. This was the reason to end the blockade right away. Not to do so would lend credence to Jefferson Davis's proclamation that the war continued as before. Yet Lincoln could not simply declare the blockade ended and all southern ports open for business. One crucial southern port remained under Confederate control: Galveston, Texas. U.S. troops occupied the other major ports but lacked the staff and ships to regulate the flow of commercial vessels. Opening these ports would invite smugglers to create new supply lines into the Confederacy. Seward's solution was to lift the blockade but close the ports. This combination would do nothing in reality but everything in terms of international law. Closing ports was not the same as instituting a blockade. It was an act of domestic law, one that Congress had authorized in 1861 because southern ports had refused to collect tariffs on behalf of the United States. It was also a temporary act. Southern ports would open as soon as Lincoln deemed that U.S. forces had sufficient power over them. Some that the United States had occupied for a long time, like New Orleans, might reopen very soon. The important thing, at least from the standpoint of international law, was to strike "blockade" from official policy. That move, coming on the heels of the capture of Richmond, would send an unmistakable message to the world that the American Civil War was over.

Seward drafted a set of wordy, legalistic blockade-ending proclamations for the president to sign. Then, on the morning of April 5, he sent the telegraph to Lincoln offering to "come down" to City Point with some "papers." He never got to see Lincoln's response, in which the president said that the decision was up to Seward. In the afternoon, during his daily carriage excursion, something spooked the horses. They sprinted wildly down the street, the driver lost the reins, and when Seward tried to grab them, he fell out. He landed headfirst on the street at high speed. His son Frederick, who had been in the carriage, got some of the onlookers to help him carry the unconscious man back to his house. The army doctor who took charge thought that the sixty-three-year-old Seward might die. His jaw was broken on both sides and his shoulder dislocated. He slowly regained consciousness but was in terrific agony and running a fever.[36] When Stanton received the report of Seward's condition from the surgeon general, he immediately telegraphed Lincoln at City Point that Seward was "dangerously injured" and that he thought Lincoln's "presence here is needed." Stanton added that, earlier in the day, Lincoln's wife had decided to return to City Point and was already on her way.[37]

The imminent arrival of Mary Todd Lincoln meant that the president had to put aside any idea he might have had of rushing to Seward's bedside. If he were not at City Point when his wife arrived, she would never forgive him. Fortunately, the next day, April 6, the news about Seward was better. He was "severely injured" but "not in danger," Stanton telegraphed.[38]

While relieved that Seward would live, Stanton was not exactly disappointed that he would be laid up for a while. With Seward bedridden and Lincoln still in City Point, the secretary of war was now effectively in charge of the executive branch, if only briefly. He was freer than usual to pursue his own plan for ending the war. At the top of his agenda was getting high-ranking Confederates convicted for the crime of treason. Using what he called "the scepter of the conqueror," Stanton meant to end the war with hangings.[39] Seward, by contrast, shared Lincoln's preference for "liberality" toward the rebels. Stanton had little patience for Seward's bloodless solution to every problem. It was a relief to him that the secretary of state would not be joining Lincoln at City Point, but the challenge remained of how to keep the president from indulging his own tendencies toward mercy.

Stanton relied on Charles A. Dana to be his eyes and ears in Virginia. A successful journalist, Dana was one of Horace Greeley's star reporters on the *New York Tribune* when war broke out. When Dana began investigating corruption and incompetence in the U.S. Army, Greeley told him to back off. Dana refused, the *Tribune* sacked him, and Stanton snatched him up. Stanton, like Dana, was worried about wrongdoing in the army. With Lincoln's blessing, Stanton used Dana as an informer. He circulated among officers in the field and reported back any misdeeds or suspicious activity. One of his first assignments was vetting Grant for a top command spot. The two men became close, and Grant, of course, was promoted. Now, in April 1865, Dana carried the title of assistant secretary of war. But his job was effectively the same: he was Stanton's special agent. The secretary of war gave him two tasks. Richmond had just fallen, and Stanton wanted Dana to search the former Confederate capital for any records that might be used in court to secure treason convictions of Jefferson Davis and the rest of the rebel leaders. Second, Stanton wanted Dana to spy on Lincoln. What was the president up to in Virginia? Was he talking to rebel leaders, perhaps promising some kind of amnesty that would stay Stanton's scepter?

Dana arrived at City Point on the morning of April 5, right when Lincoln was upriver in the *Malvern* talking to Campbell and Myers. When Dana learned where the president was, he got back on his steamboat and headed for Richmond. Once there, he learned that Lincoln had already left for City Point. His barge must have passed Dana's going in the other direction, and Dana missed it. His job of keeping watch on the president was not off to a great start.

So Dana focused on the other task that Stanton had given him: gathering records and intelligence from Richmond. Much of the official correspondence of the Davis administration was gone. The Confederate president had arranged to have the material moved onto his train, which left the city before the Yankees arrived. Dana did manage to find some records strewn about the official buildings. He had them shipped to Washington without reading or organizing them. He left that for Stanton's staff in Washington, who would be building the treason cases against the rebels. Then Dana sought out General Weitzel, commander of the occupying forces. The general told him about the conversation that he had witnessed the day before on the *Malvern*. Dana knew that Stanton would be interested in the plan for the Virginia legislature that Lincoln had put to Campbell and Myers.

In City Point over the next few days, the president uneasily came to terms with the prospect of returning to Washington without having ended the war. He was beginning to feel more like an errand boy than a peacemaker. His time was spent shuttling between the telegraph operator and his wife, who had arrived with a large party interested in touring the ruins that scarred the land between Petersburg and Richmond. At the telegraph station, all he could do was forward Grant's battlefield reports to Stanton. With Mary and her guests, he put on a good face and joined them in a few of their excursions. He was passing time, keenly aware of the absence of a sign that the war was truly over. When a telegraph arrived from Major General Philip Sheridan, Grant's top lieutenant, saying that the army was gaining ground on Lee and could bag him "if the thing is pressed," Lincoln fired back, "Let the *thing* be pressed."[40] While touring a hospital the next day, he tried to cheer up a soldier by telling him that "this dreadful war is coming to a close." To one of the doctors, he said the war would be over within six weeks.[41] He had expected a much quicker end when he left Washington ten days earlier.

Adding to his frustration was a growing awareness that he had misstepped in his conversation with Campbell and Myers. When Charles Dana finally arrived at City Point, two days after the meeting, Lincoln showed him the messages he had sent to Campbell. From Dana's reaction Lincoln could tell that he was skeptical that the Virginia legislature should—or even could—meet. Lincoln also knew that Dana would be conveying news of the plan to Stanton, who was sure to disapprove. Indeed, later that day, Dana returned to Richmond, learned the latest about Campbell's actions in response to Lincoln's proposal, and sent Stanton a report. Lincoln wanted the Virginia legislature to order the state's troops to surrender; then it would adjourn. But Campbell had devised a plan whereby the legislature would convene indefinitely and negotiate the state's future with the U.S. government. Stanton was furious—with Campbell for proposing such nonsense, and with Lincoln for having left the door open in the first place.

Stanton was not the only member of the Lincoln administration upset by talk of negotiating with rebels. At the hotel in Richmond that Weitzel was using as his headquarters, Dana ran into Andrew Johnson, who had been inaugurated as Lincoln's vice president the month before. Like many Washington politicians, the vice president had decided to visit Richmond after it fell. Maybe he hoped to visit with Lincoln during the trip, but he made no effort to do so. He did not tell the president that he was coming. The two men rarely had a word for one another. Johnson thought Lincoln's "malice toward none" approach was misguided. Growing up poor in Tennessee, he had come to despise the elites who controlled his state and the South as a whole. They were the ones responsible for the war, and they must pay. At a rally he attended in Washington before coming to Richmond, he told the crowd that there should be leniency for the southern "masses" but suffering for the leaders. "Treason must be made odious and traitors must be punished and impoverished," he declared. Now he was learning that elite Virginians might get to negotiate their way out of punishment. This must not happen, he snarled at Dana. The traitors must pay for their "sins."[42]

Thirty miles down the James, Lincoln was again on the *River Queen*, preparing for the journey from City Point back to Washington. Mary and her party would be traveling with him. As the steamer left the pier, one of Mary's guests kept his eye on the president. Lincoln was staring back at City Point, the makeshift, muddy village he had arrived at two weeks before, intent on making peace. "Mr. Lincoln's mind seemed absorbed in the many thoughts suggested by this scene," the observer later wrote. As the site began to fade from view, the president kept his eyes fixed there and continued to "pursue his meditation."[43]

The trip to Washington would take less than twenty-four hours, but for Lincoln, it would feel much longer. He was returning empty-handed. There had been no surrender by Jefferson Davis; the rebel leader was far from Richmond now, rallying his people to keep up the fight. The Confederates who had stayed behind talked about peace, but their refusal to submit without negotiating first would only prolong the war. As for the armies under Grant, they might well snare Lee's army. But the wily Virginian had slipped out of tight spots before. And even if Lee did surrender, there were other Confederate armies in the field. Would they scatter if Lee fell, or would they listen to Jeff Davis and hold firm? Still, even Lincoln had to concede that with Richmond and Petersburg now in Union hands, and Lee's army on the run, the nation was closer to peace than it had been when he left the capital weeks ago.

It was about six in the evening on April 9 when the *River Queen* arrived in Washington harbor. The president and his entourage went straightaway to the White House. While Mary oversaw the settlement of her husband's belongings back into the residence, Lincoln checked in with his secretaries. Any telegram from Grant? he asked. No. They showed him instead a stack of papers that had accumulated while he was away and needed his signature. These included the proclamations lifting the blockade that Secretary of State Seward had drafted a few days earlier. Seward: Lincoln needed to check on the state of his badly injured friend. He rushed off.

When the president arrived at Seward's house, he found his friend lying in his bed, still very much in pain from the carriage accident. Lincoln saw that Seward wanted to say something, but his broken jaw made it near impossible for him to speak. Lincoln drew his head close to his friend's mouth.

"You are back from Richmond?" Seward whispered.

Lincoln answered: "Yes, and I think we are near the end at last."[44]

He then lay down on the bed and spoke softly into his friend's ear. Now that Richmond had fallen and Lee's army was almost in the bag, Lincoln asked, should he proclaim a day of thanksgiving?

No, Seward croaked. That would be premature. The president should wait until the surrender of Joe Johnston in North Carolina.[45]

Lincoln took the point. Before declaring victory, he needed things to play out further. He especially needed to hear from Grant about his pursuit of Lee's army. The president had not heard directly from the general since April 7, two days earlier.

2

A Big Country

S ITTING AT SEWARD'S bedside on the evening of April 9, Lincoln did not know yet that Robert E. Lee had surrendered to Ulysses S. Grant earlier that day. The surrender had taken place at Appomattox Court House, a village about a hundred miles due west of City Point. Word of the event raced by telegraph across the Union. As the sun rose in Washington on April 10, residents took to the streets. They cheered, sang, and wept. Bells rang from churches and cannons blasted from army batteries. It would be days, though, before people learned the details of what had happened at Appomattox.

A few days before, on April 7, Grant had spent most of the day suffering from one of his legendary migraines. His forces had stung Lee's army fiercely over the past three days, but still the Confederates refused to give up. At 5:00 p.m., Grant sent a messenger along with an orderly to deliver to Lee a note asking for his army's surrender to cease "any further effusion of blood." On the way to Lee's headquarters, the message-bearers ran into Confederate pickets, who fired at them. The messenger survived unharmed. The orderly was shot and quickly died from blood loss. Lee eventually received the message and wrote back, asking what terms of surrender Grant was offering. Grant was dismayed: Lee was refusing to surrender unconditionally. The general's headache grew worse.

Over the next thirty-six hours, Grant and Lee engaged in a series of thrusts and parries involving both military action and diplomatic

maneuvering. In the morning of April 8, U.S. troops attacked Appomattox Station, the train depot about a mile southwest of the village
of Appomattox Court House. They successfully seized the railcars
filled with supplies sent from Lynchburg to sustain Lee's army. In
the late afternoon, Phil Sheridan launched a major assault on Lee's
army. Sheridan's men were repulsed, but they managed to inflict
heavy casualties on the Confederates and to place a contingent of
cavalry west of Lee's army, blocking the route to the mountains.
Although successful in containing Lee's forces, Sheridan had failed
to attain his personal objective of wreaking such devastation on the
enemy that Lee would beg to surrender on any terms. Grant had
taken a softer approach, writing to Lee on the morning of the eighth
that Lee could expect humane terms if he surrendered. Lee's soldiers
would be "disqualified" from taking up arms again until "properly
exchanged" with U.S. prisoners held by the Confederacy. Beyond
that one condition—a standard term of every surrender to that point
in the war—anything, it seemed, might be negotiable. Lee refused to
meet the offer head-on. Instead, he claimed that the "emergency" he
faced was not so great as to require surrender. Nevertheless, might
he meet with Grant at ten the next morning, April 9, to discuss how
the two generals might help their respective sides move toward a
"restoration of peace"?

Lee was stalling, and Grant knew it. Any "restoration of peace" in
the Confederate view had to entail a separate Confederate nation.
Lee had no wish to surrender the whole Confederacy. Nor did he
have such authority. Only Jefferson Davis, as the Confederacy's
civilian leader, had that power. Technically, Lee controlled all the
Confederacy's armies, not just the Army of Northern Virginia. He
had been appointed general in chief back in February. Yet, in the
absence of an order from Davis, he was reluctant to speak for any
army but his own. And as his note to Grant revealed, he was not
inclined to yield even that army. So why write Grant at all? Lee was
playing one of the last cards left to him. He would arrange a ceasefire by dangling the possibility of a general peace, and then use the
time to stop the hemorrhaging. His army, 40,000 strong just a week
before, had in the last few days suffered roughly 8,000 casualties and
perhaps more than 10,000 desertions. Grant saw through the ploy.

He was also following orders. A month earlier, the president had relayed to him through Secretary of War Stanton that Grant was "to have no conference with General Lee unless it be for the capitulation of Gen. Lee's army, or on some minor, and purely, military matter." The general was "not to decide, discuss, or confer upon any political question. Such questions the president holds in his own hands, and will submit them to no military conferences or conventions." Grant had telegraphed Lincoln his assent.[1] No doubt Lincoln had reiterated the strategy during his time with Grant at City Point. Now, on the night of April 8, Lincoln was still at City Point—the *River Queen* would not begin its journey back to Washington until late that night. But contacting Lincoln never crossed Grant's mind. He already knew what the president would say: Lee must surrender.

Suspecting that Grant would reject the delaying tactic, Lee called together a few of his senior staff, including his nephew Major General Fitzhugh (Fitz) Lee, to discuss a final strategy. Late on the night of April 8, they sat around an outdoor fire, most on blankets, a few propped against saddles. The commander they revered, his face drawn and voice thin, offered little hope. Grant had rebuffed delaying tactics, Lee explained. The only option left was to punch a hole through the Federals' ever-thickening lines. They would launch an assault on Sheridan's cavalry in the early morning. Those who broke through would find refuge in the mountains to the west and then swing down to join Johnston's army in North Carolina. Lee assigned his nephew Fitz to be one of the commanders leading the dawn charge.

Sunrise on Sunday, April 9, was followed by a melee of fighting and messaging. The Confederate breakout attempt pushed back Sheridan's men, though Sheridan later claimed that his troops purposefully gave way to lure the Confederates into a trap. Meanwhile, Grant's reply to Lee's message of the day before made its way to Confederate headquarters. The note rejected Lee's offer of a peace meeting. Grant had no authority to treat for peace, he explained. Grant, though, was "anxious for peace"—an unlikely sentiment from a general known for demanding "unconditional surrender." Grant's words were indeed meant to soften his image and ease a path toward reconciliation. By "laying down their arms," Grant promised, the South would "save thousands of human lives, and hundreds of millions of property." A reunited nation would be grateful, Grant implied. The

Confederate attack had begun before Grant's note got through the
lines. But the message would not have made a difference. Grant's
demand remained the same—surrender—and Lee was committed
to a final assault, if only to prove to his peers and posterity that he
had done everything he could to avoid defeat.

By 8:30 a.m., Lee knew that his army was finished. The breakout
had failed. His army was spread thin across the battlefield. He had
no way to communicate with the various elements to bring them
together to concentrate the army's remaining strength on a single
weak point. And there was no weak point. Lee's men were hemmed
in by lines of Federals, which were thickening by the hour as reinforcements arrived. His artillery commander, Edward Porter Alexander, posed the possibility of ordering the army to disperse and
"take to the woods." The longer that Lee's men could hold out, even
as isolated groups hidden across the countryside, the more liberal
terms they might secure from Grant. But if they surrendered now,
they would face "vindictive trials and punishments." Lee reassured
Alexander that Grant had already promised that the men would be
left alone if they surrendered peacefully. Alexander yielded to his
superior. He could see that the general was haggard. Like all of Lee's
confidants, he thought that the general had aged years over the past
few days. At fifty-eight, Lee was two years older than Lincoln and
fifteen years older than Grant. "I am too old to go bushwhacking,"
Lee said to Alexander with a sigh.

The exchange between Alexander and Lee grew to mythical pro-
portions in the years after Appomattox. History became legend:
Counseled to adopt a new approach, a guerrilla war, Lee rejected
the proposal and chose the more honorable route of surrender. The
story was meant to enhance Lee's mythic stature and to play up
the nobility of the South's "Lost Cause." After all, the story went,
the Confederates could have formed small bands that swooped
down upon their enemy in surprise attacks. George Washington's
army had taken this approach during the Revolution—and won!
Lee, though, as the story goes, chose honor over dirty fighting.

Facts, always nettlesome when the myth of the "Lost Cause" is
involved, tell a different story. Alexander was not proposing that
Lee fight a guerrilla war. He suggested that the troops scatter "like

rabbits and partridges." They would hold out but not necessarily fight. This was not a proposal for guerrilla war that Lee was rejecting. It was a careless catch-me-if-you-can scheme that would do nothing but keep the men away from their homes longer than necessary. Guerrilla warfare, by contrast, is a well-established military tactic involving cohesive, regulated units. Lee had no problem with guerrilla warfare in principle. His father, Major General Henry "Light-Horse Harry" Lee, had been a guerrilla leader under George Washington during the Revolution. But at this moment—pinned down by Grant's troops, short of resources, and facing low morale among his men—Lee saw that reorganizing his army into guerrilla units was not an option. Simple logistics, not vaunted southern honor, was the sticking point for Lee. As for Alexander's scheme, which was *not* a proposal for guerrilla warfare, Lee saw that it would have no military effect. Worse, he feared that it might lead his troops to become "little better than bands of robbers."[2]

Lee saw that he had only one option left: surrender. "There is nothing left for me to do but go and see General Grant," Lee said, "and I would rather die a thousand deaths."[3] His message to Grant the night before had proposed a meeting at 10:00 a.m. He had received no reply. Grant's message rejecting the proposal was still in transit. So Lee decided to proceed as if the meeting would indeed take place. Soon he encountered Grant's message-bearer carrying the note declining to "treat on the subject of peace." He sent back word that he was on his way for an "interview" with Grant to discuss the *initial* surrender terms that the U.S. general had offered.[4]

As he and a cadre of officers rode toward Grant's headquarters, word spread among his troops that surrender was near. Confederate regiments began raising white flags. U.S. commanders were unsure how to respond. Some suspected a trick. Most ordered a ceasefire. Brigadier General Joshua Lawrence Chamberlain, better known today for his heroism at Gettysburg than for his presence at Appomattox, was at once bewildered and ecstatic. "'Surrender'? What a word is this! So long so dearly fought for, so feverishly dreamed, but ever snatched away, held hidden and aloof; now smiting the senses with a dizzy flash!"[5] But the firing did not stop all at once. One of the Confederate artillery regiments assigned to support the early-morning breakout, for example, continued to shell U.S. troops even after the attack was repulsed. Major General Edward Ord, commanding the U.S. Army of the James, ordered an assault. Within minutes five hundred men lay dead, most of them Confederates who would never know that their revered leader, Robert E. Lee, had already given up the fight. "If only the white flag of surrender could have been waved five minutes sooner," one of Ord's officers later reflected, the men would have been spared. "But such is war."[6]

Grant was having trouble getting a handle on all that was transpiring. He had spent the morning riding around the main body of the U.S. troops to meet up with Sheridan. By 8:30 a.m., he knew that the Confederate breakout had failed, but he still heard fighting. He saw white flags flying in the enemy lines, yet he had received no final word from Lee about surrender. The messenger carrying Lee's request for an "interview" to discuss surrender spent the entire morning in a futile search to find Grant. Eventually, word reached Grant that Lee was waiting to meet him at the town of Appomattox Court House. Grant sent word to his senior commanders to meet him there.

Waiting with Lee was Lieutenant Colonel Charles Marshall. A great-grandnephew of former chief justice John Marshall, he was the legal expert on Lee's staff. If a surrender was to be drawn up, Marshall's keen eye would be needed. When the two men arrived at the town, Lee had dispatched Marshall to find a suitable place for the meeting with Grant. The officer asked the first civilian he saw, Wilmer McLean, if he knew of a place nearby where an important military conference might be held. McLean ended up offering his own house, the biggest in town. He had settled there only a few years before. When the war began, he was living in the eastern part of Virginia, in what turned out to be part of the Bull Run battlefield. The fighting drove him away, and he moved to remote Appomattox to avoid the war. Now the war had come again to his front door. Marshall told Grant's aide Orville Babcock, who had been escorting the Confederates since seeing them ride out of the enemy lines early in the day, that Lee would be waiting at the McLean house for Grant. Babcock found Grant and delivered the message. The general rode out to see Lee.

—

Theater now takes over from history. The mythologized meeting of the two generals would come to overshadow the actual event. Grant comes upon Lee in McLean's yard, the Confederate reposed against a freshly blooming apple tree. The white-haired warrior-sage of Virginia is stoic. The red-bearded Union commander is restless, his uniform disheveled and his boots muddy. They retire to the parlor of McLean's house. Just over an hour later, they emerge from the house. They shake hands. Or maybe they salute each other. Or maybe Grant merely removes his slouch hat and nods respectfully as Lee rides away on Traveller, the gray American Saddlebred favored by the Confederate commander. The scene allows for all manner of parting. But the meaning of the meeting is singular and certain. The American Civil War was over—at least according to the Appomattox tableau.

"Wars produce many stories of fiction, some of which are told until they are believed to be true," Grant wrote thirty years later when he recorded his version of events at the McLean house. Elements of "the purest romance" had been written into the scene, the general mused, including a fabricated tale of Lee ceremonially presenting his sword to Grant.[7] Grant's version of the surrender conference, recorded in a chapter of his war memoir (not the final chapter, by the way), remains the most unadorned account. Lee never offered his version. The "Marble Man" was not one for public reminiscences. Humiliated by having to surrender his army, he preferred not to dwell on the event. He died before Grant's memoir was published, so he never had the chance to challenge his counterpart's account of what happened on April 9. Not that he would have done so. Charles Marshall, the only other Confederate to attend the surrender conference, did offer an account, and nothing he said contradicted Grant.[8]

All who were in the McLean parlor recall that Grant spent the early part of the meeting trying to make small talk with Lee. The younger man recounted his memories of Lee when the two of them had served in the Mexican War. Lee politely indulged his onetime inferior, offering his recollections of their interactions back then. Soon, though, Lee brought the conversation to the matter at hand: surrender. What terms would Grant offer? Grant replied by repeating the same terms he had sent Lee the day before: "merely that his army should lay down their arms, not to take them up again during the continuance of the war unless duly and properly exchanged." Then Grant drifted off topic again, reflecting on the events that had led them to this moment. Lee added some thoughts but again brought Grant up short. Might they write out the actual terms of the surrender? Lee had no desire to linger. He preferred to volunteer nothing beyond what was needed to secure the best possible terms for his men.

The April 9, 1865, surrender conference between Grant and Lee at Appomattox Court House, based on a painting by Alonzo Chappel. The image captures the small size of the parlor of Wilmer McLean's house. U.S. Major General Philip Sheridan stands in the right foreground. In the background, between the windows, U.S. Brigadier General Ely S. Parker sits ready to write out the final draft of the agreement.

Grant took a pencil and wrote out the terms. Later, in his memoirs, he recalled that he "did not know the first word that I should make use of in writing the terms" and that he "only knew what was in my mind." In fact, he had ready precedents from which to draw. There was the letter already written to Lee, as well as the surrender agreements that Grant had overseen at Fort Donelson in 1862 and at Vicksburg in 1863.[9] In all of these documents, and now again in the McLean parlor, Grant relied on two controlling principles.

The first was parole. In theory at least, parole allowed those who surrendered to avoid prison. Captured soldiers who swore not to take up arms were granted paroles, documents that protected them from punishment by the enemy. Those who refused the parole were imprisoned. A "cartel" consisting of U.S. and Confederate officers oversaw prisoner exchanges: parolees and incarcerated prisoners of one side were regularly swapped with those of the other, with value attached to men depending on their rank. Thus, a side that reclaimed one of its generals might have to give back twenty parolees in the bargain. In practice, the system was clunky. Communication channels stretching from high commands through the cartel to commanders on the ground were far from perfect. Victors on the battlefield were often left wondering who went to prison and who got paroled. Some commanders arranged for prisoner exchanges without first getting the cartel's approval. Others refused to implement exchanges ordered by the cartel. The system fell apart entirely in 1863—because of race. The Confederacy responded to the U.S. enlistment of African Americans with a policy that treated Black soldiers as no different from enslaved people who had rebelled. If captured, they could be executed. They could not be exchanged. In response the Union stopped all exchanges. In early 1865, though, the Confederacy backed down and agreed to exchange Black prisoners. The cartel was fully operational by the time Lee surrendered at Appomattox, which is why Grant in his letter to Lee of April 8 and in his surrender terms of April 9 offered paroles to those who swore to lay down their arms "until properly exchanged."

If the first principle of Grant's proposed terms was about the protection of people—parolees were "not to be disturbed by U.S. authority"—the second was about the protection of property. War matériel belonging to the Confederacy, such as rifles and artillery, was "public property to be parked and stacked." Private property was different. Grant knew that Confederate officers usually owned their own sidearms and horses. He told Lee that the officers could keep these.

Both of these principles—parole-granting and retention of private property—were revisited as Grant's penciled proposal evolved into a final surrender agreement. On the issue of property, Lee explained to Grant that some of the horses in the Army of Northern Virginia were owned by enlisted men as well as by officers. Grant allowed the low-ranking men to keep their horses—they would need them back on their farms. He was not so generous when it came to privately owned weapons. As his initial message to Lee had promised, officers could keep their sidearms. But all other soldiers would have to turn over *all* their weapons, even those they owned.

The parole issue came up because of an apparent clerical error. After revising his terms based on Lee's suggestions, Grant asked Lieutenant Colonel Ely Parker, one of his top aides, to write out, in pen, the final agreement. Lee reviewed the document and spotted an omission. The first version described paroles in which soldiers swore "not to take up arms . . . unless properly exchanged"; the final one left out the words "unless properly exchanged." Lee pointed out the difference and asked Grant to fix the mistake. But was it a mistake? In transcribing the terms, Parker might have left out the bit about prisoner exchanges because he naturally assumed that there would be no more of them—at least for Lee's soldiers, who were going home for good.

Yet Lee had good reason to make sure that these three seemingly irrelevant words were included. By bringing the terms in line with prior Confederate surrenders, the general was signaling that there was nothing exceptional about this one, though of course there was, and he knew it. His was the best-known, most successful army of the Confederacy. Its demise would have a crushing effect on southern white morale. And he had reputations to consider—both his own and those of his men. Without the "exchange" provision, the Confederate soldiers would be conceding that they were going home for good rather than standing ready to return to the fight. Lee chose honor over humility. He wanted no sign that he had given up on the Confederacy. Not yet, anyway. At one point during the negotiations, Grant said to Lee that he "thought this would be the last battle of the war," or at least he "sincerely hoped so." It was the perfect opportunity for Lee to respond that he, too, hoped that the war might now be over. Instead, he said nothing.[10] His deliberate silence was deafening.

The surrender would not douse the hot tempers on both sides, the generals knew, no matter how much the war-weary might hope it would. A *New York Times* reporter present among the soldiers, for example, allowed his yearnings for peace to color his prose. "Both armies seemed instinctively to realize," he wrote, "that the last hostile shot had been fired, the last life had been taken, and that the peace long hoped for and prayed for had at last come to a reality." The quiet "was sudden and unexpected in both armies—as abrupt as the snapping of a violin string while an artist is executing a difficult bar of music."[11] The reporter failed to sense the rage that lurked below the calm. While Lee and Grant had talked terms on April 9, at least one U.S. officer, Major General George Armstrong Custer, threatened to attack the enemy in defiance of the cease-fire. At the same time, a number of Lee's lieutenants, including his nephew Fitz, slipped their men into the woods, determined to join Johnston's men in North Carolina. Fitz soon had a change of heart and led his troops back to Appomattox, but two other Confederate division commanders pressed on toward North Carolina. One of them, Thomas T. Munford, was determined to "teach our children eternal hostility to our foes."[12] With tempers on both sides simmering, Grant ordered the two armies at Appomattox to be separated, lest "unpleasant" encounters result from "a too free intercourse."[13]

Lee had asked Grant for such an order. He worried especially that his men would suffer acts of retribution. During the back-and-forth with Grant, he insisted that Confederate troops not be "disturbed" by U.S. soldiers and civilians once they were paroled. Without that assurance, Lee would not have surrendered on April 9. He would not have left his men open to abuse, torture, and murder without repercussion. Despite popular mythology, "Unconditional" Grant did not make surrender unconditional at Appomattox. He agreed to the condition that he would protect his onetime enemies. That was in line with President Lincoln's wishes that Grant "let 'em up easy," but it was also a precondition of Lee's agreement to sit down with Grant in the first place. It was the only specific term of the surrender mentioned by Lee when he issued his official farewell to his army on April 10. "Officers and men can return to their homes and remain until exchanged," Lee announced. He also used the farewell to explain that it was the Union's "overwhelming numbers and

resources," not a lack of his men's "unsurpassed courage and devotion," that led him to surrender. No amount of "valor and devotion"
could stop the "useless sacrifice" that further fighting would bring,
Lee declared.[14] The general hoped the words would shield his men
from charges of cowardice, especially from fellow southern whites.
This was the informal protection that he gave them. The formal
protection came with parole.

U.S. officers issued the paroles in the three days between the
April 9 surrender and the April 12 stacking-of-arms ceremony. Typically, commanders of Confederate units signed Union ledgers on
behalf of their men, then U.S. officers provided the parole slips that
the men could flash to any bluecoats or Union-leaning civilians who
tried to stop their safe passage home. Parolees from Lee's army thus
were assured some degree of safety.

But they also carried a stigma. Taking a parole suggested one's
acceptance of surrender. To diehard Confederates back home, that
was the coward's choice. Only later would Lee's claim that Confederate defeat was not a choice but an inevitability become central to southern white mythology. In the immediate aftermath of
Appomattox, surrender was, to many, nothing but a sign of shame.
That may explain why so few of Lee's men sought paroles before
heading home. A modern expert on the Army of Northern Virginia
estimates that as many as 20,000 men left the force without first
receiving paroles. That is a remarkably high number: Lee's army was
about 60,000 strong at the time of the fall of Richmond on April 3
and maybe half that size a week later at the Appomattox surrender.[15]
Exhausted, starving, homesick, and above all humiliated, they held
to the last sliver of pride left to them.

As for those who did take paroles, many of them assumed that
the papers were more than free passes home; they were certificates
of amnesty. Their bearers could not be prosecuted for treason. In
this reading of the parole slips, the promise "not to be disturbed
by United States authority" was permanent—assuming that parolees never again bore arms against the "Government of the United
States." As one of Lee's officers put it, Appomattox "practically gave
an amnesty to every surrendered soldier for all political offenses."[16]

Lee himself asserted this interpretation when angry northerners howled for him to be tried in the weeks and months after Appomattox. It was a suspect argument coming from the man who specifically asked for the words "until exchanged" to be included in the surrender terms. The phrase signaled that these were standard paroles and nothing more. They provided no amnesty and offered no pardon. Parolees could end up in a POW camp; they could end up prosecuted and hanged. They were supposed to end up exchanged—back with their comrades on the front lines. This was the scenario that Confederate soldiers were expected to want, for honor's sake. And if honor be damned, it was still the scenario they should prefer, seeing as their odds of staying alive were marginally better standing on a battlefield than a scaffold.

This meaning of parole had disappeared at Appomattox, former Confederates contended. By some sort of alchemy conducted in the McLean parlor, paroles had become pardons.

In fact, Appomattox made the distinction between paroles and pardons more pronounced than ever. If the war really was at an end, or at least near an end, then U.S. authorities would have to decide with finality a question that they had so far left muddled: whether Confederates were to be tried and punished as traitors. Civilians and combatants on the Union side may have been in a forgiving mood in the midst of the glorious news from Appomattox, but their forgiveness went only so far. A Portsmouth, New Hampshire, man recorded in his diary on April 10 that "the bells rang for joy" that morning; by evening, "nothing [was] talked of but . . . whether Lee will be hung as he deserves or be permitted to run at large."[17] In such a climate, Lee and his men had plenty of motive to claim that all had been forgiven by General Grant at the McLean house. Grant did his part to help, writing to Secretary of War Edwin Stanton in June that those who surrendered should not be tried for treason "so long as they observe the terms of their parole." Stanton did not agree. He wanted to see high-ranking Confederates tried and executed.[18] In addition to being Grant's superior, Stanton was, unlike Grant, a lawyer—and a very good one. This did not bode well for high-profile parolees like Robert E. Lee. At some point in the future, maybe soon, they might face vengeful justice. Appomattox would not save them.

—

Missing from the Appomattox tableau is emancipation, the defining issue of the American Civil War. The topic never came up in the communications and negotiations between Grant and Lee. What are we to make of the absence?

A simple answer is available. By April 1865, slavery had been outlawed in most of the Confederacy and certainly in the area of Virginia where the meeting between Grant and Lee took place. Even though the constitutional amendment abolishing slavery had yet to be ratified, other measures had already been adopted, most notably the Emancipation Proclamation, that prohibited slaveholding by Confederates. As part of their parole terms, Lee's men were to abide by "the laws in force where they may reside." The prohibition of slavery was one of the "laws in force" in most areas of the Confederate South. Legal abolition had been accomplished either by state legislation—such was the case in Tennessee, for example—or by military orders. Grant also had made it clear two years before Appomattox that he would not accept a surrender that allowed the possibility of continued enslavement or re-enslavement of African Americans. The occasion was Grant's taking of Vicksburg in July 1863. The surrendering Confederate commander, Lieutenant General John C. Pemberton, proposed terms that could be interpreted as allowing slaveholding to continue in the Mississippi city. Grant revised the terms to prevent such an interpretation.[19] For Grant and Lee at Appomattox, then, slavery was a dead issue. They had no reason to discuss the topic when they met in the McLean house.

Outside the McLean house, affirmations of slavery's destruction were everywhere. Three days after Lee's surrender, U.S. Major General John Gibbon, charged with overseeing the process by which Lee's soldiers were paroled, telegrammed Grant that everything was going smoothly, and further, that "all reasoning men on both sides recognize the fact that slavery is dead."[20] The fact was driven home by the presence of African American soldiers in the U.S. Army at Appomattox. Seven "colored" U.S. regiments—about 2,000 men—stood near the McLean house when Lee surrendered. Most had played a crucial role in keeping Lee's army penned in during its attempted breakout that morning. No one could imagine that any of these soldiers might be returned to slavery. "I was with General

Grant when Lee surrendered at Appomattox," an African American veteran recalled many years later. "That was freedom."[21] For African American soldiers and civilians alike, Appomattox became shorthand for the moment of emancipation.[22]

But, like so much else about the end of the war, the matter of slavery's status at the time of Lee's surrender was not so simple. The law was one thing; the reality on the ground was another. Despite the prohibitions against slaveholding, plenty of southern whites at Appomattox—both those in Lee's army and those in the surrounding community—regarded the once-enslaved as *still* enslaved. The U.S. Army at Appomattox took no formal action to disabuse southern whites of this notion.

Lee's army had impressed thousands of enslaved Blacks into service as manual laborers since the war began. After Petersburg and Richmond fell, hundreds of them escaped from Lee's army and headed for those cities, which were now occupied by U.S. troops who were lawfully bound to treat them as free people. Hundreds of others formerly impressed by Lee's army escaped to Union lines as Lee moved his army west, away from Richmond.[23] Still, by the time of the surrender at Appomattox, perhaps as many as five hundred impressed African Americans remained in the Army of Northern Virginia.[24] Along with them were hundreds of Black "body servants" of Confederate officers, used by the officers to carry their packs, cook their meals, and dig their personal latrines. All of these Black people were now free. Technically, they had been free ever since the Emancipation Proclamation of January 1, 1863, though whites had kept them enslaved. Now what should they do, and what was to become of them?

Unfortunately, no one present at Appomattox recorded the exact number or ultimate fate of the once-enslaved now held by Lee's army. Tantalizing clues abound, though. In a letter to his sister, a U.S. soldier stationed near the surrender site wrote of the trains he saw headed from Appomattox Station to Richmond and Petersburg: "Among other kinds of freight with which . . . [they] are loaded are the contrabands of all ages, sizes, sexes and colors. I saw about a hundred of them on one of the trains at the station yesterday." The soldier was taken aback by the sight of one of them: a "very good looking girl as white as you or I yet she had been a slave."[25] Enslaved women had been impressed by Confederate armies mostly for laundering and cooking, though for forced sex as well.[26] In the parole ledgers kept by U.S. officers at Appomattox, thirty-nine Black men appeared. About half of them were listed as free men serving in Lee's army as teamsters and musicians. Most of the others were listed as "slaves in public service."[27] Why these African Americans were issued paroles is a mystery. Maybe they or the U.S. officers granting paroles thought that the documents would serve as freedom papers, protecting the bearers from being re-enslaved by southern whites whose paths they crossed. Re-enslavement was a real danger to Black people who headed south or west, where plenty of whites remained whose faith was still pledged to the Confederacy and slavery. The safer route for freed people, and the one that most took, was to the east. Hundreds boarded trains bound for Union-occupied cities in eastern Virginia.

What about the African American "body servants" of individual officers? They, too, were free. Like other formerly enslaved people at Appomattox, many found their way onto trains heading east. One of them, Charley Crowley, ended up on a car with some Black U.S. soldiers. When he mentioned that he had been "a servant in the Rebel Army," he later recalled, he "came very near being shot by some of the colored soldiers."[28] Other onetime "body servants" opted instead to join their former masters in the trek back home. U.S. authorities did nothing to stop them. Maybe they believed that the once-enslaved were truly safe with their former masters, that whites would never again treat Blacks as chattel. A *New York Times* reporter on the scene had that kind of faith. White planters, he wrote, were willing to acknowledge that because they were "traitors," they must leave their plantations to their former slaves—or at least pay them fair wages.[29] U.S. troops, certainly the African American ones, could not have been so naïve. But what could they do? They had received no orders to separate formerly enslaved people from their former masters. Nor did the once-enslaved necessarily want to be separated from their former masters. Traveling with white men might offer the surest and safest way home, where family members awaited them.[30] The result was a sight that, to the modern eye, might be incomprehensible: hundreds of formerly enslaved African Americans willingly joining their former masters as they departed from Appomattox.

In the years after Appomattox, former Confederates made much of the scene. To them, here was proof of the benevolence of the slave system and the nobility of the Confederate cause. A Mississippi veteran, Billy Abernathy, recalled with sorrow that, at Appomattox, he was the only survivor of a "mess" of a dozen white friends who had joined up in 1861. He took solace that he still had "my body guard, an old Negro named Simon."[31] Thomas Devereux of North Carolina spun an even more elaborate tale. He refused to take a parole, opting instead for a POW camp. Just before the Yankees marched him away from Appomattox, he told a body servant, George, that he was free, gave him a five-dollar gold coin, and asked him to take his prized horse back home. George would have none of it: "The poor fellow looked at me a moment in silence as if hardly understanding and then blubbered out, 'Mars Thomas, I can't do it. Ise gwine to stay with you. If you can stand a Yankee prison, I can too.'" "With the big tears running down his face," George insisted on going with Thomas, but the Yankees denied his request.[32] A loyal, heartbroken slave; a proud, caring master; a heartless Yankee conqueror: Devereux's story had all the classic elements of a "Lost Cause" narrative. It gets us no closer to a real picture of what happened to the enslaved at Appomattox. They remain shadows on the periphery of the Appomattox tableau.

As with every stage of the Civil War's end, the surrender at Appomattox was full of contradictions, none so poignant as slavery's apparent survival beyond the moment when it rightly should have been dead. Years after Lee's surrender, a formerly enslaved man said that slavery was a "corpse . . . buried at Appomattox."[33] He was right—and he was wrong. A few weeks after the surrender, a slaveholder in Appomattox County named Thomas H. Flood sold sixteen enslaved women and children to Thomas S. Bocock for twenty bushels of corn and seventy-four bushels of wheat. Soon afterward, Bocock decided that he could not manage all of his purchases; he gave five to a neighbor.[34] Whatever else Lee's surrender meant to these traffickers in human flesh, it did not mean an end to slavery.

Northerners, too, were divided over the meaning of Appomattox— for slavery and even for the war itself. Some articles in the April 10 newspapers pointed out that Joe Johnston's forces remained a threat, as did the tens of thousands of Confederate soldiers west of the Mississippi. But most proclaimed Lee's surrender as the final act of the war. The *Chicago Tribune* predicted that Johnston's army "must now dissolve like the baseless fabric of a vision, or surrender to the victorious armies of the Union. The great rebellion has ended! Glory to God in the highest; peace on earth and good will toward men!"[35]

In Washington, D.C., on April 10, U.S. troops fired a 500-cannon salute at daybreak. Scores of revelers scampered to the White House and cried out for the president to say something. Twice during the day he appeared in an upstairs window and said a few words to quiet the throng, but in neither impromptu speech did he suggest that the war was over. The furthest he went was to acknowledge "the glorious news we have been receiving lately."[36] He hoped to give a fuller speech the next day, he told the revelers. Then, as was typical of Lincoln, he played the crowd for laughs. Looking at a group of musicians in the crowd, he invited them to strike up "Dixie." He had always liked the jaunty tune, he said. And the U.S. attorney general had assured him, he joked, that the Union had legally "appropriated" the song from the enemy.[37]

Other speakers in the North on April 10 gave the crowds what they wanted: unambiguous affirmation that Appomattox signaled the end of the war—and of slavery. At a massive rally in Boston, the Republican congressman George S. Boutwell, a former governor of Massachusetts, praised General Grant for having "extorted . . . from the military leader of the rebels, submission to the laws of the country." "Today," cheered Boutwell, "we can pronounce the rebellion closed under Divine Providence." Then Samuel H. Walley took the stage. The former Speaker of the state House of Representatives declared that "we have struck a death-blow to slavery." The audience erupted in applause.

Then came Richard Henry Dana, Jr., a well-known figure around Boston, and no relation to Charles A. Dana, the assistant secretary of war who had recently spent time with Lincoln in Virginia. Richard Dana, now nearly fifty years old, had become a celebrity twenty-five years earlier when he published *Two Years Before the Mast,* a bestselling, lurid tale of his sea voyages in the Pacific. He then became an attorney, eventually specializing in maritime law. Lincoln appointed him U.S. attorney, and in that role he successfully represented the

United States before the Supreme Court in the *Prize Cases*. The 1863 decision established the legality of the U.S. blockade of southern ports as well as the general principle that, while the Confederacy was not a legitimate nation, the United States could apply to it the laws of war reserved only for nations. That fancy hair-splitting helped cement Dana's reputation as one of the leading international lawyers of the day. Like the speakers who preceded him on April 10, Boutwell and Walley, Dana was a Republican and an abolitionist who demanded freedom, full citizenship, and voting rights for Blacks (though the vote was for men only, regardless of race). Yet he never had the success of Boutwell and Walley when it came to winning elections, mainly because he refused to trim principle for the sake of popularity. He ran many times for public office but won only once: he was a one-term state representative after the war, occupying a seat held safely by the Republicans. He simply was not much of a politician. In his speech in Boston on April 10, he showed why. He challenged the audience. Why were they celebrating? he asked. Was it because of the victory at Appomattox? No: there had been victories before. Was it because the victory was "glorious"? No: there had been "glorious victories" before. Was it because "peace was made" the day before? No: "peace was *not* made." And it was that fact—the absence of peace—that was the source of everyone's "intense joy."

That quieted the crowd. What did Dana mean? Hadn't Grant and Lee made peace? And if they hadn't, why was that something to celebrate?

Dana explained. Grant had accepted the surrender of Lee's army but had not agreed to peace. He could not accept a peace from "rebels in arms." Peace could be made between two nations at war, but it could not be made with a rebellion eighty years in the making. He might have added a principle from international law that he knew well: even in conflicts between nations, peace could not be made by contending generals; it had to be arranged by civilian leaders. Dana's main point, though, was that since the war's beginning, the United States had insisted on pressing terms upon the rebels rather than discussing terms with them as equals. This was the Republican position, and it had won out against proposals for open-ended negotiations with the Confederacy that had been made by northern Peace Democrats. The 1864 election had been a referendum against an arranged peace, Dana reminded the audience. The Peace Democrats had promoted "a league of free States and slave States," and they had lost. Grant had held this line at Appomattox. Lee had asked Grant, "What are to be the terms of peace?"; Grant had replied, "I have nothing to say about peace." For Dana, Appomattox affirmed the principle that "Peace must not be *made*. It must *come*." He did not suggest how or when peace might come.

Dana's speech received applause once the audience figured out that he was affirming the significance of Appomattox while taking the popular position that the United States must be firm with the rebels. Boutwell had been more magnanimous toward the defeated in his speech, but even he had said that U.S. "forgiveness" must be contingent on the rebels showing "signs of repentance." The dialogue between Lee and Grant that Dana imagined—Lee begging for peace, Grant saying not yet—went over well with an audience savoring the notion that the Confederates had been not only defeated but humiliated, and that they now must bend to the will of true Americans.[38]

By coincidence, Lee and Grant were having an actual dialogue at roughly the same time that Dana gave his speech. But the gist of the conversation was the opposite of what Dana had described. It was Grant who asked for peace, and Lee who said he could not help.

The conversation on April 10 between the two generals was starkly different from the one on April 9. It was entirely informal, nothing was written down, and no one took part except the generals themselves. Grant was going to leave that day for Washington. He decided, quite on his own, to have one last conversation with Lee. He rode to the Confederate lines carrying a white flag. Lee rode out to see him as soon as he heard of his approach. For roughly half an hour the two men sat on their horses and spoke quietly to each other. Unlike the meeting the day before, this one was private. Each general brought some senior staff members along, but the officers stayed out of earshot. The one exception was Ely Parker, who remained at Grant's side in case further terms between the generals needed to be recorded. Parker ended up writing nothing down, and he never offered an account of what was said at the meeting. The only record of the conversation from someone present comes from Grant, who described it in his memoirs, published twenty years later.

As Grant remembered the meeting, it began with his asking Lee to get the remaining Confederate armies to stand down. Lee should use his influence—not to mention his position as general in chief—to persuade Jefferson Davis to surrender the whole of the Confederacy. If Lee "would now advise the surrender of all the armies," Grant said, Davis would comply "with alacrity."

Lee refused. Davis would never give up the fight, he knew. Lee did not even know where Davis was. After the fall of Richmond, Davis had issued a public letter rallying Confederates to the cause. He said it would be easier for his forces to fight now that they did not have to defend the Confederate capital. Then he had headed by train, along with his cabinet, to southwestern Virginia. When Grant made his pitch to Lee, Davis was somewhere near the North Carolina border.

Grant had gone as far as he could to press for a general peace. Lee would not go along. He even told Grant that peace might not come for some time. "The South was a big country," Grant later recalled Lee saying at the meeting. U.S. forces "might have to march over it three or four times before the war entirely ended." But it was not Lee's war anymore. It was Grant's. Lee told him that he hoped the general "would not be called upon to cause more loss and sacrifice of life."[39] Yet it was clear that Lee thought more death and destruction might well lie in the future. Richard Henry Dana was wrong when he imagined Lee begging for peace at Appomattox. Lee did not beg, and he did not expect peace—not soon, anyway.

Dana had been right about one thing, though. Peace was not made at Appomattox. It was the one paradox hanging above all the others. The Civil War ended in Wilmer McLean's parlor. Then it went on.

3

Righteous Peace,
Fearful Retribution

RICHARD HENRY DANA said that peace could not be made. But at Appomattox Court House on April 12, three days after Grant and Lee met at the McLean house, the opposing armies performed a peacemaking ritual that put the lie to Dana's claim—or at least seemed to.

U.S. Brigadier General Joshua Lawrence Chamberlain presided over a ceremonial stacking of arms by the Confederate forces. While U.S. troops rested their rifles against their shoulders in a "marching salute," Confederate infantrymen stepped forward one at a time, placing their guns on the mounting pile. "Before us in proud humiliation stood the embodiment of manhood," Chamberlain later wrote.[1]

One Confederate officer, unnamed by Chamberlain but probably former Virginia governor Henry Wise, said to the general: "You may forgive us but we won't be forgiven. There is a rancor in our hearts . . . which you little dream of. We hate you, sir." Chamberlain tried to defuse the tension by turning the conversation to the matter of the paroles to be issued to the enlisted men. The Confederate officer's blood was still up. The oaths of loyalty to the Union required by the paroles would not end the war, he told Chamberlain. "You go home," the Confederate growled. "You take these fellows home"—meaning the U.S. soldiers. "That's what will end the war."

"Don't worry about the end of the war," Chamberlain replied testily. "We are going home pretty soon, but not till we see you home."

"Home!" scoffed the Confederate. "We haven't any. You have

destroyed them. You have invaded Virginia, and ruined her. Her curse is on you."[2]

The brief flare-up was overshadowed by the larger scene of submission and solemnity as the soldiers continued to stack arms. For years to come, the ritual of peace—not the rancor of defeat—would be remembered. Yet the sign was there from the start. Maybe Dana had been right. Peace could not be made. It had to come.

Lincoln thought peace could come quickly. Back in Washington after his trip to City Point, he did what he could to hurry it along. The morning after he arrived, April 10, he asked to meet with Francis Pierpont, the governor of the provisional, pro-Union government of Virginia. Knowing that news had leaked of his involvement in a scheme to allow the rebel legislature of the state to convene, Lincoln wanted to explain himself to Pierpont, who was sure to be chafed by the plan. All he had sought to do, the president told Pierpont, was to get the Virginia troops out of Lee's army. Because Grant had just done that at Appomattox, the governor need not worry about the Richmond legislature convening and potentially undermining Pierpont's authority in the state. Pierpont left the White House unconcerned.[3] But Lincoln had shaded the truth a bit. In fact, he was still wondering whether the best way forward—in Virginia at least—was to relegate power to the former rebel legislature, assuming that it renounced secession and committed to the Union and emancipation. "Civil government must be reestablished" in the state "as soon as possible," he told Secretary of the Navy Gideon Welles. "There must be courts, and law, and order, or society would be broken up, [and] the disbanded armies would turn into robber bands and guerrillas."[4]

The next day, April 11, the president delivered his first official act indicating that the war was over—or at least might be. He issued proclamations that lifted the naval blockade but kept most southern ports closed. Secretary of State Seward had drafted these before his near-fatal carriage accident. Even though he was bedridden and barely audible, Seward was able to convey to the president the significance of the measures. Weeks might pass before U.S. warships left southern waters. In the meantime, the proclamations would do the work of declaring to the world that even if the conflict had

once been a legal war, it now ceased to be one. That should remove
any lingering threat of France or some other foreign power lending
support to the Confederacy. The president lacked Seward's grasp of
international law, but he was wise enough to defer to his friend on
the matter.[5]

While willing to signal an end of war in law, did Lincoln think
the war was over in fact? His comment to Welles about society
being "broken up" and "robber bands" roving the South suggested
that he did not. With his guidance, peace might come soon, but
even then, he now understood, it would be fragile. In a telling bit of
inaction, the president did not rescind the order for a draft that was
about to go into effect. He had called for 300,000 volunteers back in
December, with state quotas to be filled by conscription if necessary.
Potential conscripts who thought that Lee's surrender had ended
the war were dismayed to learn that they were still on the hook. "A
draft will assuredly take place," a Baltimore paper announced. "The
hard fighting is done with, but soldiers will be required for some
time to establish law and order in those cities and towns [in the]
South where such a thing has not been known for four years."[6]

To the revelers who gathered on the White House grounds on
April 10, Lincoln had begged off giving a speech and had promised
to deliver one soon; he spent the next day composing it. It was the
longest statement that he had drafted to date about how the country would move from war to peace. But it was a sketch more than a
plan. Over time, he assumed, he would give more speeches to fill in
the details. White House messengers told city newspapers to print
notices in their afternoon editions that the president would speak
that evening. By eight o'clock on April 11, a crowd had again formed
below the north portico of the White House.

Before Lincoln appeared, Senator James Harlan of Iowa said a
few words. A good friend of the president, Harlan had visited with
Lincoln at City Point just a few days earlier. The president had
named him to be the next secretary of the interior, though he had
not yet taken up the post. Harlan spoke only briefly. He intended to
echo Lincoln's "malice toward none" theme of the Second Inaugural. Yet, as soon as he mentioned "the rebels," someone in the audience shouted out, "Hang them!" Harlan responded: "These brethren
of ours" were "comparatively innocent." "Good, good" came a weak

reply from a few in the audience. But then Harlan thought of the Confederates who were not "comparatively innocent," and rage got the better of him. "The masses" might be spared but those "who plotted and hatched this rebellion" should indeed be hanged, Harlan declared. The crowd went wild with applause.[7] Lincoln was caught off guard. The coming peace, not vengeance, was supposed to be the theme of the evening.

The president thus opened his address with a reminder that "we meet this evening, not in sorrow, but in gladness of heart." Richmond and Petersburg had fallen, and "the principal insurgent army" had surrendered. The events gave "hope of a righteous and speedy peace." In his Second Inaugural the month before, Lincoln had spoken of "a just, and a lasting peace." He was less sure now that a peace could be lasting. Yet a fragile, "speedy" peace was better than no peace at all.[8]

Replacing "just" with "righteous" was also a deliberate choice. Increasingly, northerners were using "just" and "justice" to mean the harsh punishment of rebels. The New Yorker George Templeton Strong had written in his diary that if Jefferson Davis were captured, "sound policy would probably let him live," but "justice requires his solemn public execution."[9] This was the justice of retribution, not compassion. It was the justice that James Harlan had invoked in the speech before Lincoln's when he called for the execution of rebel leaders. The president feared that such action would only rile up the enemy and prolong the war. Hence his hope, as he had hinted to Grant and Sherman at City Point, that Jeff Davis would flee the country, relieving Lincoln of the decision of whether to hang him. As for the fate of Confederate leaders who *were* captured, the president had been vague. "Judge not that ye be not judged"—the words of Jesus from the Sermon on the Mount—had been his pat response to the question in recent days.[10]

By speaking of a "righteous" rather than a "just" peace, Lincoln kept the focus on emancipation, which mattered far more to him than retribution. Early in the war, he had spoken of the Union as the "righteous" cause. After the Emancipation Proclamation of 1863, he used the word to invoke the cause of Black freedom.[11] In his April 11 address, he reminded listeners that a constitutional amendment abolishing slavery had passed Congress but still needed ratification by the states. To ensure the measure's adoption, Lincoln said, the pro-amendment votes of new, pro-Union legislatures in states like Louisiana should be counted. The president had more to say about Louisiana. Indeed, the state was the main topic of his speech. He suggested that the government there grant Black suffrage on a limited basis—to men who had served in the U.S. military and to the "very intelligent." He had urged this policy privately more than a year earlier. Now, for the first time, he publicly recommended voting rights for Black men, though in terms that were unmistakably prejudicial. He was obviously fine with whites of any intelligence voting. Why limit Black suffrage to the "very intelligent" unless he thought that some African Americans, perhaps most of them, lacked intelligence? Still, the policy that he pressed for Louisiana represented a major step for the president. He was slowly coming around to the position long advocated by abolitionists like Frederick Douglass, that long-term peace could not exist until Blacks had the vote.

Even securing a short-lived peace was "fraught with great difficulty," Lincoln said. Who, exactly, was he supposed to make peace with? "Unlike the case of a war between independent nations," he explained, "there is no authorized organ for us to treat with." He had hoped that rebel legislatures, like the one in Virginia, would serve as "authorized" organs, but he had learned from his recent trip south that his cabinet was unlikely to go along with the plan. Indeed, the cabinet scotched it at the meeting the day after the speech.[12]

Everyone found something to object to in Lincoln's address. It was not the end-of-war declaration that many had wanted. Instead of announcing peace, the president had expressed "hope" of peace. Instead of calling for a day of thanksgiving, he took Seward's advice and said such a call would be "duly promulgated." His request that Louisiana be rushed back into the Union upset Charles Sumner, who wanted the South treated as conquered territory.[13] Those who preferred compassion for the defeated, like the *New York Tribune* editor Horace Greeley, thought Lincoln could have been more explicitly magnanimous.[14] Conservatives were put off by his endorsement of Black voting rights. African Americans objected that the suffrage proposal did not go far enough. A newspaper editor in Maine complained that the president answered every question "one way" and then "about as much the other." A New York paper compared him to "a traveler in an unknown country without a map."[15] Lincoln might have agreed with the characterization. He had conceded that the situation was "unprecedented" and that "no exclusive, and inflexible plan can safely be prescribed." The words fell flat on a war-weary audience. People did not want to hear about complexity or the need for forbearance. If the president would not announce that the war was over, then the least he could do was offer a simple solution for how to end it.

There were some listening to Lincoln on April 11 who did not want the war to end. For weeks, a ring of about ten Confederate sympathizers in the Washington area had been plotting an assault on the Union high command. After plans unraveled for their first scheme—kidnapping Lincoln and holding him hostage until the United States declared the Confederacy a separate and sovereign nation—they turned to the idea of killing Lincoln, Vice President Johnson, and Secretary of State Seward. The murders would revive the spirits of defeated southern whites. Chaos in the U.S. capital would open the way for Confederate victory. Three of the conspirators were in the crowd outside the White House on April 11. When the president endorsed limited Black suffrage, one of the men, John Wilkes Booth, hissed under his breath, "That is the last speech he will ever make." He ordered one of his accomplices, Lewis Powell, to shoot the president. Powell refused. Booth turned to the third man, David Herold, and vowed, "By God, I'll put him through."[16] Eventually Booth calmed down. Killing Lincoln that evening had not been part of the plan.

It was both tragic and ironic that Booth heard Lincoln's words as proof that the president was a fanatic. So many others considered the speech not fanatical enough. Sarah Browne, a Massachusetts woman living at the time in occupied South Carolina, read the speech and was "much disappointed" by its "unmistakably conservative" quality. "Why can't he cut down the whole tree, instead of lopping off the branches?" she asked.[17]

The president was hedging in part because victory in the war still eluded him. He knew that there were still more than 100,000 Confederate soldiers in the field, well over 80,000 of them east of the

Mississippi River and as many as 50,000 beyond it.[18] The day before Lincoln's April 11 speech, Robert E. Lee had told Ulysses S. Grant at Appomattox that it might take the U.S. Army years to bring the remaining Confederates to heel. Had the president heard that, he might have been even more concerned.

Lincoln's counterpart, Jefferson Davis, was counting on his troops to hold out. For Davis, the Confederacy still lived. Its government was now contained within a single "Cabinet Car" of the train that had taken him from Richmond on April 2. Years later, some of his rail-mates looked back on the episode with bemusement. "State sovereignty, secession, foreign intervention and recognition, finance and independence," a cabinet member recalled, "gave place to the more pressing and practical questions of dinner or no dinner, and how, when and where it was to be had, and to schemes and devices for enabling a man of six feet to sleep upon a car seat four feet long."[19] But at the time, the fact that Davis was still at large and had designs of keeping the war going was no trivial matter. If he had his way, he would find new allies or some other way to revive the Confederacy, a nation on the precipice of utter defeat.

Davis had a plan. He would cross the Mississippi River, join with the armies led by Edmund Kirby Smith, and rule from Texas. Or, in a worst-case scenario, if Kirby Smith's troops were forced to surrender, he would cross the border into Mexico and rule in exile. In Mexico was a potential ally: Maximilian, the puppet emperor whom Napoleon III had installed a few years before. With the Confederacy and Mexico united, Davis reckoned, the South would regain the upper hand in the Civil War. The plan was far-fetched, to be sure. Then again, few in April 1861 had thought the Confederacy could hold out for more than a few months. Was it so absurd in April 1865 to think that the Confederacy could hold out for a few months more—long enough to build new alliances, restore confidence among southern whites, and launch new offensives against the Federals? Northerners might regard the Appomattox surrender as a decisive sign of Union victory, but as long as there were Confederate armies in the field, and as long as Davis refused to surrender and managed to elude capture, Lincoln could only say that the war was *ending*, not *ended*.

For Davis, then, Appomattox represented only a setback, not

complete defeat. The Confederate president received the news from Appomattox at a meeting of cabinet secretaries and a few military commanders at Greensboro, North Carolina, on April 13. The "late disasters" were "terrible" but not "fatal," Davis told the group, and the Confederacy would "whip the enemy yet if our people will turn out."[20] Maybe Davis secretly suspected that the end was near and simply hoped to keep morale high. More likely, he genuinely believed victory was within reach. To think otherwise was to concede the pointlessness of so much southern death and destruction. Like many wartime leaders before and after, Jefferson Davis, removed from battle and shielded from the sight of surrender, occupation, and ruin, was able to maintain the delusion of superiority even as his "nation" lay in tatters.

The Confederate generals at the Greensboro meeting did not share Davis's optimism—indeed, they were ready to surrender—but they knew that only Davis could end the war. "It would be the greatest of human crimes to continue the war," General Joe Johnston told the president, and begged him to surrender. Johnston commanded nearly 30,000 men, the largest Confederate force in the field by far, now that Lee's army had surrendered. For weeks he had been evading the forces commanded by Major General William T. Sherman. Sherman had driven Johnston's troops from Raleigh and made the North Carolina capital his headquarters. Johnston's army was now headquartered near Hillsborough, about forty miles northwest of Raleigh. Sherman could be upon them in a few days.

After hearing Johnston's plea for an end to war, Davis wrote a letter to Sherman asking for a general but temporary armistice—not a permanent peace—and gave it to Johnston, authorizing the general to begin negotiations. The president had no intention of surrendering. He was buying time, hoping to use a widespread ceasefire to consolidate the remaining Confederate forces into one large army that could maneuver about the South, occasionally striking at the Union and wearing down the country's will to fight. For Davis, the war would end only when he said it had ended, and that would happen only when the Confederacy had secured its independence.

Johnston went along with Davis, though grudgingly. Postponing capitulation would allow further destruction of the South by the Yankees, he warned the president. But Davis's mind was made up, and Johnston had to comply. Davis was his superior. Also, because of the laws of war, only Davis or other civilian leaders could negotiate matters beyond the surrender of military forces under Johnston's command. The next day, Johnston penned a message to Sherman asking to meet. He wanted to discuss a ceasefire that would "permit the *civil authorities* to enter into the needful arrangements to terminate the existing war."[21] The general gave the message to one of his captains with instructions to carry it under a flag of truce to Sherman's headquarters in Raleigh. Johnston planned to show Sherman the letter from Davis if Sherman agreed to a meeting.

The rider delivered the dispatch to Sherman on the evening of April 14. Although the general knew that his army might catch the enemy within a week, he was inclined not to wait until then to talk to Johnston. He had been thrilled to learn that Grant had accepted Lee's surrender. Now it was his turn. But Grant had waited until he had Lee's army trapped. Sherman might be acting prematurely. If Johnston did not like the terms offered, he might continue to hold out. Or worse: he might attack the U.S. forces, even though such a move would be futile. Sherman decided a meeting was worth the risk, even if it meant losing some leverage.

Sherman wanted to prevent further bloodshed. Both armies were ragged and bitter. A few days earlier, a band of Confederate cavalry scouting near Sherman's army captured a small detail of Federals, lined them up, and shot them in the backs of their heads.[22] Two days after that, a Confederate cavalryman posing as a U.S. officer joined Sherman's supply train and led fifteen wagons away from the main road. At an agreed-upon spot, next to a home owned by a local woman named Elizabeth Finch, the impostor's comrades stormed out of the woods and rode down upon the convoy. Outnumbered, the Yankees fired a volley and scattered into the woods. The Confederates made off with many of the wagons and burned the rest. When Sherman's men learned of the raid, some went looking for revenge. They went to Finch's house and accused her of being in on the plan. Then they locked her in the house and set it on fire. Don't try climbing out a window, they yelled in; if she did, they would shoot her. As the fire began to rage, Finch opened a window, hollered, "I had rather be shot than burned," and jumped. She survived the fall. The soldiers left her unmolested, but they let her house burn to the ground.[23]

Sherman also had kept in mind the words that Lincoln had spoken at the meeting in City Point with Grant two weeks earlier—that when it came time to deal with the enemy, the U.S. commanders should "let 'em up easy." As Sherman had learned, Grant had followed Lincoln's instructions in his dealings with Lee. Sherman sent word back to Johnston agreeing to a ceasefire and arranging a meeting to take place in three days' time. It would take place between the lines of the two armies, and its purpose was to work out a surrender on the "same terms and conditions as were made by Generals Grant and Lee at Appomattox Court-House."[24]

Lincoln had talked with his cabinet about the prospect of Johnston's surrender only twelve hours earlier. The cabinet meeting took place late in the morning of April 14. All were unusually cordial and optimistic. The presence of General Ulysses S. Grant bolstered their mood. Grant, too, was more pleased than he had been for months, which is to say he was only mildly sullen. The fall of Richmond and the disbanding of the Army of Northern Virginia had lifted a great load from the general. So had the news that he had received two days earlier—that Mobile had surrendered to U.S. forces. He expected to learn at any moment that Sherman had overtaken Johnston.

The president began the meeting by describing a recurring dream. In it, he "seemed to be in some singular, indescribable vessel . . . moving towards an indefinite shore."[25] The cabinet members listened patiently to Lincoln, but Secretary of War Stanton soon cut him off. The subject at hand was how to bring the country out of the war, Stanton said. To that end, he wanted to discuss a definite plan, not an "indefinite shore."

Already Stanton had sent to Lincoln a draft of his proposal. Far from promising the "speedy" peace that Lincoln hoped for, Stanton's scheme called for open-ended federal rule over the South. The operation would begin in Virginia and North Carolina. The border between the states would no longer exist. They would be merged into one "district" to be governed by the Lincoln administration. Stanton himself would oversee the most important aspect of federal rule: the military occupation of the district. Lincoln disapproved. As he had already demonstrated, especially in his handling of Louisiana, he wanted the states to stay as they were, but with new governments pledged to the Union and emancipation. He let Stanton present the plan to the cabinet anyway. His other secretaries could do the work of condemning it, which they promptly did. Quickly Lincoln cut off the discussion before it became too heated. These were matters they would explore later, he promised.

The meeting then adjourned. The mood in the room was still sunny. All were grateful for the recent Union victories and expected more good news to arrive soon from Sherman's army in North Carolina. That same day, Sherman would receive an armistice proposal from General Johnston's Confederates. Lincoln and the cabinet members did not yet know that, but they could sense nonetheless that an end to the war was coming, even if the form of that end remained foggy. Lincoln, more hopeful than ever, was buoyed in particular by the presence of Grant. He had already invited the general to join him and the First Lady at the theater that night. Grant had begged off.

Any frustration that Stanton might have felt when his plan was tabled was softened by thoughts of the abolitionist celebration going on that day miles to the south, at Fort Sumter in Charleston Harbor, South Carolina. When Union forces had retaken the fort in February 1865, a few cabinet officers had discussed the possibility of having some sort of celebration there. After years of shelling, there wasn't much left of the fort, but as the site of what most people called the "first shot" of the Civil War, it was an ideal spot for some sort of ceremony. Eventually Lincoln and Stanton caught on to the idea, and Stanton had taken charge of the planning. With Lincoln's approval, he made abolition the theme of the day. The enemies of slavery were to claim victory at ground zero of the slaveholders' rebellion.[26]

The ceremony was laden with meaning, especially for African Americans. Whether born free or enslaved, whether from the South or the North, African Americans had long seen South Carolina as the dark heart of America's most evil institution. Since sunrise, African American men and women had been huddling on the shores of the harbor, waiting to board one of the ferries shuttling people to the fort for the grand ceremony. Among them was Robert Vesey, a local celebrity. His father, Denmark Vesey, had plotted a rebellion against whites in Charleston in 1822 and then been executed when authorities caught on to it. Robert Vesey had watched Charleston become a free city. Robert Smalls, another notable African American who attended the event at Fort Sumter, had also grown up in Charleston. As a young enslaved man, he had piloted ships in and about the harbor. A year after the Civil War broke out, Smalls led a small group that hijacked the *Planter,* a Confederate transport ship, and steamed it to the Union blockade outside the harbor. Smalls thus earned his own freedom, eventually serving in the Union navy. The U.S. Navy converted the *Planter* into a Union transport ship. On the morning of the Fort Sumter ceremony, Smalls piloted the *Planter* again through the waters of Charleston Harbor—this time as a member of the U.S. Navy—ferrying passengers from the mainland to the fort. For Robert Smalls, for Robert Vesey, for the hundreds of African Americans queuing at the docks for a chance to attend the ceremony at Fort Sumter, the event to come was as much a celebration of Black freedom as of Union victory. Indeed, the two events, Black emancipation and U.S. military success, were inseparable in their minds.

Reporters at the event paid less attention to Smalls and Vesey than to the white abolitionists in attendance, William Lloyd Garrison in particular. Garrison had founded the *Liberator,* the best-known abolitionist newspaper, in 1831. "No Union with Slaveholders" was the paper's slogan. South Carolina was one of many states in the South where there was a bounty for Garrison, dead or alive.[27] His visit to the Fort Sumter ceremony was the first time he had set foot in the state. The day before the ceremony, he delivered a sermon to a community of self-governing freed people living on one of the Sea Islands south of Charleston. The day after, he visited the grave of John C. Calhoun and, standing above the corpse of the proslavery icon, declared to himself: "Down to a deeper grave than this slavery has gone, and for it there is no resurrection."[28] As the most famous abolitionist at the ceremony, Garrison was the obvious choice to deliver the main address. But Garrison's support for the Lincoln administration had been lukewarm at best in the early years of the war—the abolitionist thought the president too slow on emancipation—so Lincoln and Stanton chose not to reward him with the dais.

The honor of speaking went instead to Henry Ward Beecher, a Brooklyn pastor and brother of the novelist Harriet Beecher Stowe. Beecher may not have had Garrison's reputation for radicalism, but he shared with him a hatred of the Slave Power, the term long used by abolitionists to describe proslavery southern elites and their northern collaborators who had corrupted American democracy.[29] Like Stanton, he wanted treason trials for Confederate leaders. As for the rest of the rebels, they might receive pardons but never forgiveness. The enemy was not to be trusted, Beecher had warned Lincoln two months earlier: "It is more dangerous *to make peace than to make war.*"[30] Beecher played on this theme in his address at Fort Sumter. The "guiltiest and most remorseless traitors" would ultimately meet God's judgment and "be plunged downward for ever and for ever in an endless retribution." Until then, it was up to the U.S. government to make sure that the "armed band of pestilent conspirators" was defeated, disarmed, and disfranchised. If instead they were left in power, they would revive slavery and the war.[31] A Confederate who read Beecher's address concluded that "a hundred hangings" would not be enough for the pastor.[32]

The message was out of tune with Lincoln's "malice toward none" refrain. Beecher played up the absence of peace at the very moment that the president, in an impromptu speech at the Washington Navy Yard, expressed his belief that the war was "*so near* its end."[33]

Lincoln never got the chance to read Beecher's address. After his visit to the Navy Yard, he returned to the White House, then joined Mary at Ford's Theater. John Wilkes Booth murdered him there. The actor was known to the staff and players at the theater and so had no trouble walking into the building. He bided his time until Lincoln's bodyguard was away from the president's box, then slipped behind the president and shot him in the head. One of Lincoln's companions, Major Henry Rathbone, tried to grab the assassin. Booth stabbed him. Then he jumped to the stage, ran from the theater, and escaped into the Maryland countryside.

Across town at the Seward home, the secretary of state was also attacked. Booth's co-conspirator Lewis Powell had made the assassination attempt. The strapping former Confederate soldier brazenly strode into the house claiming to have medicine from the doctor who had been treating Seward since the carriage accident that had nearly killed him. Seward's son Frederick sensed something was off with Powell and intercepted him outside his father's bedroom. Powell tried to shoot him, but the gun misfired. Powell smashed the gun repeatedly against Frederick's head, then burst into the main bedroom and made his way toward the immobilized Seward. Seward's daughter, Fanny, was there and tried to block his way. Powell punched her in the face, knocking her to the floor. Then he leapt onto the bed and stabbed at Seward's face and neck. Seward was saved by the brace holding his jaw together, which deflected most of the thrusts. Eventually Seward's son Augustus and his attendant, George F. Robinson, pried the assassin from the bed. Powell broke free and ran from the house, screaming, "I'm mad! I'm mad!" The secretary of state lay covered in blood. Somehow, all in the house survived the attack.

Vice President Johnson was also targeted by an assassin, though he got through the night unscathed. George Atzcrodt, who had been assigned the task, had started drinking that morning to screw up the courage to make the kill. By the evening, he was so incapacitated by alcohol, fear, or both that he backed out.

Lincoln lived through the night. A doctor at the theater rushed to him and was able to feel a pulse. He had some of the men nearby carry the president to a house across the street. Rathbone, who had survived the stabbing though he had a deep gash from his elbow to his shoulder, brought Mary into the small bedroom where Lincoln lay. Others were already there. Many more would drift in and out during the dreadful hours that followed. Stanton, who suspected that the attacks on Lincoln and Seward were part of an elaborate Confederate plot, set up a command post in a nearby room. From there, he began the manhunt for the assassins, occasionally checking in on the president. Early in the morning of April 15, with Stanton at his side, Lincoln died. There was an awful silence. Then Stanton uttered something—most likely "Now he belongs to the ages."[34]

In one version of history, those words mark the end of the Civil War. Lincoln was the last fatality, his death a coda to Union victory. This view was one of the ways that Mary Todd Lincoln made sense of her husband's senseless death. Many months after the assassination, as she recalled the carriage ride that she had taken with Lincoln on the last day of his life, she embellished the scene by having her husband say, "Mary, I consider *this day*, the war has come to a close."[35]

Yet many people regarded it not as the final blow of the war but as definitive proof of the war's resurgence. Before learning of the killing, Edward B. Peirce, a Massachusetts private stationed a hundred miles east of Raleigh, had written home expressing his hope "that the rebellion will soon be crushed." Then, when he heard of the assassination, he predicted that it would have "a tendency to prolong the war."[36] In Union-occupied New Orleans, U.S. Colonel Samuel Quincy suspected that pro-Confederates were "secretly rejoicing" at the assassination even though "they seemed very much cast down."[37] A few weeks later, after he had been appointed provisional mayor of the city, he feared that these rebels who had been biding their time were about to rise up. "There will be a violent attempt made by the Secesh here to escape from military despotism," Quincy predicted. He expected that they would depose him and retake the city.[38]

Quincy was overestimating the willingness of former Confederates to take up arms again. But in the confusion of the moment, amid the torrent of emotions on all sides, it was easy to believe that the president's death was part of a plan to keep the war alive. There was no denying that the spirits of some Confederates were lifted by the assassination. When a Louisiana man serving in a Confederate cavalry unit west of the Mississippi heard the news, he cheered the assassins as "heroes of the Confederate revolution" and told his wife that their next son should be named after John Wilkes Booth.[39] In occupied Columbia, South Carolina, Emma LeConte, a young Confederate who had mourned the news of Lee's surrender, learned the next day of Lincoln's death and cheered in her diary: "Hurrah!" She was surprised to feel so "jubilant," but "after all the heaviness and the gloom" of the news from Appomattox, "this blow to our enemies comes like a gleam of light."[40]

A *New York Times* editorial on the assassination captured the way that Lincoln's death seemed to be both an ending of the war and a sign of war's endlessness. The killing was "the logical and legitimate ending of a long series of outrages" committed by "the slave system," the paper reported. But if the "promoters of this war, their agents or abettors" still possessed "dark and passion-riven hearts unsatisfied," could the nation even now hope for peace?[41] Aside from implying that the war would go on, the editorial suggested that Confederate authorities, including Jefferson Davis, were behind the assassination. No one to this day has found reliable evidence that Davis or his colleagues knew about, much less authorized, the plot to kill Lincoln, Johnson, and Seward. In the immediate aftermath of the attacks, though, when anger and confusion reigned, it was understandable that some loyal to the Union assumed that Booth and his comrades were acting under orders, and thus that Lincoln's assassination was an act of war.

This was the assumption of Secretary of War Stanton, whose opinion perhaps mattered most. The hunt for the assassins was now part of the war, he insisted. He would use war powers to find and try the killers, and the war would not be over until they swung from the gallows. The war secretary expected to find Booth and his accomplices quickly. Some were arrested within hours, but Booth and a few others evaded capture for more than ten days. Stanton was just as adamant that Jefferson Davis be treated as an accomplice. Davis had authorized if not ordered the killing, Stanton insisted, and he should be hanged along with the other assassins.

Stanton had the support of rage-filled Unionists. "Exterminate" the villains, demanded a U.S. Treasury agent in occupied South Carolina.[42] Stanton put Judge Advocate General Joseph Holt in charge of the investigation. Stanton and Holt were of one mind as to the mission ahead: prove that Davis was responsible for the assassination and, along the way, execute as many complicit rebels as possible.[43]

The new president, Andrew Johnson, would not get in their way, they assumed. The journalist Noah Brooks, one of Lincoln's former confidants, reported from Washington that the murder had "nerved the people to a demand that [Lincoln's] successor shall do a great deal of hanging." "Fearful retribution" was coming. "The people, blind with rage, demand a bloody sacrifice and will have it."[44] Brooks assumed that Johnson, too, was keen on retribution. Johnson had made his "Treason must be made odious" pronouncement more than a week *before* the assassination. Now, a week after the tragedy, Johnson shouted the words again, and again commanded that "traitors . . . be punished and impoverished."[45] In the wake of Lincoln's murder, the words took on a more menacing edge. The traitors Johnson had in mind were not just the assassins but their superiors, the aristocratic slaveholders who had led the South into war and were willing, still, to fight by any means for their unholy cause. To Johnson, they were as guilty of trying to "assassinate the nation" as Booth was of assassinating Lincoln.[46] For the new president, the assassination was not the last but merely the latest act of war.

The shock wave set off by Lincoln's death on April 15 hit North Carolina two days later. Sherman and Johnston were scheduled to discuss the possible surrender of Johnston's army on April 17 at a farmhouse belonging to James and Nancy Bennett, just outside Durham Station. That morning, just before getting on the train in Raleigh that would take him to the meeting, Sherman received word of Lincoln's assassination. He was stunned. Even more, he was terrified about the effect the news would have on his soldiers. They would want blood. Even if Sherman could secure a surrender, would his own men abide by it? They might slaughter Johnston's men in revenge. Sherman told his officers to keep the news about Lincoln from his soldiers. Then he boarded the train. At midday on April 17, Sherman and Johnston met at the Bennett house.

After exchanging pleasantries, Sherman told Johnston the news. Johnston must surrender now, Sherman said. Not only were Johnston's forces outnumbered by Sherman's; they now faced the prospect of severe retribution if they refused to stand down. Sherman might not be able to calm his troops.

Johnston agreed: the situation was perilous. But what could he do? He had promised Jefferson Davis that he would not surrender. Maybe, he wondered aloud, if he and Sherman could draft an agreement, Davis might sign off on it. And if they were going to try that, why not go further and include all the Confederate forces, not just Johnston's? The generals could "make one job of it," Johnston told Sherman.[47]

Sherman was intrigued. He knew the scheme had little chance of success. Any agreement that he reached with Johnston would be provisional, as Jefferson Davis would have to agree to it. Then, even more unlikely, Sherman's own government would have to accept Davis's authority as legitimate. Still, Sherman thought, if there were even the slightest chance of putting the nation on a road to peace, he should seize it. He recalled the words of the now-fallen Lincoln when they last met at City Point. If the enemy conceded defeat, then the match was over, and he should be let up easy. Sherman told Johnston he would consider the proposal and return the next day. Then he headed back to his headquarters in Raleigh.

There, the U.S. commander found his worst fears realized. Word of Lincoln's assassination had gotten out and ripped through the ranks. As he stepped off the train, he heard his troops holler, "Don't let the Rebels surrender!"[48] They demanded to be "let loose" on the enemy to avenge Lincoln.[49] Worried that his men would ransack Raleigh, Sherman ordered the guard posts outside the city reinforced. His commanders were "to allow no one to visit the city or wander about it, and to keep all under strict military surveillance."[50]

Soldiers ignored the orders. They took up torches and stole away toward the city. Somehow Raleigh survived the night. On one spot at the outskirts, thousands of men of the 15th Corps rallied together, determined to "clean out" the "Rebel hole." They were halted by their commander, Major General John "Black Jack" Logan. He rode to the front, pointed his sword toward a nearby cannon, and shouted that he would order the artillery to open on the men if they did not disperse. The soldiers grumbled and headed back to camp.[51]

Sherman sympathized with his men's fury but knew that it would lead to disaster if left unchecked. In the tense hours after sundown, he drafted a message to be circulated to the army the next day. Neither the Confederate army nor the Davis government was responsible for the assassination, Sherman declared. Rather, the murder was the work of dishonorable men who had moved the rebellion away from regular warfare and into a "phase ... of assassins and guerrillas." "Woe unto the people who seek to expend their wild passions in such a manner," he warned, "for there is but one dread result."[52]

For all of Sherman's tough talk, though, he knew that there was little his country could do to keep the war from entering this new "phase." The only solution he could see was to get Jefferson Davis to order all Confederates to stand down. This was now his objective.

4

The War to Cease

C OULD JEFFERSON DAVIS be persuaded to declare defeat? This was the question facing Sherman as he returned to the Bennett house on April 18 to meet with Johnston. He did not know that Ulysses S. Grant had wondered the same thing a week earlier. After securing Robert E. Lee's surrender at Appomattox Court House, Grant had asked the Confederate commander to try to convince Davis to give up the fight. Lee had refused.

Such a short time had passed since then, but everything had changed—because of the assassination of Abraham Lincoln. Hunger for retribution among Unionists represented a new threat to southerners who had supported the Confederacy. Lee sensed the change. He knew that Johnston was likely to surrender soon. To save what was left of the South, Lee believed, Davis had to dissolve all the armies. On April 20, Lee did what he had told Grant he could not do only ten days before. He wrote to the Confederate president and urged him to "recommend measures be taken for suspension of hostilities and the restoration of peace." Further fighting would lead not to a "separate independence" but to "the devastation of the country." Lee begged Davis to stop more "useless effusion of blood." The Virginian was using a phrase well known in the history of surrender. Grant had said those very same words to him just before they met at the McLean house.[1]

Did Lee think that Davis would listen to him? At Appomattox, the Confederate general had hinted to Grant that no one could budge Davis—the president would never concede that the war was unwinnable. Other southern whites were just as steadfast, Lee knew. Many hoped to "protract the struggle for an indefinite period," he told a northern reporter.[2] But Lee had to try something, and perhaps Davis would listen to Lee if no one else. Or maybe the general wrote the letter simply to save his own hide. Immediately after Appomattox, many in the North, including Lincoln, had seemed willing to give Lee a pass if there were to be any treason trials. But now, in the wake of the assassination, even some Christian ministers were calling for Lee's execution. One in Boston preached that "Booth is but a babe in iniquity compared with Lee."[3] The parole that Lee had received at Appomattox might not save him. It fell short of a grant of amnesty. The letter to Davis, though, might help his case. It showed that he stood against the rebellion when it mattered most. Whatever Lee's motivations, he knew that the prospect of an endless war was now greater than ever.

Even before receiving Lee's letter, Jefferson Davis was contemplating a surrender of all the Confederate armies. He and his cabinet were in Greensboro, North Carolina, about to depart for Charlotte, when a message arrived from Joe Johnston. The general reported that Sherman had been receptive to peace overtures when the two men met at the Bennett house on April 17. Davis would have quashed Johnston's efforts immediately had the general not also informed him about Lincoln's assassination. That news changed everything. If Lincoln had died of natural causes, Davis would have been elated: Confederates' sagging spirits would be revived. But death by murder was different. Davis feared that "it would be disastrous for our people." "I regret it deeply," he told his cabinet.[4] The assassination would rally U.S. armies to a vengeful, destructive course worse than any the Confederacy had yet seen. Davis decided to let the negotiations between Johnston and Sherman play out. The ceasefire would do Johnston's army good. Also, he was curious as to what sort of general armistice the United States might accept. To help with the negotiations, Davis sent Johnston back with John C. Breckinridge, the Confederate secretary of war, and also John H. Reagan, the postmaster general and a former state judge. Because of his legal expertise, Reagan was tasked by Davis with drafting the agreement, which he did on the train ride east. Among the terms was full amnesty—not merely parole—for all former Confederates, military and civilian. If treason trials were coming, Reagan and Breckinridge, along with Jefferson Davis, would be off the hook.[5]

On the morning of April 18, Sherman welcomed Johnston back to the Bennett house. Johnston told him that Breckinridge was outside and asked if he might join the meeting. Sherman said no: he had no authority to negotiate with a civilian leader. Johnston was prepared for the objection. He explained that Breckinridge was still a major general in the Confederate army, and in that capacity only would he take part in the discussion. Sherman consented.

Breckinridge was invited into the Bennett house—much to his relief. He had been getting hostile looks from the U.S. troops outside. To them, he was a traitor extraordinaire. The Kentuckian had been vice president to James Buchanan and then a U.S. senator before switching sides. Mary Todd Lincoln, now widowed, was his cousin.

Once inside the Bennett house, Breckinridge accepted a dram of whiskey from Sherman—the early hour did not seem to trouble anyone—then began lecturing the general on international law, specifically the rules for making peace. Sherman cut him short. Breckinridge was speaking as if this were a treaty negotiation. It was a surrender by rebels, Sherman said. If Breckinridge kept on, the general mused, he would have Sherman "sending an apology to Jeff Davis."[6]

The three men then turned to a topic that had never been discussed during the surrender at Appomattox: slavery. All agreed that the institution was effectively dead. Johnston quipped that the Confederacy had done its part to kill slavery by allowing states to enlist Black men. Breckinridge said that "the discussion of slavery is at an end" because the constitutional amendment abolishing slavery, now before the states for ratification, was sure to be "accepted by the people of the South."[7] Unsurprisingly, then, the surrender agreement drafted that day did not mention slavery.

A messenger arrived at the Bennett house carrying the proposed terms that John Reagan had finished writing that morning. Sherman read the document but insisted on drafting his own agreement. The rebels must not dictate terms. "Who is doing this surrendering, anyway?" he grumbled.[8] Yet the document that Sherman drafted was modeled on Reagan's. And when his superiors saw it, they would indeed accuse him of being the one to surrender.

The "Basis of Agreement," as Sherman called the document, was a de facto treaty meant to end the Civil War. It disbanded all Confederate armies and restored civil government to the South. Confederate units were to be "conducted" to the state capitals in the South, where they were to deposit their arms in the state arsenals and sign agreements promising to "cease from acts of war and . . . abide the action of both State and Federal authority." The "Executive" of the United States was to recognize the governments of the seceded states so long as the legislatures and leaders there pledged loyalty to the Union. If competing bodies claimed to be the true government of a state, the U.S. Supreme Court would resolve the conflict. All federal courts were to be reestablished throughout the South. But it was the "Executive" of the United States that was to guarantee, to the extent possible, the constitutional rights of "the people and inhabitants of all the States." The "Executive authority of the Government of the United States" was not to "disturb" any people "by reason of the late war so long as they live in peace and quiet, abstain from acts of armed hostility, and obey the laws in existence at the place of their residence."

The final clause summed up what Sherman had in mind: "In general terms, the war to cease."[9]

Breckinridge and Johnston agreed to the terms. Breckinridge headed to Charlotte to present them to Davis. Sherman dispatched a copy to Washington. It was April 18. Sherman and Johnston would not hear back from their superiors for nearly a week.

During that time, the two generals maintained an unsteady ceasefire. Violence between enemy lines was inevitable. As layers of weary Confederates peeled away from Johnston's army—8,000 deserted in the days after the Bennett house meeting, Johnston estimated—the diehards were left behind. "We will whip this fight yet," one of Johnston's men declared.[10] On Sherman's side were the U.S. troops still looking for an outlet for their fury over Lincoln's murder.

The far greater challenge facing the generals was their lack of control of armies that were under their command yet out of contact. What few telegraph lines had existed in the Deep South at the start of the war were now mostly gone. Sherman's army had done the greatest destruction to the lines as it had moved across the South from late 1863 through early 1865.[11] The strategy of crippling Confederate communications had worked. For example, Confederate Lieutenant General Richard Taylor commanded an army of close to 10,000 men and was technically in Johnston's department. But he was very far away—just north of Mobile, which U.S. troops had taken the week before. Communication between Taylor and Johnston was nearly nonexistent. Johnston could only hope that Taylor would do nothing rash to jeopardize the peace that he and Sherman were trying to settle. Fortunately for Johnston, Taylor was sitting idle. He knew about the negotiations in North Carolina and was waiting to learn the result.

Meanwhile, Sherman was plagued by the communication problem that he himself had created. His cavalry commander, Major General James H. Wilson, had been rampaging his way across central Alabama and western Georgia. Sherman had no idea where Wilson was or what he was up to. In March 1865, Wilson's 13,000 raiders had set out to destroy the Confederate arsenal in Selma. They took the city on April 9, the day that Lee surrendered to Grant. Wilson did not hear of Grant's victory, but even if he had, he would have kept campaigning. His eyes were set on Columbus, Georgia. Located on the east bank of the Chattahoochee River, which formed the border between Georgia and Alabama, Columbus was the last great railroad depot left in the Confederacy. It was also rich in supplies—hundreds of crates of ammunition and 20,000 sacks of corn. Most important, warehouses there held 125,000 bales of cotton, which Confederates had hoped to sell illicitly to northerners to fund the continued war effort. Wilson meant to take the city and seize its goods, crippling Confederates in the Deep South.

Columbus was defended by 5,000 Confederate soldiers under the command of Major General Howell Cobb. Unlike James Wilson, Cobb had no dash or vigor. He was overweight, with a block-shaped head and minimal experience in combat. As Wilson's raiders approached, he realized just how many of his reserve force had deserted. Quickly he conscripted hundreds of men who had already completed their military terms. He stationed most of them in Girard, Alabama, just across the Chattahoochee from Columbus.

Their task was to keep the Federals from crossing either of the two bridges that led over the river into the city, and if they failed in that, they were to burn the bridges to minimize the invasion. For nearly twenty-four hours, beginning late in the day on April 15, the Confederates kept Wilson's men off the bridges.

Then, just after sundown on April 16, Wilson's men launched a major assault. Leading the U.S. charge was Lieutenant Colonel Frederick W. Benteen, who was able to drive the Confederates back into Columbus. During the struggle, Confederate commanders on the Georgia side defied their orders and refused to burn the bridges lest they kill their own men along with the invaders. Within hours, Wilson's army had taken Columbus. Nearly 500 men had died during the battle, and hundreds more were injured. One of the wounded was Confederate Lieutenant Colonel John S. Pemberton, a pharmacist from Columbus whose injury led to a morphine addiction. Years later, to kick the habit, he developed a non-opiate-based painkiller made from coca leaves: Coca-Cola.

Once General Wilson controlled Columbus, on April 17, he began planning the city's destruction. "I resolved to destroy everything within reach that could be made useful for the further continuance of the rebellion," he later wrote.[12] Wilson's men ordered the civilians into their homes and then organized the burning of all factories and warehouses, including the massive stores of cotton and corn. When the town's cotton merchants appealed to Wilson to spare the cotton, suggesting that he take whatever amount he wanted for his personal gain, the general became incensed. He would not be bribed. He ordered the raiders to burn it all, all 125,000 bales of slave-produced cotton worth roughly $62 million (about $1 billion in today's money).[13] Wilson would later describe the burning of buildings as selective and systematic, but, as so often was the case when Civil War commanders tried to set limits to destruction, he lost control of his men. They pillaged stores, tortured civilians for their gold and goods, and coerced now-liberated African Americans into whipping their former masters.[14] This was precisely the sort of violence and destruction that Sherman had feared when he drafted the Bennett house terms. And one of his own men was responsible.

Columbus, Georgia, is considered by many to be the site of the last battle of the Civil War. A plaque there marks it as such—or,

more precisely, as "the last important land battle." But instead of
a self-contained battle, the fighting in Columbus was more in the
form of a sequence of reprisals and counter-reprisals such as Sherman had predicted would tremor the southern landscape in the
absence of a peace agreement. In the days after Columbus burned
and Wilson took his army eastward, U.S. soldiers who strayed too
far from the main force fell prey to Confederate guerrillas. One local
band of insurgents killed two stragglers from Wilson's army who
were walking across a plantation. To cover up the crime, they lay
the bodies in a pile of loose cotton and sent the whole mix through
a bale packer. They marked the resulting bale "not to be sold." Not
too long afterward, an enterprising merchant, new to the area and
not knowing the true contents of the bale, grabbed it up, took off the
sign, and sent it to market. Months later the bale was in a European
textile mill, where a worker opened it up to discover two decaying
corpses dressed in Union blue.[15]

By April 23, as Sherman and Johnston still awaited a response
from their superiors about the proposed peace terms, Wilson's men
had taken Macon, Georgia, and Talladega, Alabama. The commander "seems to have his blood up and will be hard to hold,"
Sherman wrote to Johnston.[16] Sherman apologized for Wilson's
"impetuous and rapid" movements and expressed his gratitude to
Johnston for staying true to their agreement in the face of such hostilities.[17] Wilson had little notion of the effect of his raids on Sherman and Johnston. Both commanders were more impatient than
ever to learn of their respective presidents' reactions to the Bennett
house agreement.

When Jefferson Davis received the Sherman-Johnston peace terms,
he was surprised by how far beyond the Appomattox terms they
went. He was still against surrendering the whole Confederacy, but
the extent of Sherman's generosity gave him pause. As he wrote to
his wife, Varina, the terms "freed" the South "from wanton humiliation" by "expressly recognizing the state governments, and the rights
of person and property as secured by the Constitutions of the U.S.
and the several states." In public, Davis was full of bluster about
the Confederacy's invincibility. To his wife, he admitted to being
tempted by surrender and peace. The two options he faced were

both miserable. On one side was capitulation: that way led to "the long night of oppression which will follow the return of our people to the 'Union.'" On the other was continued war: down that road was "the suffering of the women and children." He could count on a "few brave patriots" to continue to "oppose the invader," but "unless the people would rise *en masse* to sustain them," they would "die in vain."[18]

Davis decided to put the question to his cabinet. All of his secretaries advised him to accept the terms. "We have been vanquished," Secretary of State Judah P. Benjamin pronounced. Both Benjamin and Breckinridge argued that even if the Confederates moved to a purely guerrilla war—their only option if they kept up the fight—they could never win. Worse, Breckinridge worried, "irregular" warfare would bring "greater evils . . . to the South than to the enemy."[19] Davis did not know it yet, but Robert E. Lee had made these same arguments for capitulation in the letter that Davis would soon receive.

The Confederate president thought that his advisors had gone soft, but he gave in to them. He had to demonstrate that he cared about saving Confederate lives, even if he cared more about saving the Confederate nation. He took solace in the knowledge that the U.S. government would likely reject the terms, allowing him to keep the Confederacy in the fight. To Johnston on April 24, Davis sent word that he would approve the terms.

Davis had guessed right about the U.S. government's response. On the same day that Johnston received Davis's approval of the agreement, Sherman learned that Andrew Johnson and his cabinet had rejected it.

Knowing what we now know about Johnson, one might assume that he was inclined to accept it. Within a year he was articulating a vision of the country very much in line with the Sherman-Johnston treaty: the states restored to their place in the Union; the governments of those states led by the men who had controlled them for most of the war; and all former Confederates granted amnesty. The Andrew Johnson of April 1865, however, was not the president that he would soon become. When the Sherman-Johnston agreement arrived in Washington, the new president seemed very much in step

with those Republicans who blamed Confederate leaders for Lincoln's assassination and wanted to see them punished. (Only later
did it become clear that Johnson's rage at former Confederates was
short-lived, whereas his hatred of Black Americans was immutable.)
Like his secretary of war, Edwin Stanton, the new president wanted
rough justice for Lincoln's assassins. Indeed, he deferred to Stanton
on all matters—at least for now. Stanton, who always regarded himself as the smartest one in the room—and who often was—happily
took on the role of de facto commander in chief.

So it was Stanton who took control when the Sherman-Johnston
peace terms arrived in Washington, D.C., on April 21. When Stanton read Sherman's "Basis of Agreement," he insisted to President
Johnson that the cabinet meet immediately, even though night had
already fallen. When the secretaries arrived at the White House,
they all shared Stanton's dismay. When they had last heard from
Sherman, he had said that any surrender he worked out with Johnston would be on the Appomattox model. This agreement went well
beyond the terms that Grant had accepted from Lee. Stanton was
particularly critical of Sherman for violating the principle that only
civilian leaders could negotiate political matters such as the status
of southern state governments. Even before the other secretaries
arrived, Stanton had drafted a nine-point memorandum explaining why the terms were "unapproved." He now read that document
aloud.

The first of many problems, the memo explained, was that Sherman had effectively given a "practical acknowledgement of the rebel
government." The illegitimacy of the Confederacy was at the heart
of the Union's war policy, though the Lincoln administration had
fudged on this issue at times—in justifying the blockade of the
South, for example—and had dispatched informal envoys to Davis
on more than one occasion. Stanton's censure of Sherman's terms
continued. The general had exacted no toll from the rebels for the
"sacrifice of many thousands [of] loyal lives." Stanton wanted the
rebels to pay for their crimes, perhaps even with their lives. He could
not countenance an agreement like Sherman's that provided universal amnesty and thus "relieved rebels of every degree, who had
slaughtered our people, from the pains and penalties of their crimes."

Then there was the issue of slavery. Stanton despised the institution, both as a labor practice and as the cause of the war. He rightly pointed out that if the states were left under "rebel" control, as the Sherman-Johnston agreement recommended, they might "reestablish slavery."[20]

For the most part, Stanton's criticism was valid. Lincoln had told Sherman to "let 'em up easy," not to pretend the fight had never happened. Lincoln had been willing to allow a rebel legislature like the one in Richmond to govern the state, but only in the most limited possible way. The legislature could be dissolved by federal authorities at any moment, and it was to be replaced as soon as possible with a government elected by Unionists committed to emancipation. Had Lincoln been alive, he would have rejected the terms, though with none of Stanton's bile.

Yet Lincoln was not alive, and that fact more than any other accounted for the "Sherman fiasco," as some would call the episode. The general thought that he was being true to the peace that Lincoln had envisioned. Even more, he believed that the assassination of Lincoln necessitated a hasty, all-encompassing agreement to settle the chaos. Sherman had misjudged the moment. Only hours before his agreement arrived in the capital, Lincoln's funeral train had departed. The people demanded retribution. Peace could wait. "I love peace more than life"—these were the words of John Wilkes Booth, written in a letter of 1864 but published in the major newspapers just before Sherman's deal with Johnston was made public. Booth's brother-in-law had released the letter to the press. Booth himself had still not been caught, though the manhunt for him was getting closer every day. In the letter that he wrote in 1864, Booth had said it was his love of peace that turned his thoughts to blood. Lincoln alone was responsible for shattering peace in the nation, Booth had written, so he had to go.[21] Now Sherman—like Booth, it seemed to some—was putting peace above justice, and with the help of the very people who had killed the president. It was an act nearly as "astounding" as the assassination itself, a Massachusetts man wrote.[22]

In calmer times, people might have better appreciated Sherman's strategy. The general deserved some scorn, to be sure. His terms left slavery untouched, as Stanton had complained. Sherman was known to be indifferent to slavery and callous toward African Americans generally. The terms cemented that reputation. The *New York Times* mocked the general for accepting Breckinridge's claim that slavery was "defunct" and then agreeing to terms "designed to make the institution of slavery perpetual."[23] The criticism went too far. Sherman was no abolitionist, but he never thought that slavery would or should remain intact. He had written Johnston that the best move forward was for the South to "simply and publicly declare what we all feel, that slavery is dead." How to secure the actual legality of emancipation was a matter for the lawyers and politicians, Sherman said. But there was no reason the two generals could not add to their agreement a mere acknowledgment of slavery's death.[24]

Despite Stanton's accusation, Sherman had no intention of usurping civilian authority. In his letter to Johnston about slavery, he had showed respect for the line between a "military convention" and a political agreement. Over and over during the negotiations with Johnston, Sherman had made the same point. He had even been ready to dismiss Breckinridge from the Bennett house until he learned that the cabinet member also had a military appointment. When the North Carolina governor, Zebulon Vance, tried to involve himself in surrender negotiations, Sherman cordially kept him at bay. Finally, and most importantly, the agreement itself conceded the subordinate status of the generals to their presidents. "Not being fully empowered by our respective principals to fulfill these terms," the agreement read, the generals pledged "to promptly obtain the necessary authority." In a sinister bit of selective editing, Stanton did not include that line when he leaked news of Sherman's terms to the papers. Instead, he attached Lincoln's March 3 letter to Grant, in which Lincoln had said that Grant was not to discuss or decide "political questions" because "such questions the President holds in his own hands."[25] Stanton encouraged readers to draw the false conclusion that Sherman had disobeyed the order of the martyred president.

In fact, Sherman knew that "political questions" had to be decided by civilian authorities. That is why he called the terms a "Basis of Agreement." He never would have allowed the document to be called a treaty, which is what the *New York Times* called it (General Sherman "Undertakes a Treaty," the headline blared). Any encroachment that Sherman had made on civilian authority had been minimal—

and only because he did not know what civilian authority, if any, now existed in the Union. President Lincoln was dead. Were assassins still in the capital? Was the life of Lincoln's successor, Andrew Johnson, now in jeopardy? All the unknowns about the presidency led Sherman to use the term "Executive" instead of "President" in his peace terms. He might have been tempted to assign a role to Congress. Lincoln's Reconstruction Proclamation of 1863 declared that Congress must be the ultimate arbiter of the status of rebellious states. But Congress was out of session and would not reconvene until December. The president could call Congress to a special session, but—again—was there even a president to make that call? Hence Sherman's provisions giving the U.S. Supreme Court the power to determine which state governments in the South were legitimate. Even if the Court was out of session, justices could issue ex parte decisions with legal force. In many of its details, Sherman's agreement revealed the undeniable logic of the moment.

Yet by what logic could Sherman allow the very people who had led the rebellion to hold on to their power with no threat of future prosecution? They would have all the guns they needed to keep the rebellion alive. Sherman's miscalculation was in thinking that these men, if treated honorably, would return to their communities and put down any uprisings among less honorable former Confederates. To put it in modern terms, the surrendering soldiers were to be the most important safeguard against *insurgency*. Sherman had always worried that local feuds would lead diehard Confederates to rise up again in a full-on war. His fears intensified after the Lincoln assassination. He suspected that Unionists in the South would lash out in rage at former Confederates. Insurgencies against U.S. troops and their Unionist allies would result, and the army would be spread too thin to put them down. At that point, the United States would have to rely on squads of honorable former Confederates led by elite southern whites to keep the peace. Sherman's thinking was wrongheaded, and one might well wonder why he failed to foresee that the very men he trusted to save the Union would be the greatest obstacle to the "just and lasting peace" imagined by Lincoln. To understand Sherman, it may help to consider that the very same strategy for dealing with insurgents has informed U.S. foreign interventions from the Philippines in the early twentieth century to Afghanistan in the early twenty-first. Have U.S. occupiers since Sherman's time proven to be that much wiser?[26]

Whatever wisdom Sherman saw in his plan, he knew that his superiors might reject it. For that reason, he told Breckinridge at the Bennett house that he and other leaders of the Confederacy should consider leaving the country to avoid prosecution. Sherman no doubt recalled Lincoln's hint at City Point to let Jefferson Davis leave the country "unbeknown." When word arrived from Washington on April 24 informing him that the agreement was disapproved, he was disappointed but not surprised. He was stunned, though, that it was Grant who carried the message. By sending Grant, Stanton had undermined Sherman's authority, the general believed. Sherman also regarded Stanton's blistering public condemnation as unnecessarily cruel. Grant handled the encounter with Sherman deftly, making sure his subordinate understood the message and then stepping aside to allow Sherman to resume communications with Johnston. Sherman immediately informed Johnston that the agreement was rejected and the ceasefire was to end in forty-eight hours. Johnston relayed the news to Jefferson Davis in Charlotte.

When Davis received word that Johnston's peace deal had been rejected—a response he had anticipated and secretly hoped for—he took up his previous position: no surrender. He ordered Johnston to send to Davis as much of the army as could travel quickly enough to avoid capture by Sherman. This force would help Davis get to Mexico, where he would rule in exile. The Confederacy would live on.

Johnston rejected Davis's order, a remarkable act of insubordination. Instead, encouraged by the magnanimity that Sherman had shown, the Confederate general chose to surrender. "We have to save the people, spare the blood of the army, and save the high civil functionaries," Johnston wrote Davis. "Your plan, I think, can only do the last."[27]

On April 26, Sherman and Johnston had their final meeting at the Bennett house. This time, the terms that Sherman offered were exactly the same as those presented by Grant to Lee at Appomattox. Johnston signed them. As at Appomattox, only military personnel were covered by the agreement. Former Confederates were granted parole but not amnesty.

As at Appomattox, no hint of slavery appeared in the terms. If there were "body servants" in the army who belonged to Johnston's officers, they might be returning home with their masters, their legal status still in limbo. But most likely there were very few if any enslaved African Americans left in Johnston's army. The proximity of Sherman's army over the past eight months had allowed thousands of them to escape to Union lines. Any enslaved laborers left in Johnston's army by the end of April 1865 were just as likely to head into the countryside as to seek refuge in Sherman's army. There they could find hundreds of other African Americans who were making new lives for themselves away from their former plantations. Soon after the surrender, a white planter in Hillsborough, where Johnston's army was headquartered, complained to his family that all his enslaved laborers had left. He traveled the county, begging hundreds of African Americans to work on his farm. Only one man came.[28]

The surrender of Johnston's army, the last large Confederate force east of the Mississippi River, was a pivotal event. But it received much less attention than the surrender of Lee's army a few weeks earlier. One reason was obvious: Johnston was much lesser known than Lee, who had become a symbol of the Confederacy. There was another reason, though. Word of the surrender was eclipsed by the stunning news that John Wilkes Booth had been found and killed.

On the same day of the meeting at the Bennett house, U.S. soldiers cornered Booth and one of his accomplices, David Herold, in a farmhouse in Virginia, about halfway between Washington and Richmond. The detachment tried to flush them out by setting a fire that spread inside the building. A few of the soldiers were able to get inside. Herold ran out and surrendered. Booth stood amid the flames, screaming that he was prepared to die. One of the soldiers shot him in the neck. The bullet drew a torrent of blood and pierced his spine. Booth was dead in seconds. The sensational tale eclipsed the reports from North Carolina about Johnston's final surrender to Sherman.

Meanwhile, in the South, the latest news about the final surrender terms at the Bennett house was slow in coming. Unaware of the revised agreement, a number of Confederates believed that the liberal amnesty terms of the original surrender had gone into effect. They were thrilled that the war was truly over and they would suffer no penalties. Some high-ranking Confederates who had been thinking about fleeing to avoid trial and execution instead headed home, assuming that they had amnesty. One such man was Henry Wirz, the commandant of Andersonville in Georgia, the largest and most infamous prisoner-of-war camp in the Confederacy. When U.S. troops showed up at his home on May 7 to arrest him, Wirz was perplexed. Hadn't he escaped the noose because of Sherman's terms? he asked. No, came the reply: those terms had been rejected. He would have to face a trial.

In Alabama, at the end of April, Confederate General Richard Taylor assumed that he and his troops had amnesty because of the Sherman-Johnston peace agreement. He sent word to his counterpart, U.S. Major General Edward Canby, that he would take the train to Mobile to surrender his army. Canby and his senior staff, all of whom were also under the mistaken belief that Sherman's terms had been accepted, prepared to receive Taylor with a lush spread of food and a shiny brass band. Taylor's appearance was not so grand. Just before arriving at Canby's lines, the train carrying Taylor and his military escort came to a bridge impassable because of recent shelling. The Confederate general was forced to complete the journey on an old-fashioned handcar. On April 29, as Canby and his vast entourage looked on, Taylor pathetically creaked into view, a single aide at his side and two enslaved men pumping the lever that propelled the handcar. Canby's band went ahead and played "Dixie" and "Hail Columbia." All enjoyed the buffet. And the two generals signed an accord pledging to abide by the terms of the Sherman-Johnston "armistice." But within two days, they had learned about the rejection of the Bennett house peace terms. On May 4, the two generals met again—this time with no fanfare—at a small house in Citronelle, Alabama. There was no talk of a peace made in North Carolina. Instead, the Appomattox template was the basis of the surrender signed by Taylor. The general brought no enslaved laborers with him this time. Perhaps it was a sign, however dim, that he now accepted emancipation as the necessary consequence of surrender.

Back at the Bennett house, on April 26, Johnston had signed the revised surrender agreement—again, based on the Appomattox document. The event lacked the grandeur of Appomattox—there was no stacking-of-arms ceremony—but in terms of scale it was far more significant. When Lee surrendered, his agreement covered only the Army of Northern Virginia, which had fewer than 30,000 men. Johnston's surrender encompassed not only his own army in North Carolina but the units under his command in South Carolina, Georgia, and Florida. A total of nearly 90,000 Confederates were rendered inactive by the stroke of Johnston's pen. It was by far the largest surrender of the Civil War.[29]

Jefferson Davis was furious at Johnston for surrendering. Davis had tolerated Lee's surrender—the general in chief could not communicate with Davis in the days after Richmond's fall and thus could be excused for giving up his army on his own initiative—but he regarded Johnston's capitulation as betrayal, for he had willfully disregarded orders.

Johnston's action did nothing to change Davis's plan to escape to Mexico and rule from there. First, though, Davis took the "cabinet car" to Abbeville, South Carolina, where his wife, Varina, was waiting for him. The couple planned to secure some vessels on the Florida coast. When Davis headed to Mexico, Varina would go to Cuba, then perhaps Europe. Soon after Davis's train arrived in Abbeville, he learned that she had already left. Before setting out to catch up with her, he met with his remaining cabinet members and a few high-ranking officers. Breckinridge had set up the conference with the hope that Johnston's surrender would finally persuade Davis to give up. When Davis asked one of the officers if his men would still fight, he responded that they would "risk anything" for their president.

But would they fight for the *Confederacy*? asked Davis.

"Mr. Davis," the officer replied, "they think the war is over."

Davis was visibly shaken but resolute. His safety was unimportant, he told them. What mattered was the Confederacy, and he would not give it up. Things were no worse for the Confederates than they had been for the American colonists during the darker days of the Revolution, he assured the men. Davis was not entirely wrong. Kirby Smith's forces were still untouched beyond the Mississippi. But Davis's men kept quiet. No one shared the president's rosy outlook. After a few minutes of silence, Davis, now ashen, rose and spit bitterly at the men that "all was indeed lost."[30]

Yet Davis had not given up on the Confederacy—only on his

officers. He remained convinced that if he could get to safety outside the country, he could find foreign allies and rally his country
back from the brink. He gathered his things, mustered what was
left of his courage, and departed for Georgia on horseback, escorted
by a small squad of soldiers. He was intent on catching up to his
wife. Behind him lay the shards of the Confederate high command.
Ahead lay an uncertain future. But he still had a nation to lead, and
that was all that mattered.

General Sherman had learned the hard way that "peace cannot be
made"—the prophetic words spoken by Richard Henry Dana on
the day after Lee's surrender to Grant. Dana had said that "peace
must come." Even if the words were true, they were unwelcome to
the war-weary on all sides who wanted the "speedy" peace that Lincoln had promised in his final address. Americans were impatient
for peace but uncertain as to how peace could be made. The pre-
dicament will sound familiar to anyone who has lived through U.S.
conflicts of the late twentieth and early twenty-first centuries. So,
too, will the favored solution of Americans in the modern era: simply declare that war is over and peace established. A peace declared
is not peace in fact, but as a political tool, a declared peace has its
merits. It offers assurance to victor and vanquished alike that the
worst of the war is over. It orients people away from a dismal past
and toward a harmonious future.

    Familiar as the approach is today, Americans in 1865 were not
accustomed to a president declaring peace. But they were about
to be.

    In the brief period between Lee's surrender on April 9 and Lin-
coln's assassination on April 14, Lincoln sometimes came close to
declaring the war over but always stopped short. When he lifted the
blockade, he merely *signaled* peace—or at least the absence of war.
The signal was easily missed, hidden as it was within the opaque
language of international law. In his address of April 11, which
turned out to be his last, he spoke only of a "speedy and righteous"
peace to come. A more callous, artless politician in Lincoln's position might have opted for the modern method: "declare victory and
get out," a phrase attributed to Senator George Aiken during the
U.S.–Vietnam war.[31]

Andrew Johnson—callous, artless, and a hundred other things that Lincoln wasn't (bigoted, foul-tempered, and insecure, to name a few)—was now in Lincoln's position. Ten days after taking office, he rejected the approach of making a peace, or at least Sherman's method of making one. Then, in the weeks that followed, he began to toy with the idea of *declaring* a peace. Stanton and Grant went along with Johnson. Actually, they nudged him along.

The first declarations came on May 9. Johnson issued two that day. One recognized as legitimate the governments of the formerly seceded states of Arkansas, Louisiana, Tennessee, and Virginia. These were all now pro-Union governments, set up under Lincoln's supervision, so in a way Johnson was merely affirming what his predecessor had done. Unlike Lincoln, though, Johnson explicitly rejected any possibility that competing governments in these states— that is, legislatures that had been loyal to the Confederacy—would have any say in future affairs. Virginia, for example, had two governments: a tiny pro-Union body in Alexandria and a large, defunct, formerly Confederate legislature in Richmond. Lincoln officially recognized only the Alexandria government. Then, when he visited Richmond in early April, he hatched the plan of having the Richmond legislature hasten the process of reunion. Andrew Johnson, like Lincoln's cabinet, rejected the plan. Within days of Johnson taking office, Stanton authorized the arrest of John A. Campbell, Lincoln's partner in the short-lived scheme. The leaders of all the rebel state governments, Johnson ominously announced in his first May 9 declaration, would be "dealt with."[32] So, too, would Jefferson Davis, Johnson added. Indeed, just the day before, Davis had been named along with half a dozen other Confederate leaders as co-conspirators in the charges filed against those already arrested for the Lincoln assassination. Johnson's first peace declaration of May 9 thus had a warlike tone. Lincoln's "let 'em up easy" approach was gone.

The second May 9 declaration put the rebel South under control of the U.S. Executive. Each department of the Executive was to take charge of the corresponding department in every state undergoing reconstruction. The U.S. postmaster, for example, would oversee the postal service in the southern states that had rebelled. Meanwhile, the U.S. Army, under Stanton's control, would have the ultimate authority over civilian affairs in each state.

These were powerful declarations, but they were only declarations. In fact, most of the pro-Union governments that existed in the southern states were frail. As for the U.S. Executive running southern affairs, that would require the U.S. Army retaining all its current personnel and spreading forces across the South. That was not going to go over well with the hundreds of thousands of U.S. soldiers expecting to return home soon. The plan was Stanton's, and he was no doubt responsible for this part of Johnson's May 9 orders. The secretary of war had taken the proposal to the cabinet back on April 14—Lincoln's last cabinet meeting—and Lincoln had tabled it. Weeks later, Stanton had brought it again to the cabinet, this time with Johnson as president. Johnson had endorsed it, a sign again of the deference that he showed to Stanton in all military affairs.

Johnson's May 9 declarations were silent on the matter of Black voting rights. The absence did not necessarily concern advocates of Black suffrage. Nothing that Johnson had written suggested that he would stand in the way of the new state governments granting Black men the vote. (Black *women* were a different matter: Johnson, like most of those in power at the time, was against women's suffrage.) But given that Lincoln had explicitly recommended at least limited Black male suffrage in Louisiana in his last speech, the silence in Johnson's orders was audible. On the voting issue, Johnson did not defer to Stanton, who preferred a policy of Black suffrage. In a meeting with leading Republicans a few days earlier, the secretary of war had been persuaded that, as Senator Charles Sumner put it, the absence of voting rights made a "mockery" of Black freedom.[33] But Stanton chose not to press the divisive issue of suffrage on Johnson, lest it jeopardize the deference that the president was giving him. As things stood, then, Johnson seemed to be declaring that whites-only governments would be acceptable in the postwar South.

Were the May 9 proclamations a declaration by President Johnson that the war was over? They seemed to be. There was no mention of enemy armies still in the field, though there were some, and there was a clear suggestion that the U.S. government had control of the entire country, though it didn't.

A more definitive declaration of peace came the next day, on May 10, though it was buried in a tortuous order with an uninspiring title: "Ordering the Arrest of Insurgent Cruisers."[34] The "cruisers" in question were the Confederate ships *Stonewall* and *Shenandoah*, though neither was mentioned by name. Both had been European vessels repurposed by the Confederacy in 1864 to attack U.S. merchant ships. The *Stonewall*, an armored ram propelled by sail and steam, prowled the Atlantic—or was meant to. After a near encounter with U.S. ships off the coast of northwest Spain, the ship sped to the Caribbean. It was docked in Nassau when Johnson issued the proclamation. The *Shenandoah* was assigned to the Pacific. At the time of the May 10 proclamation, it was fighting storm winds just east of Japan. Intelligence about both cruisers had arrived through diplomatic channels. By international law, these were legitimate vessels that could dock and refuel in any port while the Civil War continued. Once the war was over, however, they would lose their status as warships and be classified as pirate ships. Under international law, pirates were "enemies of all mankind" (*hostis humani generis*) who were barred from all ports. To remove the threat posed by the Confederate cruisers, Secretary of the Navy Gideon Welles had been pressuring Johnson for weeks to issue a proclamation saying that they were pirate ships because the war was over.[35] This would prevent the vessels from receiving any further assistance from foreign powers.

Johnson's May 10 proclamation gave Welles what he wanted. It declared that "armed resistance to the authority of this Government in the said insurrectionary States may be regarded as virtually at an end." As a result, foreign nations now had to "refuse hospitality" to Confederate vessels. Of course, it would take some time before news of the proclamation reached foreign powers and the officers commanding the Confederate ships. By the time the crew of the *Stonewall* learned of it, they had already sailed to Havana and abandoned their ship to Cuban authorities. The captain had ended their mission after learning of the surrenders of the Confederate armies east of the Mississippi. The *Shenandoah* would not learn of the proclamation until months later.

The legal technicalities surrounding the status of the "cruisers" were nearly meaningless to the public; what mattered was the president's statement that the war was "virtually at an end." This was the closest to an end-of-war declaration that either Lincoln or Johnson had made. Between this proclamation and the orders concerning reconstruction the day before, the president had signaled that the war was over. Or so it seemed to some of the northern newspapers. The *New York Herald* announced that "in a briefer period than people dreamed of the effects of the war will have materially diminished, and unrestrained prosperity will be with us once again."[36] The *Chicago Tribune* also harped on the material benefits of the war's end: "Peace has dawned, and beside the rich consolations it brings to hearts and homes, we believe it will mark the era of an unexampled period of general national prosperity."[37]

But was a "virtual" end of war the same thing as peace? That pesky word "virtually" in Johnson's proclamation was as frustrating as the phrase "at an end" was comforting.

The expression "virtually at an end" was not new; it was new only to Johnson's pen. U.S. Major General Benjamin Butler had written Johnson on April 25 that the war was "virtually at an end" when explaining why prisoner exchanges should cease.[38] Even before that, just hours before Lincoln was shot, Chief Justice Salmon P. Chase had written to future justice Stanley Matthews that he knew of "no rebel and no sympathizer with rebellion who does not consider the insurrection as effectually, though as yet only virtually quelled." For Chase, "virtually" was not a mere qualifier; it spoke to the heart of the problem: "the hydra of rebellion" needed to be "killed not scotched."[39] By "scotched," Chase meant crippled but not finished.

Between "scotched" and "killed," between a virtual end and an actual end, lay either a tiny gap or a yawning gulf. The exact distance depended on the unknowable. How much life was left in the rebellion, and how far was the United States willing to go to crush it completely?

5

Currents Convulsive

ONE REASON FOR President Johnson declaring on May 10 that the war was only "virtually" at an end was the fact that Jefferson Davis, the president of the Confederacy, was still at large. If Davis could get out of the country, he might persuade one or more foreign powers to join his not-yet-lost cause. Failing that, he could at least issue public messages from afar, stirring diehard Confederates to fight on.

Such were indeed Davis's intentions after the surrender of the major Confederate armies in the East. While Johnson had been composing his May 10 proclamation, Davis had been making his way to the Atlantic coast, hoping to find a boat that would get him to Mexico or Cuba. From either destination, he would then get to Europe. Once there, he would orchestrate the resurgence of the Confederacy.

Plenty of southern whites shared Davis's faith that the Confederacy would live on. Nathan Bedford Forrest, the best-known cavalry officer of the Confederacy and a future leader of the Ku Klux Klan, was not one of them. Early in May, he declared that "any man who is in favor of a further prosecution of this war is a fit subject for a lunatic asylum."[1] Forrest then surrendered his troops and announced that "we are beaten . . . and any further resistance on our part would be justly regarded as the very height of folly and rashness."[2] Perhaps Forrest was thinking about Davis, the fantasist with a following.

—

On the morning of May 10, Davis was in Irwinville, Georgia, about eighty miles north of the Florida border. He was sharing a tent with his wife, Varina, the two accompanied by a small armed escort. Suddenly gunfire cracked through the dawn light.

The shots had been fired by some of U.S. Major General James Wilson's raiders. After the unit's victory at the Battle of Columbus, it had pressed into the Georgia interior. From a local Black man, the soldiers had learned that Davis was camped in Irwinville. Two of Wilson's regiments came upon the camp at roughly the same time but from different directions. It was early, the light was dim, and each group assumed that the other was the enemy and started shooting—at each other.

In the midst of the confusion, and at the urging of his soldiers, Davis tried to get away. Varina threw one of her cloaks over his shoulders and ordered one of her enslaved servants to walk alongside her husband and make as if they were fetching water from the nearby stream. One of Wilson's men thought that the duo walking away looked suspicious. He ordered them to stop. Davis spun around and ran at the man, who was on horseback. Davis planned to grab the rider's heel, pull him from the horse, mount the steed, and make his getaway. But before he reached the horse, his wife threw herself upon him and begged the rider not to kill him. The cavalryman held them at gunpoint. His comrades soon arrived on the scene. They had captured the president of the Confederacy.

For the rest of his life, Davis insisted that had his wife not intervened, he would have gotten away and continued to lead the Confederacy. The U.S. troops at the scene, wanting Davis to suffer the greatest humiliation, spread the story that he had been wearing the full regalia of a southern belle: petticoats, a hoop skirt, and a bright bonnet. That was the story that stuck, at least among Unionists. The rebel president captured and unmanned: What better symbol could there be of the completeness of Confederate defeat?[3]

Regardless of how Davis was dressed on the morning of May 10, his capture in Irwinville signified to many the true end of the war. When word of the event arrived in Atlanta, 175 miles to the north, U.S. troops occupying the city celebrated with a 200-gun salute. One of the soldiers heard the booming as a signal that "Peace is declared."[4]

Another declaration of peace. This one, like President Johnson's statement about the war being "virtually" over, took place on May 10, 1865. Maybe that should be the official end date of the war. Plenty of civilians on both sides of the conflict regarded Davis's capture as an endpoint. Most stopped recording news of the armies after May 10, if they had not stopped already. The diary of Lydia Lyman Paine of Boston was typical. On April 9, she wrote that Lee had surrendered, a "glorious end to our 4 years of dreadful war." But she kept on writing. On April 15 came news of Lincoln's assassination: "a blow alike to friends and foes!" Then, in late April, she wrote of Sherman's proposed "treaty of peace" and the "great indignation against him" it caused. Then came the actual surrender by Johnston to Sherman. Then, finally: "Jeff Davis captured!"[5] Paine's war news stopped there. Davis's capture had the same effect on his own people. When a Confederate captain imprisoned at Fort Delaware heard about Davis, he wrote, "no hope . . . nothing to cling to . . . at sea without a compass." He and a dozen other Confederate officers in the camp took the oath of allegiance to the United States and headed home.[6]

If one insists on the Civil War having an endpoint, May 10, 1865, works well—better than most of the other options, in fact. On that day, President Andrew Johnson signaled that *post*war Reconstruction had begun, and the Confederate president Jefferson Davis was on his way to prison. That sounds like a war that is over.

Yet even this endpoint was imperfect. President Johnson had said that the war was "virtually" over, but would Congress go along? When Congress convened again in December, it might reject Johnson's policy and put the whole South under military rule. Meanwhile, at least 50,000 Confederate troops were still in the field, most to the west of the Mississippi. Would they surrender when they heard that Davis had been captured? Not necessarily. Although Davis was in custody, he refused to concede defeat. U.S. authorities worried about the damage that Davis might still do. If he somehow escaped, Confederates still in the field might gain new hope. If he committed suicide, they might regard him as a martyr and lash out fiercely. When Davis arrived at Fort Monroe in southeastern Virginia, the site of his imprisonment, the U.S. officer in charge ordered extra guards to ensure that Davis stayed penned and alive.[7]

The haggard leader, half blind with an eye infection, was surly and unapologetic from the moment he arrived at Fort Monroe. His cell was small and dank. On the second day of his imprisonment, the post commander ordered him manacled. Davis managed to kick away the blacksmith assigned to fasten the chains. Four soldiers were needed to wrestle him to the ground and bind his arms. Eventually, the shackles came off. But Davis never stood down. He remained adamant that secession was legal and the Confederate cause was just.

This was all fine by Secretary of War Edwin Stanton. Stanton wanted Davis tried for treason and then executed—*that* would be the end of the war. Plenty of Union soldiers and civilians hoped for the same. "If the villain doesn't stretch hemp," a U.S. lieutenant wrote in his diary, "I shall be disappointed."[8]

Along with a hanging of the vanquished, Stanton wanted a parade for the victors. Back in April, he had persuaded President Johnson to hold a review in Washington of the major U.S. armies. Johnson waited until the Confederate armies east of the Mississippi had surrendered before allowing Stanton to move ahead with the plan. Stanton coordinated with General in Chief Grant on the timing and logistics of the event.[9] Just a week after newspapers reported Davis's capture, they announced that a "Grand Review" of the Army of the Potomac and the Army of the West would take place in Washington on May 23 and 24. The triumph of U.S. forces in the Civil War would soon be complete.

Charles Dana, the assistant secretary of war who had acted as Stanton's eyes and ears in and around Richmond, shared his boss's belief that the rebellion was dead and only needed to be declared so. "The thoroughness of the subjugation is wonderful," Dana wrote to his fellow journalist James S. Pike, now the U.S. minister at the Hague. Having spent much time recently in Virginia, Dana explained, he could testify "that no people were ever so entirely conquered, and what is true of Virginia, is true of the whole South." "Plenty of malignity is no doubt still cherished in the bosoms of individuals," Dana conceded, "but as a community, all idea and all spirit of resistance to the authority of the government, is entirely extinguished."[10]

Dana was not giving Pike the full picture. He chose to omit the presence of roughly 50,000 Confederate troops west of the Mississippi under the command of Confederate General Edmund Kirby Smith. Meanwhile, in the East, there was plenty of evidence of the "spirit of resistance" that Dana said no longer existed. On the day after Dana sent his letter to Pike, the *New York Times* reported that "irregular" armed bands remained "scattered all over the Confederacy," and one such group had just terrorized part of Indiana. These were not organized guerrillas, the *Times* reassured its readers, but rather "lawless, reckless, desperate men." U.S. authorities should declare them "outlaws, to be punished by death," the paper declared.[11]

On May 11, the day that the *Times* article appeared, General Grant issued an order announcing that after June 1, "all persons found in arms against the United States, or who may commit acts of hostility against it east of the Mississippi River, will be regarded as guerrillas and punished with death."[12] Either the *Times* had advance word about Grant's intentions or Grant had liked what he read in the paper. Grant's order showed more legal savvy than the *Times* did. Because the *Times* wanted to dispel fears that the Civil War would continue indefinitely as a guerrilla war, it argued that the "irregulars" were not guerrillas—*and* that they should be summarily executed. Grant understood that they could not be summarily executed *unless* they were guerrillas. The U.S. code of war allowed for execution of guerrillas but not civilian criminals, who were supposed to be given fair trials and sentences by civilian courts or military commissions. Grant's "guerrilla order," as it became known, avoided the question of whether these "irregulars" were actually guerrillas or not. Whatever they were, if they continued in their violent ways, they would be classified as guerrillas on June 1, 1865, and then the army could kill them indiscriminately.

Were they guerrillas? That is, were they fighting on behalf of a political cause—the Confederate rebellion? Or were they merely self-interested criminals?

Certainly some of the armed bands saw themselves as Confederate units. They wore proper uniforms and were organized under a clear command structure. These were the bands that General Sherman had hoped would disappear once his peace agreement with Johnston was approved. In the letter that he had sent to Washington along with the peace terms, Sherman had declared that the agreement represented "an absolute submission of the enemy . . . in such a manner as to prevent their breaking up into guerrilla bands."[13] Once the peace was settled, Sherman believed, there would be no guerrillas because they would have no Confederacy to fight for. There would remain some nasty marauders, Sherman understood, but these would be subdued by former Confederate regulars who had pledged their loyalty to the Union. Sherman's naïveté about the goodwill of Confederate soldiers was profound, but he was on target in predicting that some guerrilla groups would not feel bound by the surrender agreement of Confederate commanders.

Most of the armed bands covered by Grant's order fell in a hazy area between guerrillas and criminals. Some had been around for years and were known by colorful names. In Missouri, a state long plagued by violent internal strife, rural areas still dreaded attacks by "Paw-Paws" and "Black-Flag Brigades." The most notorious of the marauders in the South were William Quantrill's "raiders," responsible for an arc of savagery extending from Texas through Kansas and Missouri and into Kentucky. Some of the groups had started as local militias only and then aligned with the Confederacy. The U.S. military had also used detached militias, and although some of these pro-Union bands continued to threaten southern civilian populations well into the summer of 1865, their existence did not trouble U.S. commanders as much as the pro-Confederate groups did. They did not represent an armed pro-Confederate endeavor to keep the war alive.

In any community suffering from violence, it could be hard to tell whether the perpetrators were militias still fighting the Civil War or gangs opportunistically using the chaos wrought by the war to plunder what they could. From the perspective of southern civilians, the distinction hardly mattered. The political orientation of marauding bands—if they had any—was less important than the fact of their existence. They were armed and violent and indifferent to the fact that the major armies of the East had surrendered. In some communities, the fight seemed to be the same as ever: Unionists versus Confederates. In others, the lines were drawn between different types of Confederates: the ones who had fought and suffered in the war and those who had remained at home living a life of relative ease ("bombproofs," one local paper called them).[14] Meanwhile, in one West Virginia community, a local paper reported that the trouble the people faced—a "greater danger than at any time during the war"—had nothing to do with national or local identities. It was simple criminality: pillaging by "the immense horde of idlers, vagabonds and thieves" who had been following in the wake of the armies for years.[15] Arkansas communities faced the same problem. A diarist there wrote that the nightly battles between upright citizens and "bands of robbers" had reduced his community to "a state of perfect anarchy."[16]

Throughout the war, Confederate and U.S. authorities had struggled to come up with a policy for dealing with guerrillas, both those on their own side and those on the enemy's. The Confederacy passed the Partisan Ranger Act in 1862, which accepted guerrilla bands that fought on its behalf as legitimate. It repealed the Partisan Ranger Act in 1864 in order to condemn irregular warfare publicly and to convert guerrillas into regular Confederate army units.[17] For U.S. authorities, the vexing problem of guerrillas had led to the creation of the first U.S. code of war. Early in the rebellion, Professor Francis Lieber, a legal expert and professor at Columbia College (now Columbia University), had set out to draft a guerrilla policy for the U.S. government. He ended up writing a comprehensive code covering all aspects of war. The United States adopted Lieber's document as its official code in 1863. The code officially authorized the execution of guerrillas, defining guerrillas as soldiers who failed to wear proper military uniforms or committed acts of wanton violence. In other words, if a soldier acted or looked like a guerrilla, he would be hanged like one.[18]

Just as an ebb tide exposes rough rocks hidden below smooth waters, the receding armies left in their wake hostile bands dug into place. It was the absence of organized troops, one reporter explained, that allowed "scoundrels" to prey on "peaceable citizens" without fear of repercussion.[19] "Irregulars" were now not simply *part* of the war. They *were* the war. Near Macon, Georgia, one day in May, twelve pro-Confederate "bushwhackers" put on stolen U.S. uniforms and mingled with a local pro-Union militia tasked with rooting out Confederate guerrillas. At an agreed-upon time, the disguised guerrillas turned on the guerrilla hunters and began shooting. By the time they rode off, three of the militiamen lay dead. The commander of the U.S. outpost in Macon dispatched seventy-five soldiers to hunt down the killers.[20]

This was the post-Appomattox guerrilla war that, as legend has it, never happened. Instead, history tells us that the Confederates chose honorable surrender over guerrilla warfare.[21] At the head of the noble vanquished stands Robert E. Lee. As the story goes, Lee commanded the Confederates to lay down their arms, and they all complied. True, at Appomattox Court House, just before he surrendered, General Lee spurned the suggestion that his army disperse into the Appalachians and fight as guerrillas.

Over time, this decision became the foundation of the legend that *all* Confederates renounced guerrilla warfare after Lee's surrender. Many Confederates who fought as guerrillas after Appomattox would later take shelter under Lee's mantle, claiming that in fact they had rejected the guerrilla option because of the example set by the commander they revered. One such tale involved a scout under the command of John S. Mosby, the infamous "Gray Ghost" who led a guerrilla band attached to Lee's Army of Northern Virginia. Mosby's men had chosen not to surrender at Appomattox Court House. According to the story, when the scout happened to meet Lee in a private home near Richmond two weeks after the surrender, Lee told the young man: "Go home, all you boys who fought with me."[22] History would have us believe that the young man and all his comrades followed the command. But in fact, there were holdouts. Mosby gathered his men together on April 21 in Salem, Virginia, about eighty miles west of Appomattox Court House, and gave them the option to surrender. Most took it. Because they were part of Lee's army, they were covered by the generous Appomattox parole terms, which extended to Lee's men wherever they were. Only a few of Mosby's men, along with Mosby himself, opted against surrender.[23] Through the spring and into the early summer, Mosby evaded capture.

Then, in late June, Mosby decided to surrender—but it turned out that he was too late. The spirit of forgiveness among U.S. officers was fading. A U.S. provost marshal in Lynchburg had sent word to Mosby that he would be paroled if he turned himself in. Mosby rode into Lynchburg ready to lay down his arms, only to learn that a higher U.S. officer had countermanded the parole offer and ordered Mosby arrested and imprisoned. The Gray Ghost somehow managed to get out of Lynchburg and join other holdouts in the countryside.[24]

The incident revealed that the fate of Confederate guerrillas, even those once attached to Lee's army, had become an open question. Were they to be offered liberal terms, or were they to be tried and executed—the fate dictated by the U.S. laws of war issued in early 1863? In the immediate aftermath of Lee's surrender, anyone attached to the Army of Northern Virginia could count on paroles and safe passage home. But with every passing week, the mercy of U.S. officers waned. At the end of April, some men formerly under Lee's command sent word to nearby U.S. officers that they were willing to surrender under the terms that Lee had negotiated. These men had never been guerrillas. They had been soldiers in regular units in the Army of Northern Virginia. They received a startling reply. They were no longer part of Lee's army, a commander informed them. Rather, they were now "outlying detachments of partisans." In other words, in the eyes of U.S. authorities, they were guerrillas. Their lives were now at risk. Yet attached to the stick wielded by the U.S. commander was a carrot. Although they were now classified as guerrillas, the Confederates were told, and thus could not receive paroles automatically, they could apply individually for paroles, and most likely these would be granted—if they surrendered right away.[25]

This stick-and-carrot approach became formalized in the order eventually issued by Grant on May 11, sometimes called the "guerrilla order." It declared that "authorized troops of the enemy" had ceased to exist. All armed insurgents after June 1 were to be treated as unlawful guerrillas. They could be executed. They had three weeks to surrender and avoid the noose. This was the "cheap way to get clear of guerrillas," Grant explained in private.[26]

Grant's lieutenants reported back that the plan was going well. Still-active Confederate soldiers who feared retribution from U.S. authorities welcomed the news that they could enjoy the same surrender terms that had been granted to their comrades at Appomattox. At a U.S. provost marshal's office in Macon, Georgia, Confederates showed up in droves from the surrounding swamps to surrender. A white southern civilian, watching the penitent stream in, joked with a friend that there were more soldiers here than there had been in the entire Confederate army when Lee surrendered. Once word of the order spread farther into the southern interior, the stream of former Confederates flying the white flag became a torrent.[27]

Beyond the Mississippi River, though, far from the U.S. campaign against irregulars in the East, regular Confederate forces still had the upper hand. The U.S. Army had a minor troop presence compared to Kirby Smith's 50,000 men. And Confederates still controlled the Rio Grande, a situation particularly galling to the garrison of U.S. soldiers on Brazos Santiago, a small island just north of the river's mouth.

The commander of the U.S. troops at Brazos, Brevet Brigadier General Theodore Barrett, grew more furious with each glance toward the mouth of the great river, where European merchant ships lined up to deliver arms and supplies to the Confederacy. Their destination was the Mexican port city of Matamoros, but much of their trade was actually with Confederates. Southern agents crossed the Rio Grande with their cotton and delivered it to the waiting vessels. The more clever ship captains labeled the bales "From Mexico." That way, the cotton could not be confiscated as Confederate contraband if the ship were stopped by a U.S. cruiser. In exchange for the cotton, European merchants delivered weapons and food to the Southern agents, who brought the matériel to Confederate-occupied Brownsville, Texas. Everyone knew about the brisk trade, including U.S. civilian and military leaders, but U.S. authorities could not intervene. Mexico was a neutral, sovereign nation—albeit a puppet state controlled by France—and thus had to be left alone. By early May, though, Barrett had had enough. Was he really supposed to do nothing while the reeling Confederacy was kept afloat by goods transported right before his eyes?

On May 12, Barrett set out to take Brownsville from the Confederates. He ordered two regiments, one white and one "colored," to take pontoon boats to the mainland and then march the thirty miles to Brownsville. He then sent a message to his superiors that the Confederates were on maneuvers outside Brownsville and had left the town unguarded. That was actually just a rumor, and Barrett had no reason to believe it was true. Impatience had gotten the better of reason. Barrett's infantry stood little chance against Confederate Colonel John "Rip" Ford's cavalry, which numbered more than a thousand.[28]

Then again, Ford's crew was something of a ragtag bunch. The "Cavalry of the West," as he had christened them, consisted of former deserters and men too old or too young for the draft. The most reliable men in Ford's group were those of Mexican descent, from families who had settled in Texas back when it was a republic. Ford's cavalry had earned some renown in the summer of 1864 by retaking Brownsville from the U.S. troops who had occupied the city earlier that year.[29] By May 1865, some of Ford's men had headed for home, but he still had enough to hold on to Brownsville. His division commander, Brigadier General James Slaughter, insisted that the town must not fall. When Ford learned that Barrett's Federals were on their way, he led a contingent to meet them.

Barrett's men ran into not one but two hostile forces on their way from the coast. First, they were fired upon by some of Maximilian's troops who happened to be doing training exercises on the Mexican side of the Rio Grande. Maximilian's officers in the region had become friendly with Ford. They decided to do their part to get the Federals to turn around. But the U.S. soldiers pressed on through the bullets coming from across the river.[30] Then, on a small rise known as Palmito Ranch, they ran into Ford's cavalry. The skirmishing lasted into the next day. Finally, the U.S. troops retreated back to Brazos.

The Confederates had held the ground. They had suffered a few casualties and caused a few dozen among Barrett's troops. The whole affair hardly amounted to a battle. Yet General Slaughter hyped the engagement to stir hope among the Confederate civilians in the region. He made sure that the Galveston paper published his report, which claimed that Ford's unit of only 300 men had nearly captured the whole force of 800 Federals. Under the "sagacity" and "gallantry" of Ford, the report recounted, the Confederates had lost no men but had killed or wounded 30 of the enemy and taken 80 prisoners.[31]

Barrett told a different story. He conceded that he had been driven from the field but claimed that it was his forces who were outnumbered. He mentioned no prisoners taken by the Confederates and reported only one fatality among his men: Private John J. Williams.

To Barrett, the precise details of the Palmito Ranch engagement were not as important as its larger significance. It would be "the last engagement of the war," he wrote in his report.[32] Northern newspapers amplified Barrett's version, calling Palmito Ranch "the last ditch" of the Confederacy and "the last battle of the Rebellion." Private Williams was given the honor of being counted as the war's last fatality.[33] This spin on events gave Unionist readers what they wanted: assurance that the war was over. So hungry were they for such news that they easily overlooked the fact that the Confederates had won the "last battle" and still held on to Brownsville.

The Confederates' control of Brownsville was not lost on Ulysses Grant. The general was soon to preside over a celebratory "Grand Review" of U.S. troops in the nation's capital, yet all of Texas and some of southwest Louisiana remained in the enemy's hands. It was time for the U.S. Army to put an end to the war west of the Mississippi.

On May 17, Grant authorized Major General Phil Sheridan to take a force of up to 50,000 men to the Trans-Mississippi, the region west of the Mississippi River controlled by Kirby Smith's Confederate forces. Sheridan was to subdue the western Confederate "in the shortest practicable time, in a way most effectual for securing permanent peace." Grant's instructions were effectively a western version of the "guerrilla order" that he had issued on May 11 covering enemies east of the Mississippi. First, Sheridan was to extend Kirby Smith a surrender proposal with the same liberal terms that Grant had given Lee. If the Confederate general spurned the offer, his troops were to be denied further "belligerent" status and could be summarily executed.

Sheridan was an obvious choice for the task. Grant's top cavalry officer, "Little Phil" had led the successful campaign to wrest the Shenandoah Valley from the Confederates in late 1864. He had made himself hated in the South by encouraging the destruction of wheat fields in the valley, knowing that the move would starve Confederate soldiers and civilians. Yet he hardly looked the part of a plunderer. He was short and pudgy—a "chunky little chap," Lincoln had called him—with a kind smile and a broad, soft face warmed by a feathery mustache. At Appomattox Court House, his horsemen had encircled Lee's army, arguably doing more than any other unit to force the Confederate general to surrender. He had been present in the McLean parlor when Lee signed the terms. A West Point graduate and only thirty-four years old, Sheridan was ready for further service. He believed that the rebellion would not be over until the United States controlled the Rio Grande borderlands, and maybe a good part of Mexico as well. He gladly accepted the assignment from Grant, which he received just as he arrived in Washington to watch the Grand Review. He asked Grant if he might delay his mission until after the review. Grant said no—Sheridan must leave "at once."[34] The next day, Grant headed for the reviewing stand set up in front of the White House, where he joined the revelers celebrating victory. Sheridan in the meantime headed west, where victory had so far been elusive.

The Grand Review began at 9:00 a.m. on May 23, 1865. Major General George Meade, the victor at the Battle of Gettysburg two years before, led the 84,000 men of the Army of the Potomac down Pennsylvania Avenue. At the reviewing stand, where Grant stood next to President Johnson and Secretary of War Stanton, Meade and his top officers stopped to give their salutes. For six hours, the massive column marched between joyful, cheering crowds. Shouts of victory filled the air. "This is the Grand Union Army that put down the rebellion," one viewer cheered.[35] On the next day, General Sherman led the 65,000 men of his armies along the same route in another six-hour ordeal. When Sherman stopped before the reviewing stand, he traded sharp glances with Secretary Stanton. The fury between them, from the Bennett house peace attempt the month before, was as strong as ever. But the moment was lost amid the bellows from the throngs cheering for the hero who had taken Atlanta and then marched through Georgia.

The tens of thousands of onlookers believed they were witnessing the finale of the war. Benjamin Brown French, the commissioner of public buildings in the capital, hung a banner across his window with a quote from Isaiah that included the phrase "warfare is accomplished."[36] In a different chapter of Isaiah was the better-known passage about the Lord turning "swords into plowshares," and it was to that verse that Carl Schurz turned when he searched for words to express the meaning of the review. Schurz, a leading Republican politician as well as a former ambassador and retired general, wrote that "every man that had wielded the sword or the musket or served the cannon in terrible conflict [was] going home to his plow, or his anvil, or his loom, or his counting-room, as a peaceable citizen."[37] When the two-day parade was over, the *National Intelligencer,* the city's most widely read newspaper, declared that "the curtain has fallen on the tragedy of our civil war."[38]

The Grand Review was actually three ceremonies in one: a military review, a victory parade, and a mustering-out ceremony. After French hung his banner in the window, he climbed atop the Capitol dome and looked out over the sea of troops. "My eyes moistened with joy to think that they were on their way *home,*" he wrote.[39] Before the ceremony, while the soldiers were camped just outside the city, army administrators prepared the final muster-out lists and payrolls of the units. Each soldier would have to report to a provost marshal's office in his home state after the review as the last stage of the muster-out.[40] But that would be a quiet affair. The Grand Review was the soldiers' real farewell to the war. The demobilization that would follow the review, Schurz assumed, would encompass the entire armed forces. He was ecstatic "that this transition from the conditions of war to those of peace, this transformation of a million soldiers into a million citizen-workers, could be accomplished so suddenly, without the slightest disturbance, even without any apprehension of difficulty." For Schurz, the review "was in its way a greater triumph of the American democracy than any victory on the battlefield."[41] The assessment of the *Chicago Tribune* was less hyperbolic. "Our boys, most of them, return to their homes and the avocations of peace," it reported.[42]

Most of them? Why not *all* of them? It was easy to forget when looking out over a sea of 150,000 troops who were done with the war that more than 800,000 other U.S. soldiers did not participate in the Grand Review and would not be heading home right away—if ever. Included among these were the roughly 1,000 U.S. soldiers who had died on April 27 on board the *Sultana.* The steamship had sunk in the Mississippi River, just north of Memphis, after its boilers exploded. Most of the soldiers on board were former prisoners headed home from Confederate POW camps. Because the number of passengers far exceeded the ship's capacity, hundreds of men were trapped inside the ship when it went down. The disaster led to a War Department inquiry. The same issue of the *Chicago Tribune* that described the Grand Review—and acknowledged that some soldiers were not going home—reported that the *Sultana* inquiry had exonerated the U.S. officers in charge of the transport mission. The *Tribune* called them "murderers."[43]

Other U.S. troops who would not be returning home included the roughly 20,000 professional soldiers of the non-volunteer regular army.[44] That number was expected to increase as volunteers who mustered out opted to join the ranks of the regulars. The regular army had consisted of about 16,000 men prior to the Civil War; no one knew how large it would now become. Lincoln had written that the size of the standing army should be reduced in terms of the ratio of soldiers to civilians. But the ratio that he recommended, one soldier for every thousand civilians, would have led to a force of roughly 32,000 men, twice the size of the prewar army.[45]

Although the War Department would have no trouble recruiting tens of thousands of former volunteers into the regular army, most of the volunteers wanted to go home—but were told that they could not do so, at least not right away. They still had months, even years left in their terms of service. The typical enlistment contract required volunteers to stay on duty for the full term or until the "end of the war," so until President Johnson, as commander in chief, declared that the war was over everywhere, those who still owed time were on the hook.

Most of the U.S. volunteers expected to do some form of occupation duty in the South until they were mustered out, but few knew when that would be. William D. Guernsey, a U.S. lieutenant stationed in Atlanta at the time of the Grand Review, wrote to his mother in Iowa that he expected to be held in service "at least until fall and I think longer."[46] "We hear all sorts of rumors about being mustered out of service," a Massachusetts private wrote to his parents from outside Richmond a week after the review. He hoped to be home by the Fourth of July, he told them. A few days later, he heard that the officers meant to "hang on to us" until after the Fourth, though he was not told "why they should." Then he learned that he indeed was to be mustered out soon, but the newer recruits to his regiment were to stay on indefinitely. That seemed unfair to him. The "new" men had served a year and had seen "just as hard a time as we have."[47] The U.S. soldiers still in the field experienced a reality quite different from Carl Schurz's vision at the Grand Review of an overnight "transformation of a million soldiers into a million citizen-workers." While Schurz was enjoying the review, a U.S. private on occupation duty in Mobile confessed to his diary that he could not reconcile the talk that "Peace has unfolded her wings" with the fact that "still thousands of boys in blue" were not being allowed to return home. What disturbed him most was the news that his regiment, the 7th Massachusetts Light Artillery, was being sent to Texas, where hostile forces were still in control.[48]

Present at the Grand Review on both days was the poet Walt Whitman. He scribbled some notes as he watched the weary men march nobly by. Later, he reworked the words into a poem with the lead-off phrase "Spirit whose work is done." Whitman, it seemed, was ready to consign the war to the past. Yet, at the same time, the poet knew that the ending did not come with the speed of a closing curtain. Rather, it came by the slow dimming of stage lights. "Fade from my eyes your forests of bayonets," he wrote. "Leave me your pulses of rage," he pleaded. "Bequeath them to me! / fill me with currents convulsive!"[49]

Which was it? Was the work of the war "done"? Or were there still "currents convulsive"? Whitman knew that he was writing conflicting messages. But he was more comfortable with incongruity than most. "Do I contradict myself," he had asked in "Song of Myself" ten years earlier. "Very well then I contradict myself, / (I am large, I contain multitudes.)" Watching the Grand Review, Whitman sensed that, somehow, the war would both end and endure.

The war's most convulsive current was now in "Kirby Smithdom," the name given to the area west of the Mississippi controlled by Kirby Smith's Confederates. The region was now the object of all remaining Confederate hopes. Jefferson Davis had been captured while trying to get to Texas, but that did not stop others who hoped to get there and save the Confederacy. A Confederate soldier in Virginia told his mother that he was ready to make the journey. "I will follow the fortunes of the Confederacy," he wrote, "as long as there is any hope of retrieving our fallen fortunes." Another Confederate headed for Kirby Smithdom pondered, "Who knows but what from the ashes of the Confederacy, a new phoenix may arise, clothed with brighter hues than its parent." Confederate civilians, too, were certain that, as one young woman in Kentucky put it, "the Trans-Mississippi will save us."[50] Eliza Andrews was shocked by how many Confederate "celebrities" passed through her small town of Washington, Georgia, on their way to Kirby Smithdom, which she called "the Land of Promise."[51]

It was because the Trans-Mississippi had become the reservoir of the Confederacy's dreams—and its troops—that Ulysses Grant dispatched Phil Sheridan to put down the rebellion there. One of the officers accompanying Sheridan was George Armstrong Custer, who, like Sheridan, had been present at Appomattox when Lee surrendered. Texas "was unhappily unaware that the war was over," Custer's wife, Libbie, later wrote. She would know. She actually accompanied her husband on the mission to Texas. The "bushwhacking and lawlessness" that she witnessed would "now cease," she promised.[52]

Awaiting Sheridan, Custer, and the 25,000 Federals who ultimately went to Texas (half the number authorized by Grant) was a much larger enemy force. But the Confederate troops were dispersed over hundreds of thousands of square miles and lacked the lines of communication and command structure to make them an effective force. Confederate diehards may have put their faith in Kirby Smithdom, but Kirby Smith himself was hardly up to the task of saving the Confederacy. He spent much of late May readying for the invasion force by talking to southern governors about how best to negotiate a surrender. His lieutenants were disgusted. They discussed how he might be replaced by someone with more backbone. Once this was done, said Confederate Brigadier General Joseph "Jo" Shelby, the new commander could call together all the troops of the region—Shelby thought there were 100,000 of them—and use them in concert to repel the Federals. When Kirby Smith found out that his officers were thinking of deposing him, he promised them that he would never surrender.[53]

For Confederate civilians in Texas, confidence in victory approached the level of delusion. Few had ever seen U.S. troops, much less lived under occupation, so indulging in fantasies of triumph

through resistance came easily. The *Galveston News* was the mouthpiece of diehard certitude. It had reported Lee's surrender as a *positive* development for the Confederacy. "The late apparent successes
of the enemy are only so *in appearance,*" it had cheered. Lee "surrendered *only those points where the enemy was strongest, and where
we were weakest,* and thereby compels the enemy to encounter our
forces *where we shall be strongest and they weakest.*"[54] When word
arrived at the paper that the rest of the Confederate armies east of
the Mississippi had surrendered, the *News* did not lose a beat. "We
have a larger army, a large population, ample resources, and country
eminently susceptible of defence," it blared. Even rumors of a massive U.S. invading force on its way to Texas did nothing to dampen
spirits. If such an army appeared, Kirby Smith would organize his
forces into small guerrilla units, the *News* promised. These bands
need "only fall back into the Western prairies, and fight the enemy,
if needs be for a hundred years." Once the Confederates in the East
saw the "manly defence" in the West, they would "renew the contest
and strike heavier blows than ever for Independence."[55] The fantasy
was compelling, more so than the reality of a commander who could
barely communicate with, much less control, his troops.

Yet Kirby Smithdom might indeed hold out. There was one last
card that the general might be able to play. If he could secure an
alliance with Maximilian, the imperial forces in Mexico could help
him fend off the Yankee invaders. Ever since late 1863, Kirby Smith
had been urging his superiors to strike a deal with Maximilian or
the emperor's French handlers. If Maximilian stayed neutral and the
Confederacy fell, the general warned, then Mexico would face certain invasion by a newly enlarged U.S. Army. The argument never
led to action by authorities in Mexico or France. Kirby Smith had
the sympathies of Maximilian and his officers—hence their willingness to fire upon Federals near Palmito Ranch—but he would never
have their alliance. Yet some of Kirby Smith's men never stopped
holding out hope for Mexican intervention. The more desperate
they became, the more certain they were that Maximilian's help was
on the way. "Recognition and armed intervention" from France and
Mexico were coming, a Confederate captain wrote in his diary in
mid-May. "It has been promised." Or so he had heard from a fellow
soldier's brother. "Armies have already sailed from Mexico."[56]

Kirby Smith never got the alliance he wanted, but he had rightly assessed what the absence of such an alliance meant for both the Confederacy and Mexico. For the Confederacy, it meant certain defeat. For Mexico, it meant likely invasion by the United States, which would send its armies across the southern border once they were done with Texas.

General Ulysses Grant had made little effort to conceal the invasion of Mexico as a secondary reason for sending a massive army to Texas. In his initial order to Sheridan sending him west, he had said that "the Rio Grande should be strongly held, whether the forces in Texas surrender or not." When Sheridan sought clarification at a meeting with Grant, the general in chief told him that the United States would be out of danger only after Maximilian and his French troops had left the continent. Grant knew that Secretary of State Seward felt the same way. Yet, whereas Seward believed the solution was diplomacy—if Napoleon III could be persuaded to pull the French troops propping up Maximilian, the emperor would fall— Grant thought that military intervention was the only solution. Grant told Sheridan to act with "circumspection" when planning for a possible invasion of Mexico, lest Seward catch wind of the scheme.[57]

Even before Richmond fell, Grant had been thinking of a Mexican invasion. He had supported the plan floated by various schemers of a joint U.S.-Confederate expedition against Maximilian. The two sides in the Civil War would make a truce and come together to clear the European imperial forces from the continent. Discussing this plan was the pretext given for the Hampton Roads meeting back in early February 1865, with Lincoln and Seward on one side and three Confederate envoys on the other. Lincoln had insisted that the rebels must give up the Confederacy before any sort of venture into Mexico could take place. The Confederates refused, ending the possibility of joint invasion—officially, at least. Grant allowed informal discussions of such plans to continue. In March 1865, he listened to the scheme of U.S. Major General Lew Wallace to sail to Texas and meet with Confederate officers who might be interested in a joint operation against Mexico. Grant was no fan of Wallace. He still blamed him, wrongly, for a delay at the Battle of Shiloh in 1862 that cost thousands of U.S. troops their lives. But any plan that led to an invasion of Mexico, even one proposed by someone he regarded as a bumbler, had his ear. Grant let Wallace go to Texas. Wallace managed to persuade some Confederate officers stationed near the Rio Grande to take the proposal to their superiors. Kirby Smith rejected it. His job was to sustain the Confederacy, he insisted, and that meant keeping Maximilian as an ally. The commander needed the emperor's soldiers if he had any hope of holding on to Texas. Lew Wallace was back in Washington when he learned that Kirby Smith had thwarted his plan. With Grant's blessing, he still nursed notions of some sort of expedition to Mexico. By May, though, Wallace had other duties to attend to. He had been assigned to the military commission that was trying the accused Lincoln assassins.[58]

When Grant sent Sheridan west, the general in chief was done with Confederates and their potential involvement in his hoped-for war against Mexico. Grant told Sheridan to finish off Kirby Smith and then prepare for the conflict across the border. As one of Grant's aides put it, Sheridan was "not to be over-cautious about provoking the Imperial forces."[59]

In the American Civil War, as in all wars, a conflict that at its start had been assumed to be bounded and comprehensible evolved into a struggle unpredictable and infinite in its possibilities. Would the "currents convulsive" felt by Walt Whitman at the Grand Review light the fuse for some new war, one that would pit the United States against an ever-expanding set of enemies? Unionists and Confederates alike harbored suspicions that the end of the Civil War would be indiscernible because some other, perhaps greater conflict would take its place. Samuel T. Foster, a Texan who had served under Joe Johnston, welcomed the possibility. "Some think that the big war is about to commence," he wrote excitedly in his diary. "A war of some Magnitude. France Austria Mexico and the Confederacy on one side, against England Russia and the U.S. on the other, and the great battle ground will be in the Confederacy."[60] A newspaper editor in Wisconsin was more sober about such prospects. "The experience of this war ought never to be lost to us," he wrote, "as we may drift into another of equal dimensions."[61]

6

Almost an End

O<small>N</small> M<small>AY</small> 24, 1865, as the Grand Review drew to a close and the cheers for the war's end grew faint, U.S. and Confederate forces prepared for the war that would continue beyond the Mississippi River. U.S. Major General Phil Sheridan had already issued orders assembling the army that he would lead. The largest contingent would be the 14,000 African American men of the 25th Corps, currently on occupation duty in and around Richmond. Like all Black units, they were commanded by a white man. Major General Godfrey Weitzel had been assigned to lead the corps at the end of 1864. Ever since the fall of Richmond in early April, Weitzel had been headquartered in Richmond. It was there that he had served as go-between in the brief endeavor by Abraham Lincoln and John A. Campbell to make a hasty peace. The effort had failed. Now Weitzel, onetime peace broker, was to lead his troops to southern Texas, the heart of the war that remained. Confederate General Edmund Kirby Smith, currently headquartered in the northwest Louisiana city of Shreveport, prepared to move his base of operations to Houston. There, he would be better positioned to meet the approaching Yankee invaders. He still held out hope of recruiting Emperor Maximilian's men to his side, but overtures in that direction so far had come up empty.

One hundred miles west of Shreveport, in the town of Tyler, Texas, the loyal Confederate Kate Stone searched for signs of hope. "The war is rushing rapidly to a disastrous close," she feared.[1] Four years earlier, at the start of the war, Stone, then twenty years old, had been certain of Confederate victory. At the time, she had been helping her widowed mother manage Brokenburn, the family plantation in Louisiana. Strong-willed and sharp-witted, Stone stood out among the women of her elite white community. She was passionate about the Confederate cause and proud of her family line of "unmixed Southern blood from generation after generation of slaveholders."[2] Roughly 150 enslaved African Americans lived and toiled at Brokenburn. Stone claimed that she had nothing but "pity" for them and a "desire to help them." When word arrived at the plantation in early 1863 that Yankee armies were nearby, Stone and her mother ordered white overseers to march their charges to land owned by friends in east Texas. Slaveholders across the South had done the same thing. They, too, had said that the enslaved were better off in Texas, away from the pitiless Yankee invaders. Maybe they believed it. But their primary goal, of course, had been to avoid property loss. Soon after sending the enslaved ahead of them, Stone and her mother made their own way to Texas, eventually settling in Tyler. There, they learned of the death of Kate's two brothers in combat. By mid-May 1865, Kate Stone feared that "another month and our Confederacy will be a Nation no longer." "We will be slaves, yes slaves, of the Yankee Government," she despaired.[3] (If Stone truly believed that slavery was a benign practice, one wonders why the prospect upset her so.) All Stone could do was share in the hope of others for "a rally and one more desperate struggle for freedom." "If we cannot gain independence," she wrote in her diary, "we might compel better terms."[4]

What "better terms" could Stone and her comrades hope for? For some Confederates, anything short of national independence was unacceptable. These never-surrender types were running out of options. At one extreme was the example set by Edmund Ruffin. The notorious Virginian had written a fantasy novel before the war about a Southern nation battling its way to independence, and then had been given the honor of firing the first shot on Fort Sumter in 1861. By mid-1865, though, he could no longer sustain his faith. To his diary he pledged "unmitigated hatred to Yankee rule" and then killed himself with a rifle blast to the head.[5] Another, less lethal option was self-exile. Even before the fall of Richmond and the surrender of Lee, southern whites had started fleeing the Confederacy. Some went to Europe, but most headed for Central and South America. Those determined to maintain a life of mastery were partial to Cuba and Brazil, where slavery was still legal. The most common approach of the never-surrender types was to treat U.S. victory and occupation as merely temporary phenomena. If they refused to submit and bided their time, weary Yankee occupiers would eventually leave. White women of the South, proud of the patience and resolve they had been compelled to maintain for four years, were particularly likely to embrace this strategy. By mid-1865, white women had already earned a reputation among U.S. occupiers for being less likely than men to take loyalty oaths to the Union. Refusing to take the oath, a group of North Carolina white women declared, was but one blow in the larger fight by which women would "rise up to expel the hated invaders from the Soil."[6] Kate Stone, devastated at the news of the death of one of her brothers, took pride in his decision to keep fighting after the Yankees had given him the option of taking the oath and earning safe passage home.[7]

Stone could imagine life without a Confederate nation so long as she didn't have to yield entirely to Yankee rule. No forced "submission" to federal authority and no "Negro equality" were the "better terms" that she hoped Kirby Smith would secure if he surrendered what was left of the Confederacy. Short of that, she expected her comrades to join her in "a bloody unequal struggle to last we know not how long."[8]

Kirby Smith was as obstinate as Kate Stone. He expected that once he shifted his base of operations from Shreveport to Houston, he would be able to wear down the Yankees. If they refused to give southern rebels a nation, at least they would allow them a return to self-rule and white mastery. Unfortunately for Kirby Smith, his lieutenants did not share his delusions.

When Kirby Smith left Shreveport, he put most of the Trans-Mississippi forces under the command of Lieutenant General Simon Bolivar Buckner. Kirby Smith should have suspected that Buckner lacked his backbone. Buckner, a Kentuckian who had not pledged his loyalty to the Confederacy until late 1861, had been the first Confederate commander to surrender an army. His capitulation to Ulysses S. Grant at Fort Donelson in 1862 had given the

Union general his nickname, "Unconditional Surrender" Grant. Almost immediately after Kirby Smith's departure from Shreveport, Buckner began discussing surrender with his officers. He knew that the United States would eventually send a force to conquer the region. Desertions had already worn the ranks paper-thin. From Brownsville came news that the soldiers there had declared, "We are whipped."[9] Defeat was inevitable. It was only a matter of how long it would take.

A cadre of Confederate officers led by Brigadier General Jo Shelby was disgusted with Buckner. They thought about arresting him. Then word arrived of the capture of Jeff Davis. Even Shelby had to concede that the Confederacy was in trouble. But he and his comrades refused to surrender. Instead, they set out for Mexico. Three thousand Confederates eventually joined them in the exodus. Shelby hoped to recruit even more troops in Mexico—either former Confederates who had already emigrated or some of Maximilian's men—and then return to Texas and resume the fight against the Yankees.

Abandoned by some of his best officers and facing hundreds of desertions by the day, Buckner and the remaining commanders boarded a steamboat for New Orleans. There, on May 26, they signed a surrender agreement with U.S. Major General Edward Canby. The document was modeled on the Appomattox surrender. It would take effect, all parties agreed, only after Kirby Smith signed it. Although Buckner had brought the Confederate officers to the table, he was singled out by U.S. authorities for his treachery. Denied a parole that would allow him to return to his home state of Kentucky, he was restricted indefinitely to Louisiana.[10]

Kirby Smith knew nothing about Buckner's surrender when he arrived in Houston on May 27, the day after the agreement had been signed in New Orleans. Expecting to set up his headquarters, he had already sent word to troops in the region to report to the Confederate garrison in Houston. But only a handful of soldiers awaited him. Almost all had deserted. Civilians had run off with what few supplies his vanishing army might have used. Worst of all, he received reports that the U.S. invading force would arrive at the Texas coast within a week. Once it landed, it would scatter what few Confederate troops remained and capture the rest.

For the commanding general of the Trans-Mississippi Confederacy, the war was over—for now. He held out hope that Jo Shelby and his band would find a way to resume the fight. To Canby, Kirby Smith sent word that he would surrender. To his own troops—what few remained—he said farewell. Unlike Robert E. Lee at Appomattox, Kirby Smith was arrogant and graceless in defeat. He was surrendering not by choice, he said, but because his men's waning will had forced him to. "I am left a commander without an army—a General without troops," he wrote in his farewell address. "You have made your choice. It was unwise and unpatriotic, but it is final." From Houston he traveled to Galveston on the coast, where he had told Canby to meet him for the surrender ceremony. The city was in limbo: it was still part of the Confederacy but expected the arrival any day of a fleet of U.S. ships carrying troops of occupation. Canby's ship, the *Fort Jackson*, was already in the outer harbor, awaiting Kirby Smith's arrival. On June 2, the Confederate general had a skiff take him out to the U.S. ship. There, he signed the surrender agreement that his officers had already agreed to in New Orleans a few days before. The last major army of the Confederacy was no more.[11]

For almost a week before Kirby Smith made the surrender official, Unionists in the East had been celebrating his army's demise. On May 26, General Canby had telegraphed Secretary of War Stanton to let him know that Kirby Smith's commanders had capitulated. Within days telegraph wires from California to Maine crackled with the news. "PEACE!" declared the *New York Tribune* on the front page. "Kirby Smith Surrenders." In an unprecedented editorial move by the *Tribune*, a graphic appeared above the headline: a dove carrying an olive branch.

"PEACE," the New York diarist George Templeton Strong wrote upon hearing the news. "Peace herself at last." He reflected back on the four years that had passed since the firing on Fort Sumter. "So here I hope and believe ends, by God's great and undeserved mercy, the chapter of this journal I opened with the heading War on the night of April 13, 1861."[12]

Amid the din of the boisterous welcome to "Peace herself," deafness among Unionists to the murmurs of a possible Confederate resurgence was easily achieved. The victors could dismiss as irrel-

From the front page of the *New York Tribune*, May 29,
1865. The headline celebrates the news of the surrender of
Confederate General Edmund Kirby Smith. The use of a
graphic above a headline—here, a dove carrying an olive
branch—was a novelty in newspapers at the time. Kirby
Smith did not actually sign the surrender until June 2,
1865. He then fled to Mexico.

evant the fact that Jo Shelby and others had refused to surrender and
were headed for Mexico. Or maybe they simply had not heard the
news. Certainly many outside the Confederacy were unaware—or
chose to be so—that Kirby Smith himself was still at large. After
signing the official surrender papers, he had found a mule and set
off for Mexico.

For Unionists, these were things to worry about later, if at all.
General Grant certainly seemed unconcerned. He said nothing
publicly about Kirby Smith being on the loose—one former general
alone on a mule was hardly a Confederate resurgence, after all—
and instead used the occasion of the Texas surrender ceremony to
announce that the war was now over. In a much-publicized order
of June 2 thanking U.S. soldiers for having "overthrown all armed
opposition," Grant applauded the army for opening "the way to the

rightful authorities to restore order and inaugurate peace on a permanent and enduring basis on every foot of American soil."[13]

It all seemed so easy. The convulsive, destructive period of war, unpredictable and enervating, was at an end. Now came the mundane, technical business of securing victory, a process that would lead to the certain result of restoring the nation's strength and stature. Glossed over in this soothing scenario was the harsh reality that, for many U.S. servicemen, the war lived on, and they might not get out of it alive.

When Grant issued his June 2 thank-you message to the army, for example, thousands of U.S. soldiers were incarcerated, uncertain when their war would be over. To be sure, most of the servicemen from the Union side who had been prisoners of war in the Confederacy were heading home. Though, as the *Sultana* disaster had revealed, even they were not out of danger. At least two other transports carrying U.S. POWs northward sank in the months after the *Sultana* went down. Scores of men who had endured the travail of combat and confinement and had earned the blessing of reuniting with their families instead died by drowning.[14] Meanwhile, in parts of the South far from communication lines, confusion reigned among Confederate prison-minders over what to do with the inmates. U.S. POWs were marched from one camp to another, sometimes finding themselves returned to their original prison. "The Rebels were terribly puzzled what to do with us," one POW later remarked.[15]

The end of the war—if an end had really come—was even less visible to an entirely separate group of imprisoned U.S. servicemen: those who had been court-martialed by their own side. By the summer of 1865, as many as 10,000 U.S. soldiers and sailors were held under U.S. guard in federal penitentiaries and local jails. Their lives were unaffected by the surrender of Confederate armies. Some had committed heinous crimes such as murder and rape; they would remain in prison long after the summer of 1865, and deservedly so. But most of the inmates were guilty only of desertion. If there was no longer a war to fight, would they be released? And what would happen, if anything, to the U.S. deserters who had never been caught? One army officer estimated that 230,000 such men were still "at large."[16] Were they to be court-martialed if caught? Regardless of how an end to the war might affect them, deserters, whether imprisoned or not, could count themselves lucky in one way at least: they no longer faced the possibility of execution. In the early years of the war, military courts regularly sentenced deserters to death, though many of those sentences were commuted by Lincoln. In February 1864, Lincoln issued an order commuting the sentences of all deserters awaiting execution. These men were to be sent to a military prison for a term to last "during the war."[17] A sentence of imprisonment "during the war" or "until the end of the war" was already common among U.S. military prisoners, not only for deserters but also for servicemen convicted of other offenses. When such convicts began hearing in mid-April 1865 that the war was over, they must have assumed that they could walk right out the prison door.

They were wrong. For at least another month, even beyond the end-of-war celebration of the Grand Review, they were held behind bars. They suffered directly from the absence of any official declaration that the war was over. Finally, someone in the War Office, perhaps Secretary of War Stanton himself, decided to set these men free. Stanton no doubt could see the contradiction in keeping such men in prison while the Union celebrated victory. Not that he believed that the war was technically over. He believed that the United States was still at war with rebels who threatened the Union, such as the Lincoln assassins and diehard Confederates. But he was savvy enough to see that federal prisons swollen with U.S. soldiers whose families needed them made for bad politics. Also, who was supposed to guard these men as Stanton thinned the ranks of the army during demobilization?

On May 27, 1865, the War Department ordered the release of court-martialed soldiers whose sentences were supposed to cease when the war ended.[18] Here, then, was yet another end date—or *possible* end date—of the Civil War. On the day after the order was issued, the *New York Herald* declared it in effect "an official announcement of the termination of the rebellion."[19]

Yet, like other end dates, this one was fragile and fleeting. A few papers reprinted the notice from the *Herald*, but otherwise the order went unnoticed. Even the *Herald* offered no commentary on the order beyond the original, brief notice buried in small print amid a column of unrelated stories. Meanwhile, other prisoners who should have been released by the same logic—that the end of the war meant the end of their sentences—were left behind bars. These were the men who had received prison sentences that were to last "for the term of their enlistment." Term-of-enlistment sentences were supposed to last until the period of enlistment was completed or the war was over, *whichever came first*. However, quite a few court-martialed soldiers and sailors who had received "term-of-enlistment" sentences were still locked up in February 1866, ten months after Appomattox.[20]

Many Confederate POWs also were incarcerated long after Appomattox. Not until the first week of June would President Johnson begin to issue release policies for them. Confederates still in prison after hearing of Lee and Johnston's capitulations understandably wondered how long the war would go on for them. In early May, at the POW camp at Point Lookout, Maryland, roughly 20,000 Confederates were still imprisoned, unsure about their fate. One of the inmates, George M. Neese, wrote in his diary on May 3: "It seems that the war is over outside of the prison, but we are kept here and treated just as we have been before the war closed." Maybe, he suspected, "the Yanks are afraid to turn us loose."[21] Neese was right. Plenty of "Yanks" worried that released POWs would rejoin the fight, either as guerrillas or as members of organized armies in the West. By the end of May, however, most Unionists were ready to put aside their fears, along with the vengeful rage that had been triggered by Lincoln's assassination six weeks before.

Even President Johnson, it seemed, was ready to tone down his "traitors must be punished" refrain. On May 29, the president issued his first official statement on amnesty and reconstruction. The statement, which came in the form of two proclamations, was Johnson's clearest message to date that he regarded the Civil War as over, or nearly so.

Johnson had written the proclamations weeks before. He had waited to issue them until he learned that the last of the major Confederate armies, Kirby Smith's Trans-Mississippi force, had agreed to surrender.

The first proclamation dealt with the remaking of the governments of states that had joined the Confederacy. It focused on North Carolina, though the implication was that it would be the policy for all of the southern states. Pitched simply as a continuation of the Reconstruction policy that Lincoln had inaugurated in late 1863, Johnson's scheme, like Lincoln's, allowed for a quick reestablishment of state governments. Loyal minorities in southern states—those who had taken oaths to the Union and Constitution and received amnesty from potential treason prosecutions—would form new state governments.

As for who would be receiving amnesty, that was covered in Johnson's second proclamation. Here Johnson's policy was harsher than Lincoln's. Lincoln had offered amnesty to all but the highest-ranking military and civilian officials. Johnson denied amnesty to fourteen classes of southern whites, including a wide range of onetime Confederate officeholders and a large swath of the officer class of the Confederate army and navy. He also exempted from amnesty the wealthiest secessionists, those with more than $20,000 of property, regardless of whether they had held military or civilian positions within the Confederacy. This was the "thirteenth exemption," which was of Johnson's own devising and shocked the elite of the South. These men would have to apply in person to Johnson for a pardon. He would use the pardoning power, not the army, to bring to heel those he described as "the wealthy men of the South who dragooned the people into secession."[22] Yet, for all that the thirteenth exemption reflected Johnson's genuine resentment of the rich, a personal grudge from his days as a Tennessee workingman, the clause would prove to be a low hurdle for wealthy southerners seeking to regain political power. All but a handful would end up pardoned by the former tailor after they paid their faithless obeisance to him.

That was a future that no one could see yet. The immediate sense of Johnson's May 29 proclamations was that he, like Lincoln, blamed southern white leaders, not their followers, for the rebellion. Only elite fire-eaters would have to pay a price. The amnesty policy assured ordinary southern whites that they did not have to worry about treason trials. The point was reaffirmed in Johnson's order of June 6, which finally dealt with Confederates still in POW camps. Only prisoners below the rank of captain would be allowed to take loyalty oaths and return home.[23]

Beyond spelling out terms of amnesty and reconstruction, Johnson's May 29 proclamations had a larger purpose: to signal that the war was over. The rebuilding of the nation could now begin in earnest. The announcement was the political counterpart to the Grand Review, held just a few days earlier. That had been an end-of-war ritual orchestrated by the military. Johnson's effort of May 29 was the civil government's affirmation of the end-of-war message.

On closer inspection, though, Johnson was offering something short of a full-throated announcement that the nation had crossed the line from war to peace. His North Carolina proclamation took the form only of a recommendation. He did not assure the state that its representatives and senators would be admitted to Congress; only Congress had that power, he knew. Nor did he foreclose the possibility that he might impose further requirements on southern state governments, including voting rights for Black Americans, the policy that southern whites feared most. His tough-looking policy on amnesty seemed a continuation of his "traitors must be made odious" declaration of six weeks before. Maybe the Confederacy had ceased its fight against the Union, but Johnson, it appeared, was still fighting against the Confederacy.

In a phrase of his May 29 announcement that northerners tended to overlook—no doubt because they were so keen on immediate, universal peace—Johnson declared that the "organized and armed forces" of the rebellion "have now been almost entirely overcome." By contrast, there was no "almost" in Grant's statement that "*all* armed opposition" had been "overthrown"—the key line in the general's speech to the army delivered at roughly the same time as Johnson's May 29 proclamation. Johnson's "almost" may have been a mere stylistic decision. Much more likely, it was a deliberate move to keep the door open for further war—or at least further use of war powers.[24]

The little "almost" had big implications. It meant that some volunteers in the U.S. armed services with time still to serve would not be mustered out soon. By the terms of their enlistment, their time would be cut short only if there was an end to the war. President Johnson, the commander in chief, had effectively said that the war's end had not yet arrived. A few weeks later, a federal circuit court in Minnesota was asked to rule on whether the war was over. The case involved a man who had committed fraud against the War Department and was sentenced to serve for three years or "during the present Rebellion," whichever term was shorter. The convict had served less than two years of his sentence, but his attorney argued that he should be released because the war was over. U.S. Supreme Court Justice Samuel F. Miller, acting as one of the circuit judges, ruled that the man must stay in prison because there was only a "probability" that the rebellion was over.[25] A St. Paul paper correctly summarized the opinion as saying that "it was impossible" to determine "when the rebellion would end."[26] President Johnson's declaration that the war was not quite over—that the rebel forces were "*almost entirely overcome*"—had stymied the court. What other rebels were still out there who needed to be overcome?

An article that appeared in the *Army and Navy Journal* right after Johnson issued his proclamations spelled out the answer. Based in New York City, the newspaper had been founded by Francis and William C. Church in 1864 to provide information and commentary to men in the armed forces. Although the *Journal* gloated about Kirby Smith surrendering "without a battle," it warned that the Trans-Mississippi region, and Texas in particular, would remain a hive of armed Confederates.[27] "There must be desperadoes enough in the whole Southern Confederacy to make an irregular warfare somewhere," the *Journal* argued, and the border region with Mexico was the obvious site for them to make their stand. The region offered plenty of "places of refuge," either "within Texas, or, more probably, across the border." Between the "guerrilla operations" sure to continue in Texas and the threat posed by a possible invasion by Maximilian's army, perhaps assisted by ex-Confederates, U.S. authorities had done well to order an army led by Sheridan to the border. There was no better man for the job than "Little Phil," the *Journal* contended. The commander's 1864 campaign in the Shenandoah Valley had brought the resistance to its knees. Now, said the *Journal*, he would teach the Trans-Mississippi "the lessons of the Shenandoah Valley."[28]

Yet how was it possible to square Sheridan's massive expedition with the promise of demobilization signaled by the Grand Review? Here, too, the article in the *Journal* had an answer. The forces heading west were not "Eastern troops of importance," it reported. Only "Weitzel's Twenty-fifth (colored) corps" would be going.[29]

That was a telling remark. The implication that Black troops were less important than white ones was hard to miss. The heroism of African American soldiers and sailors had been much celebrated across the Union ever since the armed forces had begun enlisting them in early 1863. The *Army and Navy Journal* had often acknowledged the heroism of Black troops. Back in late February 1865, for example, it had noted the important role of the 25th Corps in the taking of Fort Fisher in Wilmington, North Carolina.[30] Yet the *Journal* also had published in full and without criticism the infamous letter of July 30, 1864, written by William Tecumseh Sherman, in which the general had written that "the negro is in a transition state and is not the equal of the white man."[31] The Church brothers endorsed Blacks being in the military but were dubious that their capacities were the same as those of whites. In an article in early May 1865, the *Journal* commented that "Negro artillery is not to be compared to white, because the scientific arms require a high development of prompt intelligence."[32] U.S. authorities often congratulated themselves for the egalitarian position they had arrived at when it came to African Americans in the military—and, to be sure, the admiration they had for the achievements of Black men in uniform was sincere—yet there was something disquieting about the ambivalence toward African Americans expressed in the acknowledged organ of the armed services.

Those seeking evidence of unequal treatment of African Americans in the military did not have to look hard. No African American soldiers marched in the Grand Review, for example, unless one counted the Black manual laborers—the "bummers"—who marched with Sherman's army on the second day of the review. The *Army and Navy Journal* described this group as "a grand caravan of nondescripts, led off by two small donkeys, driven by a couple of black, and smiling piccaninnies."[33] Actually, the absence of African American troops in the review was understandable: the Black regiments of the armies featured in the review had already been reassigned. Even the abolitionist William Lloyd Garrison came to the defense of the War Department when it was accused of purposely trying to downplay the role of Black troops by excluding them from the Grand

Review.[34] Still, some asked, was it fair that the War Department was putting white regiments ahead of Black ones in the mustering-out schedule? There again, the War Department had a reasonable explanation. Most of the white regiments had mustered in or re-upped before the African American regiments had been formed; it was only fair that they be released from service first. However, some of the racial disparities in the armed services were inexplicable, even indefensible. After more than two years serving their country, African Americans still could not attain the rank of commissioned officers. Their regiments were still led by white officers. Finally, there was the obvious race prejudice in the army's recruiting policy. Secretary of War Stanton ordered a halt to all recruitment of white volunteers on April 13, 1865, but he authorized the recruitment of Black volunteers in some places until June.[35]

The reason for the discrepancy had been hinted at by the comment in the *Army and Navy Journal* that no "troops of importance" were being sent west. The army was using mostly African American troops—Weitzel's 25th Corps in particular—to do the soldiering in Texas. Perhaps General Grant thought he was putting African Americans in a position of honor by sending them to the Rio Grande borderlands, where he thought the United States would soon be staging a glorious invasion of Mexico. But in the opinion of many of the African American soldiers, the assignment was nothing more than race-based punishment. The mission was likely to be thankless, arduous, and time-consuming. By the time they arrived in Texas, some feared, the last of the white volunteers would muster out and the Black troops would be forgotten.

Events did seem to be playing out that way. On June 8, as African American troops stationed in Virginia prepared to ship to Texas, the all-white 6th Corps marched in a military review in Washington. The event garnered less attention than the Grand Review two weeks earlier, but it was still a significant procession of 25,000 men. The *New York Times* called it "the Closing Pageant of War." The *Times* made no mention of the Black force being sent to Texas. It simply announced that "the last of the veterans have been reviewed."[36] Over the course of the summer, African Americans would go from representing a fifth of the volunteer force to a half. By September, 85,000 of the 180,000 volunteers still in blue were African Americans. A small number served as occupying troops in the Deep South and the Border States, but most were stationed west of the Mississippi River.[37] All of them might have rightly been offended if they knew that the *New York Times* had reported three months earlier that the "last veterans" had already mustered out.

Although African American troops at the time of the Grand Review may have been dismayed that people's attention was less on them than on victory parades and mustering-out ceremonies, many were pleased, even honored, to continue to serve their country. A correspondent for a Black newspaper reported that some of the soldiers among Weitzel's 25th Corps were excited to put on "the war-paint" for Texas.[38]

Yet plenty of African American soldiers headed for Texas were dispirited if not outright terrified. A commander of a Black regiment explained his men's concern: "Texas had been held up to them as a sort of hell to which they would be sold if they misbehaved." Slavery was more prevalent in Texas than in any of the other remaining Confederate states. Before the war, southern slaveholders regularly shipped enslaved people to newly bought land in Texas. When the war broke out, Confederates accelerated the process in order to keep the enslaved far from U.S. armies that might liberate them. Nearly 200,000 enslaved people were forcibly removed by southern whites to Texas. Told they were being deployed to the state, Black troops understandably worried about whether they would ever return from the heart of slavery. One African American soldier had a particularly frightening suspicion. The Black regiments were still commanded by white officers—this had been true since the start of Black enlistment—and he was convinced that once his regiment arrived in Texas, the officers would take him and his comrades to Cuba, where slavery was still legal, and sell them on the open market.[39]

The 1st and 2nd U.S. Colored Cavalry were two of the regiments bound for Texas. They were camped at Norfolk, Virginia, when they received word in early June 1865 that they were to be redeployed to Brazos Santiago, at the mouth of the Rio Grande. Most of the men in the Colored Cavalry regiments lived in or near Norfolk, and their wives and children, hearing that the men were stationed nearby, had walked to the camp. The white commander of the forces, Briga-dier General George W. Cole, knew that it was a mistake to let the families reunite—it would make getting the Black troops to leave their loved ones near impossible—and he had told his subordinates to keep the families away from the soldiers. But some of the white officers abandoned their posts, and at least two others let compassion get the better of them and allowed the families into the camp.

As Cole had feared, once the troops saw their families, they resolved to return home straightaway. How could they abandon their manly duties? They had not been paid for months and had no money to give their kin. All they could offer was protection and labor at home, and these they could not give if they were stationed a thousand miles away in Texas. When the commander ordered the soldiers to board the boats, about twenty immediately bolted with their families for the woods. Others refused to take a step toward the ships. The women, some of whom feared that their menfolk were being permanently colonized in Texas, wept and begged the white officers to let the men stay. Cole sympathized with the African Americans but mostly wished that the whole episode had been avoided, which it would have been if his officers had not allowed "the inflamatory [sic] stimulus of free intercourse" of the soldiers "with the howling multitude." The white officers put an end to the pitiful scene, which later was deemed a "mutiny," by shooting one soldier—not fatally—and arresting scores of others. Eventually, about a dozen of those arrested were court-martialed and sentenced to three-year terms in military prison. They had been enslaved when the war began. They were likely to be incarcerated when it ended. And they were entirely overlooked by a northern public dazzled by the gleaming bayonets carried by the white soldiers who marched in parades before going home.[40]

The precise nature of the enemy that Weitzel's 25th Corps would be facing in Texas remained a mystery. The formal Confederate armies were disintegrating. Kirby Smith was contemplating surrender even before the U.S. 25th Corps departed from Virginia; the actual surrender took place while the 25th was in transit to Texas. But thousands of Confederate troops west of the Mississippi were still at large. The best-organized contingent was the column of troops marching toward Mexico under Jo Shelby.

Born in Kentucky, Shelby had moved to Missouri as a young man and become a successful entrepreneur. During the battles over slavery's expansion in the 1850s, he discovered a passion for fighting. He left his businesses behind and led a proslavery band of Missourians in the battles over Kansas. Soon he was well-known in the region as a fierce and stubborn leader, as well as a superb horseman. When the Confederate rebellion broke out, he simply stayed at war, acting as a cavalry commander in the borderlands in and around Missouri. A string of victories in the Trans-Mississippi theater earned him wide respect among his fellow Confederates, and by 1863 he had attained the rank of brigadier general. He played down his wealth, dressing in a modest uniform and sporting the same long hair and rough-cut beard that he had worn in his days as a "border ruffian" in the Kansas wars. By early 1865, he was serving under Kirby Smith, but he was far more popular than his superior among the regular troops. Unlike Kirby Smith, Shelby believed the Confederacy was invincible. His confidence infected all around him.

Shelby and his men were prepared for a rough, improvised sort of war. Their plan was to escape with other diehard Confederates to Mexico, where they would assemble a force that would cross the Rio Grande and take back the South, or at least part of it. Such dreams had long leavened the flagging spirits of the diehards. Back in May, even before the surrender of the Trans-Mississippi forces, rumors spread from Richmond to Galveston of a scheme to remake the old Confederacy into a new "Trans-Mississippi Republic" created from parts of Texas and Arkansas as well as the northern states of Mexico. Napoleon III supposedly had already blessed the project and was ready to recognize the republic as a legitimate nation.[41] Hope of a Confederate resurrection led the military luminaries John Magruder and Sterling Price to join in Shelby's scheme. Three former state governors pledged themselves to Shelby. The small band soon became a column of thousands. Marching through southern Texas, they demanded money and goods from towns along the way. Yes, they were leaving for Mexico, they explained, but they would be back soon enough to rebuild the Confederate nation. Some of the civilians felt they were being extorted rather than asked for legitimate tribute. They mocked Shelby's men as fleeing "Confederados." Others, like a San Antonio editor who declared that "death was far preferable" to surrender, saw potential in the scheme.[42]

Shelby's men were riding south in early June when Kirby Smith surrendered, just as Shelby had expected him to. After signing the surrender on board a Union ship in Galveston harbor, Kirby Smith returned to the mainland and started having second thoughts. His prospects were grim. On one side were fellow southern whites who resented him for relinquishing the Confederacy's last major army. On the other were Yankees who might decide to hang him. Mexico began to look better as an option. Instead of waiting to be taken into custody by U.S. troops, he rode for the border.

Stopping in San Antonio, the fugitive checked into a hotel under a pseudonym. Soon after entering his room, he heard a commotion in the street below. He assumed that Federals had discovered his location and were about to storm the hotel. He piled the furniture against the door and waited for the worst. But then from below he heard joyful music—a band was playing "Dixie." A crowd was cheering his name. He stepped out onto the balcony and saw an army of friendly faces. Jo Shelby had seen Kirby Smith entering the hotel and had organized the fanfare. Shelby invited his superior to take command of the column. The general said no but agreed to join them on their southward journey. His presence was a great boost to morale. True, he was riding a mule, hardly a proper steed for a general. But he still kept a loaded pistol in his holster and a shotgun slung to his saddle. Together, Kirby Smith, Jo Shelby, and the rest of the Confederate holdouts crossed through Eagle Pass on July 1 and arrived at the northern bank of the Rio Grande.[43]

The Confederates now found themselves between two very different armies. Twelve miles behind them were U.S. troops led by Major General Frederick Steele, whom Sheridan had dispatched to seal off the Rio Grande and keep Shelby's band from escaping. In front of Shelby, across the Rio Grande, was a division of Mexican soldiers. Would they let the Confederates pass? Shelby crossed the river under a flag of truce to discuss the matter with the Mexican commander, Andrés Viesca.

Viesca served Benito Juárez, not Emperor Maximilian. To Shelby he offered an extravagant deal. The Confederates were to settle on the southern bank of the river, swear allegiance to Juárez, raise an army of thousands from the American side, and then defeat Maximilian's stronghold at Monterrey, Mexico. In return, assuming that the Juaristas were successful in driving from Mexico the Austrian autocrat and the French army, President Juárez would grant Shelby control of three provinces in the northeast corner of Mexico.

Shelby took the proposal back to his men with enthusiasm. Now, he told them, they could finally get a country they could hold on to. It would only start with three provinces. With help from former Confederates and even some sympathetic Unionists, the exiles could take over all of Mexico and maybe even seize some of the Texas land they had left behind. The original Confederate dream of 1861 would be realized—albeit south of the original Confederacy.

Shelby's men said no. If they were to ally with an army in Mexico, it had to be with Maximilian's imperialists. The reasoning of Shelby's comrades was telling. The Juaristas, they argued, unlike Maximilian, would never allow slavery back into Mexico. Peonage, a form of temporary servitude, was still practiced, but hereditary racialized slavery—what Confederate Vice President Alexander Stephens had called the "cornerstone" of the Confederacy—had been abolished by Mexico in 1829. The southern whites under Shelby hoped that Emperor Maximilian, pressured by his patron, Napoleon III of France, would make slavery legal again in Mexico. Even if Maximilian's days might be numbered, as Shelby said they were, the Confederates thought it worth the risk to align with him if it meant being able to become slaveholders once again.

The hope of ending up in a country where slavery was legal had always been a major motive behind southern whites' exodus. Slavery was still legal in Cuba and Brazil. In Mexico, it might return. Through late April and early May, an ad ran in the Galveston paper offering 585 acres of land for sale "or exchange of negroes." The landowner almost certainly meant to flee Texas, perhaps for Mexico. He could take specie or "negroes" with him but not land.[44] Plans for reestablishing southern plantations south of the U.S. border had been hatching ever since the Appomattox surrender. The scheme with the most potential was developed by Matthew Fontaine Maury. The onetime U.S. naval officer from Virginia had become renowned for his navigational innovations before the war and then joined the Confederate navy as a senior officer. He shared his vast oceanographic knowledge with Confederate sea captains, including the one now piloting the *Shenandoah* into the northern Pacific. After the surrenders of early 1865, Maury set his eyes on Mexico. He secured an appointment from Maximilian as "commissioner of emigration," tasked with recruiting former Confederates to settle in Mexico. Maury conveyed to prospective emigrants that Maximilian had agreed to allow them to remain enslavers—even though Mexico had officially abolished slavery. The plan ultimately fizzled. Even so, it revealed that plenty of Confederates were still committed to keeping slavery alive.[45]

The strength of that commitment became evident during discussions among Jo Shelby's men as they prepared to cross the Rio Grande into Mexico in early June. Shelby and a few others favored an alliance with Viesca and the Juaristas. But that meant renouncing slavery. The rest of the men wanted to side with Maximilian, in large part because they saw such an alliance as their best chance to remain enslavers. The debate between the two factions of Shelby's army centered on the same question that had faced Confederates ever since they created their republic: Was the Confederacy more about nationhood or slavery? Those who took the side of slavery had always won. They had successfully maintained the policy of refusing prisoner exchanges involving captured African American Federals—a decision that kept in Union prisons thousands of white Confederates who could have helped fend off U.S. invaders. They had voted down those who suggested a national program of freeing and arming enslaved Black men, a proposal supported even by Robert E. Lee. Then they had maligned the compromise solution, ultimately adopted, of allowing states to make their own decisions about Black enlistment. Now, on a bluff overlooking the Rio Grande, the race men won the argument again. Shelby alone liked Viesca's plan, which promised the Confederates vast lands. It also had the better chance of success, as all reports from the Mexican interior suggested that the Juaristas were gaining ground against Maximilian by the day. But Shelby was outnumbered by Confederates willing to play the long odds to achieve their dream of a permanent proslavery country.

7

Juneteenths

JUNE 1 WAS a Thursday. But in northern towns and cities it looked like a Sunday, one as mournful as the Easter Sunday six weeks earlier that had followed the assassination of Abraham Lincoln. That had been an impromptu day of mourning. Today, June 1, was the official day of mourning, deemed so by Lincoln's successor, Andrew Johnson. Businesses closed. Store owners draped black crepe across shuttered windows. Pastors called their flocks to church. Back on Easter Sunday, it had been too early to speak of an end of the war. Robert E. Lee's army had surrendered, but other Confederate forces remained at large. Now, on June 1, orators took the moment not only to mourn their fallen leader but also to celebrate the ending that Lincoln had not lived to witness.

In Cincinnati's Christ Church, Reverend John W. McCarty offered the fact of the war's ending to his congregation as solace for the loss of Lincoln. "War's long, protracted, and bloody carnival is over," McCarty assured the mourners. "The sword is sheathed. The battle-flag is furled." The war's end meant that slavery, too, had ended, McCarty declared. With "the spirit of the rebellion broken," slavery was "put to death, and the scroll of universal emancipation, [was] registered upon the nation's archives, while four millions of unfettered hands are clapping with the joyous enthusiasm of disenthrallment and liberty."[1]

The day before McCarty's sermon, on a Kentucky farm about eighty miles south of McCarty's church, an African American woman named Mary Wilson was stripped naked and whipped by white police officers. The police conducted the beating at the behest of William Adams, a white man who insisted that Wilson belonged to him. Wilson had been living in Lexington, Kentucky, when two policemen dragged her from her home to the slaughterhouse on Adams's farm three miles away. There, Wilson later testified, amid the stench of butchered hogs, one of the officers whipped her with a leather buggy trace, inflicting "upon her naked body a severe beating and bruising." Adams himself then grabbed the whip and "inflicted several stripes upon her naked body." During the torture, Wilson's hands were tied above her head to a beam in the slaughterhouse. Meanwhile, in Cincinnati, Reverend McCarty's all-white congregation put their hands together for the end of slavery.

Mary Wilson's torment did not end in the slaughterhouse. Somehow she was able to escape the plantation soon after the beating and return to Lexington. But on June 6, one of the policemen who had seized her the week before grabbed her up again from the streets of Lexington, brought her back to Adams's slaughterhouse, and, under Adams's direction, stripped and whipped her. She would take no more. This time, she went to the U.S. garrison at Camp Nelson, about twenty miles southwest of Lexington, and filed a formal complaint against her former master and the two Lexington policemen. In addition to describing the beatings, she claimed that Adams was keeping her son in "unlawful detention" at the farm. In short, she and her son were still enslaved. She also mentioned that her husband was currently away from home, serving in the 119th Regiment of the U.S. Colored Infantry.[2]

How did Mary Wilson's story make sense? The "protracted" and "bloody carnival" of the Civil War had ended, Reverend McCarty had said in his June 1 eulogy of Lincoln. Slavery had been "put to death" when the rebellion was "broken." Yet Wilson and countless other "freed" people bore witness to slavery's persistence. What if Wilson had made her way to McCarty's church on June 1 and told her tale there? What sort of cognitive dissonance would have descended on the congregation? Was slavery not abolished? Had the war not been fought to end slavery? Was the war not yet over? Mary Wilson—and millions like her—demanded a reckoning.

U.S. victory in the Civil War was supposed to mean, among other things, the destruction of slavery. When Abraham Lincoln signed the Emancipation Proclamation on January 1, 1863, he joined abolition to Union as the aim of the war. He reaffirmed that aim again and again. In December 1863, he issued a Reconstruction Proclamation requiring any rebel state seeking to restore its relations with the Union to abide by all wartime acts of emancipation. During his 1864 reelection campaign, when he was attacked by northern Democrats for refusing to relinquish the war aim of emancipation, he held firm. He rejected the advice of those who told him to play down Black freedom as a war aim. Instead, he showed even greater resolve. In a private letter that he knew would be made public and would damage him politically, he declared that he would discuss peace terms only with rebel leaders committed to Union *and* emancipation. After winning reelection, he urged Congress to pass the resolution for a constitutional amendment abolishing slavery. He worked behind the scenes for the measure and was thrilled when it was passed on January 31, 1865, though he acknowledged that it still had to be ratified by the states. In his Second Inaugural of March 4, 1865, he said that slavery was the cause of the war and that God willed the conflict to continue until the institution was destroyed. Lincoln did not live to see the end of the fighting or the end of slavery. He never had to confront the conundrum of slavery's persistence in the face of apparent U.S. victory. He never had to contend with the fundamental question facing the nation: If the war was supposed to destroy slavery, yet slavery still survived, was the war truly over?

The ordeal of Mary Wilson, the Kentucky woman twice kidnapped and beaten by the man who called himself her master and held her son in bondage, suggested that slavery had survived—at least in Kentucky.

Kentucky, like the other Border States, had been given a high degree of self-government by the Lincoln administration as a reward for not joining the Confederacy. Although the U.S. Army had a strong presence in all the Border States, and at times commanders put parts of the states under martial law, the national government regarded the legislatures of the Border States as loyal and legitimate. The legislatures of the seceded states, by contrast, were deemed treasonous. The reconstruction proclamations issued by Lincoln and Johnson were aimed at rebuilding the state governments only in the seceded states. The Border States were exempt. They also were exempt from most of the national government's wartime emancipation measures. These included Lincoln's Emancipation Proclamation and—initially—the recruitment of freed people into the armed services. U.S. soldiers were supposed to turn a blind eye to slavery in the Border States and turn away enslaved African Americans who fled to their lines.

In practice, though, as Lincoln had predicted, the "friction and abrasion of war" ground down slavery in the Border States.[3] Official policy did not stop enslaved Blacks from seeking freedom in Union army camps in the Border States, and it did not stop U.S. officers there from offering them refuge instead of returning them to their enslavers. Over time, Lincoln had opted to allow Black freedom to run its natural course in the Border States, despite his official stance that he was fine with slavery remaining in the region. He quietly condoned emancipation orders given in Kentucky and Missouri. He also lent support to the move by Maryland to abolish slavery in the state by a popular referendum in October 1864. He did the same for Missouri, which abolished slavery by an act of the legislature a few months later. In Delaware, though, neither Lincoln nor the anti-slavery activists there gained any traction. Slavery remained legal in the little state long after the Confederate surrenders. Delaware voted against ratification of the constitutional amendment abolishing slavery. U.S. authorities tended to overlook the persistence of slavery in Delaware after the Confederate surrenders, probably because the number of enslaved there—maybe 1,000—was small in comparison to the number in other southern states, including the Border State of Kentucky.

In Kentucky after surrender, somewhere between 60,000 and 250,000 African Americans remained legally enslaved. The precise number was impossible to determine because of the chaos in the state. U.S. officers in 1863 had started taking African American men into their ranks and had offered refuge to their wives and children. Violence erupted as a result. In 1864, Lincoln declared martial law in Kentucky and officially approved the policy of Black recruitment there (he had unofficially approved of it well beforehand). Some whites in the state, regardless of whether or not they were slaveholders, took out their rage on Black bodies. When they came upon

African American men making their way to U.S. armies, they sometimes hacked off their ears. But African Americans in Kentucky
stood up to the terror. Roughly 25,000 Black Kentuckians, more
than a third of the total U.S. troop population from the state, joined
the U.S. Army. Under an 1862 U.S. law that was eventually extended
to include Kentucky, enslaved African American men who served in
the military became free. The 1862 law also secured freedom to the
wives and children of soldiers, though Congress did not extend the
"wives and children" provision to Kentucky until March 1865. Like
many women in the state, Mary Wilson took advantage of the new
law. The first thing she said in her testimony at Camp Nelson was
that she was married to a U.S. soldier.[4] In June 1865, two months
after Appomattox, nothing else gave her a claim to legal freedom.
As a U.S. military commander explained to President Johnson, the
fundamental racial principle of Kentucky before the war, that "all
negroes were presumed to be slaves," still held true into the summer
of 1865.[5]

The presumption that Blacks were still enslaved was at least as
strong farther south, in the slave states that had seceded. Mary Wilson's story might just as well have come from Mississippi. Like the
other states of the Confederacy, Mississippi had no civil government
recognized by the Johnson administration. To restore its government, the state was supposed to follow the guidelines laid out in
President Johnson's proclamations of May 1865. Whites not barred
from the Reconstruction process were supposed to take loyalty
oaths and eventually vote in a state government pledged to Union
and emancipation. In the meantime, the U.S. Army ruled over civil
affairs. And because the Emancipation Proclamation applied to
the state—in contrast to the Border States—U.S. troops there were
supposed to secure the freedom of Blacks. With that objective in
mind, the commander of a U.S. garrison in Panola County, in northwestern Mississippi, issued an order on May 13 directing whites to
emancipate any of their workers still in bondage.

John S. McGehee, known to his neighbors as "Master Jack,"
refused to comply. Instead, he put his plantation on lockdown. He
declared that Black people were allowed off his land only when they
were forced to attend church on Sunday mornings. The parson of
the church collaborated. If Black people from McGehee's planta-

tion did not arrive at church at the appointed time, he was to alert "Master Jack" and his son, who had recently returned home from the Confederate army and was helping to guard the plantation. On other days, the parson sometimes joined "Master Jack" and his son in policing the plantation. Only in late June did the surveillance become lax enough to allow two Black men to escape the McGehee plantation. They made their way to a nearby U.S. army encampment. Two soldiers agreed to help them—after the escapees had paid them $10 and promised them $10 more after freedom had been secured for their friends and family back home. "Master Jack" and the parson were standing watch at the plantation when the escapees and soldiers arrived. Only when faced with military force did "Master Jack" stand down and allow Black people to leave the plantation.[6]

In nearby Arkansas, a U.S. Army colonel found "slavery everywhere." As summer gave way to fall in that state, U.S. troops continued to find masters in the state who claimed that "slavery has not been abolished by any competent authority."[7]

The more remote the region, the more likely that slavery persisted there. By June 1865, much of the vast state of Texas remained slave country. The enslaved population of the state, just under 200,000 before the war, had nearly doubled during the conflict because of the influx of enslaved laborers forced to migrate there by their owners. The U.S. Army had never penetrated far enough into the Texas interior to help disrupt slavery there. In mid-May, two months after Appomattox, a Galveston newspaper carried a runaway slave ad. A doctor in Houston was looking to reclaim Charles, a "Negro Boy" of light-colored skin, and his wife, Lucy, a "black" with "hair cut short."[8] Simon Bolivar Buckner of Kentucky had arranged for his enslaved laborers to be transported to his sister's family in Tyler, Texas. Eventually Buckner joined the high command of General Kirby Smith, the commander of the Confederate region that included Texas. When Buckner surrendered in late May, his sister remained under the impression that the people who her brother had sent to her were still enslaved. She had no reason to believe otherwise.[9] Even after Kirby Smith signed a surrender order in early June, one visitor to Texas reported that whites in the state were determined that "slavery in some form will continue to exist." They had been telling Blacks

that they were not allowed to leave the plantations; Blacks who disobeyed had been captured and returned, sometimes murdered.[10]

So long as slavery in any form existed in the country, U.S. victory in
the Civil War was incomplete. The triumph of U.S. armies by June
1865 did not make slavery magically disappear. Whites in the North
deluded themselves when they accepted at face value reports such as
one from a *New York Times* correspondent who had traveled around
Virginia and claimed that white landowners and Black workers were
living in perfect harmony. The planters were "no longer wedded to
the idol of slavery," the reporter declared. "The one absorbing idea
with all," he cheered, "was that the country was at peace again."[11] In
fact, slavery lingered on, and its presence meant the absence of peace.
For every former Confederate who took an oath pledging loyalty to
the Union and its laws, including those prohibiting slavery, there
was another saying in private, as one South Carolina planter did,
that "if the people of the South will watch and wait, take no oaths
and remain as they are, slavery will yet be saved."[12] Carl Schurz, a
prominent Republican touring the South during the summer, heard
this sentiment all the time from southern whites. They "have not
abandoned their proslavery sentiments," he wrote. He predicted that
as soon as the southern states were left alone, "the status of former
slaves will be fixed in a way as near slavery as possible."[13] For many
southern whites, defeat on the battlefield did not mean that slavery
had to die—at least not immediately, and maybe not ever.

Plenty of African Americans and white abolitionists recognized
this mindset. Back in mid-1864, the abolitionist Wendell Phillips
had worried aloud that the war might end before slavery was fully
destroyed. If that happened, he predicted, masters would keep their
grip on the bondsmen for at least a quarter century more. "If I were a
negro and a slave," Phillips declared, "I should pray God that this war
might last twenty years."[14] A year later, in the immediate aftermath
of Lee's surrender, an African American newspaper correspondent
echoed Phillips's sentiment. "With the cessation of the war our anxieties begin," he wrote.[15] Another Black correspondent who had read
about the abuses that continued to be heaped on southern African
Americans declared that those who thought "the death of slavery"

was an established fact were under "a mistaken idea."[16] With time, the truth of the statement would reveal itself fully, and U.S. officials would have to acknowledge and respond to the reality of slavery's persistence, a reality that Blacks had known all along.

Yet it was also true that, years later, when Blacks looked back at the summer of 1865, they tended to remember that slavery *did* die when the military conflict ended. Amid the hundreds of transcripts of interviews of the formerly enslaved that were conducted in the 1930s by the New Deal's Federal Writers Project are many snippets similar to the recollection of Dinah Allen of Mississippi. She recalled becoming free on "the night of the surrender."[17] (She did not specify which surrender.) When Annie Coley was asked by an interviewer in 1937 how slavery ended, she offered an answer somehow both vague and incontrovertible: "Mammy allus [always] said we was freed by the Civil War." Coley, only about eight years old in 1865, said she remembered federal soldiers coming to her farm near Camden, South Carolina, and telling her she was free.[18]

The end of slavery coincided with the end of the Civil War: this is the story that we find again and again in the interviews of the formerly enslaved that were conducted in the late 1930s. But were the memories accurate? Were Blacks simply saying what they thought whites wanted to hear? Were the interviewers asking leading questions? That question, at least, can be answered—with a resounding yes. A standard query that interviewers were given to ask was this: "What do you remember about the war that brought your freedom?"[19]

Decades before these interviews, the formerly enslaved often told a different kind of story about emancipation. Lizzie Gibson, who had been thirteen and living in Virginia during the Confederate surrenders of 1865, told an interviewer in the early 1870s that "the war came and went without my feeling it in the least. *Then* came the Emancipation."[20]

Perhaps the gap between "the war" and "the Emancipation" for Gibson was months instead of years; maybe it was only days. The point was this: at least some of the once-enslaved remembered slavery surviving the clash of armies. Or maybe they saw slavery as a war unto itself, a struggle between Blacks and whites that lasted for generations and subsumed the much shorter war between North and South.[21] In the wake of Confederate surrender, enslaved African Americans agreed with one another that they *should* be free. But they did not share a certainty that they *were* free.

Law was on the side of the doubters. Lincoln's Emancipation Proclamation, issued on January 1, 1863, exempted not only the Border States but large areas of the Deep South where Lincoln was trying to foster Unionism among slaveholders. Even in those areas covered by the Proclamation, slavery's status was uncertain. As Lincoln himself suggested late into the war, the Proclamation was a wartime measure. The courts might eventually decide that it had no effect once the rebels surrendered, or that it was never constitutional in the first place. Slavery could be abolished by state law, but by the time of Lincoln's death, only Maryland and Missouri had adopted emancipation statutes. Lincoln had insisted that the prohibition of slavery be written into the new constitutions of rebellious states seeking to reconstitute themselves as loyal states. Andrew Johnson had continued this policy and made it part of his May 1865 reconstruction proclamations. By the summer of 1865, new pro-Union governments in Louisiana, Tennessee, and Arkansas had adopted antislavery constitutions. But Congress had yet to acknowledge that these states were restored to the Union, and it would not do so anytime soon. The 38th Congress ended its term in March 1865; the new 39th Congress was not scheduled to convene until December. The Constitution authorized the president to call the new Congress into a special session before December, but Andrew Johnson had no intention of doing that. He wanted a speedy restoration of the Union. Congress might slow down the process.

Slavery could be legally abolished even before Congress came into session in December if the proposed constitutional amendment outlawing slavery were ratified by enough state legislatures. Congress had passed the resolution for the amendment on January 31, 1865. Secretary of State William Henry Seward had submitted the resolution for ratification to the state legislatures, including the pro-Union legislatures in the seceded states of Arkansas, Louisiana, Tennessee, and Virginia. Against the objection of Senator Charles Sumner, who said that the seceded states had committed "state suicide" and could not take part in ratification, Lincoln had insisted that the loyal legislatures of the South be included in the ratification process in order to make the amendment "unquestioned and unquestionable."[22] By June 1865, twenty-three of the required twenty-seven state legislatures had voted to ratify. But then ratification stalled, in part because most state legislatures had adjourned for the summer. Not until September would Seward record another vote for ratification.

If the Civil War was not over until slavery was over—the assumption at the heart of Lincoln's vision of peace—then the war persisted well beyond the solemn surrenders and triumphal parades in the spring and early summer of 1865. For slavery to end with certainty, northerners would have to remain committed to emancipation. But the motive behind that commitment for many northerners—that emancipation was crucial only as a means of winning the *military* contest, not as a moral imperative—had vanished with the military success of U.S. forces. Abolitionists warned that the Slave Power was still a threat. Southern whites would find a way to keep slavery alive, they insisted, and even a sliver of slavery left on American soil could ultimately reignite a full-blown war against slavery. But it was by no means clear that the majority of white northerners bought this argument. They had celebrated Union victory as the death of slavery as a political and legal force. Did it necessarily matter to them if slavery persisted in certain areas as a practice? Perhaps not.

Americans today rarely confront this hard truth. They prefer to assume that the death of slavery was made certain by Confederate defeat, and that northern whites remained just as committed to emancipation after Union victory as they had been beforehand. But neither of these things was true. The complete destruction of slavery would require a major commitment of national will and national resources in the months and years beyond Appomattox. Some northern whites understood this reality. Most did not—at least not yet. Weary of the military contest and the long struggle over slavery, white northerners had little trouble persuading themselves that emancipation was a fact rather than a process still underway.

Imagined in this way, emancipation was self-executing. During the debates on the antislavery constitutional amendment, congressmen expressed almost no concern that southern masters would defy the measure by refusing to abide by emancipation or by enslaving those who were now free. Indeed, the most common argument in favor of the amendment was that it prevented re-enslavement and thus provided security against further war on behalf of the Slave Power. All of this it did in its first clause, which adopted well-known legal language, in existence since the 1780s, declaring that "neither slavery nor involuntary servitude shall exist." The amendment had something new, though: its second clause, which empowered Congress to enforce emancipation "by appropriate legislation." During the debates on the amendment, the supporters of the measure said nothing about what this legislation might be. Opponents of the amendment warned that Republicans would use the enforcement clause for all manner of radicalism: to grant voting rights to the freed people, to encourage racial intermarriage, now dubbed "miscegenation," or maybe to abolish state governments. Republicans denied that the enforcement clause provided that kind of power. In truth, some did support the sort of radical program that alarmed their opponents. But most thought that the first clause of the amendment would suffice to end slavery and prevent its return.[23]

This consensus allowed the amendment to attract supporters with very different opinions and motives. Senator John Henderson of Missouri, who had proposed most of the initial language of the amendment, hated abolitionists in general and congressional Republicans in particular. He defended the amendment because in ending slavery it stopped the "slave agitation" that had given Republicans their power. He also claimed that the measure gave to anyone once enslaved "no right except his freedom."[24] Representative Isaac Arnold of Illinois was the sort of antislavery agitator that Henderson hated. A member of the Republican faction that was becoming known as the Radical Republicans or simply the Radicals, Arnold asserted that "liberty" came with more than the right not to be owned. It entailed all the legal rights enjoyed by whites, or what Republicans, whether radical or moderate, usually called "equality before the law."[25] The amendment's backers had different assumptions about the rights embedded in the measure, but all seemed to think that whatever their vision, it would become a reality as soon as the amendment was ratified.

Not everyone during the amendment debates believed that emancipation would be self-executing, however. Sumner was especially concerned about wording in the measure that allowed slavery to exist as a "punishment for a crime." Might southern whites find a way to render Blacks back into slavery by convicting them as criminals? To guard against this, Sumner proposed that the principle of "equality before the law" be written explicitly into the measure. His colleagues preferred the more traditional language and rejected the senator's proposal.[26]

Outside of Congress, James McCune Smith, an African American physician and longtime abolitionist, shared Sumner's concerns. "The word *slavery* will, of course, be wiped from the statute book," he wrote in the *Anglo-African*, "but the 'ancient relation' can be just as well maintained by cunningly devised laws."[27] Smith and other African American reformers wanted safeguards against such laws. They also called for cheap land for the freed people. Whites under the Homestead Act of 1862 had gained access to cheap land in the West. Why couldn't the government use land confiscated from rebels to give once-enslaved laborers in the South a similar deal? As one writer demanded, land held by white masters must be "parcelled out to the hardy sons of toil who have made them, under the system of slavery, what they are." Only then would war cease and "descendants of Africa . . . be received on the broad principles of their manhood."[28] Finally, abolitionists, white and Black, wanted free men to have the vote. As the editor of the *Anglo-African* put it, "emancipation without affranchisement" was "a partial emancipation unworthy of the name."[29]

Yet not all abolitionists agreed that more had to be done beyond adoption of the amendment in order to assure the end of slavery. The question split the leaders of the American Antislavery Society when the organization met in early May of 1865. On one side was William Lloyd Garrison, who had co-founded the organization more than thirty years before and was now its president. While Garrison supported land reform and voting rights—indeed all measures that might end race discrimination—he saw these measures as supplemental to emancipation. They were not needed to assure slavery's death, which he believed would be accomplished by the amendment. Garrison was not naïve. As he explained to the author and reformer Lydia Maria Child, he knew that "much of the old slaveholding spirit remains, and it will try to be as insolent and cruel as possible, especially towards its former victims." "But this cannot last long," he believed. "Every thing must gravitate towards freedom and free institutions by irresistible law."[30] The Antislavery Society therefore should be dissolved. It would be an "absurdity to maintain an anti-slavery society after slavery is dead," he declared at the annual meeting.[31] On the other side was Wendell Phillips, Garrison's old friend (Garrison had named his son after him). Phillips argued that the society must exist until "the liberty of the negro" was put "beyond peril."[32] To secure freedom required a full slate of civil and political rights for African Americans, Phillips argued. Phillips won the day, and the society lived on. Garrison stepped down from the presidency and retired from the organization.[33]

Phillips and his allies faced an uphill battle. If they could not convince Garrison that the wartime objective of emancipation had yet to be attained, how would they persuade less fervent antislavery activists? Then there was the daunting logistical problem facing them at the start of the summer of 1865. Even in the best-case scenario, it would take nearly half a year to enact their proposed reforms, such as land grants and voting rights for the formerly enslaved. The state constitutional conventions in the South that began meeting in the summer would not finish their work until the fall. Then would come elections and the convening of state legislatures, by which time 1865 would be drawing to a close. As for the federal Congress, the old one (the 38th) had adjourned in March 1865 and the new one (the 39th) would not convene until December. Johnson could call a special session of the new Congress, but he had expressed no inclination to do so. Congressional Republicans along with abolitionists outside Congress faced the reality that there would be no civil lawmaking body at the state or national level for months. What authoritative body during this period, then, could put Black freedom, in Phillips's words, "beyond peril"?

The answer, by default, was the U.S. Army. The army was demobilizing, but by the summer of 1865 there were still hundreds of thousands of troops occupying the South. They were best positioned to ensure that African Americans secured their freedom.

They also were firsthand witnesses to the efforts by white masters to deny that freedom. James A. Hawley, a white chaplain of a Black regiment stationed in Vicksburg, Mississippi, recorded a litany of abuses that his regiment had witnessed in the early summer. These included former masters whipping "freed" people, cutting off their ears, even shooting them. "The spirit of Slavery remains in a large portion of the citizens," he wrote.[34]

From Macon, Georgia, came a similar assessment by Major General James H. Wilson. Wilson's troops had captured Jefferson Davis in May. But even with Davis in prison, Wilson believed, the Union was not safe. Slavery could still destroy it. "If a single particle of life" were left of slavery, Wilson argued, southern whites would find a way to "resuscitate and perpetuate its iniquities." The war would then have to resume. The general advised President Johnson to proclaim that "all men of whatever color" should receive the same treatment by all local courts, ordinances, and legal officers. In effect, he was calling for a new, more comprehensive Emancipation Proclamation. This one, unlike Lincoln's of 1863, would assure an end to the war over slavery.

Johnson was against the idea. For one thing, he rejected the premise that Black people deserved legal equality. The president had yet to reveal the full depth of his racism, but he had already given some strong hints. In May, after meeting a delegation of Black ministers from across the South at the White House, Johnson issued a reply that started out as a ringing endorsement of emancipation. It was true, he conceded, that he was from Tennessee, a slave state, and had once been a slaveholder (he held five enslaved people in 1860). But he had never sold enslaved people and had freed his laborers soon after the war began. Then Johnson veered to the subject of his views of freed people generally. They were in a "transition state," he claimed. Too many were "loafers" and looked for government assistance "like manna from heaven" instead of adopting a proper work ethic. He also suggested that Black people were morally inferior. It was a "great fact," Johnson said, that enslaved Blacks had lived "in open and notorious concubinage." Freedom by itself did not mean that Blacks would be accepted into American society at large, the president advised. It simply meant "liberty to work and enjoy the product of your own hands." If Blacks could not get along with whites on these terms, he said, they might have to find some other "clime and country suited to you."[35] Only a few major newspapers carried the transcript of Johnson's message. Fewer still offered any commentary.

The result was that Johnson remained a cipher onto which all could project their hopes, even the Radicals. Lydia Maria Child, a longtime advocate of equal rights among all races and sexes, had anointed Johnson "exactly the man for the hour."[36] Salmon P. Chase, former treasury secretary under Lincoln and now chief justice of the U.S. Supreme Court, assumed that Johnson had told the Black delegation that he supported Black suffrage. Chase told Johnson that he, too, took that position. He asked for a transcript of the meeting—he could not find one in the *New York Herald,* the most widely circulated paper in the country.[37] Chase obviously had no clue about Johnson's actual attitudes toward African Americans.

Frederick Douglass, too, was oblivious to Johnson's true character. Like Chase, he did not know what the president had said to the Black delegation. Had he known, he would have rightly worried that the president could not be counted on to bring an end to slavery—and thus the war. Not until the fall of 1865 did Douglass begin to suspect that Johnson, if left to his own devices, would keep Blacks "in a degraded relation."[38]

On May 10, 1865, the same day that Jefferson Davis was captured and President Johnson declared the war "virtually" at an end, Douglass delivered an address in New York City titled "In What New Skin Will the Old Snake Come Forth?" This was no end-of-war speech. Douglass repeated a refrain that he had long been making: "slavery is not abolished until the black man has the ballot." More than a call for progress, the address was a warning about regression. Even the barest freedom was in jeopardy, Douglass declared. Southern whites meant to maintain slavery under "some other name." Whatever "new form" the "old monster" took, it would make "a delusion, a mockery" of Black freedom. In short, the cause of the war—slavery—was still a live issue. And by implication, the war still had to be fought.[39] To understand the state of the Civil War in May 1865, Douglass's message must be seen right alongside all the signs that the war was over—the Confederate surrenders, the capture of Davis, the Grand Review. Only then is it possible to understand why the continued fight against slavery was part of the same war that President Johnson had said was "virtually" over.

The war for Black freedom was still existential, not merely meta-
phorical. It would not be won with words spoken by reformers and
politicians. It could only be won with arms. The U.S. Army was
to play the crucial role, the *Army and Navy Journal* explained, in
"burying slavery so deep" that it could never be brought "to resurrection."[40] The fight against slavery hinged, then, on the commitment
to emancipation of whoever commanded the army. Unfortunately,
that was Andrew Johnson, in his role as commander in chief. This
was a president who told a delegation of South Carolina whites in
June 1865 that he believed that slavery had been, for the most part,
"rubbed out."[41] Fortunately, he was also a president who, for now at
least, cared little about running the army. That left the fate of slavery
in the hands of military personnel on the ground in the South.

The U.S. troops who now sought to drive a stake into the heart of
slavery had started their mission long before the summer of 1865.
Beginning in the earliest days of the war, the U.S. Army occupied
land where enslaved people worked and lived. The northeastern
counties of Virginia, the coastal stretches of the Lowcountry below
Charleston, the southernmost parishes of Louisiana—all were areas
where U.S. troops took up residence in the days and months after
the fighting began. The army became the de facto government of
these regions. It made policies for civilians, it offered military courts
in place of now-defunct civil courts, and, perhaps most importantly,
it oversaw the transition to freedom of enslaved African Americans. Already by mid-1863, if not before, the army's work was understood to be part of Reconstruction. Thus, the army's activity in the
South after the Confederate surrenders of 1865 did not represent
the beginning but rather the continuation of Reconstruction. The
surrenders meant that U.S. forces no longer had to face large-scale
organized armies, but they still had to contend with white insurrection and the persistence of Black enslavement. Remaking relations between whites and Blacks continued as before—but with two
major changes.

First, the demobilization of the U.S. Army, which had begun in
May 1865, created a lack of manpower to aid African Americans
in their emancipation. The area where slavery had existed in the
United States prior to the war comprised about one million square

miles, a region roughly the size of Western Europe. If the entire U.S. Army in the summer of 1865 had fanned out evenly across the South, each soldier would have been responsible for between 500 and 1,000 square miles of territory. Of course a perfect distribution of troops was not feasible. Nor was it strategic. An outpost needed more than a single soldier if it was to have any impact in the area. Eventually, the army managed to establish hundreds of strategically placed and decently staffed encampments across the South. But the network of outposts took more than six months after the major Confederate surrenders to take shape, and once in place, the system still left vast regions of the South under minimal supervision. Before that time, confusion more than coherence was the norm. Officers in understaffed regions had little choice but to defer to "loyal" southern white planters, many of whom had no intention of making good on their pledge to abandon slavery. Whitelaw Reid, a northern newspaper reporter who toured the South during the summer, was horrified at the flimsiness of the foundation on which the army was rebuilding the South. "The rebels whom we defeated in the field are . . . restored to full power in politics," he wrote. "No free labor system will have any fair chance. . . . Under some other name, State control, contract system, or something of the sort, slavery is certain to be re-established."[42]

The other change besides troop depletion that would affect the U.S. Army's role in securing emancipation was the creation of the Freedmen's Bureau. Lincoln had signed the legislation creating the bureau in March 1865 and then approved the bureau being placed in control of the War Department. Its full name was the Bureau of Refugees, Freedmen, and Abandoned Lands, and its role was to ensure that freed people were given access to the wage labor and cheap land they would need to sustain themselves. The law creating the bureau said that it would last for one year—a sign of white lawmakers' faith in the speed with which slavery would yield to freedom—although the term could be renewed. For all that the bureau was a novel and potentially transformative institution, it remained nearly invisible through the summer of 1865. Part of the problem was that it had to draw its staff from the existing army, which was being thinned out by demobilization. Unit commanders were reluctant to further deplete their ranks by reassigning men to the bureau. The head of the bureau, Major General Oliver O. Howard, persuaded Secretary of War Stanton to make some transfers. Yet, even by the end of 1865, only about 300 of the roughly 100,000 U.S. soldiers still serving in the South were agents of the bureau.

Then again, if the U.S. Army had had a million men in the South, with a million more staffing the Freedmen's Bureau, that would not have solved an underlying problem: the whites who ran the army, whether in Washington or on the ground in the South, were operating under fundamental misconceptions about African Americans and the means by which they sought to secure their freedom. From the perspective of those formerly enslaved, freedom required independence—or at least the possibility of independence—from their former masters. Yet too many bluecoats seemed willing to let the old bonds remain. The result was that African Americans sometimes wondered just how committed the U.S. Army was to seeing the war for emancipation through to the finish.

In the South after surrender, occupying armies waged a different kind of war than the one they had fought against armed Confederates. The objective before had been to remove enemy combatants from the field by killing or capturing them. Now, for the most part, the enemies were civilian slaveholders, and they were to be left in place. They were to be transformed into fair, wage-paying employers—at the point of a bayonet if necessary. This approach did not go far enough for many freed people. Some in Virginia, for example, said they would never work for "those who sold their children, and then fought and killed their husbands and sons to keep them slaves!"[43] Freed people told by their former masters to put their name or mark on labor contracts naturally suspected that the papers in question were consigning them back to slavery. Some demanded that a U.S. soldier be present to assure them that this was not the case.[44]

Freed people had alternatives to staying with their former masters, but those all required proactive measures by the army. One option, for example, was to seek housing and paid work from someone who was not a former master. Southern whites conspired against such efforts by policing the countryside, much as "slave patrollers" had done before the war, forcing Black people to return to their former masters' farms or plantations. If U.S. officers chose to interfere in this vestige of slavery—most did, and they were under orders from Howard or Stanton to do so—they issued travel passes to freed people. Passes became emblems of freedom. They protected those who carried them from re-enslavement. Passes allowed African Americans to search for lost relatives or return to whatever place they called home. The army officer who signed them effectively ordered the bearers to be left unmolested. Without passes, a group of African Americans from Norfolk, Virginia, explained, "we are defenceless before our enemies."[45] The pass system was effective in protecting freedom but still kept freed people in a form of dependency. They had to rely on others to issue passes.

Another alternative for freed people who sought an escape from former masters was to seek out land on which to settle. But there again, African Americans were forced to rely on U.S. authorities for assistance. For most freed people, the only land available to them that was beyond the reach of their former masters was property confiscated by the U.S. Army. The U.S. government held about 850,000 acres of confiscated land by the summer of 1865. If all that acreage was gathered into one landmass, it would be only slightly larger than the state of Rhode Island. But the acres were not in one place. They were distributed unevenly across the lower South. Also, perhaps half the land at best could sustain long-term crops. Nonetheless, plenty of freed people were interested in settling on the land, and the Freedmen's Bureau was authorized to work out agreements with African Americans so that they could rent and perhaps eventually own confiscated land.

Back in January 1865, before the Freedmen's Bureau was created, the U.S. Army had signaled its backing for land redistribution. With Stanton's encouragement, Major General William T. Sherman had issued a special order from Savannah reserving confiscated land in the lowcountry of South Carolina, Georgia, and Florida for Black settlement. Sherman actually had little interest in the welfare of African Americans. His major purpose had been to shed his army of the thousands of once-enslaved who had come within his lines during his march through Georgia. But the order was nonetheless momentous. It used about 400,000 acres, nearly half the total land confiscated in the South. Forty thousand African Americans would avail themselves of the opportunity to settle on the forty-acre plots created by Sherman's order. Word spread of the order, and African Americans across the South eagerly awaited news of when the army would give them their chance at "forty acres."

Some were not in a waiting mood. As Black people learned of one Confederate capitulation after another, many decided to act on the freedom that they believed was now theirs. With or without army-issued passes, they left their former masters. Or they stayed with their masters and refused to work. Putting a halt to the routines that had brutalized them was one thing that they could do—or at least try to do—without waiting for army intervention.

Army officers and Freedmen's Bureau agents who learned of such behavior too often misunderstood it. They failed to recognize work stoppage and escape from the plantation as the only means by which freed people on their own steam could remind former masters that the war had been fought over slavery and the masters had lost. White reformers and army officers instead interpreted freed people's actions as signs that they were "loafers." This was the word that President Johnson had used to describe freed people in his reply to a Black delegation in May 1865. General Howard did not use the word, but he might as well have. A week after Johnson met with the delegation, Howard issued a circular to Freedmen's Bureau agents warning that they must "correct the false impressions sometimes entertained by the freedmen that they can live without labor." "While a generous provision should be made for the aged, infirm and sick," Howard advised, "the able bodied should be encouraged and if necessary compelled to labor for their own support."[46] Howard genuinely wanted slaveholders to lose their grip on the South. He wanted Blacks to thrive. But he had used the language of compulsion. And to the formerly enslaved, that sounded too much like slavery.

Eventually, bureau agents and the rest of the army would learn more about the realities of what it took to end slavery. They would press for more laws assuring civil and political rights for Blacks, and they would arrest whites who refused to abide by them.[47] But in this early period, the first year of occupation following the major Confederate surrenders, the occupiers were still trying to figure out their proper role. As an officer stationed in South Carolina put it, "The free labor system can be managed much more easily in the lecture room or an editor's sanctum ... *[t]heoretically* [in the] north, than in the field practically here."[48]

From Blacks' perspective, wrong-footed moves by the occupiers suggested that they were not truly committed to ending the war against slavery. The most galling signs of their lack of commitment were the orders sent down by U.S. commanders that Black civilians living in military encampments were to be evicted unless they could find work with the army.[49] It was no longer the army's responsibility to provide assistance to the once-enslaved, a U.S. major stationed in Kentucky declared. Instead, "the masters of Kentucky should be compelled to provide for these people."[50]

Yet all the compulsion seemed to fall on the freed people. They were being forced by northern soldiers back to plantations owned by the enemy. Once there, the masters might talk of contracts and wages, but day-to-day life could feel no different from how it had been before the war. "All that is needed to restore slavery in full," a group of Black Virginians wrote to the *New York Tribune* in June 1865, "is the auction block as it used to be."[51]

One of the most common actions that U.S. commanders took on behalf of Black freedom was simply to declare slavery dead. Armies penetrating into the interior of the South came upon slaveholders who had tried to stifle reports of Confederate surrenders and had told Black workers on their plantations that the institution was as secure as ever. But long-established African American communication networks carried news to the contrary. Yankee soldiers took on the job of removing any doubt. They marched across farms and plantations announcing to enslaved workers that they were free. The announcements offered a tangible end to slavery—and to the war. Whether they had any actual force behind them was another matter.

The freedom declarations originated in separate command posts, with the ranking officer deciding on the exact wording. Soldiers took copies of the orders and posted them on town halls and courthouses or distributed them to former masters and the formerly enslaved. Often, in ceremonies described by generations of African Americans to come, an officer gave a public reading of the order, sometimes at a town square, sometimes at individual plantations. On some plantations, officers insisted that former slaveholders read the order aloud to signal their compliance.

The ritual usually made a significant impression on the freed people. Like many Black southerners in the late nineteenth century, Bill Homer of Texas remembered when the owner of his plantation— a woman—gathered the workers together "after surrender": "Missy reads de paper" that told "we'uns is free."[52] Booker T. Washington recalled the scene from his childhood in rural western Virginia when "some man who seemed to be a stranger (a United States officer, I presume) made a little speech and then read a rather long paper. . . . After the reading we were told that we were all free."[53]

What exactly did the paper say? Washington did not remember, but he "presumed" that it was the Emancipation Proclamation. That was a reasonable presumption, as it had been common ever since Lincoln signed the Proclamation on January 1, 1863, for U.S. soldiers entering areas formerly controlled by rebels to read the Proclamation aloud on farms and plantations. Usually, though, if an officer read the Emancipation Proclamation, he also read an accompanying order detailing what freedom meant—to the army, that is.

On May 20, 1865, Brigadier General Edwin McCook held an emancipation ceremony in Tallahassee on May 20, 1865. He began by reading the Emancipation Proclamation. Then he announced that freed people living within or close to army posts must decamp. McCook was acting on an order that he had received from division headquarters in Macon, Georgia. The commander there had told McCook: "Turn them out." This was the only thing that "can be done with the negroes," the order read. "We have no provisions for them. . . . They can return to their former masters."[54]

When asked by freed people where they were to find employment, U.S. officers again and again told them to trust their former masters to pay them wages and treat them well. If they were not already living on their old plantations, they should return to them. Major General Henry W. Halleck explained to his officers: freed people must be "impressed" with "the idea that slavery has ceased," but they "should not be permitted to leave the plantations and flock to the large cities, where they can get no labor." Neither, said Halleck, should they be given the passes that many had requested to travel to Washington so they could meet with the president and state their wishes. Johnson did not want to see them, Halleck said.[55]

In Selma, Alabama, on May 9, 1865, Brigadier General C. C. Andrews delivered a freedom proclamation that echoed Halleck's instructions. "You are free," Andrews declared. "I expect and certainly hope you will never again be slaves. I do not believe you hazard your liberty by remaining where you are and working for such compensation as your employers are able to give."[56]

Such words cast a shadow on freedom declarations that were supposed to signal the end of the war on slavery. To "expect" and "hope" that Blacks would not be re-enslaved—the words of General Andrews—was a far cry from the promise of Lincoln's Emancipation Proclamation that they were "forever free." To make matters worse, army units delivering freedom declarations often did not stick around to ensure that former slaveholders abided by the orders. As soon as the army moved on, masters reimposed the discipline of slavery, including the use of the whip. Maybe other U.S. troops would arrive soon after and issue another emancipation declaration. But then they, too, would leave. And slavery would return. The pattern was one of the reasons that some former slaves would later recall emancipation as a fleeting moment rather than a firm temporal divide.[57]

Ambrose Douglass, a Black man living on a North Carolina plantation in mid-1865, eventually lost patience with the cycle of jubilee followed by re-enslavement. First he heard rumors that the war was over. Then came a squad of U.S. soldiers who told his people that they were free. We "begin celebratin'," he recalled. But then the soldiers left, and the whites on the plantation told Douglass and the others that they were slaves once again. More soldiers came, declared freedom, then again left Douglass in thrall to his former master. "We musta celebrated 'Mancipation about twelve times," he guessed. On the final occasion, he gave up and "lit out" from the plantation. "I didn't take no chances on 'em taking back" freedom, he explained.[58]

Accounts like that of Ambrose Douglass are a necessary reminder that the Civil War was not over for everyone by the summer of 1865. If we continue to insist that the Civil War was a war to destroy slavery—and we should insist this—then how justified are we in saying that the war was over for *anyone* by then?

—

African Americans naturally sought stronger assurances that slavery and its vestiges were gone for good. Many were encouraged by news of an expansive-sounding freedom proclamation delivered in Galveston, Texas, on June 19, 1865. Of all the emancipation orders issued by the army during the summer, this one became the best known. Within a few years, the day of the order was known by Black Texans as "Juneteenth." In 2021, Juneteenth became a federal holiday.[59]

The army order commemorated by Juneteenth is associated most with U.S. Major General Gordon Granger, though he did not sign the measure. U.S Major General Phil Sheridan had given Granger command of the massive U.S. expedition to Texas of nearly 50,000 men. Granger's troops began landing in Galveston in mid-June. On June 19, from the headquarters that Granger had set up in downtown Galveston, the army issued General Order 3. The order announced that "all slaves are free" because of the Emancipation Proclamation, issued more than two years earlier. But it went further, declaring that "this involves an absolute equality of personal rights, and rights of property between former master and slaves, and the connection heretofore existing between them becomes that of employer and free laborer."[60] The powerful phrase "absolute equality" attracted the attention and approval of African Americans across the nation.

Despite the promise of "absolute equality," the order, along with Granger's subsequent actions, tarnished this remarkable moment of Black freedom. Like emancipation orders delivered by U.S. officers in other southern states, this one "advised" freed people "to remain quietly at their present homes, and work for wages. . . . They will not be allowed to collect at military posts and they will not be supported in idleness either there or elsewhere."[61] Behind the order lay the wrong-headed assumption, common among occupying commanders, that white employers were prepared to adjust to the new system while Black laborers would have to be disciplined to follow it.

It was unsurprising, then, that Granger had his soldiers enforce the order only against Black people. The U.S. provost marshal in Galveston, whose job it was to establish order in the city so that civilian government could resume its rule, told the mayor of the city, a former Confederate, that "idleness on the part of the colored population would not be tolerated." Then Granger's men rounded up freed people from the city streets and asked them "who they belong to." Those who provided names of former masters were told to return to them. Those who claimed "no home or master" were compelled to work for the army. "We do not hear that the masters were also called up one by one and asked whom *they* belonged to," a reporter from the *New York Times* scoffed. He asked, "What has become of the 'absolute equality of personal rights'... of which Gen. Granger's order speaks?"[62]

The announcement of "absolute equality" was meaningful not only in terms of the status of Blacks but also in terms of the status of the war. If there now existed "absolute equality" between Blacks and whites in the South, then all residue of enslavement was gone, and the danger of a reignited war over slavery had passed. "Absolute equality" meant an absolute end of the war.

Yet the opposite was also true. If "absolute equality" was merely an empty promise, then the end of the war was illusory. A declaration of "absolute equality" was revolutionary, to be sure—Blacks elsewhere in the country came to expect U.S. officers to issue these same words—but, precisely because it was only a declaration, it was a thin foundation on which to build the egalitarian society that Blacks expected the end of the war to bring. The order out of Galveston, though innovative in its use of the phrase "absolute equality," was little different from the military emancipation orders that had preceded it. It contained the condescension and skepticism toward Blacks that marked the earlier orders. Likewise, it lacked the forceful measures needed to make Black freedom a reality—namely, provisions punishing whites who mistreated Blacks. As one general said a few days after the Galveston order, "To announce their freedom is not to make them free."[63]

Slavery—actual slavery, not just its shadow—still lurked in the South. So long as that was the case, the prospect remained that the war now smoldering could flare back into an inferno. Until slavery was ended in fact, not merely by declaration, the war to end slavery still had to be fought.

8

A Short Time in Peace

THE SURRENDER AGREED TO by Lee and Grant at Appomattox Court House said nothing about Native Americans. But the issue of Native Americans inhabited the room—in the person of Ely S. Parker. A member of the Seneca tribe of upstate New York and a lieutenant colonel on Grant's staff, Parker wrote out the final draft of the surrender agreement with a careful, steady hand. It was this act, more than any other, that earned him a place in the history books. Thus it was that Parker, a trained lawyer, a leader of his tribe, an accomplished military engineer, and a respected negotiator, became known in American history textbooks mainly for his good penmanship.

The stout and severe officer took the job of writing out the terms seriously. He set up a writing table at the back of the parlor and got to work, leaving Grant in the awkward position of wondering how to fill the time as Lee, stoic and silent, waited to be presented with the final document. Grant decided to introduce Lee to the U.S. officers in the room. The Confederate commander was cordial but reserved as Grant moved him about the men, lightening up only a little when he shook hands with an officer he had known years before at West Point. Eventually, the two generals stood before Parker, who rose to shake Lee's hand.

What happened next remains something of a mystery. A few accounts of the exchange between Lee and Parker were published many years later. None is reliable. One, however, became a staple of

Appomattox lore. It was the story that Parker himself most liked to tell when asked to recount every detail of the historic surrender. According to Parker, Lee looked at him and quickly surmised he was of Native descent. "I am glad to see one real American here," the general said.

Without losing a beat, Parker looked deeply into Lee's eyes and replied, "We are all Americans."[1]

Even if the story is pure fabrication, it is too rich, too poetic ever to be erased from the tableau of Appomattox. Here was a noble moment indeed. All the warring peoples of the continent—northerners and southerners, whites and Indians—were finally, even if fleetingly, at peace. And they were one people.

Yet if Parker did say such a thing, he could not have meant it in the way that it has been mythologized. He could not have believed—or wanted—that all Native peoples would become "American." This would have required the annihilation of all indigenous sovereignties and identities. A proud Seneca, Parker respected the principle that North America contained a plurality of peoples who need not assimilate with one another. He also knew that wars between the United States and Native peoples were far from over. His people, the Seneca, as well as the league to which they belonged, the Iroquois Confederacy (or Haudenosaunee), had long been at peace with the United States, but many Native peoples west of the Mississippi were at war with the United States when Lee surrendered. As one of Grant's military attachés, Parker read the correspondence from the U.S. commanders in the West. Every day, letters and telegrams arrived at Grant's headquarters telling of the latest skirmish between U.S. troops and Native warriors or the newest plan by some U.S. officer to neutralize the Indian threat.

These missives did not arrive in some sort of separate inbox from the accounts of ongoing fights with white Confederates. All the reports were jumbled together as wartime operations. Many of the thousands of U.S. volunteers at war with Native Americans at the time of Appomattox had enlisted in the army at the same times and under the same terms as the soldiers fighting Confederates. They may not have expected to fight Native Americans—most likely they anticipated facing white Confederates—but their service in the Civil War was as real and potentially lethal as that given by their comrades charged with putting down the secessionists' rebellion.

Appomattox signaled the end or at least the approaching end of the U.S. war against armed Confederates. Did it also portend an even grander finale, one that included the end of hostilities between the United States and Native Americans? A message of national harmony embracing not only all sections but all *peoples* lay at the heart of Parker's now-famous if apocryphal remark. Yet that message did not square with the reality of continued "Indian Wars" in the West—conflicts that, like so much else in post-Appomattox America, kept peace elusive.

In early May 1865, for example, at the very moment that U.S. leaders were planning the victory parade that would become the Grand Review, Confederate officials in the West were arranging a meeting with leaders of all the major tribes in the region. If the Confederate plan worked, and the Natives agreed to come together and join the Confederate fight against the Union, the U.S. Army would face a military force greater than any it had seen since Lee's surrender. Any end-of-war celebration would have to be postponed.

The "U.S.-Indian Wars" began well before 1861 and continued long after 1865. They did not stop between 1861 and 1865 to make way for the war between the United States and the Confederacy. Nor did they become mere sideshows to the main drama of the Civil War. During the years of the Confederate rebellion, skirmishes, raids, massacres, and full-pitched battles involving Native Americans pockmarked a vast arc of territory from Minnesota down through the Great Plains and into the Southwest desert.[2]

To be sure, many indigenous peoples avoided the conflict between the United States and the Confederacy—or at least tried to do so. From the perspective of some tribes, like the Nez Perce of the Northwest, the Confederate insurrection was a peripheral, near-meaningless affair. Other tribes closer to the fighting of the Civil War better appreciated the scale and significance of the conflict, but that only gave them more reason to steer clear. Why risk the lives of their people in a fight that wasn't theirs? Many of the tribes had treaties with the U.S. government, but these agreements did not commit them to support the United States against the country's foes. So long as the United States held to its end of the treaties, which typically promised the tribes annuities (cash payments) as well as reservations (land they could occupy but not own), the tribes were generally happy to stay on the sidelines.

For its part, the U.S. government showed little interest, at least at first, in enlisting the assistance of Native Americans in the fight against the Confederates. Some Native Americans tried to join the U.S. armed forces at the outbreak of the war. Almost all were turned away. U.S. authorities tended to regard them as savages incapable of loyalty or "civilized" warfare. Like whites generally, U.S. officers often bought into the myth that all Native Americans tortured their enemies, took no prisoners, and scalped the dead. Robert Gould Shaw, the white commander of the famous 54th Massachusetts regiment of African American soldiers, once criticized a fellow white officer for his cruel methods by calling him "an Indian in his mode of warfare."[3]

Yet some U.S. commanders did not carry such prejudice and welcomed Native Americans into their armies. The War Department approved the use of members of certain tribes as scouts, and it allowed indigenous groups to create "Indian Home Guards" tasked with protecting their people and land. These units were officially part of the U.S. Army but only rarely deployed by the War Department beyond the boundaries of reservations. The solicitor general of the U.S. Army eventually ruled that Native Americans could not serve in the U.S. Army unless they had become U.S. citizens.[4] In theory, the policy represented an obstacle to Native American enlistment in the U.S. Army, as most Native Americans were disinclined to renounce their allegiance to their tribes, which was a requirement of acquiring U.S. citizenship. In practice, the policy had only a minimal impact, as it was not widely known and certainly not rigorously followed. In general, U.S. Army units and Native Americans were able to work out alliances on the ground without waiting for official approval from authorities in Washington. Only a small number of Native Americans threw in with U.S. forces, however. If indigenous groups were inclined to choose a side—and most were not—they were just as likely to favor the Confederacy as the Union.

The so-called Five Civilized Tribes in particular had good reason to sympathize with the Confederacy. These Native Americans—the Cherokee, Chickasaw, Choctaw, Creek, and Seminole—had originally lived in the Southeast. Now almost all of them lived in "Indian Territory," the name given by the United States to the region between Kansas and Texas stretching west to the southern Great Plains. About 70 percent of the roughly 100,000 indigenous Americans living in Indian Territory were members of the Five Civilized Tribes. They had been deported to the region in the 1830s after white Americans and their government representatives had manipulated and coerced them into signing treaties requiring what was euphemistically termed their "removal." Prior to deportation, they had been deemed civilized according to the dictates of U.S. Indian policy. They created their own alphabet, learned to read and write English, and earned their livelihood from farming instead of nomadic, large-scale hunting (a practice that European Americans disparaged as "the chase"). Some of the wealthiest among them were slaveholders. That, too, was a sign of civilization—to most whites of the South, at least.[5] Being civilized in the eyes of U.S. officials carried benefits. While still in the Southeast, the tribes had been rewarded with a decision by the U.S. Supreme Court that gave them near-sovereign status (the Court deemed them "dependent nations"). But in the end, their status as "civilized" failed to stave off the schemes of white settlers, land speculators, gold seekers, and U.S. authorities (including President Andrew Jackson) to remove them from their homelands. By the time of the Civil War, resentment against the United States still ran high among many members of the tribes.[6]

For the Cherokee in particular, removal had been devastating. Aside from causing the mass death and suffering of the Cherokee during the infamous Trail of Tears, the U.S. removal policy fostered rivalries within the tribe that led to bloody feuds and assassinations. The tribe was divided most fiercely on the question of whether it should resist removal or embrace it. Pro-migration Cherokee contended that the tribe would be better off if relocated away from dense populations of whites. Anti-removal Cherokee said the true tribal members would never leave. They called themselves "full bloods"—race-pure traditionalists—and their rivals "mixed bloods." The terms were taunts, not accurate descriptors. Natives in both sections were of mixed ancestry. The principal chief of the whole tribe,

Wilmer McLean commissioned this lithograph from the firm of Major & Knapp in 1867. During the day of Lee's surrender, April 9, 1865, a number of officers walked in and out of the McLean house. The image puts all of these people in the same room at once, transforming the small parlor into a massive office.

The meeting between Lee and Grant on April 10, 1865, the day after Lee's surrender, as depicted in a 1922 painting by Stanley M. Arthurs. No one was near enough to the men to hear their conversation. The only close-to-reliable source that we have of what was said is an entry from Grant's *Memoirs*, published twenty years after the event. The scene of the civilians and soldiers surrounding the generals was entirely the invention of the artist. Arthurs titled the painting *The First Day of Peace*.

Lincoln entering the Confederate executive mansion on the day that he toured Richmond, April 4, 1865.

Jefferson Davis was not in the Confederate "White House" when Lincoln visited the building on April 4, 1865. Just before Richmond fell to U.S. troops, Davis and his cabinet fled the city on a train bound for Danville, Virginia. The artist depicts the escape as cowardly. Davis leads a horse away from Richmond. Davis's wife, Varina, rides on top of saddle bags carrying $300,000 of coin, all that is left of the Confederate treasury.

The Last Days of the Confederate Government, from *The Illustrated London News,* July 22, 1865. As Davis and his cabinet headed away from Richmond, they stopped occasionally and conducted official business. Davis, here sitting against a tree and signing papers, declared that his government was as functional as ever.

THE CONFEDERACY IN PETTICOATS.

The Confederacy in Petticoats was one of many caricatures depicting the capture of Jefferson Davis. As in most such caricatures, Davis wields a knife and wears a dress. He is both an assassin in disguise—meant to suggest a connection to the killing of Lincoln—and an emasculated, cowardly leader, fleeing his country for Mexico (note the satchel). Davis's wife, Varina, pictured at right, had lent her husband a shawl to hide his face when the U.S. troops arrived; he was not, in fact, wearing a dress at the time of his capture.

A Currier & Ives lithograph: "The surrender of Genl. Joe Johnston near Greensborough N.C. April 26th 1865." The surrender was in fact near Durham Station, North Carolina, at Bennett Place. The date given, April 26, 1865, while accurate, obscures the fact that a first surrender by Johnston had occurred more than a week earlier, but the terms agreed to by Sherman were disapproved of by his superiors.

Stand Watie, a Cherokee leader and brigadier general in the Confederate army, was the last Confederate commander to surrender in the Civil War. He surrendered to U.S. Colonel Asa Matthews on June 23, 1865, near modern-day Fort Towson, Oklahoma.

A plaque at the site of Stand Watie's surrender commemorates the event, identifying Doaksville as the name of the town. Doaksville no longer exists. At the time of the surrender, it was a small settlement in the Choctaw Nation.

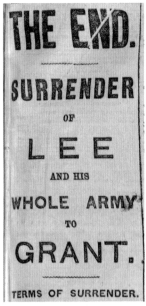

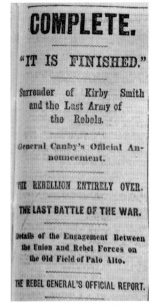

Two headlines from the *New York Herald*, separated by seven weeks, suggest the challenge of finding one true endpoint of the Civil War. On the left, a headline from April 10, 1865, announces the surrender of Robert E. Lee as "The End." On the right, a headline from May 28, 1865, declares that the surrender of Edmund Kirby Smith makes the Civil War "Complete."

LAST LAND BATTLE
IN WAR OF 1861 - 65

The last important land battle of the War
Between the States was fought here April 16,
1865, resulting in the capture of Columbus by
Federal forces.

The engagement began directly west of Columbus
in Alabama and ended on the Georgia side of
the Chattahoochee. The defending line of en-
trenchments (in Alabama) was more than a mile
in length.

Artillery mounted on high hills was used in the
action. Both cavalry and infantry engaged in the
battle.

BATTLE OF PALMITO RANCH
THE LAST LAND ENGAGEMENT OF THE CIVIL WAR WAS
FOUGHT NEAR THIS SITE ON MAY 12-13, 1865, THIRTY-FOUR
DAYS AFTER ROBERT E. LEE SURRENDERED AT APPOMATTOX.

COL. THEODORE H. BARRETT COMMANDED FEDERAL TROOPS ON
BRAZOS ISLAND 12 MILES TO THE EAST. THE CONFEDERATES
OCCUPIED FORT BROWN 12 MILES TO THE WEST, COM-
MANDED BY GEN. JAMES E. SLAUGHTER AND COL. JOHN S. (RIP)
FORD, WHOSE TROOPS HAD CAPTURED FORT BROWN FROM
THE FEDERALS IN 1864.

The last battle of the Civil War, like the war's end date, is not obvious. Two different places, separated by one thousand miles, compete for the distinction of being the site of the last battle. On the left, a plaque identifies the Battle of Columbus (Georgia) on April 16, 1865, as the last battle. On the right, a plaque in Brownsville, Texas, declares that the Battle of Palmito Ranch on May 12–13, 1865, was the last battle.

Mathew Brady took this photograph of U.S. troops marching down Pennsylvania Avenue in Washington, D.C., during the Grand Review of May 23–24, 1865. The parade gave Union civilians the chance to celebrate victory, and it also conveyed the message that the armies would soon be mustering out.

HARPER'S WEEKLY.
JOURNAL OF CIVILIZATION

This image, published in *Harper's Weekly* on July 8, 1865, depicts an angel of peace leading U.S. troops out of the war and home to their families as part of the nation's Fourth of July celebration.

Fort Sumner, Bosque Redondo, New Mexico Territory. As people in the East celebrated the Confederate surrenders in mid-1865, Native Americans in the West felt the heightened presence of the U.S. Army. At the Bosque Redondo, U.S. forces under Brig. Gen. James H. Carleton fought to keep Navajo and Mescalero Apaches penned on the reservation there. A year before, Carleton's troops had started the forced relocation of Navajo from their homelands to the Bosque. The Navajo would later call the episode "The Long Walk."

Fort Smith, Arkansas, in the fall of 1865, as depicted in *Frank Leslie's Illustrated Newspaper*. Some U.S. civilian leaders, most notably the Republican senator James R. Doolittle of Wisconsin, hoped that the surrender of Confederate armies would be followed by an end of the "U.S.-Indian" wars, leaving the country in complete peace. Doolittle led a peace commission through Native American lands in the West during the summer of 1865. U.S. agents arranged a meeting with tribal leaders at Fort Smith to take place in August 1865, but the peace mission failed.

On July 7, 1865, four of the people convicted of conspiring to kill Abraham Lincoln and members of his administration were hanged at the Old Arsenal in Washington, D.C. Alexander Gardner took a number of photographs of the scene, including this one of soldiers and civilians (most of them reporters) gathered in front of the hanging bodies of Mary Surratt, Lewis Powell, David Herold, and George Atzerodt.

A month after the hangings of the Lincoln conspirators, the trial of Henry Wirz began. Wirz had been the commandant of the infamous Confederate prisoner-of-war camp at Andersonville. The proceedings attracted hundreds of spectators. Wirz, weak and feverish through much of the trial, lay on a settee in the middle of the courtroom as a military commission decided his fate. He was convicted and sentenced to death in November 1865.

Captain James Waddell of the Confederate ship *Shenandoah,* which destroyed much of the New England whaling fleet in the Pacific Ocean during the summer of 1865, dismissed rumors told to him by other ship captains that the Confederate government had fallen. A cartoonist for *Harper's Weekly* later portrayed him as a Rip Van Winkle figure who woke up to learn, unbelievingly, that the war was over.

The *Shenandoah* arrived in Liverpool in early November 1865, almost seven months after Lee's surrender. The *London Illustrated News* published an image of the Confederate warship at anchor in the River Mersey and described the debate among American and British authorities about whether the crew should be released or hanged as pirates.

This lithograph from late 1865 contrasts the reconciliatory Lincoln with the recalcitrant South. The former president extends a hand of friendship to Jefferson Davis. Davis turns his palm downward, rejecting the offer. Behind Davis, Robert E. Lee consorts with John Wilkes Booth. An enslaved man in the background remains in chains.

Titled *The End of the Rebellion,* this lithograph shows that the fight to end the rebellion still continues. Lady Justice wields a sword against unrepentant rebels, including John Wilkes Booth and Jefferson Davis, who hides in darkness, still carrying the Confederate treasury. Robert E. Lee tries to surrender his sword, but he stands alone. The new president, Andrew Johnson, stands with Justice, ready to fight alongside the Black soldier to his right in order to secure the freedom of the formerly enslaved Black man who kneels in front of him.

By September 1866, when this illustration by Thomas Nast appeared in *Harper's Weekly,* President Johnson had revealed that he was not interested in continuing the war for Black freedom. As Shakespeare's Iago, Johnson betrays the Black veteran Othello. He pardons rebels and allows them to attack defenseless Black families during the massacres in Memphis and New Orleans.

Appomattox, Virginia, remains at the heart of the story that the Civil War ended neatly, with perfect reconciliation. Signs like this one, speaking of "our nation reunited" and showing stacked arms, stand next to every major road entering Appomattox County.

In early 2021, Reginald C. Adams led a team of artists in creating the "Absolute Equality" mural in Galveston, Texas. The mural features crucial episodes in Black history, including the Atlantic slave trade, the work of Harriet Tubman on the Underground Railroad, and the civil rights movement of the mid- to late twentieth century. Abraham Lincoln and U.S. Maj. Gen. Gordon Granger are at the center, surrounded by Black U.S. soldiers. On June 19, 1865, Granger signed the emancipation order for Texas, declaring "Absolute Equality." The day would come to be celebrated as Juneteenth, now a federal holiday. The mural puts Black freedom and equality, not white reconciliation, at the heart of the story of the ending of the Civil War.

for example, was John Ross, a "full blood" whose father and maternal grandmother were from Scotland. Ross remained chief for decades after removal and still held the position when the Confederate rebellion began. His leading rival among the "mixed bloods" was Stand Watie, a younger leader with a loyal following. Ross had managed to broker an uneasy peace among the factions, and plenty of Cherokee were thriving—Ross and Watie included—when the armies to the east began warring. Ross rightly worried that entanglement in the war would reignite hostilities among his people.[7]

The "civilized" tribes of Indian Territory represented a small population compared to the indigenous groups who had always lived in the West. Most of these peoples were known by U.S. officials as "wild" or "blanket" Indians ("blanket" for the customary robes they wore instead of the European-style garb worn by many "civilized" Indians). The efforts of the U.S. government to convert the Native peoples outside Indian Territory into place-bound farmers had met with little success. In a number of treaties brokered in the 1850s, the government promised lands for pasture if Natives promised to give up hunting, to stop raiding other tribes and white emigrant parties, and to renounce their claims to ancestral lands now settled by white Americans. U.S. Indian agents, members of the Interior Department's Bureau of Indian Affairs, sweetened the deals with promised annuities. The treaties rarely held. The pastures promised by the U.S. government were usually of poor quality and uncomfortably close to U.S. troop encampments. U.S. authorities said that it was in the Natives' best interest to settle close to federal forts: the army would protect them from raids by white settlers and enemy Natives. But Natives had good reason to suspect that the army would not always be on their side.

In New Mexico Territory on the eve of the Civil War, for example, Navajo who had settled near Fort Defiance fell victim not to indigenous enemies or white emigrants but to the army itself. By the terms of an 1855 treaty, the garrison was allowed to graze its horses and mules on the Navajo land near the fort. To conserve pasturage next to the fort, the army had overgrazed the pastures of the Navajo. With their grass nearly depleted, the Navajo moved their stock onto the fields next to the fort. The army responded by driving off the animals, killing some of the cattle in the process, and offering no restitution to the Navajo. Further depredations by the army followed, and in 1860 the Navajo finally responded by attacking the garrison. About 1,000 Navajo warriors seized the fort but were driven back by the U.S. soldiers. When news of the attack reached Washington, U.S. authorities ordered troops to the Southwest, claiming that the Navajo had broken the treaty.[8]

On the northern plains, a similar pattern of accusation-attack-counterattack played out between the United States on one side and the Cheyenne and Sioux on the other. At the heart of the dispute—and of most of the conflicts that shattered U.S.-indigenous treaties—was confusion over how much control Native peoples had over the land granted them by the U.S. government. Native groups often assumed that the land was theirs exclusively: they could keep others from using it for grazing or from traveling through it. U.S. authorities had a different view. They believed that whites could encroach upon the land when necessary, such as when emigrant parties needed to cross it to get to their destinations farther to the west. For the Lakota Sioux of the northern Great Plains, white encroachment of any kind, including by civilians passing through, represented a treaty violation. Sioux war parties felt within their rights when they attacked white emigrants. On such occasions, the U.S. Army felt justified in launching retaliatory attacks. Amid the hostilities Interior Department officials tried to renegotiate treaties, sometimes successfully, but they always met opposition from army men, who generally regarded the treaty system as futile. The Lakota and other powerful tribes of the northern plains also grew skeptical of treaties. They felt that force alone could secure the sovereignty they sought over their people and their land.

The Civil War created opportunities for some Natives in the West and catastrophes for others. Everything depended on the existing relationship a particular indigenous group had with the U.S. government. Prior to the war, about 15,000 U.S. troops—most of the country's regular army—served in the West. Some groups, like Ross's faction of the Cherokee, depended on the army to protect them from rivals from within the tribe as well as indigenous foes farther to the west. The U.S. Army also oversaw treaty provisions, including the delivery of federal annuities. The outbreak of the Civil War led the War Department to shift many of the soldiers to the east. Not even the invasion of Indian Territory in May 1861 by the Confederate forces stopped the exodus of the Federals. Ross declared neutrality, hoping in vain that this would prevent the Confederacy from interfering in the affairs of his tribe. But Watie's faction saw in the Confederate troops the chance for an alliance that would put Ross on his heels.

Meanwhile, for the Native peoples outside Indian Territory, the transfer of U.S. troops from west to east represented a welcome shedding of restraints. Those who had been moved by the army from their homelands to reservations saw a chance to turn the tables on the United States. When U.S. army recruiters showed up on a Dakota Sioux reservation in Minnesota seeking recruits to fight the Confederacy, some of the Sioux saw it as a sign that "the whites must be pretty hard up for men to fight the South." "Now would be a good time to go to war with the whites and get the lands back," one suggested.[9] By coincidence—or divine intervention, as some Sioux saw it—the rains returned to the northern Great Plains after nearly a decade of drought. The region thickened with grass, then with the buffalo that came to graze. The Lakota Sioux, located just west of the Dakota Sioux, found the hunting better than ever as they rode unchecked beyond treaty-prescribed boundaries.[10]

In Indian Territory, well to the southeast of the Sioux hunting grounds, the absence of U.S. troops was proving to be an increasing problem for John Ross. Confederate troops could travel wherever they wanted across the Territory. So could Confederate envoys sent by Jefferson Davis to make alliances with tribal leaders. One by one the tribes of the Territory joined with the southern rebels. Ross's Cherokee were the last holdouts.

Ross's determination was no match for the wiles of Albert Pike, the lead Confederate envoy. A longtime Arkansas resident, though born and raised in Massachusetts, Pike had contacts among the tribes of the southern plains and was a natural choice to be the Confederacy's commissioner of Indian affairs. Broad-girthed and white-bearded, with gray locks that tumbled onto his back, Pike reveled in his flamboyance. He had written the anthem "Dixie to Arms!" and insisted on having musicians in his coterie who could play the tune whenever his whim commanded. Pike had persuaded Jeffer-

son Davis that if Indian warriors joined with the Confederacy and
attacked U.S. armies in the West, they would force the United States
to divert men and matériel from the East. Then, with their ranks
thinned and vulnerable, the Federals would recognize the hopeless-
ness of defeating the Confederates. To Ross's people, Pike offered
the same deal that he had given the other tribes: resumption of the
annuity payments that the United States had stopped making; protection from common enemies, including the United States; noninterference with governance of tribal territory, which was deemed a
"protectorate" of the Confederacy; and non-voting representation in
the Confederate House of Representatives.[11]

There was an unstated term in the agreement that was at least
as important as those that were explicit: the Confederacy, as a proslavery republic, would always support the enslavement of African
Americans by Native Americans. Support of Black enslavement was
the clearest common cause between the Confederacy and the Five
Civilized Tribes. Thousands of enslaved African Americans lived
in Indian Territory, mostly among the Cherokee, Choctaws, and
Creeks.[12] Some Native Americans in the territory despised Black
slavery—and thus the Confederacy. They were members of or at
least sympathetic to the Keetoowah Society, a longtime Cherokee
antislavery organization reviled by the majority of indigenous people in the region. The Keetoowah were also known as "Pins" because
of the X-shaped pins they wore on their lapels.[13] The hostility of
the Pins against Natives who collaborated with Confederates added
yet another explosive charge to the powder keg that John Ross was
determined to disarm. By October 1861, Ross saw no option for
saving his tribe except to sign a treaty with the Confederacy. After
he signed it, the Cherokee National Council ratified it and then
issued a declaration that the "interests" of the tribe were "identical"
to those of "the Southern States." "The war now raging" between
the Union and the Confederacy, pronounced the Council, was "a
war of Northern cupidity and fanaticism against the institution of
African servitude."[14]

Under the terms of the treaty, Ross remained the principal chief
of the Cherokee, but Watie's people regarded Ross as an impostor whose fidelity to the Confederacy was false. Ross was indeed
hedging his bets. He kept up his communication with U.S. offi-

cials, telling them that he was open to breaking with the Confederacy and signing a new treaty with the United States.[15] That turned out to be a wise move. Although the Cherokee scored some early military victories against the Federals, they suffered a crushing loss in March 1862 at the Battle of Pea Ridge in northwestern Arkansas. The defeated commander was none other than Albert Pike, the Confederate envoy to the western tribes. His defeated force of 3,500 Confederates consisted of roughly 1,000 Native Americans. The Confederate high command convicted and imprisoned Pike for military incompetence and mismanagement of Indian affairs.[16]

Chief Ross responded by declaring for the Union. To improve the standing of the Cherokee with the United States, he promoted an act emancipating Black people in Cherokee territory. The measure was adopted a few months after the Emancipation Proclamation. He then traveled east to negotiate a new treaty with U.S. authorities. With him went a large coterie of fellow Cherokee dignitaries, along with his wife, Mary, and a few Black servants to help Mary keep house in her family home in Philadelphia. The Cherokee emancipation act affected only those on Cherokee land, so the legal status of enslaved Black servants in the Ross household was unchanged. Also, the near-sovereign status of the Cherokee gave Ross and his family immunity from the antislavery laws of Pennsylvania. From 1863 to 1865, enslaved African Americans lived in the Ross nook of the City of Brotherly Love.

Stand Watie stayed loyal to the Confederacy, eventually receiving a commission as brigadier general. He commanded the Confederacy's 1st Indian Cavalry Brigade, which consisted mostly of Cherokee but also included members of other tribes from Indian Territory. Watie was fighting two wars, one against the United States and one against Ross's faction of the Cherokee. To punish Ross's faction, Watie led his troops on a raid of Tahlequah, the Cherokee Nation capital, burning down much of the town, including Ross's home. U.S. troops eventually arrived on the Cherokee land. They denounced Watie's actions, declared him a guerrilla, and joined with the Pins to drive pro-Confederate Cherokee civilians from their land.

By 1863, most of Watie's people were refugees in northeast Texas. Included among them were his wife, Sarah, who went by Sallie, and three of their children (one of their sons, Saladin, had enlisted in his father's brigade). Enslaved Black people lived among the refugees. Because they were off Cherokee land, they were legally unemancipated, like the Black people living in the Ross household in Philadelphia. All of the Cherokee refugees in Texas lived in constant threat of attack by U.S. soldiers, local white militias, and the Cherokee Pins, whose loyalty was to Ross. "I would like to live a short time in peace just to see how it would be," Sallie Watie wrote her husband in mid-1864.[17] It would be another two years, well after the major Confederate surrenders of 1865, before she would get her wish.

In part because they were so divided, the Cherokee were never as much a threat to the U.S. Army as the "wild" Natives farther west. The Navajo of New Mexico Territory and the Sioux of the Dakota Territory in particular kept the U.S. Army fighting in the West from early on in the war until long after the surrenders of the major Confederate armies.

The Navajo, whose agreements with the federal government had always been tenuous, had seized the opportunity presented by the southern rebellion to leave their settlements near federal forts and return to their homelands in the mountains of northern New Mexico Territory. Then, in September 1862, U.S. Major General James Carleton arrived in New Mexico.

Carleton had grown up an aspiring author in the Northeast, sympathetic to reform causes touted by New England elites—including Native American "civilization." Unsuccessful as a writer, he joined the U.S. Army and spent most of his early military career in the Far West. When the Civil War broke out, Carleton, by that point a colonel, took command of U.S. forces in southern California. In 1862, he responded to news that Texas Confederates had invaded New Mexico by brazenly marching his cavalry regiment from Fort Yuma on the California-Arizona border across the desert and into Santa Fe. By the time he arrived in New Mexico, the Confederates had already turned back for Texas. Carleton pursued them but found only a few stragglers with whom to skirmish. He was now a commander with an army but no enemy.

He turned his sights on two Native groups in the area: the Navajo and a smaller band of Mescalero Apache. Neither had sided with the Confederacy, though each had skirmished with U.S. soldiers near the Mexican border. The two groups were enemies with one another, and by the time Carleton arrived in New Mexico, the Navajo had gotten the better of the fight. The weakened Mescaleros were vulnerable. So Carleton attacked them first. He had help from Kit Carson, a wizened western explorer and self-promoting "Indian fighter" now serving as an officer under Carleton's command. There were to be no peace negotiations with the Mescaleros, Carleton told Carson. The women and children were to be captured and the men "to be slain whenever and wherever they can be found."[18] Quickly the Mescaleros surrendered.

For the Navajo, Carleton adopted a different plan: forced relocation. Beginning in late 1863, the commander ordered his men to drive the Navajo to the Bosque Redondo, a forested area about 150 miles southeast of Santa Fe. Carleton touted the plan as cost-effective. "You can feed them cheaper than you can fight them," Carleton said of the Navajo.[19] He decided that the captured Mescaleros would also be sent to the Bosque. Although thousands of Native Americans were able to evade the roundup, the effects of Carleton's policy on the Navajo and Mescaleros were devastating. By late 1864, Carleton's soldiers had arrived at the Bosque with roughly 10,000 Natives. At least 2,500 others had died during the forced march. Carleton hid the number of fatalities from his superiors. The full details of the deadly trek—what the Navajo came to call the "Long Walk"—were suppressed by the army for years.[20]

The region of the fiercest fighting between U.S. forces and Native Americans was the northern Great Plains. As in the Southwest, most of the U.S. troops in the area had been recalled to the East to deal with Confederates, leaving the tribes largely untrammeled. The Lakota Sioux and Cheyenne, who dominated the region, were now free to hunt where they pleased. The recent growth of the buffalo herds meant that the tribes did not have to resort to raiding white emigrant parties. By mid-1862, the northern plains were generally peaceful. There was no sign of the full-blown war to come.

The crisis began in southwestern Minnesota, far from the hunting grounds of the plains. In the summer of 1862, about 2,000 Dakota Sioux faced starvation on their reservations in Minnesota. The environment was partly to blame. A long winter had delayed the planting of crops. But the fault lay mainly with the U.S. government. Long-standing bureaucratic holdups and more immediate logistical snags resulting from the U.S. war with the Confederacy kept the government from delivering promised annuities to the reservations. When the Dakota complained, a local white storekeeper named Andrew Myrick retorted, "Let them eat grass." He would regret the words. A few of the Dakota attacked Myrick's store and shot his clerk. They killed Myrick as he tried to flee and stuffed his mouth full of grass. Retaliation and counter-retaliation followed. In response, the War Department dispatched Major General John Pope to Minnesota with orders to organize federal troops from Minnesota into an army to put down what the government now called "the Sioux rebellion."[21]

Pope was known as a hothead who thought that the only way to bring an enemy to submission was by massive force instead of careful strategy. With such an approach he had taken the Army of the Potomac, the major U.S. force in the East, and marched it directly at Richmond in August 1862. The result was the Second Battle of Bull Run, a devastating defeat for the U.S. forces. Many U.S. soldiers in the East were no doubt glad to see Pope dispatched to Minnesota. Before arriving there, the general sent word that the Natives were "to be treated as maniacs or wild beasts, and by no means as people with whom treaties or compromises can be made."[22]

Once in Minnesota, Pope ordered the arrest of hundreds of Dakota men and forced all of the Dakota in the area to march west and settle in the shadow of U.S. forts at the edge of Dakota Territory. U.S. officials declared that the Dakota had broken the treaty and that all annuity payments would cease. The governor banned from the state all Sioux not living in proximity to U.S. forts. The arrested men were hauled before military courts, most of them on charges of murder or rape or both, and hastily convicted. Just over three hundred were sentenced to death. President Lincoln reviewed the cases and reduced many of the sentences, but an extraordinary number still faced a death sentence. On December 26, 1862, in Mankato, Minnesota, thirty-eight Dakota men were hanged simultaneously from a single massive gallows surrounded by U.S. troops. It was the largest criminal execution in U.S. history.

The hangings did not end the hostilities. Instead, they turned a small state-level conflict into a full-scale regional war. Well over a thousand Dakota had evaded capture and headed west into Dakota Territory, where they were welcomed by the Lakota Sioux. The combined groups were bent on vengeance, and together with the Cheyenne and Arapaho they staged strikes against white civilians and U.S. army patrols. Authorities in Washington demanded that the tribes be subdued or slaughtered. For the government, this was about more than demonstrating its military might. The nation's economic destiny was at stake. Congress had passed legislation in 1862 for a transcontinental railroad. The line was supposed to run through the heart of Sioux and Cheyenne country. The war on the northern plains had to end. Pope's lieutenants launched campaign after campaign against the tribes in the summers of 1863 and 1864 but failed to bring them to heel. In frustration, Union forces—sometimes regular army units, but more often local militias—lashed out at peaceful Natives who were easy to target and posed no threat at all.

The most notorious attack by white soldiers occurred in late November 1864, when a militia of 800 men led by Colonel John Chivington massacred more than 200 Cheyenne and Arapaho at Sand Creek in southeastern Colorado Territory. The leader of the settlement was the Cheyenne chief Black Kettle. Earlier that year he had led his people to U.S. Army lines and promised to live peacefully. When Chivington's men attacked, Black Kettle's people were under the protection of the U.S. garrison at Fort Lyon, about forty miles from Sand Creek. A U.S. flag flew above the village. Chivington was not acting under the command of his army superiors. It was the territorial governor, John Evans, who authorized the attack—and who praised Chivington's men afterward for their "valor." More than half of those killed were women and children. Soldiers raped many of the women before murdering them, and they mutilated scores of dead bodies. Black Kettle managed to escape with his wife, who survived multiple gunshot wounds.

Word of the massacre traveled north to Dakota Territory, where Lakota warriors, already disgusted by the whites' treatment of the Dakota, now became enraged. Even before the snows melted in early 1865, they raided army outposts and attacked white emigrants on the Bozeman Trail, a new throughway to Oregon that—to the frustration of the Lakota—cut right through the land that was theirs by treaty.

In response, Pope resolved that he would conquer the Plains Natives during the summer of 1865. He had come to consider them an enemy as formidable as the Confederacy, which had begun to collapse in April 1865 in the East but remained a threat in the West. As far as Pope was concerned, until the nation's western enemies, Natives and Confederates alike, were crushed beyond hope of resurrection, the United States remained at war.[23]

Neither Pope nor his superiors knew in May 1865 that the nation's western enemies were attempting to ally with one another. If successful, the alliance between Trans-Mississippi Confederates and Plains Natives might keep the United States at war for years to come.

General Edmund Kirby Smith, commander of the Confederacy's Trans-Mississippi forces, backed the plan. His goal was a "tripartite" agreement that would add "the wild prairie Indians," most notably the Comanche, to the alliance between white Confederates and pro-Confederate tribes from Indian Territory.[24] Together, the new coalition would launch a multipronged attack on U.S. armies from the West.

When Kirby Smith put the plan into motion in April and early May 1865, he had no idea of the major Confederate surrenders in the East. Because U.S. forces had destroyed Confederate telegraph communication with the East and had made Confederate sea travel between southern ports nearly impossible, messages from the East about the fall of the armies under Lee and Johnston did not reach Kirby Smith until mid-May. Though even then, for almost two weeks, the general still thought he could keep the fight alive. One of the reasons that he would hold on to this seemingly absurd notion was that he understood the potential power of a pan-tribal force of Native Americans. His plan had always been to use that force to negate any Confederate setbacks in the East and to put the U.S. Army on its heels.

In early April, Kirby Smith set to work creating the "tripartite" alliance. He asked none other than Albert Pike to lead the effort. The self-anointed Indian expert had been released from a Confederate prison in 1863 and returned to the West to try to broker more deals between indigenous groups and the southern rebels who had deemed him a criminal. Pike made little headway at first. Then, in the spring of 1865, with the prospect of a massive U.S. military expedition to the West likely, increasing numbers of Native Americans were willing to consider any alliance that could help stave off the coming invaders. A few bands of Comanche on the southern plains offered to meet with Pike. On April 8, 1865, Kirby Smith appointed him commissioner to the Comanche.[25] But when he asked Pike to oversee the broader "tripartite" alliance that Kirby Smith envisioned, Pike said no. He preferred to negotiate with Natives tribe by tribe. That made deception easier: he could promise different things to different groups but tell them all that they were getting the best deal. When Pike refused Kirby Smith's offer, the general turned to some of his own officers to act as negotiators. They began organizing a meeting of Confederates and representatives from all the tribes to take place on May 15 near the Washita River at the center of Indian Territory.[26]

Stand Watie, the Cherokee leader and Confederate brigadier general, urged his "red Brothers of the prairie" and his "red brethren of the South West" to attend the May 15 meeting. He expected the assembled to adopt "a plan, for a united and more efficient and vigorous prosecution of the War . . . a unity of action, that when we strike it may be felt."[27]

To lead the army that would result from the alliance with the Natives, Kirby Smith turned to Major General Douglas H. Cooper. Cooper had military experience—he had served in the Mexican-American War alongside his friend Jefferson Davis—and he had been a federal agent to the Choctaw and Chickasaw in the 1850s. He had helped those tribes repel raids by the Comanche. The Chickasaws had made Cooper a citizen of their nation.[28] When Kirby Smith contacted him, he was living in the Chickasaw Nation—at Fort Washita, just a few miles up the Washita River from the Texas border. Knowing firsthand the history of animosity between Native peoples outside Indian Territory and those within, Cooper had his doubts about the tripartite scheme. He worried especially that the Confederacy would not be able to control the tribes outside Indian Territory once the fighting began. Cooper was loyal to the Confederate cause, though, and he did his best to execute the mission that Kirby Smith had given him. Even as rumors trickled in from the East in early May that Lee and Johnston had surrendered, Cooper told his staff to act "as if no bad news had reached us." They should "keep everything rocking along just as usual."[29]

Privately, though, Cooper's skepticism was growing. On May 15, he wired Kirby Smith's headquarters at Shreveport that a peace council between the "allied nations" (pro-Confederate members of the Five Civilized Tribes) and the "Indians of the plains" was soon to take place. Was the Confederate high command certain, Cooper asked, that it was "proper and politic to turn loose these savages"— the Plains Indians—"upon the Federal settlements"?[30] For the four weeks between mid-May and mid-June, Cooper continued on his mission, despite his misgivings. If things went well, a massive multi-tribal army guided by the Confederacy would soon attack U.S. forts in the West.

First came the meeting of Native Americans to secure an alliance among themselves. On May 26 at Camp Napoleon, upriver from Cooper's post at Fort Washita, delegates from all the Native peoples involved in the scheme agreed to end disputes. Once united, they agreed, they "would present a body that would afford sufficient strength to command respect and assert and maintain our rights."[31] The resolves did not mention an alliance with the Confederacy, but Cooper read them as a step in that direction.

He now worked on the next phase: an agreement between the Confederacy and the new tribal alliance. Tribal delegates were set to meet again on June 10. To a Choctaw commander already allied with the Confederacy, Cooper issued an order to fend off a U.S. force that was rumored to be planning to disrupt the June 10 meeting.[32] To Stand Watie, the general in command of the Cherokee Confederates, he sent an encouraging note asking him to hold firm to his loyalties and ignore the "thousands of rumors afloat" that Kirby Smith had surrendered.[33] From Kirby Smith, who Cooper assumed had not surrendered, he pleaded for money. Many of the Native delegates who would be meeting on June 10 represented tribes that years before had been promised annuities by the Confederacy. If there was any hope of an alliance, Cooper wrote, the annuities now had to be paid, either in cotton or in gold certificates.

The Natives were well aware that Confederate currency was nearly worthless.[34]

Soon after sending the message, Cooper learned that the rumors were true: Kirby Smith had surrendered. By the time that the tribal delegates had their meeting on June 10, the general was hustling his way to Mexico. The last-ditch scheme overseen by Cooper collapsed. Cooper himself was actually relieved. Only out of loyalty to the Confederacy had he managed a project that he thought might set the country ablaze. The Confederacy was now gone, but apocalypse had been averted. "By the blessing of God," he wrote to one of his lieutenants, "I believe the most dangerous crisis of the late war has been safely passed."[35]

Cooper was surprised and a bit frightened when he learned that the tribal delegates had gone ahead with their June 10 meeting even though there was no longer a Confederacy for them to ally with. He assumed that they meant to use the alliance to attack all whites in the West, whether pro-Confederate or pro-Union. To a U.S. officer in the region, Cooper, the former Confederate, offered his services as a negotiator. He knew the delegates and thought he could halt the violence. The U.S. officer thanked Cooper for the offer but never acted on it.[36]

The tribes were not planning the attack that Cooper feared, but neither were they planning to disperse, and certainly not to surrender. Anticipating that U.S. authorities would be alarmed by their new intertribal agreement, they hoped to leverage the threat to secure a commitment from the United States to respect the sovereign boundaries and governments of all the Native groups. In other words, they wanted precisely what the Confederates had failed to attain after four years of war.[37]

Stand Watie now found himself in an odd spot. As a Confederate officer, he was under the command of Kirby Smith and was expected by the U.S. Army to abide by the surrender that his superior had signed. But Watie had always operated with some autonomy, and he might well decide to keep fighting. Watie was also a Cherokee chief, or at least regarded as chief by his faction. He had to consider whether keeping up the fight was best for his people and for the other tribes that had allied with the Cherokee. In both his roles, as

Confederate brigadier general and as Cherokee chief, the decision to surrender was not obvious. He had the military might to stay in the field indefinitely. Operating with close to 1,000 troops in the border region between Indian Territory and the United States, Watie had staged a number of successful raids on Unionist communities in Arkansas and Kansas in late 1864 and early 1865. He was planning more raids when word of Kirby Smith's surrender arrived in early June. Knowing that many of his troops now thought the war—or at least *their* war—was over, he furloughed hundreds of them, mostly the non-Cherokee. But he kept a core army of Cherokee under his command.

Meanwhile, talk of surrender was everywhere in Indian Territory. After the capitulation of Kirby Smith's forces, a U.S. commission led by Colonel Asa C. Matthews traveled through Indian Territory offering to discuss official surrender terms with any tribe that so wished. On June 18, Peter P. Pitchlynn, the chief of the Choctaw Nation, signed terms with Matthews. The flimsiness of the agreement made among the tribes a few weeks earlier was now exposed.

If his loyalty had been only to the Confederacy, Watie might have continued to hold out, simply out of military pride. But to do so was to neglect his duty as a civilian leader of the Cherokee. At stake was the future of his people, including the matter of who would be their acknowledged chief. Watie's rival, John Ross, had been at the game for more than two years, though the United States had yet to enter into negotiations with him. Now, with the major armies of the Confederacy having surrendered, the United States was ready to turn to the matter of treaty negotiations with tribes formerly allied with the Confederacy. If Ross were allowed to make a treaty on behalf of all the Cherokee, he was sure to blame Watie's faction as being solely responsible for the Cherokee-Confederate alliance. Watie's faction would then take the fall for the actions of the whole tribe. Already most of Watie's people were in exile in Texas. Now they could lose their tribal lands permanently.

Watie's instinct was to keep fighting—not against U.S. troops but against the Ross faction. That was the surest way to remove Ross as a threat. He planned to use his army as he had been using it for many months: as a guerrilla force attacking rival Cherokee. Once he had brought the Ross faction to submission and regained his people's lands, then he would think about settling a peace with the United States. And when that time came, he would be the undisputed, sole chief of the Cherokee.

Watie's plan was rash. He failed at first to appreciate the effect his actions would have on U.S. officials in the region. The longer that he fought, the less likely the United States would ever treat him as anything other than an outlaw guerrilla leader. Robert M. Jones, a Choctaw leader, a friend of Watie, and perhaps the wealthiest Native American in Indian Territory, met with the Cherokee general to explain the awful risks of keeping up the fight. Jones was successful. He persuaded his friend that *General* Watie had to surrender so that *Chief* Watie could get to the bargaining table. Jones then acted as intermediary between Watie and Colonel Matthews. He sent a message to Matthews that Watie was ready to discuss terms, and he suggested that a surrender conference take place in the Choctaw Nation. Jones could protect Watie there. If the meeting took place in the Cherokee Nation, Ross's people might catch word that Watie was there—they might assassinate him.

Matthews sent Watie an official invitation to meet at Jones's home, a large estate far from any town.[38] Jones thought it was more convenient to meet somewhere more accessible. A high-ranking Mason, the Choctaw leader chose the Masonic Lodge in Doaksville. He sent word to Matthews that the meeting would take place there. Then he and Watie rode for the town.[39]

On June 23, 1865, Stand Watie met Colonel Matthews in Doaksville and presented his sword as a sign of surrender. Jones stood next to Watie and reviewed the terms that Matthews presented to him.[40] As in the other Confederate surrenders, the enemy soldiers vowed to return home and refrain from taking up arms against the Union.[41] Sallie Watie might now get her wish to live at least a "short time in peace."

But peace would be a long time in coming. The agreement that Watie signed protected his people only from the U.S. Army, not from Ross's faction of Cherokee. Whether Watie's people would be able to return safely to their tribal lands remained an open question. Watie would spend the coming months in the exhausting work of vying with Ross to establish a treaty with the United States that allowed his people to return to their homes. During this period,

Sallie Watie saw her husband barely at all. She and her family continued to live in exile, fearing attacks from Ross's people that could come at any moment.

Stand Watie would go down in history as the last Confederate general to surrender in the Civil War.[42] Ten weeks had gone by since Lee surrendered to Grant at Appomattox Court House. After accepting Watie's surrender, Colonel Matthews wrote that "the war between the United States and the Confederate States is at an end."[43] Did he know that U.S. officers had made the same pronouncement after Lee's surrender? And then after Johnston's? And then again after Kirby Smith's? How many times did the war with the Confederacy have to be declared over before it really was so? Did Matthews really think that this surrender somehow carried more finality than the ones that had preceded it?

In fact, the surrender agreement that Watie signed was indeed different, though not in its terms concerning Confederate soldiers. The Doaksville agreement was the first surrender to encompass civilians. Because Watie was a civilian leader of Native Americans as well as an officer of the Confederacy, he was able to sign the surrender on behalf of his army *and* the Cherokee people he represented. Also included in the agreement were the tribes of Indian Territory that had not yet surrendered: the Creek, Seminole, and Osage. The surrender declared that new treaties between the United States and the tribes of the Territory would be signed after the tribes held their next Grand Council meeting, scheduled to take place on September 1, 1865.

The Doaksville surrender thus accomplished what the Appomattox surrender had not: it looked beyond the surrender of one army and toward an actual peace.[44] Of course it covered only the tribes within Indian Territory, thus leaving the potential for continued warfare between the United States and tribes outside the Territory, such as the Sioux. These groups mattered little to Watie. To some U.S. authorities, though, those most optimistic and naïve, the Doaksville agreement was a template that would be reproduced in future treaties with all Native Americans. The blessings of peace had flowed from Appomattox to Doaksville and soon would cover the entire continent.

PART II

THE GRASP OF WAR

A war is over when its purpose is secured. It is a fatal mistake to hold that this war is over because the fighting has ceased. This war is not over. . . . Suppose a man has attacked your life . . . and after a death struggle, you get him down—what then? When he says he has done fighting, are you obliged to release him? Can you not hold him until you have got some security against his weapons? Can you not hold him until you have searched him, and taken his weapons from him? Are you obliged to let him up to begin a new fight for your life? The same principle governs war between nations. When one nation has conquered another, in a war, the victorious nation does not retreat from the country and give up possession of it, because the fighting has ceased. No; it holds the conquered enemy in the grasp of war until it has secured whatever it has a right to require. I put that proposition fearlessly—*The conquering party may hold the other in the grasp of war until it has secured whatever it has a right to require.*

Richard Henry Dana, Jr., Speech at
Faneuil Hall, Boston, June 21, 1865[1]

9

Complete and Perfect Freedom

LET 'EM UP EASY. That was the message delivered by President Abraham Lincoln to his top commanders on board the *River Queen* a few weeks before his death. Lincoln had assumed that the Confederates would reward clemency with a concession of defeat. In a proper wrestling match on the frontier, which is where Lincoln picked up the phrase, that was how things worked. When one's opponent gave up the fight, the fight was over and mutual respect stepped in to take the place of hostility. The philosophy imbued Lincoln's writings in the last months of his life. In his December 1864 message to Congress, he offered the simple proposition that "the war will cease on the part of the government, whenever it shall have ceased on the part of those who began it." Diehards would remain, Lincoln knew—those few who "cannot reaccept the Union." But the number of "Southern people" who "desire peace and reunion" was on the rise, Lincoln believed.[1] Their ranks would ultimately dwarf those of the diehards, but only if they knew that they would be "let up easy." This was why the victors must show "malice toward none"—Lincoln's plea of the Second Inaugural, delivered three months after his address to Congress.

Lincoln had a good heart. But he was a terrible judge of the enemy. Yes, the Confederates were willing to go through the motions of surrender. Yes, they were willing to give up secession and their dream of a separate nation. But their commitment to white supremacy was something else. It was the fuel that had powered their fighting spirit. They did not leave it behind, like blood pooled from a wound, when the victors "let 'em up easy." It stayed with them. Force alone could drive it away. Lincoln died before having to confront this grim reality. Indeed, the plot that killed him bore witness to the truth. If the nation were to achieve the "just and lasting peace" that Lincoln had called for in his Second Inaugural, the enemy had to be held down, not helped up.

The experience that Richard Henry Dana, Jr., had with fighting was wholly different from Lincoln's. Dana himself was no wrestler. As a young man from a well-established Massachusetts family, he shied away from physical combat, though he was easily drawn in by rowdy protests against authority. That rambunctious streak got him kicked out of Harvard during his freshman year. He returned after the suspension but left again in his junior year, this time because of an eye ailment. Somehow a rash idea took hold of him: he should forget about college and join the crew of a merchant ship bound for California. The notion led to a two-year voyage, the details of which he would recount in the 1840 memoir *Two Years Before the Mast,* a bestseller. As a lowly crewman, he saw the raging seas of Cape Horn, the green paradise of the Monterey Peninsula, and the fiercest fighting of his life. One impromptu "boxing-match" was etched in his memory. The combatants had gotten into a scuffle belowdecks. The chief mate separated them and told them to make peace. They refused. So the chief brought them topside and staged a proper match. The fighter with the weaker physique had the stronger spirit. Again and again he was knocked to the deck. His shirt torn, his face bloodied and bruised, he refused to yield, surprising the crew with a cry that he would fight to the death. "Well crowed," his comrades cheered. "Never say die, while there's a shot in the locker!" More bloodshed and bone-cracking ensued. The bigger man finally hobbled away, deciding that he had less to prove. He was "cowed," Dana later wrote, but refused to concede. The two men never made peace. An unspoken, uneasy truce was all they could muster.[2]

Thirty years had passed since Dana witnessed the fight, but the lesson stayed with him. It was the summer of 1865. The enemy he faced had even more resolve than the wiry seaman. The sailor that day had fought out of pride. So had the Confederates. But they had also fought for slavery. Dana had long despised the institution, not only because of the abuses it inflicted upon Black bodies but also because of the monsters it made of its white devotees. He had seen enough of white brutality at sea to know the violent capacities of slave masters.

A ship captain he recalled was a terrifying figure who flogged sailors on a whim. On one occasion, a crewman refused the punishment. "I'm no negro slave," he challenged.

"Then I'll make you one," the captain sneered.

He whipped the man to near unconsciousness. Then he did the same to a sailor who had questioned the flogging of the first man. He "danced about the deck" as he beat the new victim, Dana recalled. Working himself into a frenzy, the captain hissed, "If you want to know what I flog you for, I'll tell you. It's because I like to do it!— because I like to do it!—It suits me! That's what I do it for!"[3]

Dominating, exuberant violence, incapable of admitting error and infinite in its appetite for a fight: this was the enemy that the Union fought during the Civil War, Dana believed.

The fight that Dana had witnessed as a young man did not end the way that it should have, he thought: the crewmen should have risen up, beaten the tyrant, and lashed him to the deck. Instead, the chief mate stepped in, set up a rope at waist level, and told the two men that all blows had to be delivered above the line. Every time the bigger man knocked his foe to the deck, he had to let him up rather than dropping down and applying a hold. At one point when he tried to finish the fight in this way, the chief intervened. The rules allowed the weaker man to win the day. They also allowed the fight to end without any genuine resolution: hostility continued to simmer between the two men. Maybe this sort of fight was suitable for sailors temporarily at sea, Dana thought. But it would not work in a Union that was meant to be perpetual, and especially when the enemy was slavery.

Lincoln had always been reluctant to treat the enemy this way, and not merely because it ran against his philosophy as a fighter. It also violated his sense of who the enemy was. The real culprit, he believed, was a small group of slaveholding hotheads. In his 1864 Annual Message, he distinguished this group from the "Southern people" who "desire peace and reunion."

Lincoln's understanding of the South was deeply flawed. First, when he spoke of "Southern people," he had in mind whites only. Lincoln saw African Americans in the South as southern people, but not as part of *the* "Southern people." Even in his last year, when he came to accept that some African Americans in the South should be able to vote, he still put non-slaveholding whites over Blacks as the more crucial constituency in the South. This first assumption by Lincoln and like-minded Union leaders, which was to have grave consequences for the process of Reconstruction, was coupled with a second, equally flawed notion: that non-slaveholding whites lacked a firm commitment to slavery. Theirs was the devotion of the deceived, Lincoln thought. Confederate defeat would turn them against the proslavery elite who had led them into war. Then the scales would fall from their eyes and they would accept the end of slavery.

African Americans knew better. As one writer for a Black newspaper explained, ordinary white people in the South would have supported Black enslavement regardless of what they had heard from elite whites. Lincoln had put his faith in the common "white loyalists" of the South; the Black writer said that most of these folk were "ignorant" and thought that Blacks were "made to be slaves."[4]

Richard Henry Dana agreed. A devotion to Black enslavement was wired into the souls of southern whites, Dana believed. For this reason, as he would say in the summer of 1865, putting down the rebellion required not merely "an emancipation of the actual, living slaves, but . . . an abolition of the slave system."[5]

Dana did not count himself among the ardent abolitionists of Massachusetts, like William Lloyd Garrison and Wendell Phillips, who thought that the rule of law must be put aside if it allowed for slavery or racial discrimination. Rather, he believed that law, when properly interpreted and applied, could secure the justice that African Americans deserved. In 1854, that faith had led him to defend Anthony Burns in the most famous fugitive slave case in U.S. history. His work with Burns furthered an education that had begun years earlier about the nature of the Slave Power, the insidious power bloc consisting of slaveholders and their non-slaveholding allies, South and North. Dana had learned from African Americans about white overseers who knew how to beat enslaved people without leaving scars that might reduce their price on the auction block. He saw in

Boston the non-slaveholding whites hired by slaveholders to hunt down fugitives. If the "slave catchers" could get away with kidnapping Black people who were legally free, that, too, served the interests of the Slave Power.

One night during the Burns trial, while walking home alone, Dana was nearly murdered by a few whites, though he never learned whether they were from the South or North.[6] Dana was undeterred. The defense that he provided Burns was applauded by African Americans and white antislavery activists everywhere. But he lost the case. "Massachusetts lay at the foot of the slave power," Dana thundered.[7] Burns was marched through the city to the harbor and shipped to slavery in Virginia. Residents of the city protested in fury. Even before the final verdict was rendered, U.S. troops had arrived in Boston to prevent a riot. They were sent there by the secretary of war, Jefferson Davis.

By the time of the Civil War, Dana was a sturdy member of the Republican Party—the affiliation helped secure him an appointment as a U.S. attorney—but he was a different sort of Republican than Abraham Lincoln. Dana distrusted all southern whites as real or potential agents of the Slave Power. Lincoln, by contrast, never abandoned the sentiment expressed in his First Inaugural—"We are not enemies, but friends"—at least when it came to the white non-elites of the South. His faith in the independence of the non-elites, their ability to act in their own self-interest, made Lincoln skeptical of the notion that all whites in the South and some in the North were part of a single Slave Power. Unlike Dana, he never used the expression. He acknowledged the evil of slavery and the outsized influence of slaveholders but had confidence that he could bring the non-slaveholding whites to his side.

The differing views of the South represented by Dana and Lincoln reflected one of the differences between radical and moderate Republicans. The clearest policy difference between the two factions concerned African American voting rights. Radicals supported Black suffrage. Moderates were more tentative, if not outright opposed. The divide was due only partly to competing ideas about Blacks' capacities, though opinions on that subject did indeed differ and the difference mattered a great deal. The deeper disagreement was about the *white* South, specifically how much force, if any, was needed to bring white southerners to heel. Or, to put it as one Republican broadside did in 1864: "How shall we end the Rebellion—Shall we Coax it, or Crush it?"[8] At the time, the question had been aimed at the Democrats; Republicans during the 1864 election had been united in calling the opposing party too soft-hearted in its approach to the Confederates. A year later, in mid-1865, the "coax or crush" question now divided the Republicans. Moderates—the coaxers—worried that Black suffrage would prolong the rebellion by stirring up southern white animosity. Radicals—the crushers—saw Black suffrage as a crucial tool to end the rebellion by subduing white power.

The Appomattox surrender exposed the difference between Lincoln and Dana—and between Republican moderates and radicals—on the subject of making peace with rebels. Lincoln applauded Grant's conciliatory approach. Indeed, he had ordered it. Dana thought it was a terrible misstep. At the celebration in Boston after the surrender, he mocked those who thought peace had been "made" at Appomattox. Peace had to "come," he declared: it would arrive not in an instant but over time. He had not been explicit about *how* peace would come, but his meaning was hard to miss: rebellious whites had to be subdued while enslaved Blacks had to be emancipated and enfranchised. In short, the Slave Power had to be crushed. Edward Kent, a judge and former governor from Maine, praised Dana for noting that the Appomattox agreement fell far short of preventing a "relapse into the state where the old leaders of the slave power shall resume their plantation manners and their tyrannical sway in our councils."[9] A week after the Lincoln assassination, Dana asked his friend William Cullen Bryant, the famous poet and newsman, whether "Lincoln ordered the terms with Lee." Dana hoped it was the case. "Far better is it that it should have been a mistake of the dead," he wrote, "than of a man still living and in power."[10]

In the weeks after Appomattox, Dana started working on a speech that spelled out how peace might come, seeing as he thought it could not be made. He conceded that the war between enemy armies was over. To his son in boarding school in New Hampshire, Dana wrote, "The rebellion is broken up and our great country stands nobly before the world."[11] He used a similar phrase—the "sudden and complete breaking up of the Confederacy"—in a letter to his friend Charles Francis Adams, the son of former president John Quincy Adams. But to Adams, Dana added a wry note of doubt. Was this indeed the perfect "winding up" to the war, he asked, "reading so like a novel"? "Well, sir," he wrote facetiously, "so our people believe it to be!"[12]

Dana believed something else. The major armies might have retired from the field, but the nation was still at war. "White power" in the South aimed to keep Blacks "in a servile and degraded position," he warned Adams. "This will give us the old, troublesome, oligarchal spirit to deal with." The United States therefore was still at war against the Slave Power. "The war does *not* cease because the fighting ends," he told Adams.[13]

Dana had found support for this position in long-standing theories of international law. The Dutch legal theorist Hugo Grotius, whose seventeenth-century work on the law of war was foundational, had written that war "can exist even when it does not carry forward its operations."[14] Grotius had rooted this proposition in the "law of conquest," under which "everything can be taken" from the conquered by the victor.[15] Dana, though, believed that there was a limit to conquest, at least in the context of the Civil War—namely, that the United States could not deprive the defeated states of their status as states. Some of his contemporaries, Senator Charles Sumner most prominent among them, had taken the opposite approach. Since at least 1863, the Massachusetts senator had argued that the governments of the seceded states had "vacated" their power when they rebelled.[16] Congress could therefore rule over the region much as it governed over federal territories. This "territorial" approach, also known as the "state suicide" theory, went too far for Dana. Secession was unconstitutional, Dana agreed, but it did not "vacate" state government. While he admired Sumner's "great moral energy," he thought the senator's approach "never had any logic."[17] The states must remain as states, Dana thought.

Here Dana and Lincoln had agreed—to a point. They both believed that the states had neither left the Union nor extinguished themselves. Rather, the states had fallen under enemy control. By the terms of the U.S. Constitution (Article 4, section 4), the nation guaranteed to every state a "republican form of government." The "guarantee clause," not the law of conquest, was the legal basis for reconstructing the states that was preferred by most Republicans, including Lincoln and Dana. Lincoln thought that seceded states became "republican" again when they adopted constitutions accepting the Union and emancipation. Dana agreed. But he thought the United States must demand more. At the very least, he expected seceded states to grant voting rights to some of the Black men who had been enslaved. Lincoln approved of limited Black suffrage—he had endorsed it in his final speech—but not as a precondition for a state resuming what he called its "practical relations" with the Union. Demanding Black suffrage went beyond what the guarantee clause allowed, Lincoln thought. That might be true, Dana contended, but the United States had more in its arsenal than the guarantee clause. It had the "war power," and it could use that power to impose conditions on the enemy beyond what the guarantee clause allowed. Lincoln disagreed, though he died before he could develop a full rebuttal. The message that he had given to Congress in 1864, that "the war will cease on the part of the government, whenever it shall have ceased on the part of those who began it," could hardly have been clearer. The United States lost its war power when the enemy stopped fighting. Dana contended that the United States kept its war power until the nation was secure.

Dana grounded his argument in international law—not the old law of conquest but the more modern law of national security. The crucial theorist for national security was—and is—Emmerich de Vattel, the eighteenth-century European philosopher whose writings remain required reading for international relations experts. When dealing with a "perfidious enemy," Vattel argued, "we should avail ourselves of a successful war, and follow up our advantages, till we have humbled a dangerous and excessive power, or compelled the enemy to give us sufficient security for the time to come."[18] The United States must take this approach to the rebellious South, Dana wrote Adams: "We can hold the region and its people in the grasp of war until we have obtained such securities for the future as it is reasonable for us to require." Keeping the enemy in a "grasp of war" was for Dana the only way to assure that peace would come. The "grasp of war" approach refined Vattel's theory and imbued it with Dana's personal experience. He had seen enough combat, like the bloody contest between two sailors decades before, to know the importance of keeping one's foe pinned until all threat of further fighting was removed. Was "the grasp of war" nothing more than "coercion"? he asked Adams rhetorically. "Of course it is," Adams answered. "War is coercion."[19]

More than thirty years before, the Prussian general Carl von Clausewitz had made a strikingly similar assertion: "War is an act of force, and there is no logical limit to the application of that force."[20] Clausewitz, too, had acknowledged the cold brutality of the position. There was no place for "kind-hearted people" in war, he wrote. "War is such a dangerous business that the mistakes which come from kindness are the very worst."[21] Clausewitz had no patience for a "let 'em up easy" approach like Lincoln's. Neither did Dana. It is tempting to think that Dana was influenced by Clausewitz, but he probably had never heard of him. The Prussian's theories were studied in military academies, not law schools, and they were known barely at all in the United States (English translations of Clausewitz did not proliferate until the twentieth century). Most likely, Dana arrived on his own at the conclusion already reached by Clausewitz. He certainly seemed to be channeling him when he wrote the final draft of the speech. There, Dana offered the "fearful proposition" that war was "an appeal from the force of law to the law of force."[22]

The occasion to deliver the address came sooner than Dana expected. He was invited to be one of the speakers at a rally for Black suffrage to be held at Faneuil Hall in Boston on June 21, 1865. Dana was not as ardent as some on the specific issue at hand. As he wrote to Adams, he rejected the idea of the "crazy radicals, who hold that the ballot is the inalienable right of every human being."[23] But he did believe Black suffrage of some sort was needed in the South to overcome the old Slave Power. The main reason he accepted the invitation, though, was to make public his broader ideas about the United States still being at war. For weeks before the event, he polished his ideas and practiced his lines as if he were preparing the closing argument of the case of a lifetime. His son, home from boarding school, recalled him preparing diligently, "walking up and down the room, his head a little to one side, his eyes slightly raised . . . developing the arguments."[24]

When the Faneuil Hall event took place on June 21, Dana was

ready. Soon into his speech, he arrived at the central premise: that the United States must hold the "enemy in the grasp of war until it has secured whatever it has a right to require." Before his one-hour oration was done, he had used the "grasp of war" metaphor no fewer than six times. The address, which would become famous within weeks, was known by all as the "Grasp of War" speech. The "grasp of war" approach became the foundation of Republicans' Reconstruction policy, though it took the party more than a year to coalesce around the position.

Reconstructing the nation, Dana argued, was not a peacetime endeavor but a continuation of the war. "When a nation goes into war," he explained, "she does it to secure an end, and the war does not cease until the end is secured."[25] Dana reminded his audience what that end was: the "complete and perfect freedom" of the once-enslaved.[26] This meant that the war continued until the enemy granted to Black Americans "equality before the law," landholding rights, and "an impartial ballot."[27]

The innovation in Dana's argument lay not in his call for the "complete and perfect" freedom of Black Americans, though that position did mark him as among the more progressive of white Republicans. Even before the war, Blacks had contended that freedom required not merely the prohibition of slavery but the granting of positive rights, including the right to vote. "Slavery is not abolished until the black man has the ballot," Frederick Douglass had repeatedly insisted in the months and years following Lincoln's Emancipation Proclamation.[28] In a mourning oration for Abraham Lincoln delivered a few weeks before Dana's Faneuil Hall speech, Douglass declared that the country had still not reached "the desired condition of peace" and would not do so until the emancipated were "enfranchised and clothed with the dignity of American citizenship."[29] The novelty of Dana's speech was that it grounded goals like those demanded by Douglass in the actual law of war. In this formulation, the "complete and perfect freedom" of Black Americans was not a consequence of war but rather a prerequisite for the war to be deemed over. Until the rebel states enacted legal equality, Dana proclaimed, "we are in a state of war."[30]

That a "state of war" could exist after the main armies had disbanded was a concept that would reverberate with power for years to come. Even more profound, for our own time as much as for Dana's, was the contention that slavery, or even its mere vestige, kept the country in a state of war.

Dana's speech was a sensation. It was reprinted in newspapers across the country as well as in the *Times of London*. As an international lawyer, Dana was particularly interested in the opinions of intellectuals familiar with his field. He was no doubt thrilled when Francis Lieber asked if he could reprint the speech. Lieber was one of the foremost theorists on the law of war and the author of the code of war that the United States had adopted in 1863. He also was chair of the Loyal Publication Society, which meant that Dana's speech was sure to get wide distribution. Lieber heard in Dana's words echoes of his own recent tirades calling rebellion an act of treason punishable by death. He told Dana that he had always been "for crushing the Rebellion by shot and powder, and for keeping the conquered states for a time sufficient to lead the waters into the right channels, under sword and bayonet."[31] From Paris came high praise from John Bigelow, the U.S. minister to France, who wrote that he, like Dana, thought that the war would cease only when "a decided majority of the nation were opposed to Slavery [and] ... prepared to recognize the fraternity of the African."[32] John L. Motley, the U.S. minister to Austria, wrote that Dana had pierced the heart of the problem facing the nation. Even if the constitutional amendment abolishing slavery was ratified, he wrote, that would not be enough to assure the end of the war. To prohibit slavery "and then to restore the whole powers of government to the 'chivalry' without taking guarantees is only to reestablish the Oligarchy and Slavery along with it," Motley wrote. "It is as if the Inquisition should have been declared abolished in Spain and then the whole government of the country placed in the hands of Torquemada and his familiars."[33]

Amid the chorus of praise, Dana heard a sour note from his closest friend in the diplomatic corps, Charles Francis Adams. Adams rejected the idea that war persisted. "The rebellion is put down," he declared. "The States resume their ancient status of perfect equality and perfect obedience to the general law."[34] If the national government wanted something changed in state law, it had to rely on the "voluntary agency of the people" of that state. As for Blacks within those states, the war power had made them free. They could not be turned back into "chattel" by the states. The Constitution offered them nothing more than that.[35]

Dana had tried to use international law to get around the Constitution's protection of the power of the states. Adams was having none of it. If Dana's theory was put into practice, Adams told him, "the Constitution is virtually annulled—and the law of force is established."[36] Even Francis Lieber, a leading advocate of international law, especially in the practice of war, put the letter of the Constitution above all else. For this reason, Lieber advised Dana that his proposal would be stronger if molded into an amendment to the U.S. Constitution. Only after the adoption of such a measure could the "grasp of war" theory become law, Lieber argued.[37] Lieber himself had taken that approach and was currently promoting a slate of constitutional amendments. Some dealt with prohibitions against treason and secession. Some dealt with rights for freed people. All were aimed at rooting out slavery, which Lieber, like Dana, regarded as the "deplorable anachronism" that had caused the war and continued to threaten the nation's security.[38]

"The grasp of war" immediately entered the parlance of Reconstruction politics. A few days after Dana's speech, the business leader John Murray Forbes encouraged a friend to read the address so he might better understand why the "safety and honor" of the nation depended on holding rebels in a "war grip."[39] In mid-July, the *Chicago Tribune* published the speech with an approving editorial endorsing the "right and duty" to hold the rebel states "in the grasp of military authority . . . until the scepter of the old slave barons is rusted by disuse."[40] In response to the editorial, former Maryland congressman Henry Winter Davis fired off an angry private letter to the *Tribune*'s editor, Joseph Medill. It was Davis who had first put forward the notion of the Constitution's guarantee clause as the foundation of Reconstruction. He had argued that Reconstruction happened outside the sphere of war. Congress required state governments to be "republican" and defined what "republican" meant (for example, whether it required a state to grant voting rights to Blacks). Then it was up to the states to meet the standard set by Congress—by consent, not coercion. If lawmakers instead adopted Dana's approach, Davis argued, "the Republicans will go down before the just cry of the people against military and despotic power."[41]

The reaction to Dana's address that mattered most was Andrew Johnson's. But Johnson was hard to read. On June 24, three days after Dana's speech, he met with a delegation of South Carolina whites at the White House. The delegation tried to pin the president down on what exactly the loyal whites of their state had to do to restore self-government and free South Carolina from military rule. Johnson began by saying he would "speak clearly." Then he obfuscated on every point. He said he was "a better State rights man" than they were. But then he said that the U.S. military would continue to rule the state. He seemed to demand ratification of the constitutional amendment abolishing slavery as a prerequisite to restoration. Yet, when pressed on this point, he replied that he could "only advise" ratification. On African Americans, Johnson seemed to advocate equal rights. Blacks "went into the rebellion" as slaves but came out as "freemen of color." Whites must "stand simply as equals" to them. Later, though, he said that the state government could leave Blacks "out in the cold" once it ratified the abolition amendment.[42] The *Albany Argus,* a Democratic newspaper, chose to read Johnson's words as a rebuke to Dana and the "agitators" in Boston who had recently "demanded that the Southern States should continue to be controlled by military power."[43] But Johnson probably did not know of the speech. The interpretation offered by the *Argus* also assumed a coherence to Johnson's views. There was none. Indeed, because Johnson did not explicitly renounce the "grasp of war" theory, Dana could indulge in the belief that the president's "course" followed "the same principle" as Dana had laid out in Boston.[44]

Dana's friends suspected otherwise. Forbes worried that Johnson had a "haste for reconstruction."[45] Lieber, too, suspected that "the hurry of Presdt Johnson may give us much trouble."[46] Medill wanted Johnson to commit explicitly to "absolute equality before the law," with Black suffrage "thrown in."[47] Johnson's coolness on Black suffrage was undeniable. But that may not have troubled Dana, who thought that only some African Americans should get the vote. The reality was that at the time of Dana's address, no one really knew what Johnson stood for, including Johnson himself.

As it turned out, Johnson's opinions, whatever they were, did not matter—at least in the summer of 1865. For more than six weeks after his meeting with the whites from South Carolina, Johnson was little seen and rarely heard from. He was bedridden with illness.

Johnson's body was as sickly as his soul. Unlike his predecessor, he drank and took tobacco (mostly by chewing it). Where Lincoln had liked to be on the move—striding between the White House and the War Department telegraph office, or riding his carriage to the Soldiers' Home—Johnson rarely emerged from the White House residence. Either he was dealing with his own ailments or with those of his wife, Eliza, chronically ill with tuberculosis (she would make only two public appearances, both brief, during her time as First Lady). The camera was kind to Johnson, much kinder than history would be, and the photographs taken of him by Mathew Brady in his first year in office suggest a young, even vigorous man. But he was actually a bit older than Lincoln. And for much of his first half year as president, he was sicker than Lincoln ever had been.

For those wanting Dana's "grasp of war" theory to be put into action, the president's indisposition during the summer of 1865 was perfectly timed. It allowed Secretary of War Edwin Stanton, who shared Dana's preference for rule by force, to take charge. No one stood in Stanton's way. Johnson had not named a vice president— and never would. Typically the secretary of state was regarded as the highest-ranking cabinet officer. But Seward was still recovering from the injuries that he had sustained in April. Also, on June 21, the day of Dana's "Grasp of War" address, Seward's beloved wife, Frances, had died. Seward, incapacitated by grief, rarely appeared at cabinet meetings during the rest of the summer. That left Stanton, already regarded by Secretary of the Navy Gideon Welles as "intriguing and tyrannical," effectively unchecked.[48]

Even before this moment, Stanton had been gaining firmer control over the army. The decentralized structure of the army had long been an impediment to Stanton using the troops efficiently in the management of the occupied South. The army's provost marshals were in charge of civilian affairs. But they were spread out across hundreds of units, and they operated independently of one another. The result was a patchwork of conflicting policies. For example, provost marshals in different regions set different standards for what counted as arrestable offenses by former rebels. Meanwhile, the Freedmen's Bureau, created in March 1865, acted as a distinct agency within the army. It had the top-down structure that Stanton preferred. But by midsummer of 1865, the bureau was in its infancy, still recruiting officers from existing units and setting up posts across the South. U.S. troops in the region still lacked a uniform policy for establishing order and ensuring emancipation. Stanton would gladly have held the South in a "grasp of war," but he was working with a fist of sand.[49]

While Lincoln was alive, Stanton had developed a plan to remedy the problem. Under his system, provost marshals would follow a single set of guidelines, to be drawn up by Stanton himself, of course. The South would be divided into military districts superimposed over existing state lines. The civil affairs of each district would be overseen by a military department, with all the department heads reporting to Stanton. Lincoln was assassinated before he could render his final verdict on the plan, but during what turned out to be his final cabinet meeting, he expressed reservations and tabled it.[50]

In Johnson, Stanton saw a more pliable ally. He liked that Johnson, unlike Lincoln, showed no inclination to interfere in army affairs. He assumed that the new president was deferring to Stanton out of trust. In fact, Johnson did not know whom to trust. The self-important Stanton mistook his superior's indecision for endorsement. In May, Stanton brought to the cabinet the new plan for the army that had been tabled by Lincoln the month before. He sat by passively as his fellow secretaries shot it down for being too autocratic. Stanton's old foe Gideon Welles was mystified by the "alacrity and cheerfulness" with which the war secretary surrendered.[51] The navy secretary failed to note that Johnson had said nothing. That silence was all that Stanton was looking for: he assumed the president was signaling approval. The opposition of the rest of the cabinet was irrelevant to him. He intended to put the plan into effect anyway, at the right moment.

The moment came with the absence of Johnson and Seward beginning in late June. On June 27, less than a week after Dana's "Grasp of War" speech, Stanton implemented his scheme.[52] Knowing that he would need major manpower, he slowed the process of demobilization. The army was nowhere near its peak size of one million men, but with 200,000 troops still in the field, it was more than twelve times its prewar strength. Lincoln had assumed that the volunteers would muster out quickly, leaving a regular army of roughly 35,000 troops, twice the size of the prewar army but only a fraction of what Stanton now expected to work with.[53] Stanton also left the size of the capital's War Department unchanged. Early on under Stanton's leadership, for example, Congress had authorized the creation of three new assistant secretaries of war to help manage the army. Stanton kept the three assistants, along with hundreds of other wartime hires, at his disposal.[54] The increased size of the army and the War Department because of the Civil War created its own logic, at least for Stanton. Now that the United States had more military resources than usual, he thought, why not push the war beyond the point where others might have seen a natural end? The reasoning should be familiar to anyone who has paid attention to the way that the United States has managed its armed forces in the last eighty years.

Secretary of the Navy Gideon Welles, unlike Stanton, thought retrenchment should be the order of the day. Welles was furious when he found that Stanton was still managing a "vast concourse of generals" and now sat atop more than a dozen "departments" imposed on the South.[55] He found just as "notorious" the expenditures of Stanton's War Department. While Welles had been severe in cutting the navy's costs, Stanton had made no similar effort to "retrench expenses" in the army.[56]

Welles was wrong to think of Stanton as a mere power-grabber. There was a higher purpose to the secretary of war's autocratic moves: the destruction of slavery and all its vestiges. Quite rightly, he did not trust the civil governments that were forming in the southern states to do the job. Like Richard Henry Dana, Stanton believed that the war continued until the nation was secured against the reemergence of the old Slave Power. Military rule was for Stanton a moral imperative. He expected the commanders in the field to share that view. Many did, including General in Chief Ulysses S. Grant and Major General Oliver O. Howard, head of the Freedmen's Bureau. Those with softer spines, the officers who cozied up to former Confederates at the expense of Black freedom, did not fare well after midsummer 1865, when Stanton's power reached its peak.

Consider Gordon Granger, the U.S. officer who had landed in Galveston and proclaimed freedom and "absolute equality of personal rights" for all Black Texans on June 19—or "Juneteenth," as the day came to be called. The *New York Times* mocked Granger's promise of "absolute equality" when word came north that Granger's men had forcibly rounded up Black people in the city and delivered them to their former masters or put them to work for the army.[57] General Howard sent notice to Granger that the earliest that a contingent from the Freedmen's Bureau would arrive there was September; until then, Granger was to act on behalf of the bureau and ensure that Black laborers received fair treatment. Granger ignored the message. He allowed former masters to dictate the terms of contracts with freed people. Workers who complained were warned by Granger's men not to "abuse" the rights bestowed upon them. While stories of white "employers" whipping Black "employees" filtered back to Granger's headquarters, Granger himself socialized with elite former Confederates who were drawing up plans for the new state government. With Stanton's blessing, Phil Sheridan, Granger's superior, had the general transferred out of Texas.[58]

Across the occupied South, U.S. commanders who favored a strong hand were emboldened by Stanton's directive that military rule trumped civilian authority. In Louisiana, Major General Edward Canby ran out of patience with southern whites who complained about the continuing presence of bluecoats among them. "It is scarcely reasonable to expect," he jeered at one civilian, "that we shall get out of the wilderness in forty days."[59]

The officers of Howard's Freedmen's Bureau ventured into the wilderness. Howard knew that a commander's declaration of emancipation, such as Granger's in Galveston, was by itself meaningless, even if, like Granger's, it carried a pledge of "equality." The bureau's job, Howard believed, was to use the army to give teeth to such proclamations. This was not a *postwar* mission but rather a continuation of the war against slavery. Created back in March 1865, while Lincoln was still alive and the prospect of Confederate surrender anything but certain, the bureau was to exist for a one-year, renewable term, regardless of how the U.S. armies fared against the rebels. The southern whites in mid-1865 who assumed that the United States would remove occupying troops as part of the deal for their surrender were in for a surprise. Although the total number of U.S. military *men* decreased rapidly during the summer, the number of U.S. military *posts* across the South increased.[60]

Meanwhile, Freedmen's Bureau agents became more visible at the army posts, as did their power. In a circular issued to his agents on May 30, General Howard declared that the bureau would have jurisdiction over any matters involving African Americans that came before U.S. occupying troops. This meant that crimes involving Black victims could be tried in military courts. "Equality before the law" was to be enforced, Howard declared, not merely promised. He explained: "A black, red, yellow or white thief should have punishment without regard to the color of his skin."[61] Howard wasn't really talking about theft, though. He was talking about violence: white violence against Blacks, including efforts by whites to re-enslave Blacks. Southern whites could no longer count on judicial immunity because of the color of their skin. Whiteness as a license for violence was at the core of slavery. Howard, following the lead of Stanton and Dana, meant to put slaveholders in the grasp of war and take that license away.

Richmond, Virginia, fallen capital of the Confederacy, became a symbol of the shift in policy by the U.S. military toward the grasp-of-war approach. Up until late June 1865, the U.S. commanders overseeing civilian affairs in and around the city, Major Generals Henry Halleck and Edward Ord, allowed former masters free rein to hold African Americans in place and to impose on them whatever labor arrangements they wished. Halleck told his superiors in Washington that the elite whites he met with in Richmond accepted slavery's end. They were more loyal to the Union than their counterparts in Baltimore and the nation's capital, the general gushed. Stanton knew better. He had heard about the protests lodged by African Americans against their former masters. The secretary of war reassigned Ord to the Midwest, banished Halleck to California, and brought in Major General Alfred Terry. Stanton instructed Terry to investigate complaints that Black people were being held in bondage. Stanton meant to aim his war power right at the heart of slavery, the cause of the Civil War.

Within weeks of taking command, General Terry, a Yale Law School graduate, established a code of equal rights more progressive than could be found in many northern states. "The people of color will henceforth enjoy the same personal liberty which other citizens and inhabitants enjoy," it declared. They were to receive "the same restraints and same punishments for crime that are imposed on whites, and no others." Freed people could look for work wherever they wanted. They could testify against whites in military courts. Indeed, civilian courts not only in Richmond but throughout Virginia were deemed inoperative until they allowed Blacks the same testimonial rights as whites. This was a stunning legal reversal. Prior to the war, Blacks in the southern states and even some of the northern ones could not testify against whites. This was still the law in Kentucky, which had avoided radical intervention by federal authorities by staying loyal to the Union. The rule against Black testimony still existed even in Indiana, an ostensibly "free" state, and would not be overturned there until 1866.[62] General Howard thought the order that Terry had issued to Virginia should be "universal." He ordered one hundred copies of it printed and distributed to Freedmen's Bureau officers across the South.[63]

It was the ongoing presence of African American troops in southern communities, even more than shifts in the military's administration of law, that signaled to victors and vanquished alike that the United States was still waging a war for emancipation. In Charleston, South Carolina, Black soldiers of the 54th and 55th Massachusetts made the poignant choice of The Citadel as their barracks. The military academy, created in the wake of the 1822 Denmark Vesey conspiracy, had been a training ground for white paramilitary forces. African American troops gladly enforced military curfews that prohibited social and political gatherings of Charleston's white residents. They turned the racial deference of the antebellum era on its head. Black soldiers claimed the sidewalks, forcing white women to tread the muddy streets. A few strode up to men of the former master class, held out cigars, and demanded a light. Local whites were disgusted. Some assumed, wrongly, that the soldiers were all from the North—that their lack of "attachments to masters," as one South Carolina planter suggested, was the reason for such insolence.[64]

In North Carolina, the recent aggressive approach by the U.S. Army against the remnants of slavery troubled former governor David L. Swain. Using language that affirmed the need for a grasp-of-war approach, Swain wrote to a friend: "With reference to Emancipation, we are but at the beginning of the war." The former governor was especially horrified by events at the recent Fourth of July celebration in Raleigh. With many white society ladies in attendance, placid white men at the rally had been overwhelmed by "rowdy" Black men carrying political signs and casting "their white brothers entirely in the shade."[65]

The Fourth of July of 1865—in all communities, not only Raleigh— was a momentous holiday indeed. It was the first Independence Day since the surrender of the Confederate armies. The prospect of national rebirth, or at least national reunion, gave all Americans who had been loyal to the Union reason to regard this July 4 as special.

The holiday was most poignant for African Americans. Although the Declaration of Independence declared all Americans "free people" and all men "created equal," the country that emerged from the American Revolution had been committed to the preservation of slavery. In his 1852 address titled "What to the Slave Is the Fourth of July?," Frederick Douglass had called out the hypocrisy of whites who celebrated freedom while four million Black people were held in bondage and hundreds of thousands of others were technically free but confined to a separate caste from whites. The seismic shifts in freedom and equality that had begun during the war were rumbling as powerfully as ever by July 4, 1865, offering hope to African Americans that their country might soon measure up to the promise of the Declaration. Douglass penned a message from his home in Rochester, New York, endorsing a Fourth of July celebration in Washington, D.C., and expressing his regret that he could not attend in person. Now, it seemed to Douglass, the day *did* have meaning to Black people, some of whom would join with whites on the grounds of the White House to rejoice. But the event's organizers would do well to remember, he wrote, that the "prophecy of 1776" was still unfulfilled. Americans would not "stand equal before the laws" until "the colored people of the whole country" had "immediate, complete, and universal enfranchisement," including the right to vote.[66] Senator Henry Wilson of Massachusetts, one of the speakers at the event, echoed Douglass. The rebel states must put an end to "property in man," he declared, along with discriminatory laws, and they must "give suffrage to the loyal men of the country without distinction of color." Drawing directly from Dana's "Grasp of War" speech, Wilson announced that until these reforms were enacted, "we shall hold your rebellious States with the military power of the nation."[67]

"That's the doctrine!" the audience cheered.[68] The Fourth of July event in the nation's capital was less a celebration of the end of war than of the continuing grasp of war.

As the Fourth of July approached in 1865, Blacks in Kentucky, like those elsewhere, decided to use the occasion to demand an end to racial injustice. At the very least, they felt, the U.S. Army should declare Blacks in the state free. The army had done as much for Blacks in rebel states as far away as Texas. No Juneteenth had come to Kentucky, though. Slavery was still technically legal in the state because it had been exempted from the Emancipation Proclamation. Some whites in Kentucky still treated Blacks traveling through the countryside as if they were enslaved. They snared them and took them to their former masters. Sometimes they tortured them on the spot, usually by cropping their ears. Blacks had little remedy against the violence. There was no Freedmen's Bureau to turn to in the state. Although the bureau officially had authority in Kentucky, it would not begin operations there until June 1866.[69]

Major General John M. Palmer, the commander of U.S. forces in Kentucky, knew that Blacks in the state expected him to issue some kind of emancipation order on the Fourth of July 1865. Because the state was under martial law, Palmer had the authority to do so. Like his predecessors, he had deferred to civilian authorities in the state when it came to emancipation. Yet their inaction increasingly gnawed at him. Every week, he read new reports of whites dragging Black people back to plantations, of beatings and forced labor, of rape and murder. As a Freedmen's Bureau officer across the border in Tennessee put it, Kentucky's "devotees" of slavery were clinging "to its putrid carcass with astonishing tenacity."[70]

Much to the dismay of the "devotees," Palmer started to show signs in the early summer of 1865 that he might be ready to turn firmly against slavery. When asked if he intended to order emancipation, he denied it. But inside, he knew that he was a general, and that this was a war. Because Kentucky had not seceded, it had never been categorized as an enemy state. But tens of thousands of slaveholders lived in Kentucky. Some had supported the Confederacy. All had supported slavery. Palmer could not accept an end of the war that left these people in power. At the very least, he thought, slavery had to be outlawed in Kentucky before the Civil War could be said to be over.

A few weeks before the Fourth of July 1865, Palmer authorized his officers to issue travel passes to "colored persons" seeking employment. Thousands of African Americans used the documents to cross the Ohio River into the free states.[71] Former masters blamed Palmer for the exodus, even though it was African Americans who were carrying themselves to freedom. Whites demanded that President Johnson remove the general. But Johnson was still largely absent from his duties. Secretary of War Stanton along with General in Chief Grant remained in control of the army. Both lent tacit approval to the pass system, left Palmer in command, and kept Kentucky under martial law. Palmer then pushed a little harder against the slave system. In an order of June 18, he deftly authorized wage payments for Black laborers without suggesting that they were free. He claimed that some slaveholders had asked him to declare the workers free so that they could be hired for wages. Slaveholders themselves could not emancipate Black laborers because of the anti-manumission laws still in effect in the state. Palmer's order announced that he could not comply with such requests because he, too, lacked the authority to emancipate anyone. The result was a strange, inherently contradictory declaration: slavery was not abolished in the state, but the army was to promote and uphold wage-based contracts in which "slaves" were treated as "hired servants." He advised but did not compel "colored persons" to enter such agreements with those they regarded as "just and humane masters." Palmer was walking a fine line. He refused to declare African Americans in Kentucky free even as he ordered his soldiers to treat them "as if free"[72]

How could the war be over if Blacks in any state were only "as if" free? Blacks in Kentucky were furious. Like Blacks across the nation, they knew that in Galveston, Texas, the U.S. Army had declared that Blacks had both freedom *and* "absolute equality" with whites. Yet in Kentucky, a state that had stayed loyal and where Blacks had joined the U.S. Army by the thousands, Blacks were supposed to accept continued enslavement? John Mercer Langston, a well-known Black lawyer and abolitionist from nearby Ohio, had had enough. He spurred a movement among Black people in northern Kentucky to use the upcoming Fourth of July holiday to force Palmer to make an unequivocal commitment to Black freedom. Langston and his allies organized a grand emancipation festival to take place near Louisville on the Fourth. Without saying a word to Palmer, they spread the word that the general would appear at the event to issue a freedom decree for Kentucky.

Palmer knew about the plan and was prepared to go along with it. But he feigned surprise when an angry white man showed up at his headquarters on Independence Day to tell him that 20,000 Black people were assembled nearby, awaiting the general's arrival. "What in the h-ll do you mean by telling the negroes . . . you will set them free?" the man thundered. Palmer denied the accusation and repeated the official line that he lacked the authority to emancipate. In fact, the general knew about the event and had arranged to attend. He arrived in a gold-painted chariot. The throng exploded in cheers, anticipating that Palmer had come to play the role of grand liberator. According to many witnesses, the general stepped from the chariot, strode to the center of the stage, and bellowed, "My countrymen, *you are free*, and while I command in this department the military forces of the United States will defend your right to freedom." Palmer later tried to downplay the story to his white critics. He said that he had happened on the chariot by chance— a circus performing in Louisville had offered it to him. Then, when he arrived at the rally, he merely declared that Blacks in the state were "*substantially* free," by which he meant that they were effectively already living as free people, not that he was actually granting them legal freedom.[73]

Whatever Palmer did or said that July 4, he obviously felt caught in a bind. He believed that the grasp of war, at least when it came to emancipation, should reach into all the states, regardless of whether or not they had seceded. But he also knew that the law was on the side of the masters, at least in Kentucky. The once-enslaved were only "substantially" free. "Substantial" freedom fell well short of the "complete and perfect freedom" that Richard Henry Dana had said the United States could require as part of the grasp of war. To Blacks, Palmer had signaled that their freedom was indeed complete, even if perhaps not perfect. To whites, he said that Black freedom was only "substantial." The general had been walking a tightrope, and he fell off it at the July 4 rally.

As a result, Palmer nearly ended up in prison. A month after the rally, an all-white electorate delivered a judgeship to George Johnston, a Confederate sympathizer determined to reverse all of Palmer's actions. Johnston instructed the grand jury that Palmer's orders granting passes to freed people were illegal. In effect, the judge explained, the general had committed the crime of abetting slave escapes. Whites were authorized to reclaim Blacks who had left—even those now residing in free states—and Palmer should go to jail. The grand jury indicted Palmer and ordered the sheriff to arrest him. Palmer told the sheriff not to comply. "I cannot command a department through the grates of a jail," the general declared. If the sheriff locked him up, he warned, his soldiers would seize the prison, release the general, and arrest the sheriff as well as any grand jury members they could find. The threat worked. The sheriff opted not to arrest Palmer or even to make him pay bail. To save face, he announced that Palmer would have to stand trial. A local judge approved the indictment of the general.[74]

Palmer was never convicted, and the African Americans who had crossed the Ohio were never dragged back to Kentucky and forced back into bondage. Yet the whole series of events surrounding the Fourth of July in Kentucky raised questions about the firmness and reach of the U.S. military's grasp of war. Dana's approach called for an end to slavery and its vestiges in the defeated states of the Confederacy. But what about slavery and its vestiges in other areas of the country? Legal enslavement in Kentucky, bans against Black testimony in the Midwest, prohibitions of Black voting in nearly every state in the Union: Why were these breaches of legal equality any less threatening to the security of the nation than similar practices in the states of the crumbling Confederacy? Also, who had the final say as to when the threat of a resurgent Slave Power was gone and the war therefore over? The president? Commanders in the field? Congress? Local civilian authorities? Why not the freed people themselves?

The notion of a "state of war" at the heart of Dana's "grasp of war" theory was a conundrum masked as coherence. A state of war authorized the continued use of force without specifying how the force would be applied and when it would be withdrawn. Contours of the conundrum would become clearer in the months to come, but answers would be elusive—and would remain so long into the future.

10

Armies of Observation

JUST HOW FAR was the reach of the U.S. "grasp of war"? It extended to the states that had rebelled. But did it cover the rest of the continent as well?

In Mexico, Emperor Maximilian remained in power. The United States had opted not to send its armies across the Rio Grande. Some leaders, Ulysses S. Grant in particular, had long harbored hopes for a war with the European invaders of Mexico. Lincoln had been against the idea. So had Secretary of State Seward. They had calculated that the threat from Mexico did not amount to much. But Lincoln was now gone. Grant held more sway than Seward. And the exodus of Confederates to Mexico after surrender changed the calculations. If Confederates could persuade Maximilian to invade the United States, or at least to lend them troops so that they could invade, then Mexico would become as much a threat to the United States as any of the rebel states had been. The United States would have to extend its war grasp beyond its southern border. Plenty of Americans anticipated that result. The Associated Press announced that the thousands of U.S. troops sent to Texas in the summer of 1865 were meant to form an "Army of Observation to Be Established on the Mexican Frontier."[1] The wording purposely evoked events of twenty years before. In the summer of 1845, General Zachary Taylor had taken an army to the Mexican border in anticipation of the likely annexation of the independent republic of Texas by the United States. Once it arrived, Taylor's force became known as the "Army of Observation." Soon afterward, Texas was annexed, war broke out with Mexico, and the army of observation became an army of invasion. The Associated Press obviously expected a repeat of history during the summer of 1865.

In addition to facing a potential war with Mexico, the United States had to fight actual wars already in progress against Native Americans in the West. The surrender of Stand Watie's Cherokee as well as the other tribes of Indian Territory had had no ripple effect. Outside Indian Territory, fighting between U.S. troops and Native warriors continued. The Sioux and their allies on the Great Plains in particular refused to be subdued. From his headquarters in St. Louis, Major General John Pope, who oversaw all operations on the plains, wrote that the continued presence of hostile Natives in the West made it "debatable" whether the region was "in a condition of war" or "a condition of peace."[2] Only force applied by his armies would bring peace and end the debate, Pope believed. Yet if his critics had their way, the troops under his command would be like those at the Mexican border: merely an "Army of Observation." Civilian leaders in Washington, like those in charge of the Interior Department, which controlled the Bureau of Indian Affairs, demanded that the army stand down so that peace treaties could be negotiated. Even Pope's superiors in the War Department had their doubts about the efficacy of further military campaigns. Across the plains and even into the Southwest, the U.S. war against hostile indigenous enemies, which had become entangled in the war against Confederate rebels, seemed to some unwinnable—or at least not worth fighting. But Pope, never a doubter when it came to his own prowess, remained certain that the army must apply the grasp of war to Native Americans in the West.

Like many crucial actors in the months after the major Confederate surrenders in the spring of 1865, John Pope was rewriting the script of the Civil War. He was adding a new act. In its earliest draft, the war was about putting an end to rebellion. The drama ended when the rebels renounced their demand for a separate nation. In that script, Appomattox was the final scene, perhaps with the surrender of Johnston and Kirby Smith as a kind of coda. The persistence of slavery and its vestiges beyond the rebel surrenders made some Americans demand a rewrite of the end. For Blacks in particular, the drama wasn't over until the animating force behind it—slavery—was resolved (which is to say "killed"). This was the script that Richard Henry Dana had in mind when he delivered his "Grasp of War" speech. John Pope's script had yet a different finale: the extension of U.S. sovereignty across the West, bringing an end to *all* warfare in the country. If Grant had been writing the play, he would have tweaked Pope's script so that the end came with Mexico also at peace and under U.S. control.

Which script would the United States follow? When would the country say, decisively and with unity, that the Civil War was over?

In the summer of 1865, most Americans believed that the Civil War already *was* over. Yet members of the armies of observation looked across America—west into the plains and the deserts, south into the Mexican borderlands—and they saw landscapes of war. At any moment, these wars could be their wars. When that happened, what would it matter whether the conflicts were counted as part of the Civil War? What mattered more—to them, at least—was where and when they would have to fight, and whether they would come out of the fight alive.

For U.S. soldiers still in the field in the summer of 1865, the scariest enemies were the Sioux. In the escalation of violence on the plains following the Sand Creek massacre in 1864, the Sioux had bested U.S. troops at nearly every engagement. John Pope was determined to destroy their resolve using any means possible. For the summer of 1865, he planned a military campaign that would target Sioux settlements along the Powder River, which ran between the Black Hills to the east and the Bozeman Trail to the west. He put Brigadier General Patrick Connor in charge of the expedition.

Connor was a career officer with a sordid, murderous history when it came to Native Americans. Born in Ireland, he had emigrated to the United States in his teens and immediately enlisted in the war against the Seminoles in Florida. Early on in the Civil War, he was stationed in Utah, where he oversaw the signing of treaties with tribes in the region while ordering his men to slaughter those Natives who interfered with U.S. mail and telegraph lines. Throughout the war, Connor was frustrated that the high command in Washington refused his many requests to serve in the East against the Confederates. He channeled his fury against indigenous peoples. By mid-1865, there were few Confederates left to fight, and once again his superiors were sending him against Natives, this time along the Powder River. When he arrived in the Dakota Territory, he announced that the enemy "must be hunted like wolves."[3] He ordered one of his colonels to kill all male Natives over the age of twelve.[4]

Connor was accompanied by Major General Grenville Dodge. A railroad engineer who had joined the U.S. Army at the start of the Civil War and risen quickly through the ranks, Dodge was one of General Sherman's star commanders in the campaign to capture Atlanta. His background as a railroad man made him particularly interested in the coming campaign. He ordered his soldiers to scout locations for the transcontinental line as they "whipped out" of the Natives their "false notions" of holding out against the U.S. Army.[5]

Secretary of the Interior John Harlan was disgusted by the army's crass and vicious approach to Native Americans. Too many soldiers, he declared, had abandoned the ideal of "kindness" in favor of the goal of "extermination."[6] He told the commissioner of Indian affairs, William P. Dole, that even President Andrew Johnson favored diplomacy over war as the best way of getting western Natives to abandon "their wild and roving habits" and to adopt "the more peaceful and industrial arts of civilized life."[7] In fact, Johnson never showed any interest in Native American affairs and cared not at all about their fate. His actual message to Harlan, no doubt issued simply to placate the secretary, spoke only of the banal objective "to terminate hostilities, and to secure a more cordial and lasting peace."[8]

While the Interior Department and the U.S. Army squabbled, the U.S. Congress was taking its own course on Native American affairs. In March 1865, Congress had approved the plan of Senator James R. Doolittle of Wisconsin to lead a commission of congressmen to investigate the treatment of Natives across the West. In a stunning move, the commissioners decided to see for themselves what was going on. They boarded trains and by the end of May had arrived in Kansas. There, they broke into teams, each assigned to a different part of the West. Beyond compiling reports of their investigations, the congressmen were supposed to settle treaties with tribes that remained at war against the United States. Doolittle was confident of success. He wrote James Harlan that he expected treaties to be quickly signed by all the "hostile" tribes except for the Cheyenne, who were "still for war to the knife" because of the massacre of their people at Sand Creek the year before. Yet even the Cheyenne could be brought to terms, Doolittle believed, so long as they were offered some type of compensation for the massacre.[9]

Doolittle assigned to himself the task of inspecting Native American affairs in New Mexico. He was fascinated in particular by the project undertaken by Major General James Carleton at the Bosque Redondo.

Carleton had painted an Edenic picture of the Bosque in his letters to Washington, D.C. He described the forced march of the Navajo to the reservation—what history would record as the infamous "Long Walk"—as a peaceful migration. He gushed about how the Navajo and the Mescalero Apache had settled happily into agrarian pursuits. All that was needed, he wrote, was a crew of surveyors to divide the land into neatly defined farms.[10]

In fact, the only satisfied residents at the Bosque were the voracious grasshoppers and corn worms who repeatedly devastated the crops. Carleton's experiment had been a failure, though he refused to admit it. The effects on the Natives had been lethal. Carleton did not have enough rations to make up for the loss of crops. When Natives begged soldiers for food, they were beaten. What little water they could find tasted like chalk because of the high alkali content. Nearly a quarter of the 8,000 Navajo and Apache attempted escape.

This was the situation at the Bosque when Carleton learned that Senator Doolittle intended to visit and see for himself the wonders that the general had orchestrated there.

Carleton moved quickly to hide the truth. Knowing that the Natives who had left the Bosque would seek out livestock for food, he told ranchers in the area to lead their sheep and cattle far away and to use any method they wished to repel Indian raiders. Carleton predicted that "all absent Indians" would return to the Bosque before Doolittle arrived because it was the only place where they had a chance to survive. Meanwhile, to stop further departures, the general had his men inform the Natives who were still at the Bosque that marauders were killing those who had left. The message should be clear, the general ordered: "They will be exterminated unless they come in."[11] The plan worked, though it exacted a lethal toll.

By the time Doolittle arrived at the Bosque, hundreds of Natives had returned. But hundreds of others had been murdered or died of starvation.[12]

Doolittle was easily duped by Carleton. At the Bosque, the senator was convinced that the general was indeed turning the Navajo and Mescalero Apache into productive farmers. This was the only way to save them, Carleton persuaded Doolittle, or at least to stave off for a bit their ultimate fate, determined by the Almighty, to "disappear off the face of the earth." Doolittle would quote the general's words at length, and approvingly, in the opening pages of his final report.[13] But soon the truth came out. When officials in the War Department learned about the crop failures and the continued suffering and resistance of the Natives, they removed Carleton from command.[14]

Elsewhere in the West, Doolittle's fellow commissioners were more clear-eyed than Doolittle when it came to seeing the reality of the poor treatment that Native Americans had received from whites. They collected damning accounts of corrupt Indian agents and brutal army commanders. The picture they painted was so grim that Doolittle ended up sitting on the report for nearly two years out of fear that it would destroy any remaining hope among white and Native leaders that meaningful treaties could be negotiated.[15]

Even without the damning Doolittle report, faith in the treaty-making process was badly shaken over the summer of 1865. No meaningful, lasting treaties were settled in the Far West, either by Doolittle's commissioners or the agents of the Interior Department. The most likely chance of a settled peace—a meeting at Fort Smith, Arkansas, in August 1865 between officials of the Bureau of Indian Affairs on one side and envoys from dozens of tribes on the other—became the most glaring failure.

The gathering at Fort Smith had originally been planned by the Confederacy. It was the follow-up to the meeting on the Washita River back in May, which Confederate General Edmund Kirby Smith had hoped would lead to a pan-Indian alliance with the Confederacy. Kirby Smith's fantasy had long ago evaporated, but the loose alliance among the tribes still held. Dennis Cooley, who had succeeded William P. Dole as the U.S. commissioner of Indian affairs, planned to step into the vacuum left by Kirby Smith, who had fled to Mexico, and secure a settlement between the tribes and the United States. At Cooley's side was Ely S. Parker, the Seneca who had written out the surrender terms at Appomattox.

Just before leaving Washington for Fort Smith, Cooley and Parker received final instructions from Secretary of the Interior Harlan. The treaty they arranged at the fort was to cover all the tribes now living in Indian Territory. The Natives were to renounce their tribal affiliations and promise to become U.S. citizens. Indian Territory was to become an official federal territory and would be represented by a single delegate in the House of Representatives. Slavery would be prohibited there. Then, said Harlan, once the peace at Fort Smith had been settled, Cooley and Parker would travel west to the Great Plains to make agreements with tribes that had not been represented at Fort Smith. When it came to the Plains Indians, Harlan wrote, the improvement of "their moral, intellectual, and physical condition" was the goal. The commission was to establish tribal districts on the plains that would be overseen by the federal government. Each district would have clear and permanent boundaries. All would be set up far from "the great routes of travel" (the existing emigrant trails and the transcontinental railroad to come). If this required forced relocation of some of the tribes, so be it. They would be compensated—not with cash annuities, which they would surely squander, Harlan wrote, but with food, clothing, and the tools and animals they needed to become self-sustaining farmers. In closing, Harlan blessed the mission. Cooley and Parker would be traveling "under the guidance of an overruling providence."[16]

Providence did not show up. The meeting at Fort Smith, which began just before the end of August, was a failure in almost every way. Some tribal delegates came late. Some never came at all. Among the Native peoples who did attend, fierce disputes arose between those who had stayed loyal to the Union and those who had sided with the Confederacy. Cooley showed no favoritism to the loyalists, which only enraged that group further. John Ross of the Cherokee attended the meeting expecting a warm welcome from the U.S. representatives. He had steered his faction back to the Union, after all. But Cooley berated him for his betrayal early in the Civil War, and he refused to acknowledge him as the principal chief of the Cherokee. Cooley also rejected the chiefdom of Stand Watie, who opted to send delegates rather than attend in person. In the view of the U.S. negotiators, the Cherokee and other Natives were beginning at square one, and the first step they had to take was to pledge fealty to the United States. The Natives were dismayed. They had expected to receive an offer similar to what Kirby Smith had promised: recognition as distinct sovereigns. Instead, they were being told that they had to dissolve their tribes and become "Americans." The meeting at Fort Smith dissolved in early September in shambles. The promise of a peace settlement was gone. So was the uneasy alliance between the tribes. Each tribe was now on its own to make a treaty with the United States—if any could be made at all.[17]

The United States could not negotiate its way to peace with Native Americans; nor, it turned out, could it subdue Natives with further war. The summer campaign that John Pope had launched against the Sioux along the Powder River was a failure. U.S. forces could not overcome the challenge that they had always faced when campaigning on the plains: Natives were able to move faster than they could. U.S. scouts would report a Sioux encampment on the river, and by the time the army arrived, the enemy, who knew that the army was coming, had moved away. Pope now had to decide whether to plan a new campaign or simply to declare the war at an end.

Pope's soldiers already had made up their minds on that question. Ever since the Powder River campaign began, they had been deserting by the hundreds. The reason? They claimed that *their* war had already ended.

Most of the soldiers on the Powder River Expedition were volunteers who had joined the army in late 1862 or afterward. The terms of their enlistment seemed straightforward when they signed on. They were to serve "during the war" or for three years, whichever period was shorter. The three-year term was not over. But the war was—the war against Confederate rebels, that is. It was this war that soldiers had signed up to fight. Instead of going home, they had been told that they were being sent far away to fight the Sioux. Their frustration was understandable. Like many, they had assumed that the volunteer army was to be disbanded. Wasn't that the message signaled by the Grand Review in Washington at the end of May? But then, a month after the review, Pope announced that his men would not be mustering out. They were off to the West to fight Indians. Techni-cally, Pope was in the right. The enlistment papers signed by his sol-diers did not specify which enemies they were required to fight. Nor did the papers distinguish between one U.S. war and another. From the perspective of Pope and his commanders, the enlistees were still on the hook. They were a "force on hand," Grenville Dodge wrote, "ready to be thrown" against Native Americans. It made no sense, he said, to send them home and miss the chance to win multiple wars for the price of one.[18] For the sake of expedience if nothing else, U.S. commanders were willing to combine all conflicts into one. The approach rightly amounted to deception in the view of many in the army's rank and file. They had been asked to serve their country for one purpose and now they were being ordered to fight and die for another.

Men known for their loyalty now bucked. The 6th Michigan Cavalry had been formed in October 1862 and had been present at the surrender at Appomattox Court House in April 1865. After nearly three years of service—the length of the cavalrymen's term—and the apparent defeat of the rebels, the men expected to muster out. Instead, they were sent to the West. On July 25, the regiment arrived at Fort Laramie on the northern Great Plains. Colonel James Harvey Kidd confided to his diary that he did not "want to see any more of this god forsaken vicinity" and "would be satisfied to see a flood sink the whole concern."[19] When troops at the fort received word that they were to fight the Sioux along the Powder River, Kidd heard grumblings everywhere of mutiny. Kidd's men decided to join the expedition, but only after receiving assurances from General Connor that they would be allowed to go home when their terms were up in October.[20] Other units with longer to serve refused to fight. The men of the 1st Nebraska Cavalry told Connor they were done because "the war is over." Connor ordered one of his commanders to suppress the mutiny with "grape and canister" and then to court-martial the leaders.[21] The men of the 16th Kansas Cavalry deserted on the journey from Fort Leavenworth to Fort Laramie as soon as rumors arrived that they would have to fight the Sioux. An officer tasked with finding the missing regiment wryly remarked that the unit's disappearance was "the most miraculous event of the war."[22]

In mid-August 1865, Pope conceded to his superiors that "nearly all of the volunteer regiments" serving under him believed that there had been a "conclusion of the war." They were "dissatisfied, not to say insubordinate and mutinous, from the fact that they believe their terms of service to have expired." "Whether right or wrong," Pope continued, "they are so possessed with this belief, and their officers so heartily sympathize with them in it, that they are nearly altogether inefficient, and are deserting so rapidly as to threaten disintegration of the organized forces in this department."[23] Pope begged for reinforcements. Stanton and Grant said no.[24] When word came back to Pope that no more troops were coming, he told Connor to abandon the Powder River Expedition. The "pressure from Washington" to end the campaign was too great, Pope explained.[25] But it was really the conviction of his own men that the war was over that was most to blame for the failure.

When Stanton and Grant decided to halt troop movements to the plains, it was not because they, like the common soldiers under Pope, thought that the war was over. They believed that the war continued, but that its most important theater was in the borderlands with Mexico. That was an ulterior motive for sending 50,000 men to south Texas back in May. This "Army of Observation," it turned out, would end up beset by the same trouble that had infected Pope's army: a rampant resistance to service by soldiers who believed that *their* war was over.

At the time that the massive U.S. army under Phil Sheridan had been ordered to Texas, Confederate General Kirby Smith had yet to surrender. Sheridan's stated objective was thus to defeat Kirby Smith's armies west of the Mississippi. But from the start Ulysses Grant had hoped that Sheridan would find some excuse to invade Mexico. Sheridan was keen to oblige. The French troops who were propping up Maximilian and welcoming Confederates into their ranks had to be driven from Mexico, Sheridan insisted. Otherwise, he wrote, "we never can have a fully restored Union, and give a total and final blow to all malcontents."[26]

Of the U.S. officers assigned to Sheridan, his favorite was George A. Custer. The cavalry officer, only twenty-six years old when sent to Texas, had gone out of his way during the war to cement his reputation as a show-off. His long, curly blond hair and red kerchief made him hard to miss. He liked that people spoke of him, no matter what they said. Sheridan had been impressed by Custer's ferocity during their campaign together in 1864 to clear the rebels out of the Shenandoah Valley. At Appomattox Court House on April 9, 1865, while Grant and Lee engaged in their surrender discussion, Custer decided not to wait to learn of the results. Instead, he rode under a flag of truce to see his opposite across the lines, Confederate Lieutenant General James Longstreet, telling him to surrender his force right away or expect more "blood upon the field." Longstreet, nearly twenty years Custer's senior, was unimpressed by the bravado. He shooed the hothead away. They must wait for Grant and Lee to finish their talk, Longstreet told Custer. Though if the circumstances were different, Longstreet jibed, he would gladly have taken up the challenge and trounced the impertinent fellow. Sheridan was so taken by Custer that he presented the young officer's wife, Libbie, with the table on which the Appomattox surrender agreement was signed. It was the least he could do, he told her, to express his appreciation for her "gallant husband."[27]

Libbie accompanied her husband on the Texas campaign. The troops were less than thrilled to have her along. They grumbled that she would slow them down and that she was an attention-seeker like her husband. For her part, Libbie had no trouble keeping up, was much more enthusiastic about the rough, overland ride than the enlisted men were, and did a fantastic service to later historians by chronicling every stage of the journey. The Texans she met she found to be kind and generous. But stories of outlaws met her everywhere. Simmering hostilities in the state both troubled and titillated her. Texas was a "go-as-you-please" state, she wrote.[28]

Sheridan was far less generous in his assessment. If he "owned Texas and hell," he reportedly quipped, "he would rent out Texas and live in the other place." Diehard Confederates shot back that the arrangement would suit them just fine—though "there may be some objections in the other place."[29]

The general actually spent little time in Texas. When he was dispatched to the Southwest by Grant, he decided to set up his headquarters in New Orleans. To get there, Sheridan took the overland route, traveling by way of St. Louis. There, on May 26, he crossed paths with John Pope. The two commanders faced different enemies—Plains Indians in the Dakota Territory for Pope; French imperialists on the Mexican border for Sheridan—but they shared a common view that the fighting that lay ahead was part of the same struggle for the nation's security that had begun four years earlier as a war to suppress the Confederate rebellion.

When Sheridan arrived in New Orleans in early June, he learned about the surrender of Kirby Smith's troops, the force that he ostensibly had been tasked with defeating. The news led to rejoicing among U.S. troops in the Southwest, who assumed that they would now be sent home. They were in for disappointment. Sheridan, whose eye had been on Mexico from the start, had no intention of mustering them out. The news that Kirby Smith along with a number of his officers and a column of Confederate soldiers—Sheridan put their number at 6,000—were heading for Mexico instead of surrendering bolstered Sheridan's case that the threat to the Union was as great as ever. He suspected, rightly, that many of the Confederates would be offering their services to Maximilian in his war against the Juaristas. Once the puppet emperor had defeated the opposition, Sheridan assumed, he would return the favor by sending a combined force of Confederates and French imperials into Texas.

Grant described the same scenario to President Johnson's cabinet on June 16. "The Rebels were crossing the Rio Grande and entering the imperial service," Grant warned, and they meant "to provoke differences, create animosity, and precipitate hostilities." The only way to avert a crisis, Grant advised, was to use the threat of military force to "warn" Maximilian and his French imperial troops out of Mexico.

Secretary of State Seward advised restraint. From the start of France's intervention in Mexico, Seward had been playing a delicate diplomatic game. The United States had refused to accept Maximilian's legitimacy, even when Napoleon III offered to remove his troops from Mexico if the United States would recognize the installed despot. The official position of the Lincoln administration had been that the Benito Juárez regime, which Maximilian had deposed, was the only true government of Mexico. Yet the United States opted not to lend material assistance to the Juaristas. Seward feared that funneling guns across the border would provoke Maximilian and his French backers to ally with the Confederacy. Fending off the overtures of the Juaristas had consumed much of Seward's energy since 1863. Juárez's wife, Margarita Maza de Juárez, had moved to New York City when her husband was deposed (Benito Juárez remained in Mexico to lead the opposition). Mrs. Juárez charmed many influential Americans in New York and Washington; they in turn pressured Seward to give more than vocal support to the Juaristas. Seward was able to hold the line. The Lincoln administration acknowledged Mrs. Juárez as the "First Lady of Mexico," and the president even met with her. But noninterference in Mexico had remained U.S. policy. During the spring of 1865, when Seward had been temporarily put out of commission by a carriage accident, an attempt on his life, and the death of his wife, the lobbyists for Juárez were able to gain more traction in Washington. Having Grant's support helped their case. But now, in late June, Seward was nearly fully recovered, and he again applied a firm, staying hand. When Grant asked the cabinet to prepare for war against Maximilian, Seward countered with a prediction that Maximilian's government would fall in two to six months, but only if the United States stayed out of the conflict. Seward won the day. The cabinet agreed that the U.S. military should not stir up trouble on the border.[30]

The meeting worried Grant. What would his superiors think when they learned that he had dispatched nearly 50,000 men to Texas? Kirby Smith's recent surrender had led to celebrations of the war's end across the Union and proclamations by President Johnson that effectively put the war in the past. Seeing what he was up against, Grant tried to pare down the force assigned to the border. He wrote to Sheridan that when the army landed he should muster out the cavalry units. Sheridan ignored the order. Grant decided not to push the issue further with his lieutenant.

Instead, Grant continued to plead his case to his superiors. To President Johnson in mid-July, he wrote that the interlopers in Mexico were "part and parcel of the late rebellion in the United States, and a necessary part of it to suppress before entire peace can be assured." He advised that a U.S. officer be dispatched to Mexico to monitor the Confederates who were seeking an alliance with Maximilian. He also broached the delicate subject of selling arms to the Juaristas, a move that might provoke the French. The United States sold weapons to other governments, Grant pointed out. So why not sell them to "the only Government we recognize on Mexican soil"?[31] With Seward's assent, Johnson gave way on this point a bit. The United States still would provide no direct military assistance to the Juaristas, but it would lift the embargo on private arms sales.

On July 22, Grant issued his rosy "final" report on the U.S. Army, praising it for restoring "the supremacy of law over every foot of territory belonging to the United States." The statement went well beyond embellishment. There was no civil government in half the states of the former Confederacy, and outside of the South, fighting with Native Americans prevented anything like "the supremacy of law." Grant knew all this, of course. The reason for his statement was not to deceive Americans but to lay the groundwork for an invasion of Mexico. If the army's work on U.S. soil was done, Grant's report implied, it could now move on to Mexican soil. The report spoke of the general's "hope for perpetual peace."[32] Grant had already told President Johnson that peace would remain *only* a hope unless the army subdued the nation's enemies south of the Rio Grande.

By the end of July, word had spread back to Washington from Texas that more than 40,000 U.S. troops were amassing there. Secretary of the Navy Gideon Welles was shocked by the news. "This on the part of the military means war, and we are in no condition for war," he wrote in his diary.[33] For army leaders, especially Grant and Sheridan, the Civil War was not over. It was simply moving to the Mexican borderlands.

The prospect that troubled Grant and Sheridan the most, an alliance between diehard Confederates and Maximilian, was in fact not such a dire threat. Not yet, at least. After reaching the northern bank of the Rio Grande in mid-June, Jo Shelby and his comrades had indeed decided to approach Maximilian. But they faced many obstacles in their plan to revive the Confederacy.

Not least of these was the fact that they could not claim to represent the Confederacy. Jefferson Davis, who might well have supported Shelby's crew if he could have, was in prison at Fort Monroe in Virginia. Alexander Stephens, vice president of the Confederacy, had been arrested and was in prison at Fort Warren in Boston Harbor. Most of the other leaders were trying to get to Europe, and none seemed particularly interested in finding a way to get the Confederacy back on its feet.

Kirby Smith, for example, who was still technically Shelby's superior and had joined the Confederate column bound for Mexico, never put much faith in the diehards' scheme. He eventually left Shelby and headed for Havana. The Cuban city had long been an offshore haven for Confederates. Blockade runners operated from the port. Slaveholders in the interior maintained business relationships that predated the rebellion, including illegal slave-trading, with their counterparts in the American South. At the luxurious Hotel Cubano, Kirby Smith mingled with fellow Confederate elites. Most were trying to get even farther from home. Some were headed to Brazil, which, like Cuba, still permitted slaveholding. Others, like former Confederate secretary of state Judah Benjamin, sought refuge in Europe. Benjamin actually had left Cuba for England just before Kirby Smith arrived on the island. Kirby Smith's hope was to return to the United States, though he would do so only if he knew he could avoid a trial for treason. His wife, Cassie, and their children were making their way to Virginia, where Cassie's family lived. From Havana, Kirby Smith wrote to his old acquaintance Ulysses Grant, not as a Confederate commander but as a civilian, asking whether he would be safe if he returned and took the oath of allegiance. Months passed as he vainly waited for a reply. Grant never wrote back.[34]

When Kirby Smith first arrived in Havana, he spent much time with John Breckinridge. The onetime U.S. vice president was technically still the Confederate secretary of war. Like Kirby Smith, he had given up on the Confederacy. Unlike the general, he entertained little hope that the United States would allow him to return without facing prosecution. During the negotiations with William T. Sherman at the Bennett house back in April, Breckinridge had tried to salvage what he could of the Confederacy, proposing terms that would allow all of his comrades to return home safely and even obtain positions of authority in their states. When the United States disapproved the peace deal, Breckinridge decided he had done all he could. He made his way to Havana. High-society Cubans loved having the dignitary in their company. They even offered him a house where he could stay permanently. But he decided instead to sail for England.

Just before boarding, Breckinridge invited some newspaper correspondents to his side. According to one of them, he relayed a message to "his friends" who still held out hope for Confederate victory that they should "throw themselves on the clemency of the president and ask for pardon."[35] This was as close to an official declaration of capitulation by the Confederacy that would ever take place. Breckinridge was the last high-ranking civilian leader who was not in prison or remote exile (though he had England in his sights). A general can surrender an army; only a civilian official can surrender a nation. Whether Breckinridge intended his message as a national surrender we will never know. He may have hoped simply to buy some goodwill from those back in the United States who meant to hang him. Whatever his purpose, the message, barely noticed, made no difference. If Jo Shelby and his Confederate comrades at the Mexican border had heard about it—and they almost certainly hadn't—they would not have wavered. On July 1, 1865, Shelby's men set out to cross the Rio Grande, many of them determined to persuade Maximilian to help rekindle the Confederate war effort.

They had to cross the river as civilians, however. If they met Maximilian's men as uniformed Confederates, the emperor could be accused by the United States of allying with known rebels in violation of Mexico's official position of neutrality. Clad in civilian garb, Shelby and his men waded into the Rio Grande with the battle flag they had carried for more than two years of fighting for the Confederacy. Stopping in the shallow water, they lay the emblem of the Confederacy in the mud. A few spoke sorrowful words as the flag disappeared beneath layers of silt deposited by the indifferent brown ripples. By sundown they were across the river.

Shelby's men joined other Confederate dreamers who had already made their way to Mexico. Jubal Early, for example, a lieutenant general who had led a near-successful raid on Washington, D.C., in the summer of 1864, had disguised himself as a farmer and snuck across the Mexican border. He had escaped to Mexico to "get out from the rule of the infernal Yankees," he claimed.[36] His motives were actually more complicated. Relieved of command by Robert E.

Lee in late March 1865, he was hoping for redemption in the eyes of his former comrades. Once in Mexico, he sought out Maximilian's subordinates, sounding them out on a plan to create a breakaway army that would invade Texas. Meanwhile, he pretended to Maximilian that his only wish was to join the other Confederate émigrés who sought a permanent settlement in the country. Maximilian welcomed the creation of such colonies. He was especially taken by the one that Confederates had named Carlota, after the emperor's wife. Early, though, never intended to stay long in Mexico. In his mind, at least, he was still on the warpath against the United States.[37]

Early and like-minded Confederates would have to rein in their dreams. Maximilian was never going to lend them any of his troops to fight the United States. To do so was to start a war that his benefactor, Napoleon III, did not support. Maximilian already had trouble enough with the French emperor, who had good reason to doubt his puppet's capacity for putting down the Juárez opposition, much less winning a war against the more powerful neighbor to the north. Yet even as Maximilian rebuffed overtures for an alliance with the Confederacy—or what remained of it—he welcomed former Confederates into his imperial army. Specifically, he approved their enlistment in the French Foreign Legion units serving in Mexico. When Phil Sheridan heard about that, he naturally assumed that the southerners meant to worm their way into command of these units and then lead them across the Rio Grande to rekindle the Confederate war.[38]

Sheridan persuaded Grant and President Johnson that the Confederate presence in Mexico was a powder keg ready to blow. At the very least, Sheridan insisted, the United States had to slow the flow of Confederates across the border. The army should require special passports for those passing from Texas to Mexico, Sheridan suggested. Grant backed the plan, as did President Johnson. Johnson implemented a related measure requiring former Confederates to apply for U.S. passports if they traveled abroad, regardless of their destination. Even if they were granted passports, once they left the country, they had to apply to the president for readmission.[39] The moment was filled with irony, at least from our perspective in the early twenty-first century. Seething American white supremacists, filled with the resentment of defeat and displacement, were *not* obsessed with the prospect of Mexicans streaming into the United States. Rather, they were the ones who wanted to cross the border—*into* Mexico. Standing in their way was a U.S. policy barring emigration from within, not immigration from without.

The border wall was even more illusory in 1865 than it is today. Grateful as he was for President Johnson's passport orders, Sheridan knew that enforcement was impossible. Even if all the 42,000 troops that Grant had promised arrived and stayed, they could not maintain order in the region *and* stop the Confederate exodus. The border was too long and the ferryboats across the Gulf too many, Sheridan conceded. The only way to negate the threat with certainty was to drive Maximilian's armies from Mexico. As he later explained, he had always seen those armies as "part of the rebellion," and he never thought the Civil War would be over "until Maximilian was compelled to leave."[40] Sheridan overestimated the likelihood of a Confederate alliance with the imperial forces in Mexico. But his read of the dark intentions of the diehard Confederates—or of some of them, at least—was on the mark.

The real threat at the border came from the whites who stayed in Texas, not the ones who fled to Mexico. Although his eye was mainly on Mexico, Sheridan had to pay attention to the reports he received regularly from the U.S.-appointed provisional governor of Texas, Andrew Hamilton, who clamored for help suppressing violence from pro-Confederate reactionaries. Without the intervention of the U.S. Army, the governor warned, "freedmen would be killed and Union men driven from the State." Sheridan knew that Hamilton was not exaggerating. "The trial of a white man for the murder of a freedman in Texas would be a farce," the general reported to his superiors.[41] Libbie Custer, still camped with her husband's troops, offered a similar assessment. "The restless throng let loose over the State from the Confederate service," she wrote, made it impossible for U.S. commanders "to act in perfect justice to citizen, soldier and negro."[42]

Keeping white insurgents at bay would be especially challenging for U.S. commanders who faced disgruntlement in their ranks. The thousands of U.S. soldiers who arrived in Texas during the summer were understandably upset about being kept in the army and sent to such a hot, dismal locale. A dynamic played out at the Mexican border similar to the one on the Great Plains during the ill-fated Powder River Expedition. Army commanders insisted that there was no distinction between the service now demanded of the troops and their original stated mission: the suppression of the Confederate rebellion. Whether commanders genuinely believed this was an open question. Some surely did. They took the line that Richard Henry Dana had taken in the "Grasp of War" speech, that there was a single ongoing war that would not end until "the conquering party . . . has secured whatever it has a right to secure."[43] Other commanders may have doubted the "one war" line but went along with it for expediency's sake. They wanted to use the troops that they already had on hand. Regardless of any division of opinion among commanders on the question of whether the Civil War was over, they presented a united front to their soldiers: the men remained in service to their country, no matter the talk in the ranks and around the country about the "end" of war. The troops themselves were inclined to see things differently, of course. Some grew increasingly vocal that the war they were in now—or were about to be in—was not the same war that they had signed up for. The rebellion was over, so "I know of no need for us there," one white soldier wrote of his assignment to Texas.[44] "We did not enlist for two wars," griped another.[45]

Many of the U.S. soldiers who ended up in Texas were African Americans. One Black regiment that had been dispatched there, the 109th U.S. Colored Infantry, had been present at Appomattox Court House when Grant accepted Lee's surrender on April 9. Most of the white regiments at the surrender mustered out within a month or so. Not so the 109th, which boarded a vessel for Texas six weeks after Appomattox. Tempers were hot among the Black enlisted men, many of whom assumed that the war was over and they should be going home. The ship was still at sea on June 6 when one of the soldiers got "saucy" with some of the white officers. The officers tied him up and left him on the deck for all to see. His comrades were furious. One reportedly thundered, "These officers think they can do just as they have a mind to with us." "Now the war is over," he continued, "but we will show them." Another soldier went belowdecks and came up with his rifle. The men were going to cut loose their friend, the soldier said, and he would shoot anyone who stopped them. No one got shot that day, but when the ship docked, the soldiers involved were charged with mutiny. Two were acquitted. One did a year of hard labor at Fort Pickens in Pensacola— the first six months with a cannonball chained to his ankle—before he was released when his former master intervened on his behalf. The others ended up serving more than two years at Fort Jefferson. The fort, which one scholar would later call "the Guantanamo of the Nineteenth Century," occupied the main island of the Dry Tortugas, a tiny archipelago in the middle of the Gulf of Mexico. The prison population at Fort Jefferson swelled to nearly 1,000 in the latter months of 1865. Many of the imprisoned were soldiers like those of the 109th, furious at being forced to serve when the war was supposed to be over. Although soldiers of all races were crammed into the fort's casements, a disproportionate number of the inmates were African American.[46]

The growing number of incarcerated Black soldiers who had been stationed on the Gulf Coast was a symptom of a larger, systemic mistreatment of African American troops in Texas. The men were caught in a vise. On one side was a hostile population of white civilians appalled by the presence of armed African Americans. "The idea of a gallant and highminded people being ordered and pushed about by an inferior, ignorant race is shocking to the senses," a local newspaper editorialized.[47] This was a state where mass lynchings of Black civilians were common. They happened "by the half dozens of the time, for the crime of leaving their former masters," the state's provisional governor reported in July 1865.[48] Black soldiers in the state always faced a greater risk of assassination than their white comrades. They met the peril with courage. When a soldier of the all-Black 25th Corps first saw some of "the Texan desperadoes of whom we have heard," he predicted with confidence: "I do not think we will have any trouble in teaching them their true level."[49] But if Black soldiers acted out such thoughts against unreconstructed Texans, they felt the other side of the vise: white U.S. officers who insisted on Black docility. Despite more than two years of African Americans proving themselves as disciplined, effective, and brave soldiers, a number of white officers still believed that Black soldiers, especially those who had recently been enslaved, needed to be policed with extra severity. African American soldiers who spoke sharply or raised a hand to insolent white civilians might find themselves bucked and gagged or thrown into a "sweat box" by their superiors. Sometimes the punishment was for show. Commanders of U.S. occupying forces needed white civilians to believe that the armed Black men were under control. Whatever the reason behind the brutal, unequal treatment, the effect was to make Black soldiers question how free they really were.

African Americans on occupation duty grew even more frustrated as the summer wore on. All the soldiers in Texas, regardless of race, faced nasty physical conditions ranging from venomous snakes and insects to outbreaks of scurvy. Water shortages were common. A soldier reported being charged a dollar for every mouthful.[50] Another soldier got all the water he needed but found that it tasted foul and was filled with stuff that looked like silt but turned out to be a sludge of living organisms.[51]

African American soldiers might have been willing to suffer in silence if they had seen white soldiers suffering alongside them. But from the moment that the occupation of Texas began, the army began mustering out white units while dodging questions from Black units about when their turn would come. General in Chief Ulysses Grant was behind the policy. His stated rationale was simple: the white units had served longer and therefore should get to go home sooner. But other, race-based considerations seem to have come into play. Some white officers thought that because the recently enslaved might not have a home to go to, Black men were better off serving in the army. Often entangled in such professed benevolence was a darker motive. Whites assumed that freed people might get violent. What better method to impose discipline than to keep them under the watch of white officers? When the army did start mustering out the Black units from Texas, it kept in the ranks the recently emancipated from the South and sent home Black soldiers from the North.[52]

As the end of 1865 approached, U.S. Army leaders like Grant still viewed the situation at the Texas-Mexico border as potentially explosive, but not for the same reasons that they had seen it that way back in the summer. An alliance between diehard Confederates and Maximilian's army was no longer a threat. The Mexican emperor was now in trouble. Seward's diplomatic maneuverings finally had borne fruit: Napoleon III had agreed to remove his troops from Mexico. Declawed and humiliated by his patron, Maximilian spent most of 1866 evading capture by the Juaristas. In early 1867, his luck ran out: he was arrested and then executed by a firing squad. Although Maximilian's fortunes had begun to fall in late 1865, the U.S. Army still needed troops in Texas to police white insurgency. In part because of the deliberate mustering-out decisions made by Grant and other top commanders, nearly 80 percent of the 25,000 U.S. troops left in Texas by the end of 1865 were African Americans, and almost all of those men had been enslaved at the start of the war.[53] Rumors began to circulate among whites in Texas that freed people in the state were planning an armed attack against them. The fact that there already had been violence across the South involving Black troops lent credence to white fears. In Jacksonville, Florida, in October 1865, a protest by Black soldiers turned bloody. The white officer in charge had five of the men executed immediately.[54] When Grant heard about white southerners in Texas who thought they were about to be massacred by Black troops, he feared that violence might indeed explode in the area. The biggest threat in Texas, he believed, was now a race war, not a French-backed Confederate invasion.

With Grant's blessing, white commanders in the area moved to thwart an imagined Black uprising. A white regiment stationed in Alabama was dispatched to south Texas.[55] Meanwhile, military units across the state and elsewhere in the South instituted a change in policy regarding African Americans carrying weapons. Typically when U.S. soldiers were mustered out, they were allowed to buy their government-issued rifles. Beginning in the fall of 1865, the option was denied to African American soldiers in a number of occupied areas, including all of Texas. Phil Sheridan explained that "the purchase will create some uneasiness in this section of the country."[56] African Americans receiving discharge orders learned that their loyal service was being rewarded with confiscation of their guns.

There was no massive Black insurrection in the works in Texas or anywhere else in the South, for that matter. Fears of such revolts—shared among white southern civilians and white U.S. authorities alike—revealed how incomplete the war and emancipation still were by the end of 1865. Rumors of planned Black rebellions gained traction amid the precarity. They were inflamed by stories of actual race warfare coming from Jamaica. There, beginning in October 1865 in Morant Bay, armed Black protesters stood up to British officials and militias. The rebels killed or wounded more than fifty people and burned down five buildings and a number of nearby plantations. News of the violence ripped into the headlines of U.S. newspapers. A Virginia editor wrote of "terrible massacres of the whites" and blamed events on the same abolitionists who were, in his view, responsible for the Civil War. These men now meant to "transfer the scenes of Jamaica and San Domingo to the Southern States of this Union."[57] The editor had nothing disapproving to say about the reprisals by British authorities, which included the hanging of more than 350 Black Jamaicans.

The racial anxieties of white Americans were unfounded: African American soldiers for the most part remained loyal and deferential. But by the end of 1865, they had grown weary and understandably confused about their status. Members of the 1st U.S. Colored Cavalry, most of them from Virginia, sent a pleading message to the War Department in December from Brazos Santiago, a desolate outpost at the mouth of the Rio Grande. They had been in Texas since June, when General Granger had issued his now-famous order declaring all Blacks in the state free. But now they were being told that they could not go home, not even on temporary furlough. They were desperate to see their families and make sure that they were safe. "Wee have come in as U.S. Soldiers and are treated as Slaves," they wrote. "Never was wee any more treated Like slaves then wee are now in our Lives." If the army was "good hearted" it would "turn us out of servis to the pertecttion of our be loved wifes."[58] No response came. The regiment would languish at the border for another two months before being discharged. This was not the war for freedom that they had signed up for, and that supposedly had already ended.

11

Demons Incarnate

A FRICAN AMERICANS STATIONED in the South contended that it was time for them to go home because the war was over. Their superiors disagreed. So did plenty of southern whites—about the war not being over, at least. As for African American troops staying in the South, the white southerners under occupation would have welcomed their departure. For Rodney Dorman, a relentlessly bitter Confederate from Jacksonville, every day that dawned with Black occupiers in his city was another day of war. A slaveholder at the start of the war whose enslaved workers had escaped early on in the conflict, Dorman was enraged at being bossed around by armed Black men in Yankee blue. "War, with all its horrors, is preferable" to this so-called peace, he ranted to his diary. He stood ready for a white uprising against the Black troops. The rest of the nation might "pretend" that the war was over, he sneered, but in fact "the war has just commenced."[1] Dark dreams of endless war were some of the last possessions of the diehards.

John R. Kelso, a pro-Union guerrilla leader from Missouri, warned of the doom that would follow if those with devilish designs of rekindling the secessionist spirit were not hanged, or at least stripped of their property and thrown into prison. They were "like Milton's Satan," Kelso thundered in a speech in western Missouri. "Cast down from the high positions they once occupied, maddened by disappointment, and burning with revenge, they are now endeavoring to accomplish by *guile* those dark designs which they long attempted to accomplish by *force*."[2] He quoted from Patrick

Henry's famous "Liberty or Death" speech: "*Let us not deceive our-selves! Gentlemen may cry peace! peace! but there is no peace.*" There could be no "permanent peace in this nation," Kelso continued, until slavery was truly destroyed (it was "dead in name" but still existed "in reality") and the secessionists "rendered totally powerless." The rebels were like "the serpent of old in Paradise," biding their time, the former minister warned. The rage of Unionists, which had led President Johnson to demand that "traitors" be hanged and treason "made odious," was fading. Even the president had been becalmed by their professions of "frankness and honor." Seduced by the ser-pent's charm, Unionists would soon feel its strike.[3]

Yet even the vengeful and hypervigilant Kelso saw the war no longer as a military but rather a "political contest." War continued, but armies no longer "hurled" themselves at one another and "the thunders of battle" no longer sounded.[4]

For others, though, the war remained a military struggle. Espe-cially in regions where the Federals' "grasp of war" was weak—from the hard-to-reach backcountry, where rebel guerrillas still lurked, to the vast Pacific, where a Confederate cruiser mercilessly targeted U.S. ships—the killing and depredation continued.

Much of the inspiration for the insurgents came from Jefferson Davis, who remained unrepentant. Humiliated in capture and an obvious failure as president, Davis was having a second life as a model diehard Confederate. He refused to ask for a pardon, pre-ferring instead to stay imprisoned in Fort Monroe. He never con-ceded that the Confederacy had given up. He said nothing about the surrender statement that his secretary of war, John Breckinridge, had issued from Cuba. Most likely he had not heard about it. If he had, he would not have agreed with it. Though he might have liked Breckinridge's suggestion to use whatever was left of the Confeder-ate "treasury" to pay for Davis's defense. He was going to need some good lawyers.

Davis welcomed a trial. It would give him the public venue he wanted to proclaim yet again that secession was legitimate and legal. He might even boast, as he had done even after Richmond fell, that the Confederacy—and the war—were not yet finished. His fellow diehards would be thrilled.

Plenty of northerners wanted a trial, too, but merely as a formality that would precede Davis's inevitable execution. "Let him be hung!" cried thirty Massachusetts women in a petition to President Andrew Johnson.[5] Johnson, they assumed, would comply. Charles A. Dana, assistant secretary of war, wrote privately that he had "no doubt that some men will be hanged under him, who would have escaped the halter under Mr. Lincoln."[6] Northerners had not forgotten Johnson's cry that "traitors must be punished."

Inside the Johnson administration, though, opinion was far from united on how—or even if—Davis could be hanged. The issue dominated the cabinet meeting on July 18. Secretary of the Navy Gideon Welles argued that Davis should be tried for treason as soon as possible. Even if he were acquitted, Welles reasoned, the trial would do the important work of persuading the public that the rule of law reigned again—the disruption of war was over. Seward urged postponing a trial until evidence of treason was irrefutable. Stanton agreed—because he expected such evidence would soon arrive. The secretary of war had endorsed the move by his ally Joseph Holt, the army's judge advocate general, deputizing Francis Lieber to scour what remained of the records of the rebel government for documents proving that Davis's true motive—beyond secession—was the destruction of the United States.[7]

Lieber was the right man for the job. As author in 1863 of the new U.S. code of war, he was widely known and respected for his legal expertise. Even before he set out to do the bidding of Stanton and Holt in 1865, he had already decided on his own that rebel leaders like Davis were the worst sort of criminals. They were guilty of both "treason" and "high crimes," he had concluded in a pamphlet that he drafted in 1864.

The pamphlet had begun as an endeavor by Lieber to propose amendments to the U.S. Constitution that would help bring the present Civil War to a close and prevent the eruption of a new one. Lieber wanted the revised Constitution to state explicitly that slaveholding and secessionism, the sources of the current conflict in his view, were "treason" and "high crimes." These terms, "treason" and "high crimes," appeared in the current Constitution but with no definition—much to Lieber's frustration. (He was equally flummoxed by "citizenship," another word used but left ambiguous in the Constitution.) The pamphlet that Lieber penned offered seven amendments to the Constitution. Three of them defined "treason" and "high crimes" in such a way that snared Davis along with other rebel leaders and most of the Confederate rank and file. In early 1865, the pamphlet was published. The amendments, though, never gained traction, leaving Americans still wondering, even today, what constitutes "treason" and how "high crimes" differ from other types of crimes.

Yet, in mid-1865, Lieber had every reason to hope that his measures would be adopted. (Indeed, versions of his other amendments, the ones outlawing slavery and defining citizenship to include African Americans, *did* become part of the Constitution—as the 13th and 14th Amendments.) While waiting for the Constitution to be changed, Lieber was happy to help find some other way of sending Davis to the gallows. Thus he welcomed the opportunity provided to him by Holt and Stanton to search the Confederate archives for evidence that would doom the Confederate president.[8]

Because the meanings of "treason" and "high crimes" were nebulous, a better-defined capital offense was needed to nail Davis: murder, perhaps, or maybe one of the more vile transgressions in Lieber's code of war, such as mistreatment and killing of prisoners of war. Following this logic, Stanton and Holt would eventually seek to pin on Davis the deaths of U.S. soldiers that took place at Andersonville and other Confederate POW camps.

The surest and swiftest way to hang Davis and other rebel leaders, though, was to implicate them in the Lincoln assassination. Fury about the assassination still ran red-hot through the North, and many southerners as well thought that those involved in the plot should suffer severely. Trying rebel leaders for murder rather than treason had another advantage. It made it easier for U.S. authorities to extradite former Confederates who had fled the country. Former U.S. attorney general Edward Bates noted this point in his diary— that treaties typically allowed extradition for murder but not necessarily for treason or other "political offences." Yet Bates did not speculate on whether the current administration was thinking along these lines. Would the United States, for example, demand that the British government turn over Judah Benjamin, the former Confederate secretary of state who was making his way across the Atlantic with a plan to settle in England?[9]

Stanton and Holt had yet to confront the extradition question, if only because they were singularly focused on enemies still in the country, beginning with the Lincoln assassins. From the start of the manhunt, Stanton and Holt had assumed that Jefferson Davis and other Confederate leaders were complicit in the assassination. On May 9, 1865, when the trial of the assassins began, Davis was listed as a co-conspirator, though he was not yet in U.S. custody (he was captured the next day). Stanton and Holt expected Lieber to find evidence of Davis's involvement in the plot, or at least his knowledge of it, in the Confederate records. Even the flimsiest hint of complicity would do.

John A. Campbell got a taste of what Stanton and Holt had in mind for Davis. The former U.S. Supreme Court justice, who had left the Court to become an assistant secretary of war in the Confederacy, was at home with his wife, Anne, in Richmond on May 22 when U.S. soldiers barged in, put his arms and legs in irons, and hauled him away. No one told him why he had been arrested. It turned out that Lieber's researchers had uncovered a letter from 1864 in which a state representative from Alabama offered to assassinate Lincoln. Although the letter was addressed to Jefferson Davis, there was no sign that the Confederate president had seen it. Nor was there any connection between the Alabama man and the Booth team. But Campbell's signature was on the document—simply as an official sign of receipt. Campbell had forwarded the letter to the office of the Confederate adjutant, and there the document had sat until Lieber uncovered it. Campbell had no memory of the letter. Crackpot schemes and unsolicited military advice had come across his desk all the time. The idea that he had wanted Lincoln killed was outlandish. He had been part of the delegation that met with Lincoln in February at Hampton Roads to talk peace, and he had worked with the president in the days after Appomattox on a failed scheme to bring Virginia out of the Confederacy. Yet his signature was on an assassination scheme, and that was enough to hold him on board a U.S. naval vessel for eight days, after which he was sent to Fort Pulaski off the coast of Savannah, Georgia. No one told him why he was there. His wife pleaded for his release and finally got a meeting with Stanton in Washington. The secretary of war sent her away. Her husband sat in prison for more than four months.[10]

Meanwhile, the trial of the actual assassins of Abraham Lincoln continued in Washington. The proceedings were held at the Old Arsenal, an army base and penitentiary at the southern tip of the District of Columbia. John Wilkes Booth was not present, as he had been killed during the manhunt. But his shadow hung over the trial. As for his body, or what remained of it, that lay buried in the Arsenal's courtyard. Stanton had quietly arranged for the interment. He planned to see Booth's accomplices hanged in the same spot and then buried next to their ringleader.[11] When that day came, Stanton hoped, Jefferson Davis would be standing on the scaffold as well. It was in large part because of Stanton's urging that Judge Advocate Joseph Holt, who was in charge of the trial of the assassins, named Davis as a co-conspirator.

Determined to make the charge against Davis stick, Holt allowed a dubious witness to testify because the man claimed that Davis had been in on the plot. The witness called himself Sanford Conover. Had Holt vetted him, he would have learned that Conover was not his real name. Soon the press was onto the fact that "Conover" was a freelance journalist and publicity-seeker who used many aliases and lied frequently and poorly. Holt was embarrassed, and the case against Davis as an assassin fell apart.

There was still plenty of legitimate evidence to convict the rest of the accused, though. Four of the conspirators were sentenced to hang. Another four were sentenced to life in prison. One other, John Surratt, had evaded capture and fled to Quebec. There he had found sanctuary in a Catholic church outside of Montreal. Eventually he fled to England. His mother, Mary Surratt, had not been so fortunate. She had been arrested and was now one of the four eventually sentenced to hang. Her lawyers had argued that she had only run the boardinghouse where the assassins had their meetings and had no inkling of the plots hatched beneath her roof. Her twenty-two-year-old daughter Anna came before the commission to plead her mother's innocence and beg against the noose. But Holt stood firm. On July 7, 1865, Mary Surratt became the first woman to be executed by the federal government. She was hanged along with George

Atzerodt, David Herold, and Lewis Powell. The *Nation* declared that "the bloody deed of the 14th of April has been expiated."[12]

Not all those who mourned Lincoln supported the hangings. Horace Greeley, the editor of the *New York Tribune,* published a column criticizing the way that the War Department had skirted procedural norms in its trial of the conspirators. Like many in the North, Greeley found particularly distasteful the hanging of Mary Surratt, a middle-aged mother of three. Stanton was furious with Greeley. He saw any challenge to his efforts at retribution as tantamount to collusion with the enemy. The war secretary hired a lawyer to assemble a case against Greeley, who Stanton believed meant "to incite assassins to finish their work by murdering me."[13] Stanton genuinely believed that assassins were still at large who meant to kill the new president, Andrew Johnson, as well as the cabinet. Stanton now traveled everywhere with a menacing bodyguard and told the other cabinet members to do the same. None took his advice.[14]

One of Greeley's complaints about the trial of the assassins was that it had taken place in a military rather than a civilian court. If none of the assassins were on active duty in the Confederate military service, asked Greeley, and no one in the Confederate high command had ordered the killing, why were the accused denied a civilian trial? A number of civilian courts were operational in the District of Columbia and northern Virginia. Yet, instead of being judged by a jury of their peers, the accused had faced a commission of U.S. officers. Every part of the proceedings, from trial to executions, took place at a military facility. The convicted men who were spared the noose were sent to a military prison—the U.S. fort in the Dry Tortugas, Florida—rather than to a civilian jail. Former attorney general Edward Bates was likewise appalled by the use of a military system to try civilians. The current attorney general, James Speed, also had doubts—at first, anyway. Then he had been browbeaten by Stanton and Holt, who bullied him into issuing an opinion that justified the use of military instead of civilian law. Speed grudgingly wrote that Booth had been an agent of the Confederacy. He had "acted as a public foe" and "not an assassin from private malice."[15] The only evidence that Speed offered for the claim was the unsubstantiated story that Booth, just before dying, uttered, "Say to my mother that I died for my country." Serving the Confederacy,

Speed reasoned, must therefore have been the aim of Booth and his accomplices.[16] Bates recognized Stanton's handiwork behind the attorney general's opinion. The war secretary believed only in "mere force," Bates wrote in his diary.[17]

Mary Surratt's lawyer had also objected to the use of the military system. His argument was that military courts should be used only during wartime, and the war was over. In his final, futile plea to President Johnson, he argued that Surratt had been a civilian living in the postwar, peacetime city of Washington when she had been arrested. Why, then, had she been tried as if the country were still at war? Attorney General Speed offered the answer: "This country is now in the midst of a great war." The statement came on July 7, nearly three months after the capital city had celebrated U.S. victory in the wake of Appomattox. Few at the time noted the conundrum raised by Speed's claim. Mary Surratt barely had time to consider it. Fifteen minutes after Speed issued the statement, she was led to the scaffold.[18]

Was the country still "in the midst of a great war," as the U.S. attorney general had declared? By early July 1865, when Speed had made the statement, organized armies engaged in full-on combat had disappeared from the landscape. Yet, at the same time, the prevailing opinion among U.S. military leaders was the same as that of Richard Henry Dana: the United States held the former Confederacy in a "grasp of war," and the "war" in question was the same one that the nation had been fighting for four years.

Maybe what these people meant was that the country was in a *state* of war only, and that the existential war—uniformed soldiers on opposite sides trying to kill one another—was over. Today in the United States it has become commonplace to think in such terms: a state of war can exist even when an actual war does not. A vocabulary has even emerged to describe armed conflicts that don't quite count as full-blown wars. We hear of "police actions," "peacekeeping missions," and "small wars." But in mid-1865, such categorial thinking was embryonic at best. There was simply "the war." It might be over, it might be ongoing. Or it could be both things at once. Cognitive dissonance about war was the norm, not the exception.

The dissonance was embodied in—or, rather, woven into—a

woolen suit: the Confederate army uniform. In the days following the surrender at Appomattox, many of Lee's men continued to
wear their uniforms. Maybe they believed that the war was over
and simply had nothing else to wear. Maybe they wore it because,
though they had officially surrendered, in their hearts they refused
to relinquish the cause. Or maybe they wavered between accepting and rejecting that the war was over. U.S. policy allowed little
room for ambivalence. On April 22, 1865, Attorney General James
Speed issued an opinion declaring that those who had surrendered
must cease wearing the "traitor's garb." Refusal to do so, he said, was
"an act of hostility against the Government."[19] U.S. officers did not
apply the policy rigidly, at least at first. By midsummer, though, the
grace period was over. The order in late July issued by a U.S. lieutenant colonel stationed in northern Mississippi was typical. It threatened arrest of those who wore "military buttons, insignia of rank,
and distinctive badges of the late Confederate Army."[20]

Was everyone in Confederate uniform necessarily an enemy of
the United States? Certainly some seemed like they were, like the
"Gray Ghost," John Mosby. In an infamous episode on April 9,
1866, the one-year anniversary of Lee's surrender to Grant, the
fabled "raider" commander appeared in Leesburg, Virginia, sporting two pistols and wearing full Confederate regalia. A federal officer ordered him to remove his uniform or at least the distinctive
regimental buttons. Mosby refused, taunting that "there were not
enough damn Yankees in Leesburg" to strip him. Shooting ensued,
though no one knows for sure who started it. Mosby fled the town
unharmed.[21] Was Mosby still at war with the United States? Perhaps. Just as likely, he staged the episode to counter rumors among
his former comrades that he had been sidling up to federal officers,
including Ulysses Grant himself. (The rumors, it turned out, were
true: by 1868, Mosby was full-throated in his support of the Republican Party.)

Wearing a Confederate uniform was as likely a sign of pov-
erty as hostility. When Confederate veterans returned home, they
often found that they had no proper civilian garb. Some had had
their wardrobes ransacked by U.S. and Confederate armies that
had marched through their neighborhoods. Most had little money
to buy new clothes. Their army uniforms were the only suits they

owned. A visitor to a church service in Fredericksburg, Virginia, in October 1865 was initially shocked to see the male congregants all in Confederate uniform. Then he learned that the men simply had no other respectable church wear.[22]

Southern whites who wanted to wear their old uniforms, or who had no choice but to do so, came up with clever solutions. Some replaced their old buttons with plain ones. But that took work, along with the money to buy new buttons. It also suggested a renunciation of the Confederacy, which could offend old comrades. A preferred solution was button covers. Using small bits of cloth that could easily be removed, southern whites covered up their Confederate buttons when U.S. troops were nearby. Old comrades would understand that their renunciation of the Confederacy was merely expedient and temporary. As soon as the Yankees left, the covers could come off.[23]

Button covers seemed such light and trivial things, but they were weighty in their meanings. For the men who wore them, they signaled ambivalence toward the idea of a Confederate cause that was truly lost, as opposed to merely dormant. For the occupying U.S. soldiers, they epitomized the sometimes impossible challenge of weeding poisonous diehards from upright ex-Confederates in a field where the stalks all looked the same.[24]

Of course, U.S. occupiers had no trouble identifying diehards when they took the form of enemy guerrillas. The Confederate surrenders that began at Appomattox had curbed but hardly ended guerrilla activity. Pro-Confederate guerrillas continued to strike at U.S. troops and Unionist civilians from the backcountry of Virginia and the Carolinas to the swamps of southern Louisiana. The worst of the guerrilla violence remained where it always had been: in the rough borderlands of Arkansas, Missouri, and Kansas. Pro-Union guerrillas were as lethal as those still loyal to the Confederacy, and with the dispersal of Confederate regulars, they now had the upper hand. Yet plenty of pro-Confederate guerrillas still believed that the tide would turn their way. A band of Missourians who heard the rumors that Jo Shelby was making an alliance with the Mexican emperor started calling themselves "Maximilian bushwhackers."[25] The daily murderous skirmishing in one Arkansas community led a resident there to declare, "We are now experiencing a state of perfect anarchy."[26]

However, by late summer, guerrilla activity had dropped off significantly. The most notorious of the Confederate guerrillas, William Quantrill, was gone. A onetime drifter unable to figure out whether he wanted to be a schoolteacher or a professional gambler, Quantrill had found his identity as a leader of "bushwhackers" during the Kansas wars of the 1850s. Then he fought for the Confederacy, becoming lionized by southern whites for his military exploits, real or exaggerated. Along with his lieutenant "Bloody Bill" Anderson, Quantrill led raids across Kansas, Missouri, and Kentucky, killing hundreds without worrying whether the dead were legitimate enemies of the Confederacy or not. Anderson was killed by U.S. troops in Missouri in October 1864. Quantrill lived beyond Lee's surrender at Appomattox. After a sojourn in Texas and his home state of Missouri, Quantrill was caught in an ambush by U.S. troops in western Kentucky in May 1865. He was shot in the back and lingered a few weeks before dying in a prison hospital in Louisville.

Helping to staunch the bloodletting of guerrilla warfare was an olive branch offered by General in Chief Ulysses Grant in mid-May. The general's "guerrilla order" declared that armed Confederate sympathizers east of the Mississippi River who turned themselves in before June 1 would be treated as ordinary soldiers. In other words, surrendering guerrillas would receive paroles. Then, most likely, they would receive amnesty or have the opportunity to apply for a pardon. Either way, their lives would be spared. Those who came in after June 1 might not be so lucky. They would be treated as operating outside of official Confederate authority, which meant they had no protection under the laws of war and could be executed. The order applied only to the East because it was issued at a time when major Confederate armies still operated in the West. Implicitly, when the western armies surrendered, guerrillas there, too, would be denied official enemy status and be subject to hanging. The announcement that U.S. protections offered to enemies during wartime would soon not apply to guerrillas sent a chilling message. It also signaled— yet again—that, in some respects at least, U.S. authorities regarded "wartime" as over.

Grant soon received reports that the order was proving effective.

Guerrillas were surrendering in greater numbers than before, though not without some bristling. A U.S. commander in Missouri received a letter in late May from a Confederate guerrilla leader who agreed to surrender only if his men were allowed to keep their guns. *Their* guns, the U.S. officer scoffed. Those weapons had been stolen from Union sympathizers. They would have to be relinquished before any surrender could be discussed. The guerrilla captain grumbled but eventually gave in.[27]

The leniency offered by Grant's guerrilla order did not sit well with some U.S. commanders. One in central Tennessee asked Grant whether he was really supposed to extend a warm hand to the brutal diehards. Some of these "demons incarnate," the officer wrote Grant, had just murdered his scouts and shot some local men. They also had raped a pro-Union woman and tried to rape a sixteen-year-old orphan huddled near the corpse of her murdered cousin. Grant agreed that the offenders deserved severe punishment. Yet he did not insist that they be executed.[28]

Guerrillas who were caught after Grant's June 1 deadline faced an uncertain future. Joseph Holt, the U.S. judge advocate general, wanted those who had committed the most severe crimes to be hanged—regardless of when they were apprehended. No surprise there. A gallows man all around, Holt was the loudest voice calling for the execution of Jefferson Davis and other high-ranking Confederate officials. Grant's more moderate approach reflected his concern that hanging guerrillas, even those who deserved it most, would antagonize local populations. Holt agreed with Grant only when it came to the youngest offenders, teenagers whose crimes could be written off as youthful indiscretion—and whose execution might trigger local riots.[29] President Johnson, as Holt would learn, was fine applying the softer touch even to older guerrillas. In the months following the June 1 deadline of Grant's guerrilla order, Johnson commuted the sentences of at least half a dozen guerrillas who had been sentenced to death by military commissions. Holt was furious. Some of the men had committed rape and murder. One had killed a U.S. lieutenant. Another had tried to assassinate U.S. Major General Edward Canby, the officer who had overseen the surrender of Kirby Smith's forces. Holt suspected, rightly, that the ferocity that Johnson had shown toward Lincoln's assassins was tempering.[30]

Yet even Johnson would not stand in the way of the execution of the most notorious of the Confederate outlaws. Two were executed on the same day—October 20, 1865—though in different cities. Louisville hosted the hanging of Henry Magruder. The Kentuckian had served in a few regular Confederate units before joining up with a band of guerrillas who committed various atrocities against Unionists living near Louisville. These included burning an African American alive and raping a group of students at a local girls' school. He and some of his accomplices were captured and convicted in early 1865. Magruder was shot multiple times and nearly died. While he was recovering, one of his comrades, Marcellus Jerome Clarke, was tried and sentenced to hang. At the trial, some claimed that Clarke had dressed as a woman during a number of his crimes. That spawned rumors that Clarke was in fact Sue Mundy, a legendary female guerrilla of the region. Legendary indeed. She did not exist but rather was a fictional creation of a pro-Confederate newspaper editor. Locals swarmed to Louisville to see the hanging of a woman—brave, brutal Sue Mundy. What they got instead was a callow, long-haired figure, clearly male, who pleaded for his life, denying he had ever been a guerrilla. When Magruder's turn on the gallows came in October (authorities had decided to wait for his injuries to heal before killing him), *he* claimed to be the true Sue Mundy. Always something of a showman, Magruder had decided to add some sensation to the event.[31]

Yet most of the attention of the press that day was on the hanging in Nashville, 170 miles to the south. There, crowds turned out to see the last of Champ Ferguson, the most notorious guerrilla next to William Quantrill.

Born in Kentucky, Ferguson had settled in the Cumberland Plateau, a rugged mountainous region north of Chattanooga. The area was the scene of fierce local feuding before and during the war, with Ferguson a leader among those partial to the Confederates, and David "Tinker Dave" Beaty his lethal Unionist counterpart. Ferguson raised a company of guerrillas that partnered with regular Confederate armies in operations across the South. He was responsible for the murder of well over fifty civilians, though his most reprehensible act was a mass killing of defenseless U.S. soldiers hospitalized in Saltville, Virginia, in October 1864. Historians dispute how many were killed by Ferguson's band at the Saltville Massacre—estimates range between twenty and fifty—but they agree that most of the victims were African Americans from the 5th and 6th U.S. Colored Cavalry.

In May 1865, Ferguson and his men surrendered near Nashville. U.S. army officials paroled most of Ferguson's band but decided to make an example of some of the leaders. Ferguson's lawyer argued that his client was a lawful guerrilla and therefore deserved the same lenient treatment that the army had afforded other Confederate combatants. It was a reasonable argument, especially in light of the fact that plenty of guerrillas who surrendered *after* Ferguson had been treated kindly under Grant's guerrilla order. But Ferguson's crimes were too ghastly, and the man himself was entirely unapologetic. He claimed to be just an ordinary Confederate soldier. Yet even Confederate authorities had jailed him after the Saltville Massacre, though for the murder of a single white U.S. officer, not the killing of dozens of African American enlistees. A crowd of hundreds turned out to see the hanging. U.S. authorities assigned troops to make sure that those sympathetic to Ferguson did not rise up in riot. One of the regiments was the 15th U.S. Colored Infantry. Their faces were among the last that Ferguson saw before the noose pulled taut.[32]

Even before the hangings of Magruder and Ferguson, guerrillas had learned that their lives were at greater risk than ever before, especially after the June 1 deadline of the guerrilla order had passed. The danger for them lay not only in being captured and sentenced to death by U.S. soldiers. They could just as likely be hunted down and hanged by pro-Union civilians, who knew that U.S. officers were unlikely to punish Unionists for reprisals.[33] "In my opinion," a U.S. captain said of guerrillas still at large, "killing them is the best method of procuring their surrender." "This is being quite rapidly done at present."[34]

The officer's words stated something that U.S. authorities knew but were understandably reluctant to report: U.S. soldiers were taking justice into their own hands. They were murdering guerrillas without allowing them to surrender or summarily executing those who had surrendered. Before the major Confederate armies had begun to disperse, guerrillas were a secondary concern for U.S.

troops. Now, though, guerrillas were the sole enemy. Upon them the Federals could unleash all of their pent-up fury. It was a scenario that had worried General William Sherman back in 1862. He had told a Confederate officer that a time would come when U.S. armies could devote all their energy against Confederate irregulars. At that point, Sherman said, "your guerrillas would meet their equals, and the world would be shocked by the acts of atrocity resulting from such warfare."[35]

In fact, nothing so apocalyptic occurred. Policies had been in place since 1863, such as Francis Lieber's treatise on guerrillas and his broader code of war, published as U.S. General Order 100, that prohibited arbitrary reprisals against guerrillas. Also helping to keep U.S. soldiers in check was the knowledge, among some at least, that they would undermine their legitimacy and authority if they resorted to the most vicious practices of the enemy. This "citizen-soldier" ideal had crystallized particularly among the units tasked with occupation duty from the start of the war.[36] But by the summer of 1865, kindness among occupying troops was in short supply. Veteran occupiers were wondering what they were still doing in the South if the war was over. Meanwhile, the thousands of troops newly assigned to occupation duty were untrained in the ways of winning the hearts and minds of local civilians. They were also anxious to find new enemies. In such an atmosphere, it was inevitable that some U.S. soldiers adopted a take-no-prisoners approach to guerrillas.

Jesse James had already witnessed this approach in the spring of 1865. The seventeen-year-old had tried to surrender to Federals at Lexington, Missouri. Some of the soldiers who recognized him as one of the men who had ridden with "Bloody Bill" Anderson started shooting. James was hit in the chest by a bullet but managed to get away. When his older brother, Frank, heard the news, he resolved to take revenge. With his fellow Missourians (and distant cousins) Cole and Jim Younger, he formed a band of outlaws set on menacing U.S. authority in the region. Jesse James joined them once he had recovered from his injuries. The Youngers and Jameses—known eventually as the James Gang—had never had much passion for the Confederacy. Like most insurgents, they were driven by hatred of outside occupiers, no matter their political affiliation. Sometimes they attacked Federals directly. More often they embarrassed them by committing brazen crimes in broad daylight. In the early afternoon of February 13, 1866, the gang donned U.S. army uniforms and robbed a bank in Liberty, Missouri. The episode now is remembered as a beginning: the start of the much-romanticized banditry of the "Wild West." But it was just as much an ending: a closing chapter, though perhaps not the final chapter, of the guerrilla fighting of the Civil War.[37]

Faced with the impossibility of defeating U.S. occupiers in direct battle, onetime Confederate guerrillas found other ways to carry out their insurgency. The James Gang robbed banks. Most other bands of outlaws chose a course less risky but far more lethal: they tortured and murdered African Americans. Defenseless African Americans had always been targeted by Confederate guerrillas. No one could deny the racial animus behind the Saltville Massacre led by Champ Ferguson. Guerrillas might have lost their status as legitimate soldiers, but their methods and motives remained the same. In the summer of 1865, the members of a group in Freestone County, Texas, calling itself "the Brotherhood" swore an oath to use any means possible—whips, torches, and rifles—to drive every last Black person from the county. This was nearly a year before another white supremacist paramilitary band with similar goals formed in Giles County, Tennessee. That organization called itself the Ku Klux Klan.[38]

Officially, the guerrilla war was over. Whites who acted as guerrillas could no longer claim the status of legitimate combatants. But this fact must have seemed trivial—if it was known at all—to newly free African Americans in more remote areas of the South. In such places, there were neither U.S. troops to hunt down guerrillas nor military courts to try them. Black Americans, now as before the most likely targets of brutal, coordinated violence, would come to hear new names for their persecutors: Ku Kluxers, Night Riders, Knights of the White Camellia. By the 1870s, such groups might be called "insurgents" or "terrorists"—terms that were technically more accurate than "guerrillas" and are still favored today in the taxonomy of collective, racially motivated violence.[39] But for Black people, terminology mattered far less than the fact of racial violence—its unprecedented scale and horrific everydayness.[40] Assigning a correct name to the category of perpetrators was almost beside the point. "Guerrillas" would do as well as any other term.

Secretary of the Navy Gideon Welles did not trouble himself much about guerrillas. That was the army's problem, a *land* problem. His focus was on rivers and oceans. Also, as he stated more than once in the weeks after Appomattox, he believed that the war was over. For that reason, he had recalled most of the gunboats used on the rivers and the warships used on the seas. No doubt he agreed with the policy of clemency toward guerrillas, believing that they, no less than Robert E. Lee's men, accepted defeat and wanted to go home. Reality then shook Welles's world. He came to see that there was still a dangerous number of guerrillas determined to carry on the rebellion against the United States. Worse, at least for him, he learned that guerrillas were not afraid of the water.

When Welles removed all but a few gunboats from the South, he left the river system largely unprotected. Guerrillas infested the waters like an invasive species. They stole small steamboats and steered them upriver into the backcountry of Arkansas and Missouri. From the water, they could easily prey on riverside communities. They also hijacked larger transport boats and robbed the passengers. In one instance, a few guerrillas pretending to be cotton speculators talked their way onto a merchant vessel loaded with bales of the crop. Once on board, they seized the ship, tied up the crew, and made off with most of its cargo. One of Welles's admirals tried to assure the navy secretary that the episode was an anomaly. "The apprehension that lawlessness would ... allow predatory bands to come in to the river has not been realized," the officer wrote. A few weeks later, the same officer had to eat his words. He told Welles that numerous rebel bands now traveled freely along the tributaries of the Mississippi. The few U.S. gunboats still in the region drew too much water to follow. Without military assistance, the officer warned, "great harm will result to the citizens." Welles had assumed that rebel guerrillas were no longer a problem—or at least scant enough in numbers not to be *his* problem—and that any concerns about a resurgence of rebellion were absurd. Now he had to concede—at least privately to his diary—that the guerrilla activity was evidence of a dangerous "banding together of the Rebel element."[41] Maybe Richard Henry Dana had been right. Rebels, or

The Voyage of the *Shenandoah*, 1865

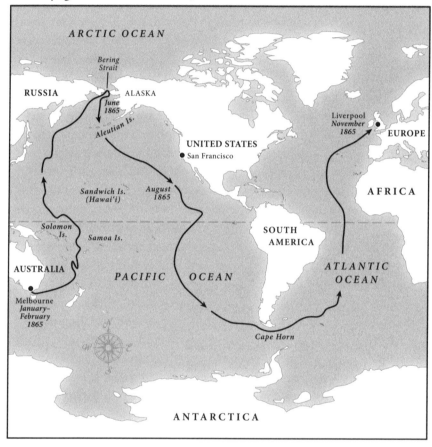

at least some of them, needed to be held by the United States in a "grasp of war." But how was *Welles* supposed to do that, especially with a shrinking navy? The "Rebel element" on the waters was out of his grasp.

There was one ship more than any other that the navy secretary was desperate to catch: the *Shenandoah*. The 230-foot, 1,000-ton Confederate armed cruiser had arrived in the North Pacific by the summer of 1865. Cut off from communication with the Confederacy, the ship's crew had yet to learn that the "nation" it served no longer had major armies or a functional government. They assumed that the war was in full swing, and they were as intent as ever on completing their mission: the destruction of U.S. merchant vessels. In particular, they hunted the whaling ships of New England that plied the seas below the Bering Strait. Sinking these ships and the whale oil in their holds would strike a devastating financial blow to the U.S. economy.

Like other prominent Confederate warships, the *Shenandoah* had been acquired from foreigners. The Confederacy had no major shipbuilding works of its own. It relied on purchasing war-worthy vessels from neutral powers or capturing them from the United States. The ironclad CSS *Virginia* fell into the latter category. It had been the USS *Merrimack* at the start of the war, stationed off Norfolk, Virginia. U.S. naval officers had tried to keep it from falling into Confederate hands by burning and sinking it. But Confederate engineers had been able to salvage the wreck and convert it into the *Virginia*. A year later, after its most famous fight against the USS *Monitor* off Hampton Roads, Confederates destroyed the ship to prevent it from falling back into the hands of the enemy. Two years later, in the spring of 1864, Confederate naval officers disguised as civilians boarded the *Salvador*, a small U.S. coastal trader operating along the Pacific coast of the Panama isthmus. They planned to hijack the ship once it was at sea and put it under the Confederate flag. U.S. agents foiled the scheme. They had learned about it in advance and, like the Confederates, had boarded the *Salvador* dressed as civilians. As soon as the ship put to sea, the U.S. agents arrested the Confederates, finding in their possession guns, a Confederate flag, and instructions from the Confederate secretary of

the navy, Stephen Mallory. The agents transferred the Confederates to a waiting U.S. naval ship, which carried the prisoners to San
Francisco. There, because the United States did not recognize the
Confederacy as a legitimate nation, the sailors were to be tried for
violating the laws of war. The trial of the "*Salvador* pirates," as they
became known, began in late May 1865.[42]

Buying ships from outside North America proved to be a more
successful method for the Confederacy to secure ships, especially
large, seagoing vessels. The trick in this method was to buy them
from civilians, not foreign governments. England, France, and the
other sea powers had all pledged neutrality: their governments
could not sell ships to the Confederacy that might be used for warring purposes. "Neutrality" also required these nations to keep their
civilians from selling ships to Confederates. But how vigilant the
foreign authorities were supposed to be in policing private transactions remained a gray area. Confederate agents looked to exploit
the ambiguity. They sought out European shipping magnates who
were willing to skirt the law in order to make a profit and to win the
favor of Confederate authorities, who, for now at least, controlled
the largest supply of the world's cotton.

The first major Confederate acquisition using this method was
the *Alabama*. The Confederate agent James Bulloch arranged with
an English shipbuilding company to construct the sloop on the sly,
never allowing its true purpose to be revealed. Launched in mid-1862
and commanded by Raphael Semmes, the *Alabama* spent two years
destroying U.S. merchant vessels from the Gulf of Mexico to the
Indian Ocean. It was finally sunk by a U.S. warship off the coast of
France in June 1864. Semmes escaped capture by boarding a nearby
British yacht. Eventually he made his way back to North America
and headed up a Confederate army unit composed in part of other
Alabama survivors. In the meantime, the Confederacy had found
other ships to buy. In October 1864, it acquired from a French ship-
builder the *Stonewall,* a massive ironclad ram with two masts and
two steam-powered propellers. That same month, it secured from
a British cotton merchant the *Shenandoah*. The *Stonewall* ended up
doing no damage to the Union, though it terrified the commanders of two U.S. warships who came upon it off the northwest coast

of Spain in March 1865 and decided to keep their distance from the indestructible-looking vessel. The *Stonewall* was provisioning in Havana two months later when the crew learned of the surrender of the major Confederate armies. The captain abandoned his plan to shell U.S. coastal fortifications. He had his crew abandon the ship, then sold it to a Cuban general. That left the *Shenandoah* as the only Confederate warship still in action.

Unlike the *Stonewall*, the *Shenandoah* was far from any port when the major Confederate army surrenders took place. Its last anchorage at a major city had been at Melbourne in early 1865. There, the crew had heard conflicting stories about affairs back home. One rumor (true) told of the fall of Wilmington, North Carolina, the last open Confederate port. Another rumor (false) told of Lee scoring a decisive victory against U.S. forces in Virginia. The ship's captain, James I. Waddell, assumed the best and took his ship into the northern Pacific to fulfill its mission.

Although the *Shenandoah* was not as well armed as the *Alabama* and lacked the protective ironsides of the *Stonewall*, it turned out to be the most destructive vessel ever to fly the Confederate flag. With a full complement of broad sails along with a retractable propeller and smokestack, it could run on wind or coal-fired steam or both. Before becoming the *Shenandoah*, it flew the British flag as the *Sea King*, a merchant vessel that had set the speed record for the round-trip voyage between London and Bombay. The *Sea King* had left Liverpool in early October 1864, ostensibly to travel back to India. On board, disguised as a coal trader, was William Conway Whittle, a lieutenant in the Confederate navy who was to become the *Shenandoah*'s executive officer. Only Whittle and the *Sea King*'s captain, a British civilian, knew that the vessel had been secretly purchased by the Confederacy. The captain piloted the ship to the Desertas Islands, about eight hundred miles west of the Strait of Gibraltar, where it rendezvoused with a small vessel carrying the Confederate officers who would take charge of the ship. One of the officers was Captain Waddell. Another was Sydney Smith Lee, Jr., Robert E. Lee's nephew, who went by his middle name, Smith. On October 19, 1864, the officers boarded the *Sea King* and oversaw the transfer of supplies and arms from the transport ship. Cannons were affixed to the decks. The British merchant ship *Sea King* was now the Confederate raider *Shenandoah*. It carried two flags, the British Union Jack and the Confederate Stars and Bars.

The methods of the *Shenandoah* were devious, bordering on illegal. If it spotted other ships, it pretended to be a British trading vessel. The crew hoisted the Union Jack, pulled up its propeller, and dropped its smokestack—a steam-powered vessel was more likely to be suspected of being a warship. The *Shenandoah* left all but U.S. ships alone. If a ship flew the U.S. flag, however, the *Shenandoah* raised the Confederate banner, added steam power if necessary, and chased down its prey. If the U.S. vessel refused to yield, the *Shenandoah* fired a warning shot, which almost always brought it to heel. The enemy crew was brought aboard along with any provisions that could be found. Finally, the *Shenandoah*'s crew covered the vessel's hull with tar and any other flammable substance found on the captured ship. Then it set the vessel on fire. The *Shenandoah*'s mission was destruction, not pillaging. It did not have room on board to hold captured cargo. (On a few occasions it did "bond" a captured ship, claiming its cargo as Confederate property and ordering its captain to sail it to a neutral port.) Also, the flaming ship offered immediate gratification of a blow inflicted on the enemy. Whittle in particular had a creepy passion for the sight, confessing to his diary that he had "rarely seen anything which is more beautifully grand than a ship burning at sea."[43] The flames became most spectacular when they touched the hundreds of barrels of sperm oil aboard. Each exploding barrel represented a loss to the Union of roughly $100 (about $2,000 in twenty-first-century dollars). The *Shenandoah*'s Pacific voyage of destruction ended up being the most costly campaign against the Union, and almost all of the destruction took place after most Americans back home thought the Civil War was over.

Oddly, the Confederate menace that was the *Shenandoah* had very few actual Confederates aboard. The handful of officers were members of the Confederate navy, but the rest of the crew had little or no attachment to the American South or its cause. Almost all of the regular crew members of the original *Sea King* were British subjects. When Captain Waddell took command of the vessel, now rechristened the *Shenandoah*, he told the sailors that they had a choice: leave or "ship"—meaning join the crew. If they "shipped," they would receive a regular salary plus a bounty. All but four of the fifty-five sailors begged off. To join the *Shenandoah* was to violate their country's Foreign Enlistment Act, which prohibited them from providing military service to any country except England. Violating the act was treason. If captured by British authorities, they could be hanged. The men who refused to join were sent to shore by Waddell. They would have to find their own way home. The *Shenandoah* ideally needed a crew of at least 100 sailors. It started with fewer than a dozen. Waddell's objective, then, was not simply to chase down U.S. ships and strip and sink them; he also had to persuade captured crew members to join the *Shenandoah*. In the months to come, Waddell successfully took on about 120 sailors willing to "ship." Of course, the sailors did not have much of a choice. If they refused, they would be chained on deck until the ship reached a port where they could be offloaded, and no one knew when that would be. Dozens of captured sailors chose that grim option rather than sign on with the Confederacy. But eventually Waddell built a crew of adequate size. Most of the sailors were European. The largest group were British subjects willing to risk the treason charge. There were also a good number of sailors from the North of the United States. They, too, risked treason, but they could always argue that they had been forced to join—not technically true, perhaps, but true enough. The *Shenandoah*, then, was a Confederate ship only in name. The officers were Confederates, to be sure, and maybe some of the captured men who "shipped" ended up sympathizing with the rebels. But most of the regular sailors acted out of some combination of survival, compulsion, and the slim chance of a payday. The white sailors, that is. For the Black sailors—there were four who served aboard the *Shenandoah*—coercion played the leading role.

On November 8, 1864, the day that Abraham Lincoln was reelected to the U.S. presidency on a platform pledged to the abolition of slavery, the African American sailor John Williams came aboard the *Shenandoah*. His ship, the U.S. merchant vessel *D. Godfrey*, had left Boston the month before and was sailing into the South Atlantic, bound for Valparaiso, Chile, when it was captured by the *Shenandoah*. Five men from the *Godfrey* voluntarily "shipped" to the *Shenandoah*. Four refused and were allowed to transfer to a

passing vessel headed for Rio de Janeiro. Williams also refused—
but Waddell made him serve anyway. He declared that Williams
was now the ship's cook. Waddell, adopted and raised by an elite
slaveholding family in North Carolina, never gave the four African
Americans captured by the *Shenandoah* any option except to serve
the ship.[44] He told Williams that he was doing a service by bringing "coloreds" aboard, as they would be better off on the *Shenandoah*
than anywhere else on the high seas. Williams, who had done a stint
on a U.S. naval vessel before joining the *Godfrey*, refused to go along
without a fight. To Waddell's endless exasperation, he tussled with
anyone who bullied him. He sneered and swore at the officers who
tried—and failed—to render him docile through beatings and tric-
ings. In tricing, a sailor was displayed on deck with his limbs excru-
ciatingly bound together in a stretched position for hours. Smith
Lee triced John Williams at least once. Williams bolted from the
ship the first chance he got, which came in late January 1865, when
the *Shenandoah* docked in Melbourne. He leapt overboard, swam
to the pier, found the U.S. consul, and told him of the *Shenandoah*'s
plans to destroy American whalers in the North Pacific.[45]

If Williams had hoped to foil the ship's mission, he was disappointed. The U.S. consul, William Blanchard, knew that Williams
was telling the truth—other sailors from the ship had told him
the same story. But he could not persuade the British governor at
Melbourne, Charles Darling, to hold the *Shenandoah*. The ship had
entered the port with guns stowed and the Confederate flag on
display. (To sail under the British flag while commanded by non-
British officers would have led the British authorities in the port
to lock down the ship for good.) Neutrality, the official policy of
Great Britain toward both sides in the U.S. Civil War, meant noninterference, the governor told Blanchard. The consul was furious.
With British subjects aboard and British provisions being added
to the cargo, he insisted, the Crown was *already* interfering. Some
U.S. sailors aboard a ship docked nearby took matters into their own
hands. One night they floated a massive makeshift bomb up to the
raider's hull. But the line that triggered the device snapped when
they pulled it. Eventually, Governor Darling did decide to intervene.
He was convinced by Blanchard that the *Shenandoah* was gaining
new recruits from the British sailors on the docks. Port authorities

stormed down the pier to board the ship. Waddell held them at bay, claiming the ship as sovereign Confederate territory. The ploy worked. The *Shenandoah* was able to slip out of the port on February 18, 1865.

It would not enter a major port again for nearly nine months. A month after the Australia sojourn, Executive Officer Whittle wrote in his journal: "We are almost out of the world."[46] From Melbourne the *Shenandoah* had sailed east then north, reaching the Bering Sea in early June. Navigating around the perilous ice floes off Siberia, the crew had little idea of what was happening back in North America. No one knew that the Confederacy was in shambles.

On June 22, the *Shenandoah* finally began encountering New England whaling ships. A sailor from New Bedford, Massachusetts, taken from one of the first whalers captured and destroyed by the *Shenandoah*, told the crew what had happened at Appomattox back in April. The Confederate officers refused to believe that Robert E. Lee would ever surrender. Waddell told his men not to believe Yankees: they would say anything to get the *Shenandoah* to stand down. Then the *Shenandoah* captured a vessel carrying old newspapers from San Francisco that reported Lee's surrender as well as the assassination of Lincoln. The news about Lee was shocking, but Waddell refused to give up the mission. Other Confederate armies were still active, he assumed, and Jefferson Davis was still at large. As a later report told it, he "scoffed at the idea of the collapse of the rebellion." If anything, the news hardened the resolve of the Confederate officers. Waddell fantasized that Lincoln's death had led to riots in the North that had crippled the U.S. war effort. Whittle, furious with the Yankees for humiliating Lee's army, now took special pleasure in burning the whalers. Any compassion for the enemy was gone, he wrote in his journal, replaced with "intense hatred, and a determination in this cruel and relentless war to fight the devil with fire."[47] On June 28, the *Shenandoah* captured eleven whaling ships and set nine of them aflame. In terms of financial loss, it was the most destructive day of the Civil War. Assuming, that is, that there still *was* a Civil War. Certainly Whittle assumed so. He wrote a hopeful note in his journal that the Union's loss would be "encouraging [to] our noble people" back home.[48]

Whittle did not know—there was no way that he could know—

that a week before the *Shenandoah* brought an inferno of destruction to the Bering Sea, the ship had been ordered by Confederate authorities to cease its attacks. James Bulloch, the Confederate agent in Liverpool who had helped orchestrate the *Shenandoah*'s mission, penned a letter to Waddell on June 19 directing him to "desist from any further destruction of United States property." The letter detailed the events of the past ten weeks, from Lee's surrender to the arrest of Jefferson Davis. "President Johnson has formally declared the war to be at an end," Bulloch wrote. That was not technically true—Johnson's proclamation at the end of May had said that the war was "almost" at an end—but the technicality made no difference when it came to the *Shenandoah*. The proclamation denied further legitimacy to Confederate warships. Secretary of State Seward had buttressed the order with a promise from foreign powers that they would withdraw their policies of treating Confederates as lawful belligerents. Bulloch explained all this in his letter to Waddell. The meaning was inescapable: there were no more friendly ports for the *Shenandoah;* it had no official protection; its crew members could be executed. Bulloch gave the message to British diplomats, who sent copies to ports around the Pacific with instructions to show the letter to Waddell if the *Shenandoah* should appear.[49]

Unmentioned in Bulloch's letter was the fact that U.S. warships had been hunting the *Shenandoah* for more than three months.[50] U.S. Secretary of the Navy Gideon Welles was especially distraught that the ship was still at large, not simply because of the damage that it might do but because its mere presence on the seas gave the lie to his claim, so often made in cabinet meetings, that the Civil War was over. He refused to call the *Shenandoah* a Confederate ship. The Confederacy was dead, Welles believed, and even when it was alive, it had never been a legitimate nation. At the same time, he knew that the officers commanding the vessel were more than mere brigands. He opted to call the *Shenandoah* a "rebel pirate."[51] It was half stateless marauder and half national enemy, a hybrid vessel sailing in the murky waters between war and peace.

For the officers aboard the *Shenandoah,* there was no ambiguity. They were Confederates. The destruction they had wrought at the end of June was legitimate warfare. It would revive Confederate spirits enough to hold their nation together.

The *Shenandoah* never received the letter from Bulloch spelling out the doom of the Confederacy. After laying waste to the New England whaling fleet in the Bering Sea, the *Shenandoah* had sailed southeast toward the west coast of the United States. Waddell sought to inflict further damage on the Union. He briefly contemplated shelling San Francisco. He knew that he could not get the city to surrender—that would take a bombardment by a whole fleet—but hoped the attack would nonetheless shock and demoralize the enemy.

On August 2, 1865, all such schemes evaporated. That day, the *Shenandoah* pulled aside the *Barracouta*, a British naval vessel. The officers provided Waddell's crew with newspapers that removed any doubt that the Confederate government had fallen. Whittle immediately realized that "nearly all our work in the Arctic" had taken place after the fall. "God knows we were ignorant," he wrote in his diary. Even so, God might not save the crew. The timing of their attacks meant that they could be tried as pirates. One of the midshipmen imagined his execution. He "could hang as gracefully as any other man," he reflected, but when he pictured the moment, he felt "a sort of choking sensation."[52] Waddell ordered the crew to strip and stow the *Shenandoah*'s guns. They removed all emblems of the Confederacy. To stay alive, they had to pretend, once again, to be sailing a British merchant ship. But where would they go? A British port seemed the safest option. Some well-connected Englishmen had been in on the plot from the beginning. Maybe they could save the sailors from the gallows. A few officers suggested returning to Melbourne, but most preferred Cape Town, which was farther away but faster to reach because of prevailing winds. Waddell took the ship around Cape Horn and into the South Atlantic.

Then, to the dismay of his officers, Waddell ordered a course for Liverpool. That would add a month and close to ten thousand miles to their voyage. The reason for Waddell's choice remains unknown. Probably he hoped that bringing the ship back to Liverpool would put it close to the businessmen who had financed the venture and make them more likely to come to their defense. Also, they could pay off the crew. The *Shenandoah* had only enough coin aboard to pay the sailors a reduced rate. Custom dictated that the crew receive its pay before the ship docked. If the sailors were shorted, they might mutiny. Whatever Waddell's reasons for steering for Liverpool, his decision may have saved the lives of his crew. Unbeknownst to those aboard the *Shenandoah*, the USS *Wachusett* had left Rio de Janeiro on September 21 to hunt for the Confederate raider. The captain of the Union warship assumed that Waddell was making for Cape Town and focused his search efforts on the shipping lane between Cape Horn and South Africa. Had the *Wachusett* caught the *Shenandoah*, Waddell and his crew would have been tried as pirates in a U.S. court. Instead, just before midnight on November 5, they arrived safely at the mouth of the River Mersey, the gateway to Liverpool.

The *Shenandoah*, still flying the British flag, pulled alongside a small boat at anchor. It was one of the vessels used to pilot large ships to the harbor. Waddell's crew hailed the pilot, claiming that their ship was called *America*. The pilot came aboard so that he could steer the vessel to the harbor. As soon as the Englishman arrived, the crew told him the truth: their ship was the Confederate raider *Shenandoah*. They asked him for "news from the war in America."

"It has been over so long people have got through talking about it," came the response.[53]

Confirmation that the Confederacy had fallen hit the crew hard. Waddell ordered the Confederate flag hoisted. The days of flying false flags were over. He had the pilot sail the ship to the harbor and anchor it next to a British warship, the HMS *Donegal*. The Confederate flag was then lowered, and Waddell presented it to the *Donegal*'s captain. The *Shenandoah* was surrendering and placing itself under the protection of the British Crown, Waddell informed the officer.

For two days, U.S. and British authorities in Liverpool argued about what should happen next. The crew of the *Shenandoah* knew that they might be hanged, either here in England or back in the United States. They hoped that enough time had passed to soften the vengeful sentiments of their onetime enemies. Waddell already had anticipated that the Americans would want any Confederates on board extradited to the United States to be tried, either for piracy or some violation of the laws of war. As soon as the *Shenandoah* surrendered, Waddell had a letter transmitted to Earl Russell, England's prime minister, claiming that the crew was innocent. During all the time the *Shenandoah* was sinking U.S. ships, Waddell claimed, he had been "ignorant of the reverses suffered by the Confederates and the total obliteration of the government under which I acted."[54] That was only a partial truth, of course. On June 24, Waddell had seen San Francisco newspapers that reported the fall of Richmond and the surrender of Lee, but he had gone ahead and destroyed more than fifteen U.S. vessels in the four days that followed. Waddell claimed that it was not until August 2, when they encountered the British ship *Barracouta,* that he had learned of the full extent of the Confederate defeat. The U.S. consul at Liverpool, Thomas H. Dudley, was furious when he learned that British officials believed Waddell and were inclined toward clemency. Regardless of what the crew had known or when they had known it, they were guilty, he insisted. Either they were guilty of piracy, in which case the British authorities should hang them, or they were guilty of violating the laws of war, in which case they should be sent to the United States to stand trial there. But Dudley could do little more than rage aloud. If he ordered the men arrested on English soil, he was sure to set off a diplomatic crisis.

In the end, all the men who served aboard the *Shenandoah* went free. The British government declared that their acts of war had taken place when—to the knowledge of the sailors, at least—they were still lawful belligerents. In a meager act of contrition, British authorities turned over to Dudley the *Shenandoah,* which was now barely seaworthy. Even the British subjects aboard, who were guilty of violating England's Foreign Enlistment Act, escaped punishment. They did so by claiming their nationality as "Confederate" rather than British. All the sailors, in fact, including those from the U.S. North, shielded themselves from potential prosecution by their home countries by declaring themselves Confederates. One after another, in an English accent, or an Irish one, or one from Germany, France, or even New York, each of the seamen who had shipped aboard the *Shenandoah* pledged fealty to the Confederacy, though few, if any, had ever set foot in the American South.

The genuine Confederates, the officers who had commanded the ship, were relieved to have escaped the noose, yet they could not return home. At least not anytime soon. They were almost certain to be arrested as soon as they touched U.S. soil. The Confederates who had tried and failed to commandeer the *Salvador* back in 1864

had just been given a death sentence by a military commission—
and they had not done *any* damage to the Union. Ultimately the
"*Salvador* pirates" had their sentences commuted to prison terms
ranging from ten years to life, a price still too high to pay for the
Shenandoah officers.[55] Raphael Semmes, the most notorious Confederate sea captain of all, had initially been granted a parole but
then was arrested in December 1865. Gideon Welles, usually one
of the more lenient U.S. leaders, had ordered the arrest. He hoped
to see Semmes imprisoned, even hanged, for having robbed and
destroyed "the ships and property of his unarmed countrymen
engaged in peaceful commerce"—exactly the crime committed by
the crew of the *Shenandoah*.[56] Northern newspapers in the United
States were filled with outrage at the *Shenandoah*'s crew. A letter to
a Boston editor demanded that British authorities compensate U.S.
shipowners for their losses and called the men of the *Shenandoah* no
better than "corsairs" with "the greed of unhallowed gain by piracy."[57]
An Albany, New York, editor was disgusted that the British had
handed over "the worthless hulk" of the *Shenandoah* but refused to
render up the "freebooters" and "criminals" who had manned it. "It is
as if a murderer should be set at liberty," the editor wrote, "while the
pistol with which he did his deed was condemned and sold for the
benefit of his victim's heirs."[58]

Sure to face prosecution if they returned to the United States,
the officers of the Confederate raider sought out new homes. James
Waddell stayed in Liverpool. He sent for his wife, who had spent a
bit of time in prison during the summer of 1865 after U.S. Secretary of War Stanton had ordered her arrest. A few of the officers,
including William Whittle and Smith Lee, fled to Rosario, Argen-
tina, about a hundred miles up the Paraná River from Buenos Aires.
There, the onetime mariners bought and worked a farm. A few others went to Mexico. They had heard about the colonies that had
been set up there by Jo Shelby and other "Confederados."

Like the Confederados who had left the South yet schemed to
resurrect the Confederacy, like the "demons incarnate" who had
stayed behind and fought as guerrillas, the *Shenandoah* Confederates had failed to leave the stage when U.S. officials had declared the
show over. Maybe they were different. Maybe, as they claimed when

their lives were at stake, they were simply unaware that the curtain had come down. Even so, at least some of them had found glory in keeping up the fight when others had surrendered. In deviating from the standard script of war, they had earned their enemies' contempt, yet managed to escape with their lives.

12

The Final Trial

O N N O V E M B E R 10, 1865, just a few days after the decision was made in Liverpool not to hang any of the Confederate naval officers from the *Shenandoah,* Henry Wirz, a Confederate army captain, was hanged in Washington, D.C.

Wirz had become infamous as the last officer to command the POW camp at Andersonville, Georgia. Reports of the suffering and death of U.S. soldiers at Andersonville had circulated long before Confederate armies started surrendering. Then, in the summer of 1865, grotesque images of emaciated U.S. POWs began appearing as photos in northern storefronts and sketches in popular magazines. The men pictured were not from Andersonville but from other Confederate POW camps, but that did not matter. Viewers assumed that prisoners from Andersonville looked the same—or worse. The wrecked bodies of northerners kept aflame Unionists' rage, which had only been brought to a simmer by the hanging of the Lincoln assassins back in July.

The hanging of Wirz took place at the Old Capitol Prison, a few hundred yards from the U.S. Capitol. Although the scaffold was shielded by prison walls, the execution was very much a public event. Secretary of War Stanton allowed members of the press to attend— or at least those who were friendly to the current administration. Stanton also oversaw the distribution of 250 tickets to dignitaries as well as selected family members of those who had died at Andersonville. The secretary of war invited Alexander Gardner, who had gained fame during the war for his photographic records of battlefields and luminaries like Lincoln. Stanton arranged for Gardner to set up his equipment near the scaffold and asked him to photograph all the stages of the execution. Washingtonians outside the walls did not want to wait for the pictures and newspaper reports. They climbed atop the prison walls or perched on high tree branches nearby.

From a photograph by Alexander Gardner: a U.S. officer reads the death warrant to Henry Wirz before he is hanged. The gallows were within sight of the U.S. Capitol.

No one knew it at the time, but Wirz would be the last Confederate to be executed by the United States government. The hanging, then, might take a place in history next to other "lasts" of the Civil War: the last battle, the last shot, the last surrender (that is, if historians could agree on which battle, shot, or surrender was truly the "last"). Although some hoped for further executions—when would Jeff Davis be hanged from that "sour apple tree"?—a sense of finality still pervaded the scene. Wirz's death, it seemed, might be blood atonement enough for the sins of the rebels. The *Chicago Tribune* led off its front-page account of the event with a large-print, single-word pronouncement: "Expiation."[1]

In any war, the execution of perpetrators can serve the function of marking the end of the war, or at least *an* end. Wirz's hanging, which drew national attention, certainly played such a role. Yet no plaque or stone marks the place where Wirz died. The site of the scaffold is now covered up by a building erected seventy years after the hanging: the U.S. Supreme Court.

One of those who wanted more hangings to follow was U.S. Judge Advocate General Joseph Holt. His boss, Secretary Stanton, was firmly in support. Stanton had appointed Holt to his position and put him in charge of the Bureau of Military Justice, which was created to punish those guilty of crimes connected to the war. Holt, with Stanton looking over his shoulder, had overseen the prosecution of the Lincoln assassins. The two men had revealed their ultimate goal during that trial by having the military commission name Jefferson Davis and Robert E. Lee as co-conspirators. The strategy had proved an embarrassment. Yet Stanton and Holt remained convinced that, if not the assassination, they could find something else to pin on Davis and other high officials of the Confederacy. With this purpose in mind, Stanton created the Bureau of Rebel Archives in late July 1865. The idea was to gather all Confederate records in one place and then search them for evidence of crimes by Davis and his cohort.

Stanton put Francis Lieber in charge of the project. It was an inspired choice. Lieber, the legal expert who had drafted the U.S. code of war implemented in 1863, had taken on as his next project the establishment of a law of treason. He believed that Davis and other Confederate leaders were guilty, if not of treason then of violating the norms of warfare that his code had spelled out. The code had declared assassination an "intentional outlawry" and "outrage."[2] Lieber welcomed the opportunity to search for links between the Confederate government and the Lincoln assassins. For similar reasons, he scoured the record for evidence that the Davis administration was complicit in the mistreatment of POWs. His code condemned as a "barbarity" the "intentional infliction of any suffering" on prisoners of war, including "cruel imprisonment" and "want of food."[3] For Lieber, the hanging of Wirz would be an affirmation of the justice embedded in his code of war. And like Stanton and Holt, he assumed that justice must also include the execution of Jefferson Davis.[4]

The idea of hanging Davis was still popular among the more bitter Unionists. Magazines and periodicals printed sketches of Davis strung up. A Boston printer distributed "Metamorphosis," a multi-folded broadside that enabled the user to create a motion picture by flipping through the frames, showing Davis going from begging for a pardon, to weeping atop his as-yet-unfilled coffin, to hanging from the gallows.

The imagined death of Jefferson Davis. This 1865 print was designed to be folded into parts and then opened in sequence. The first part shows Davis pleading vainly for a pardon; the second shows him weeping on his coffin, a noose around his neck; the third shows him hanging. The desire to hang Davis, powerful among many northerners by mid-1865, would fade by 1866.

Yet the rage for Davis's execution was losing its intensity. It had been sated somewhat by the rollicking (and largely exaggerated) stories of Davis's humiliating capture in May. Maybe it was better to leave Davis reduced to a laughingstock, remembered as running away from his pursuers dressed as a woman, instead of elevating him to a martyr by putting him on the scaffold. Davis's wife, Varina, spent the summer of 1865 helping to spread the word that her husband was already suffering plenty. Even though she had not been allowed to visit him, she knew that he was in poor shape. Locked up in a damp casement within one of the walls of Fort Monroe in Virginia, he was constantly sick and losing weight. He had dark visions. Varina used her connections to get southern papers to report on his poor conditions—and hers. She had been denied visitation rights. When she asked one of the officers in the fort if she might move in to be close to her husband, he scoffed that she was welcome to take a spot in the area where prostitutes from the outside were set up to ply their trade. Davis was still unrepentant. He refused to ask President Johnson for a pardon. But his wife's labors were having some effect. The Confederate leader, once known for his swagger, now cut a more pathetic figure in the public eye. Varina reported that he had finally forgiven her for restraining him from attacking his pursuers at the moment of his capture. She probably had saved his life. But she also had marred his legacy. If he had died that day in an act of combat, he might have been remembered by all Confederates as a hero.[5]

Holt and Stanton, too, must have wished sometimes that Davis had died that day in Irwinville. Killing him now was going to take some finesse. The number of petitions calling for his pardon was on the rise. One of the few that President Johnson chose to respond to had been signed by 15,000 "Baltimore Ladies." The president gave a reply that was a far cry from the "traitors must be punished" refrain that had once been his trademark. He sympathized with Davis "in his sufferings," he responded. If the matter were merely a question "between man and man," he would release Davis from prison "at once." But the law called for a trial.[6]

A trial for what, though? That was one of the problems that Holt and Stanton faced—and one of the reasons that the Wirz prosecution became so important to them. The obvious crime was treason. But Holt, Stanton, and other members of the Johnson administration had already figured out that a treason trial for Davis would raise all sorts of legal, political, and logistical problems.

Legally, a treason charge against Davis might hold up in court. But if Davis were tried for treason, then thousands of other rebels must be tried for treason as well. This logic followed from "constructive treason," the reigning principle of the day that dictated that anyone involved in a treason, not just the leaders, was culpable. President

Johnson's amnesty proclamation of May 29, 1865, protected most but not all former Confederates from prosecution. High-ranking soldiers and sailors were exempted from amnesty and had to apply to Johnson for pardons. So did Confederate soldiers and sailors who had once been members of the U.S. regular forces, or who had been educated at West Point or the U.S. Naval Academy. Civilians who had lived in U.S. jurisdictions at the start of the war but ended up serving the Confederacy were also fair game for treason prosecution.

In June 1865, a federal judge in Virginia, John C. Underwood, made real the possibility of mass treason prosecutions. In his instructions to the grand jury, he declared that Confederate soldiers and sailors who had received paroles after surrendering might still be tried for treason. He acknowledged that it would be impractical to try all such men. He even suggested that most of them were "not morally responsible for the Rebellion," a generous position considering that the principle of "constructive treason" did make them *legally* responsible. But the overall severity of Underwood's message was unmistakable. Former Confederates who thought that their paroles would save them from the noose now had to think again. Robert E. Lee immediately applied to Johnson for a pardon. Some of the paperwork was lost by U.S. clerks, however. Lee never received a pardon from Johnson—only because the request never crossed the president's desk.[7]

Lee and other paroled Confederates need not have worried much. The crucial architect of the Appomattox arrangement, Ulysses S. Grant, now general in chief of the U.S. Army, was livid when he heard that parolees might be tried for treason. He knew that the law allowed for such trials, but the implicit understanding reached at Appomattox, he claimed, was that they would go free. The opinion of Grant, the most revered war hero in the Union, carried serious weight. Grant even told Johnson that he would resign if Lee and other parolees were tried for treason. Johnson, fearing the political fallout if he crossed the hero of Appomattox, and also more inclined toward leniency than he had been after the Lincoln assassination, took Grant's side. Some in the Johnson administration, most notably Stanton and Holt, still believed that high-ranking Confederate military leaders like Lee should be tried for treason, but they were in the minority.

The public stance of Johnson and Grant against trying Confederate combatants for treason still left the fate of Jefferson Davis an open question. Although Davis had technically been the Confederacy's commander in chief, he was first and foremost a civilian leader, not a combatant. A treason trial for Davis was viable, then, but it would lead inevitably to difficult-to-answer questions. Why should Davis be hanged while Lee went free? Or, put more generally: Where did one draw the line between the guilty and the innocent?

A treason trial for Davis would raise other problems. If Davis were put in the dock, he was sure to use the legality of secession as a defense. He was no more a traitor than George Washington had been, the argument would run. He and other Confederates had reacted logically and legally, under the well-established "right of revolution" sanctified by the Declaration of Independence, to a government they had deemed tyrannical and unconstitutional. The country would be subjected to the secession debate once again. It wouldn't matter that secession had lost on the battlefield. It could still win in the court of public opinion. And it could win in the actual court hearing Davis's case. A few jury members persuaded by the secession argument were all that would be needed to acquit Davis. Then Davis would go free. Worse, secessionists might use the ruling to justify a new call to arms. The war would resume in full force, this time with the law on the rebels' side. The United States would be forced again to settle the matter with arms, seeing as it had failed to do so with logic.[8]

This nightmare scenario could be avoided by rigging the trial to guarantee a verdict that equated secession with treason. A court presided over by a judge like Virginia's John Underwood, who had already made public his willingness to see rebels tried as traitors, might do the trick. Little surprise, then, that U.S. authorities eventually chose Underwood's court as the site to indict Davis—though that was still a year away. Even in that court, a conviction was not a sure bet. As a civilian court, specifically a U.S. district court, a jury would render the judgment. U.S. authorities could pack the jury with loyal Unionists, including Black men (that was already Underwood's plan), but all that it would take for Davis to be acquitted, and thus secession to be upheld, was one wayward juror.[9]

The surest way to secure a unanimous guilty verdict was to try

Davis by a military commission. U.S. officers would be the "jury" in such an instance. They could be counted on—especially if selected for the purpose by Holt and Stanton—to quash the secession defense and convict Davis of treason. In the unlikely event that they took Davis's side, Holt, as judge advocate general, had the authority to set aside the proceedings. In Johnson's cabinet, Secretary of the Navy Gideon Welles thought that a military commission for Davis was unlawful and impolitic. He preferred a civilian trial somewhere in Virginia. But Welles was a lone voice, easily drowned out by Stanton and Seward. They doubted that a jury of Virginians, even one composed solely of men who had sworn loyalty to the United States, would deliver a guilty verdict. As Seward put it, "there could be no conviction of such a man, for any offense, before any civil tribunal." A military prosecution might fail too, Stanton and Seward feared, if the evidence against Davis was insufficient. For this reason, they hoped to find airtight proof in the rebel archives, which Francis Lieber was now inspecting.[10]

The cabinet member who mattered most when it came to legal questions was the attorney general, James Speed. Speed supported treason trials for Davis and other rebel leaders. He was also open to using military commissions for the prosecutions. But unlike Seward and Stanton, he preferred a long delay before Davis and his associates were tried. Even if damning evidence against Davis and others was found, he told Lieber, the time for trials was only after "the political and military power of the government shall proclaim that the rebellion has been suppressed." Otherwise, Speed wrote, the trials would have the illegitimate look of proceedings "presided over by bayonets." A definitive end of the war had to precede the trials. He predicted that "some time must elapse" before the endpoint.[11] But Speed did not tell Lieber how anyone would recognize the endpoint when it came.

If Holt and Stanton were going to get Davis executed, and soon, they needed a strategy that did not involve a treason prosecution. The Wirz trial offered a solution. If during the trial of Wirz, Davis could be implicated in the crimes that took place at Andersonville, then he could be tried separately from Wirz and end up suffering the same punishment—inevitably, a hanging. Trying Davis for violating the laws of war, maybe even for murder, would be easier and less politically dangerous than trying him for treason. The strategy was not simply a legal work-around to ensure that Davis was killed one way or another. Stanton genuinely believed that Davis approved of—maybe even facilitated—the horrors experienced by U.S. prisoners across the South. For that alone, Stanton thought, regardless of how things might play out with a separate charge of treason, the Confederate president should be convicted and hanged. Stanton knew that others inside the Davis administration had tried to relieve the suffering while Davis did nothing. He had evidence, for example, that Alexander H. Stephens, Davis's vice president, had complained about conditions at Andersonville. On that basis alone, Stanton helped secure the release of Stephens from his confinement at Fort Warren in Boston Harbor.[12] Davis must have known whatever Stephens knew about the horrors of Andersonville, Stanton reasoned, but he had never lifted a finger to intervene. For this, and for so many other reasons as well, Stanton thought that Davis deserved to die.

The Wirz trial was the perfect venue to condemn not only the most infamous prison-keeper of the Confederacy but also his superior, Jefferson Davis. By August 1865, when the trial began, everyone had heard about atrocities at POW camps in the South. No camp was more notorious than Andersonville. No commandant was more despised than Henry Wirz.

Back before the Confederate surrenders of spring 1865, U.S. soldiers who had served time in Andersonville and managed to get out had described countless miseries at the prison. A U.S. officer in August 1864 reported that he had learned from former prisoners there that conditions were "pitiful in the extreme." The men there were "but half fed . . . naked, suffering, sick, and dying."[13]

More powerful than such reports were the images. U.S. medical officers in 1864 interested in the effects of starvation had requested photographs of the most emaciated U.S. soldiers who had spent time in Confederate prisons. Eight former prisoners were photographed. They had been in Belle Isle prison near Richmond, not Andersonville. Artists converted the images to engravings. *Harper's Weekly* and *Frank Leslie's Illustrated Magazine,* the two most widely read magazines in the North, featured the images as evidence of "diabolical barbarities of the rebels" on their covers on June 18, 1864. By 1865, it had become commonplace for Union politicians and officials to distribute reproductions of these "living skeletons" at any debate or inquiry where vengeance against Confederates was called for. Although the men pictured had not been at Andersonville, that detail generally went unnoticed because Andersonville had gained more notoriety than any other POW camp.[14]

By the summer of 1865, northerners already enraged by the assassination of Lincoln regarded Andersonville as further evidence that Confederates, or at least the leaders among them, deserved to die. Lucretia Bancroft Farnum, the sister of the famous historian George Bancroft, told her brother that Jefferson Davis should end up "on the gallows"—"if not for treason, for cruelty towards our prisoners."[15] Another genteel Massachusetts woman, Sarah Browne, wanted to see Davis "unclothed—unprotected and fed after the manner in which the sufferers at Andersonville lived and died."[16]

Yet it was Wirz, much more than Davis, who northerners held responsible for Andersonville. The publication of prisoners' accounts of Andersonville surged in the early summer of 1865, before the trial began, and all fingered Wirz as the primary villain. A U.S. captain reported having seen more than 5,000 former Andersonville prisoners who were "nothing but mere skeletons, having been almost starved to death." "If there is a hell on this earth, it is Andersonville," he wrote. "And the chief devil is Capt. Wirz."[17]

Wirz had never intended to be a prison-keeper. Born in Switzerland, he emigrated to the United States in the 1840s, settling first in Kentucky and then in Louisiana. He trained to be a doctor and for a short time had a medical practice in New Orleans. Eventually, he and his family moved to a plantation outside the city that was owned by an acquaintance. In exchange for living there, Wirz was tasked with maintaining the medical well-being of the enslaved people on the plantation.[18]

When the Civil War broke out, Wirz mustered into the Confederate army as a private. At some point in mid-1862, he began keeping his right arm in a sling. His version of events was that he had been shot in the arm during the Battle of Seven Pines. During his trial in 1865, his detractors said that he had faked the injury to get out of combat duty.[19] Because of his condition, he was reassigned to the command of Brigadier General John H. Winder, who oversaw a number of non-combat operations, including some prisons. The transfer came with a promotion to the rank of captain. When Camp Sumter at Andersonville was built by the Confederacy as a POW camp in early 1864, Winder sent Wirz to run the place. Winder remained Wirz's superior. By the end of 1864, Winder was in charge of all Confederate prisons. He spent most of his time at the Camp Sumter POW camp, which by then was known simply as Andersonville. So it was Winder, not Wirz, who was the top officer at Andersonville.

Then, on February 7, 1865, Winder died suddenly of a heart attack. Henry Wirz was promoted to major and put in command of the prison. He remained in that post until early May 1865, when U.S. troops arrived at Andersonville and took charge of the remaining prisoners there.

Well before Wirz took command of Andersonville, the place was horrific. Prison gangs known as "raiders" stole rations and clothing from the weak. Inmates picked through corpses rotting in the open air, looking for bits of food, and then stripped the bodies of clothing that they might use to keep warm. One POW later recalled seeing a comrade "with not only the lice and fleas feeding on him, but out of every aperture of his body the maggots were crawling."[20]

Overcrowding was the cause of most of the deaths. The prison had been designed to accommodate 10,000 inmates when it opened in early 1864; by late spring, it held twice that number. In August, when Winder was still in charge, the population hit its peak of roughly 33,000. By the time the facility closed, well over 40,000 U.S. soldiers had served at some point as inmates there, and about 13,000 of them had died. Insufficient supplies led to starvation. Living in close, ramshackle quarters—hovels known as "shebangs" that prisoners constructed themselves—the inmates were constantly exposed to the elements and to the diseases that spread unchecked through the camp. Water was limited and its quality was poor. A shallow creek running through the camp was the prison's only source of water. The water was clean enough when it entered, but it then picked up poisonous runoff: the urine, feces, and detritus of thousands of squalid men. The clean water at the point of entry was off-limits to prisoners. It ran behind a hastily constructed barrier made of posts and planks. Guards told prisoners that they would be killed if they crossed the boundary. When desperately dehydrated POWs crawled below the planks and made for the fresh water, at least some were indeed shot. The barrier became known as the "dead line." Sensationalized accounts of men being gunned down at Andersonville simply for trying to get a drink appeared in newspapers before, during, and after the Wirz trial. The phrase "dead line" became known to all, quickly evolving into one word: "deadline." Reporters with a morbid sense of humor began using the term to describe due dates imposed on them by editors.

Henry Wirz stayed at his post through April 1865 and into early May. When he heard of Lee's surrender at Appomattox, he did not assume that the war was over. He waited for news from Johnston's army, which was larger than Lee's and closer to the camp. When news of the peace terms offered by Sherman to Johnston arrived, Wirz was dismayed at the Confederate general's surrender but pleased that the terms provided a blanket amnesty. He was not to be prosecuted, or so he thought. Communication between North Carolina and central Georgia being slow, Wirz did not know that those terms were disapproved by Sherman's superiors. Had he known, he might have tried to flee the country. Instead, on May 7, 1865, he was arrested by a squad of U.S. soldiers.

From Andersonville, Wirz was transported to Macon, Georgia. Jefferson Davis arrived at the town under guard soon after Wirz did. Northern newspaper correspondents rushed to the camp when they heard that the two villains were in one place.[21] The two men did not see or speak to one another. Indeed, they had never met or had any contact, and they would never communicate or cross paths in the future. Yet by the time that Wirz and Davis ended up in their final sites of confinement—Wirz at the Old Capitol Prison in Washington; Davis at Fort Monroe in Virginia—U.S. Judge Advocate General Joseph Holt and U.S. Secretary of War Edwin Stanton were certain that they could establish a link between the two men and send both to the gallows.

The Wirz trial began on August 21, 1865. Crammed into a small room in the Old Capitol Prison were Wirz and his two attorneys; a nine-member military commission presided over by Major General

Lew Wallace; and Colonel Norton P. Chipman, who served as judge advocate of the commission, a position analogous to a civilian prosecutor. Stanton and Holt were also there. Hundreds of others tried to attend—newspaper reporters, former prisoners and their relatives, and the generally curious—but only a few were able to gain entry. There simply were not enough seats.

Stanton and Holt wanted the trial to create a sensation. They hoped that the northern fury that would result from the proceedings could be harnessed and used to mount a similar prosecution of Jefferson Davis and other former high-ranking members of the Confederate government. At Stanton's request, Henry Raymond, the editor of the *New York Times,* published daily proceedings in his paper.[22] To enlarge the spectacle, Holt had the trial moved to a larger venue: the court of claims in the basement of the Capitol. Attendees were sickened by the tales they heard—and could not get enough of them. Susan Wallace, the wife of the presiding commissioner, Lew Wallace, told her brother of a female spectator who attended every day of the trial "and whenever there is anything particularly horrible sits and cries."[23]

The new site of the proceedings, a civilian courtroom in a non-military building, conveyed the impression that Wirz would get a fair trial. When Wirz's attorneys told the commissioners that their client was chronically weak and feverish, the authorities set up a comfortable settee for the defendant in the middle of the courtroom. Lying there, pale and small, Wirz looked pathetic. Somehow, this only made the crowd hate him more.

In the proceedings against him, the commission offered no kindness. It gave only the slightest nod to the regular rules of criminal procedure. It allowed hearsay testimony—for the prosecution only. Judge Advocate Chipman listed dozens of "victims" in the written charges against Wirz; next to each, he simply wrote "whose name is unknown." The two attorneys assigned to represent Wirz could barely mount a defense. Chipman told defense witnesses prior to their testimony that any support that they showed for Wirz would be treated as sympathy for the Confederacy. They could be prosecuted as a result. Some of the scheduled defense witnesses bowed out. Others were denounced by Chipman as disloyal or untrustworthy; they were dismissed by the commission. The president of the commission, Lew Wallace, ended the proceedings before the defense finished presenting its case.[24]

Members of the commission had made up their minds at the start: Wirz deserved to die. It was the result that most northerners expected and demanded. Even Walt Whitman, that lover of humanity, said that Wirz should suffer "blackest, escapeless, endless damnation."[25] Wirz was doomed from the beginning.

The trial of Henry Wirz was also, in effect, a trial of the Confederacy. The military commission, along with the northern public generally, came to link Wirz's evil deeds to the sins of slaveholding and secession. In condemning Wirz, the victors of the war meant also to condemn the Slave Power. In hanging Wirz, they would kill the Confederacy completely. Then, perhaps, they could feel that the war was truly over.

Chipman, along with his superior Joseph Holt, implicated the entire Confederacy in Wirz's crimes. Only by studying the suffering at Andersonville, Holt declared, could one truly "understand the inner and real life of the Rebellion, and the hellish criminality and brutality of the traitors who maintained it."[26] Chipman formally charged Wirz with murder and violation of the "laws and customs" of war. But he laced the charging document with scathing, prejudicial pronouncements of the moral transgressions of Wirz and the Confederacy. Wirz and his superiors, Chipman declared, were infected by "wickedness," a word that appeared dozens of times in the official charges.

Although it was not the case, as some would later record, that Wirz was accused of "war crimes"—that phrase did not appear with any regularity in the United States until the twentieth century—the atrocities that Wirz supposedly committed do sound like war crimes to the modern ear. At Andersonville during the winter months, Chipman claimed, Wirz arbitrarily removed clothes and blankets from prisoners and let them freeze. In summer, he offered no refuge to those without hovels. He let them languish under the "burning sun." He starved them all. He stuck some with poison, claiming that it was vaccination. And, most infamously, he forced them to drink foul water and shot those who sought clean water across the "dead line."[27]

Many of the horrific acts described by Chipman and his witnesses were meant to evoke the horrors of slavery. By linking the crimes of Andersonville to the crimes of slavery, the architects of the prosecution amplified the evils of Wirz—and of the Confederacy. In recounting the sins of the vanquished, the victors were performing a common end-of-war ritual.

Tales of the use of bloodhounds at Andersonville contained perhaps the most familiar echoes of slavery. Chipman offered a preview of these stories in one of his opening charges: "Wirz, still pursuing his evil purpose, did keep and use ferocious and bloodthirsty beasts, dangerous to human life, called bloodhounds, to hunt down prisoners of war . . . and encourage the said beasts to seize, tear, mangle, and maim the bodies and limbs of said fugitive prisoners of war."[28]

Chipman asked every former prisoner who testified about the bloodhounds. One former prisoner spoke of some friendly nose-rubbing with a dog during his escape. Other than that, every story about bloodhounds presented at the trial was hearsay. Former prisoners had *heard* that Wirz kept ferocious dogs but had never seen them. They had *heard* of an unnamed escapee who had been tracked down and mauled by one of the dogs. As with all the hearsay evidence against Wirz, the commission let the testimonies stand. Why was Chipman so insistent that stories of bloodhounds at Andersonville appear in the record? Because he knew they would make northerners think about southern slavery.

Southern slaveholders and the northern antislavery activists who wrote about them had made plantation bloodhounds notorious. These were not modern-day bloodhounds, the name of an actual breed known for cute droopy ears, friendly faces, and cuddly dispositions. "Bloodhound" in the nineteenth century was a generic term. It applied to any dog used to hunt. When used in connection with the Slave South, it described a dog used to hunt the enslaved. The animals were not violent by nature. They were trained to be ferocious by slaveholders. In the words of the historian Walter Johnson, they were "weaponized dogs."[29] Frederick Douglass had written in his widely read narrative, published in 1845, that anyone enslaved was haunted by the specter of being "torn to pieces by the fangs of the terrible bloodhound."[30] Harriet Beecher Stowe's *Uncle Tom's Cabin,* the bestselling American novel before the Civil War, featured many dogs trained to track and attack human beings. The terror that the hounds inspired was a crucial part of the many stage adaptations of the novel.[31]

The stories of bloodhounds at the Wirz trial fused the horrors of slavery with the evil of the Confederate prison at Andersonville. Sometimes the testimony made the connection explicit. One former prisoner, a U.S. soldier originally from Virginia, said that he was "acquainted with blood-hounds" such as those purportedly at Andersonville because he had used them himself before the war to help slaveholders hunt escapees. "I caught negroes in Hardie county, Virginia," he explained. "I used to have real good sport there at it."[32]

Eliciting tales of what one witness termed "negro hounds" was only one way that the prosecution kept the shadow of slavery lurking over Wirz's trial.[33] Chipman made a special effort to get witnesses to recount how Wirz forced white inmates, regardless of their ethnicity, to do hard labor alongside enslaved people who had been brought to the prison from neighboring farms. Chipman wanted all to know that Confederates like Wirz were capable of treating white soldiers like Black slaves. One witness, a Black civilian, recounted hearing that Wirz told captured Black soldiers that he would release them only if they disavowed the Union and performed manual labor for the Confederacy. If they refused, Wirz threatened, then he would block all prisoners, regardless of race, from ever being exchanged. In other words, Wirz tried to enslave free Black soldiers.[34]

Chipman also solicited testimony about whippings. Guards most often used the whip against Black men, either enslaved workers or Black U.S. soldiers.[35] But whites, too, were whipped. Witnesses told of white U.S. soldiers living in such filth at Andersonville that they looked like Blacks.[36] "White negroes" was the way that one witness described two such prisoners.[37] Other witnesses told of white prisoners who blackened their skin before attempting to escape so that they might pass as enslaved Blacks once they were in the Georgia countryside. When such escapees were caught, Wirz ordered them whipped, even though he knew that they were white. Such had always been the fate of runaways, he once supposedly remarked.[38] Chipman insisted on hearing more about the whippings. How many lashes were given? How long did the torture last? What did the whip look like? Did the victim scream in pain? Did he die?[39]

Chipman fed the audience a pornography of pain, a strategy long used by antislavery reformers.[40]

With one witness, a white man, Chipman asked for confirmation of the story that a Black soldier had been whipped simply for talking to a white woman who had been touring the prison. The witness did not play along. He replied that he knew of no such motive given for a whipping.[41] But the question served its purpose. It raised the old antislavery argument that slavery was both a cause and a consequence of southern white men's pathological insecurity about their manhood—hence their need to torture Black men in the name of protecting white women.[42]

Chipman and his superiors wanted northerners to see Andersonville as something more than a POW camp. It was part of the larger slave system that was responsible for the war. A similar argument had appeared in *Frank Leslie's Illustrated Newspaper* in an article accompanying images of skeletal POWs. The article, titled "Southern Inhumanity," contended that "the barbarism of slavery" was to blame for the treatment of the prisoners.[43] In his closing statement to the Wirz commission, Chipman declared that Andersonville, like slavery, was a "relic of the dark ages now happily passed away."[44] By executing Wirz, Americans could put "the dark ages" behind them.

As the Wirz trial broadened its focus and became a condemnation of the Slave South as a whole, Jefferson Davis nearly dropped from sight. Yet it was Davis whom Holt and Stanton had hoped would suffer most as a result of the trial—aside from Wirz himself, of course. In his closing statement, Chipman tried to bring Davis back into the picture, but it was too late. He suggested that Wirz was but one member of a conspiracy run by Jefferson Davis. The claim now seemed absurd. When Davis was in the Confederate White House, did he transmit specific instructions to Wirz to carry out the whippings, the dog attacks, and the poisonings? These were the atrocities of the entire Confederacy, not merely its president. Someone had to pay for the crimes, to be sure, but that person already had been selected: Henry Wirz. Chipman had no evidence that Davis was directly involved in the suffering that had been inflicted at Andersonville. Holt's staff along with Francis Lieber had scoured the prison records and the rebel archives looking for evidence of Davis's complicity. They had found nothing. The best that Chipman could do was to argue that it would have been impossible for Davis not to know about the situation at the prison.[45] In Holt's final report on the trial, he dismissed the absence of proof against Davis and thundered that the atrocities of Andersonville were the work of the "chiefs of the rebel confederacy." They would "be held responsible by the judgment of history and by the abhorrence of the civilized world."[46]

In Wirz's statement to the commission, which he delivered near the end of the proceedings, he ridiculed the efforts by U.S. authorities to blame Andersonville on a small ring of conspirators led by Davis. Wirz rightly pointed out that the trial had delivered a version of crimes "outraging humanity" so epic in scale that "every general, colonel, and captain in the rebel service" would have to be held accountable.[47] How could Chipman now single out only Davis, Wirz, and a few others? he asked.

Wirz could have tried to save himself by blaming Davis for Andersonville. He knew that this was what Chipman and his superiors wanted him to do. According to one account, which has never been verified, Stanton offered the commandant a deal the night before the execution: you pin Andersonville on Davis, we'll save your neck. If Stanton tried such a gambit, it obviously did not work. Wirz went to the gallows never having implicated Davis in any misdeed. For this he would be revered as a hero and martyr by Confederates and then neo-Confederates for decades to come.[48]

It was not from love of the Confederacy that Wirz refused to implicate Davis. Already Wirz was hated by Unionists; if he named Davis, he would be scorned by Confederates as well. More important, he knew that nothing he said would save his life. If Stanton did in fact offer Wirz a deal, Wirz must have known that the war secretary could never have kept his side of the bargain. The clamor for the commandant's death was too loud. Also, because any death sentence issued by a military court had to be reviewed by the president, a commutation of Wirz's sentence to imprisonment—the carrot purportedly dangled by Stanton—had to come officially from Andrew Johnson, and that was never going to happen. Johnson had stepped back a bit from his "traitors must be punished" line in his May 1865 amnesty proclamation, but a commutation of Wirz's sentence would have been too complete a retreat. The May proclamation had explicitly denied amnesty to Confederate commandants like Wirz.[49]

On October 31, 1865, Holt officially approved the death sentence that the military commission had given Wirz. "The annals of our race present nowhere and at no time a darker field of crime than that of Andersonville," he sermonized. "And it is fortunate for the interests alike of public justice and of historic truth, that from this field the veil has been so faithfully and so completely laid bare."[50] Had Holt replaced the word "Andersonville" with "the Slave Power"—or, better yet, "the Confederacy"—few northerners would have objected. The "veil" in question had covered all of rebeldom. Now that it had been removed, it was time to apply the noose, though only to Henry Wirz.

The only real chance that Wirz ever had of evading execution was on procedural grounds. From the start of the trial his lawyers had claimed that he could not be tried by a military commission. Military trials of non-U.S. servicemen like Wirz could only be held in a time of war, they argued, but "the United States are now at peace." "The lately existing civil war is ended."[51]

Nothing put forward by the prosecution challenged this narrative. Everyone, from Stanton to Holt to Chipman to the hundreds of witnesses brought to the stand, had spoken of the war as an event of the past, not the present. The charges against Wirz even included an actual end date. They spoke of his crimes having occurred "on or about the first day of March, A.D. 1864, and on divers other days between that day and the tenth day of April, 1865."[52] The start date was the point when Wirz took up his post at Andersonville. The end date was, of course, the day after Lee's surrender. But at Andersonville, the war had not ended with the Appomattox surrender. If the closing of Andersonville was linked to an event, it was not Lee's surrender but Johnston's, which came weeks afterward. Maybe the prosecution had taken liberties with the closing date of the war, but it had nonetheless implied all along that the war had, at some point, come to a close. If that were true, then Wirz's point about the illegitimacy of a trial by military commission had merit.

This was not the first time that U.S. military authorities had to engage with the argument. Lawyers for the Lincoln assassins, who also had been tried by a military commission, had made a similar point. At that trial, the argument was comparatively easy to parry. The prosecution left open the possibility that other assassins might still be at large and planning further attacks—a situation that suggested that, in a narrow way at least, the war continued. No similar argument could be made at the Wirz trial.

Holt therefore offered a different sort of argument, one that he had rehearsed in his discussions with Stanton about how a military commission might be used to try Jefferson Davis. Holt fed the words to Chipman, who read them to the commission. "As we recede from a state of actual war and approach a condition of profound peace," Chipman recited, "we doubtless travel away from the corner-stone upon which the military commission as a judicial tribunal rests." But the transition from war to peace was incomplete, Chipman said: no one should be fooled by the "mere suspension of hostilities on the part of rebels in the field." "The spirit of rebellion is still rampant," Chipman declared, channeling Holt.[53] For Holt, the war consisted of two overlapping conflicts, one against the armies of rebellion, the other against the "spirit" of rebellion. The first conflict was over; the second was not. So the war had never ceased. The army still had the power to try to punish its foes. Holt no doubt wished it were Davis that was heading for the executioner. But Wirz would do for now.

On November 10, 1865, the scaffold door was sprung, and Wirz dropped through. With him went the "spirit of the rebellion," a reporter wrote; "another sanguinary agent of the slave power" was gone.[54]

An agent had been slain, but the Slave Power itself, the animus of the "spirit of the rebellion," lived on. It would not be killed by hangings alone. After Wirz, the public lost its taste for executions. Less than a year after the hanging, a U.S. military commission tried the commandant of a different Confederate POW camp and acquitted him of all charges.[55] By then, the tide of northern sentiment had turned against executing even Jefferson Davis—though Stanton and Holt still hoped to see him swing. How, then, was the "spirit of the rebellion" to be snuffed out? How would the country know when the war against the "spirit" was over? There was no obvious answer. Such a war would abide no deadline.

13

Imperfectly Closed

THE RESILIENCE OF the Slave Power was much on the mind of Frederick Douglass as he prepared an address to deliver at the end of 1865. The subject of the speech was Abraham Lincoln, but Douglass planned to cover much broader ground. He would argue that although the Confederacy had experienced a "sudden collapse and downfall," the desire and power remained among "a privileged class in the Southern States to make slavery perpetual in this continent." Lincoln would be vindicated, Douglass wrote, and the Civil War truly over, only with "the utter extinction of every root and fibre, not merely of slavery, but of the insolent, aggressive, and malignant oligarchy . . . founded upon it."[1]

Douglass was hardly alone in the belief that the Slave Power remained a threat. The notion was at the heart of proposals by Radical Republicans like Thaddeus Stevens and Charles Sumner to punish or at least disempower southern white elites. The Radicals' enemies attacked them as vengeful extremists who put retribution over the good of the nation. In fact, the Radicals were not extremists but realists. They understood that the true end of the war came not with ceasefires and surrenders but with the removal of the war's cause. That might mean property confiscation and exclusion from the polls for whites. It definitely meant emancipation for Blacks: not only the formal end of slavery but the end of anti-Black laws that had given all southern whites an undue purchase on power. The Radicals differed on the details of how to proceed. Stevens wanted rebel land confiscated and distributed to freed people. Douglass prioritized voting rights. Regardless of their priorities, Radicals in general accepted Richard Henry Dana's stance that the war against the Slave Power continued. The Indiana congressman George W. Julian invoked Dana in a speech in November 1865, contending that "you can hold the rebels in the strong grasp of war till the end and purpose of the war, which is a lasting peace, shall be made sure." Julian mocked the notion that Appomattox marked an immediate end of war. Had we fought the Confederacy "as a mighty public foe . . . up to the moment of the surrender of Gen. Lee," Julian asked, "and then, by some devilish necromancy, were we forced to make a dead halt, and recognize in the rebels the very rights they had sinned away?" The notion was ridiculous. Dana agreed, of course, though he did not share Julian's opinion on when the grasp of war could be released. For Dana, as for Douglass, equal rights and Black suffrage would suffice as a barrier to future war. For Julian, trials and executions of "a score or two of the most conspicuous of the rebel leaders" also were necessary—"not for vengeance, but to satisfy public justice, and make expensive the enterprise of treason for all time to come."[2]

Specifics differed among proposals for how to crush what Douglass called the "malignant oligarchy" that had started the war. But the premise behind every plan was the same: the war against Confederate rebellion may have been won, but the war against the greater evil—slavery and the Slave Power—still continued.

When Douglass drafted his address, slavery still existed in the United States not merely as a rhetorical construct but as an actual practice of racialized forced labor. The constitutional amendment abolishing slavery, sent to the states for ratification by Congress early in 1865, had yet to be adopted. A number of northern state legislatures had voted for ratification immediately, but then there had been a lull. Some northern state legislators, even those who supported emancipation, were troubled by the amendment's second clause, which gave Congress the power to enforce the prohibition of slavery "by appropriate legislation." The clause had received almost no attention during the congressional debate of the measure, but opponents now fixated on it. What federal legislation might Congress deem "appropriate"? they asked. They insisted that Republicans meant to use the clause to force Black suffrage on the states—even those that had stayed loyal to the Union. Republicans had denied that Black freedom must entail Black suffrage during the amendment debate, but they were not to be trusted, opponents insisted.

White fear of the Black ballot is what kept New York from ratifying the abolition amendment, despite the fact that the state had abolished slavery nearly forty years earlier. New York still had a law limiting Black suffrage to men with $250 worth of property—a significant restriction (the 2025 equivalent would be about $5,000). Every attempt by New York African Americans and white abolitionists to remove the qualification, including a statewide referendum in 1860, had failed. Anti-amendment legislators finally yielded in late April 1865, not because of any change of heart toward Black rights but rather because of Lincoln's death. The shocking assassination of the president made opponents of the amendment vulnerable to the charge that they were defiling the memory of the slain emancipator. As Lincoln's funeral train approached Albany, a Democratic editor in the city advised Manton Marble, the powerful editor of the *New York World*, the most widely circulated Democratic newspaper in the country, "from this point let us refuse to allow the Dem. party to ever *seem* in a disloyal position or as the defenders of Slavery."[3] The next day, the Democrats in the legislature allowed the vote for the amendment to carry.

Other loyal states opposed to the amendment held their ground. New Jersey, firmly under the control of the Democratic Party, voted against ratification. So did Delaware and Kentucky. All of these states had African American residents who were still legally enslaved. Delaware and Kentucky were two of the four Border States, states where slavery was legal when the war began but which had never seceded. (The other two, Maryland and Missouri, had passed state measures abolishing slavery prior to congressional passage of the antislavery amendment.) New Jersey, unlike Delaware and Kentucky, had passed an abolition law prior to the Civil War, but the measure emancipated the enslaved gradually, not immediately. The result was that some Black people in New Jersey were still enslaved at the time the war broke out. Slavery was nearly defunct in Delaware as well, though white legislators in the state were set on blocking any measure, including the antislavery amendment, that might be used by Republicans to overturn the state's proscriptions against

Black rights and Black suffrage. Not until 1901 did Delaware vote to ratify the amendment.[4] In early July 1865, a former North Carolina governor had privately written that while the organized rebellion had been defeated, "with reference to Emancipation, we are but at the beginning of the war." He was thinking of slavery in the former states of the Confederacy when he wrote that, but the statement held true as well in some of the states that had stayed in the Union.

Of these, Kentucky was the site of the fiercest battles in the war against slavery. Back in July, the U.S. general in charge of the state, John M. Palmer, had gone only so far as to declare Blacks in the state "substantially free"—a status of de facto freedom that carried no formal rights. Kentucky Blacks claimed official freedom rights anyway. They took travel passes issued to them by the U.S. Army and held them up as "freedom papers" that severed any obligation to their masters. Hundreds of Black families headed north across the Ohio River into the land of undisputed freedom. The risk they took was enormous. Whites patrolled the countryside, capturing and torturing Blacks who claimed that they were free. Sometimes the patrollers cropped the ears of their captives, an old punishment to mark Blacks permanently as enslaved. An officer of the Freedmen's Bureau in Kentucky wrote that "the devotees of the barbarism" were clinging to slavery's "putrid carcass with astonishing tenacity."[5]

General Palmer wrongly assumed that Kentucky whites would back down once they saw that their actions were driving their primary labor force across the Ohio. But the prospect of slavery's end only made whites more committed to using any means necessary to keep the institution alive in their state. They made the state election in August a referendum on the antislavery amendment— and defeated the pro-amendment faction soundly. They wrote to President Johnson demanding that he stop the army from issuing passes that enabled Blacks to leave their masters. Because Kentucky had remained loyal to the Union, Johnson, like Lincoln before him, was inclined to reward the state with promises of noninterference with slavery. He demanded and received assurances from Palmer that Blacks were not receiving "freedom papers" from the army. State judges ruled that passes already issued by the army were illegitimate—and certainly not to be regarded as "freedom papers." One judge even indicted Palmer for securing a pass for an African

American woman named Ellen a few months earlier. Palmer ended up avoiding prosecution. But the events of late summer 1865 had their effect on the general. He had lost all confidence that Kentucky whites would come around on the issue of slavery. As he wrote to a friend in September, every time he informed white Kentuckians that Blacks were free, he was told he was wrong.[6]

South of Kentucky, in the slave states of the former Confederacy, the army had a freer hand to wage war on behalf of emancipation. But there as well, whites found ways to keep slavery alive, or at least to maintain the antebellum racial order. In Louisiana, arcane local assemblies known as "police juries" revived the old "patrol" system that had undergirded slavery. Black people found off their plantations without permission could be arrested and imprisoned. They could even be subjected to corporal punishment, including whipping.[7] In Mississippi, a reporter for the *Army and Navy Journal* was chagrined to see a slate of measures designed to ensure the abuse of freed people. Among these was a law preventing Blacks from testifying against whites (Kentucky had the same law and would hold on to it for years to come). The ban effectively ensured that any white act of violence against an African American would go unpunished—at least by the civil authorities. The news item from Mississippi was one of many offered by the *Journal*'s reporter as evidence that the army was still needed in the South and that there was validity to the much-maligned "hypothesis" that "the war is not ended."[8]

In areas of the South outside the army's control, there could be no war against slavery, at least none waged by U.S. soldiers. The vast swaths of Texas hinterlands offered chilling examples. In DeWitt County, not far from San Antonio, a sheriff shot a Black man for whistling "Yankee Doodle."[9] U.S. General Gordon Granger's "Juneteenth" proclamation issued from the coastal city of Galveston during the summer had little impact on the belief of masters in the Texas interior that slavery still existed. They faced no challenge from the U.S. Army, which was not able to move significant numbers of troops into the area until late 1865. Blacks were left to fight their own battles against slavery. Leaving the plantation was an obvious first step, but even that basic act of self-liberation carried a lethal risk. In Rusk County in eastern Texas, whites shot and hanged Blacks who had left their plantations to attempt to cross the Sabine River, where they had heard there was freedom.[10]

Northerners knew little about the persistence of slavery. Stories from remote areas of the South rarely reached northern newspapers. To be sure, dozens of northern reporters and freelance writers traveled to the South in mid-1865 to report on conditions there, but for the most part they chose routes that were well protected by occupying U.S. troops. That meant they were unlikely to see or hear about the practice of slavery in regions far away from occupation zones. But they saw enough to raise concerns in the North that some form of racial servitude akin to slavery might emerge to take the place of the old, formal system of chattel slavery. All of the correspondents who earned fame for their dispatches from the South—Sidney Andrews, John Richard Dennett, J. T. Trowbridge, and Whitelaw Reid foremost among them—told of plans afoot by whites to keep Blacks in some form of bondage. The prospect did not seem to trouble many of the correspondents, all of whom were white, as the dominant view among them was that the freed people were as yet unready for freedom. Reporting from South Carolina in early September, Andrews concluded that "the white man must be taught what the negro's rights are, and the negro must be taught to wait patiently and wisely for the full recognition of those rights in his own old home."[11] The overall sense conveyed by the reports was that the southern labor system was in a transition away from slavery, even if the pace of the change was regrettably slow in places.[12]

A profoundly different view of the South, one much more attuned to Blacks' experience there of continuity rather than change when it came to slavery, was offered by Carl Schurz, a former major general in the U.S. Army. According to Schurz, even those southern whites who accepted the logic that slavery died with the rebellion could not get their heads around a new reality in which Blacks were actually free. They might say in public that slavery was dead, one southern white told Schurz in Vicksburg, but in private "it is so difficult for our people to realize that the negro is a free man."[13]

Schurz mentioned this exchange in a private letter to President Johnson. Johnson had asked Schurz to make the trip early in the summer. The two men had become acquainted the year before, when Johnson had been the provisional governor of Tennessee and Schurz had been stationed in Nashville as a major general. Schurz had been reluctant to accept the assignment from the president—a journey through the Deep South in the miasma of midsummer held little appeal—but friends, including Charles Sumner, had persuaded him to go.

Schurz, well-known for his abolitionist leanings, was an odd choice for Johnson, who was growing more conservative by the day. Schurz had already made public his disappointment with the president's policies on race. He believed that Black men should have the right to vote and should participate in the re-forming of southern state governments. Johnson thought Blacks were unfit for entry into the American body politic—maybe permanently so—though he had been careful not to express his opinions publicly. Why, then, did Johnson tap Schurz? The decision was based on a political miscalculation by Johnson, one of many that he would make in the months to come. This one, though, turned out to have particular significance in the ongoing debate, soon to be a full-blown battle, over whether or not the Civil War was over.

Johnson's plan was to use the growing rift within the Republican Party on issues like Black suffrage to his political advantage. He thought that he could get Republicans opposed to progressive measures to break from their party and fuse with Democrats, the party that Johnson had been loyal to all his life. (The ticket that he had joined with Lincoln in 1864 was Republican but had billed itself as a broader coalition, the *National Union* Party; Johnson had been added to the ticket to lend credence to the idea that the party was a safe haven for pro-war Democrats.) Johnson was prodded toward his scheme by some of the most inept political strategists of the day. One was Montgomery Blair, a former Democrat from Maryland who had been Lincoln's postmaster general. Another was James Gordon Bennett, the editor of the popular *New York Herald*, who claimed to be a political independent but whose sympathies were unquestionably with the Democrats. Carl Schurz was to be a pawn in the scheme. Johnson counted on him to send the president a report after the trip that touted Black suffrage and other measures that moderate Republicans opposed. Johnson would then use the document as a wedge to split the Republicans and drive the conservatives among them into an alliance with the Democrats. For months Blair had been pushing the strategy of using "the Negro equality question" to bring the Democratic Party back into power.[14] Johnson knew that the coalition he envisioned would face opposition from Republicans in Congress when that body convened in December. But he was confident in his abilities to win over ordinary white Americans, northern and southern, and turn them against any opposition he might face, whether Republicans in Congress or oligarchs in the South. His inflated sense that he could become a populist leader like his hero (and namesake) Andrew Jackson was fueled by fawning courtiers like Blair.

Johnson's confidence was also boosted by dispatches that he received from his true emissary to the South—not Schurz but Harvey M. Watterson, a newspaper editor, longtime friend, and fellow Tennessee Democrat. Johnson had secretly sent Watterson south weeks before dispatching Schurz. The newsman confirmed what Johnson already chose to believe, that "an undivided South and every conservative man in the North, will ere long be rallying around and sustaining" Johnson's presidency.[15]

The part of Johnson's plan involving Schurz depended on the abolitionist issuing his dispatches only to the president. Johnson could then repackage the material and present it to the American people—*his* people—as evidence of a plot by extremist Republicans to revolutionize the country.

Johnson's scheme threatened to come undone when Schurz began sending dispatches to the *Boston Advertiser*. The newspaper published the reports, and other papers began reprinting them. The president was enraged. He had lost control of the flow of information. This would not have been a problem if the reports by Schurz had contained only radical proposals of the sort that Johnson meant to use to discredit extremist Republicans. But they also contained stories of white southern intransigence that all northerners, no matter their opinion of radicalism, would likely find unacceptable.

Most former Confederates, Schurz reported, had not accepted defeat—or emancipation. The majority of white planters he met declared that Blacks could only be made to work through "physical compulsion"—meaning whipping.[16] Planters expected Blacks to accept coercion and torture as if there had never been a war against slavery. One white man in Georgia told Schurz that when he learned that a Black woman on his farm had refused to be whipped, he reasoned that Black people in the neighborhood must be planning an insurrection.[17] In Mississippi, Schurz learned of rampant violence against Blacks, including assassinations. Instead of hunting down the offenders, the conservative governor, William Sharkey, had called up a state militia consisting only of whites, most of them ex-Confederates. The U.S. Army commander in the state had countermanded the order. Schurz's report from Mississippi, which ended up being reprinted in papers across the North, read as an argument that the South was still in rebellion. Johnson in a fury telegraphed Schurz, ordering him to publish a retraction and to keep his future reports private.

Schurz refused. His final report forced readers to wonder whether it might be too soon to say that the war was over. If southern whites could still behave as slaveholders, then what exactly had the war accomplished? According to a U.S. officer stationed in the South who was quoted by Schurz, it was just as true now as before the war that "the whites esteem the blacks their property by natural right."[18] Schurz concluded that the U.S. government must declare that "national control in the south will not cease" until there was a visible "new order of things" in place of the old system of slavery. Until then, "security" in the South remained uncertain.[19] He had restated Richard Henry Dana's now-familiar dictum: until the South was secure, the United States must hold it in a grasp of war.

Johnson now had to reframe his political strategy. He might score points by attacking radical-sounding propositions for Black equality, but he could lose the game altogether if the people believed that rebellious slaveholders still threatened the Union. He needed proof that slavery was dead and the South secure. In short, he had to convince the country that the Civil War was over.

Johnson called on Ulysses Grant for help in the endeavor. He asked the general in chief to tour the South and confirm that all was well there. Grant was savvy enough to know that the purpose of the trip was to generate a narrative of sectional harmony that would counter Schurz's report of continued hostilities. For Johnson, General Grant, the most revered American of the moment, was the

perfect man to do his bidding. Grant had a good reason to make his
countrymen believe that the nation was at peace, not war. His reputation as the Appomattox peacemaker was jeopardized by reports
like those of Schurz that focused on continuing hostilities. Grant
had never liked Schurz. The abolitionist had no military training,
only political connections, and he used his undeserved rank to spout
policy positions. In Grant's view, that all made Schurz "a political
general" of the worst sort. Unlike Schurz, Grant believed that little
more had to be done in the South aside from a brief period of army
occupation while the southern state governments got back on their
feet. In his farewell speech to the army in July 1865, he had promised "perpetual peace." He remained untroubled as reports of a surge
of white violence against Blacks arrived at his headquarters in late
summer and early fall.

Only much later, in May 1866, would Grant begin to take seriously the reports of white insurgency in the South. At that point, he
would turn against the elites of the South, telling them angrily that
they no longer deserved the goodwill that he had shown them at
Appomattox. The "golden moment" of leniency had passed, he told
a reporter, as had the prospect of perpetual peace.[20] Later still, after
he became president in 1869, his resurgent anger against the white
South turned to action. He sent army units into the most hostile
regions of South Carolina, ordering them to break the grip of the
Ku Klux Klan.[21]

But all that lay in the future. In the fall of 1865, when Grant
agreed to President Johnson's request that he tour the South, he still
believed that southern whites had accepted their defeat with dignity.
In October, he assured a U.S. commander stationed in the South
that "we are now at peace." He told Secretary of War Stanton that
the South's "submission" was "perfect."[22] Johnson knew that he could
count on Grant to put the lie to Schurz's report and persuade the
people that no further grasp of war was needed.

Grant dutifully complied. He donned civilian clothes to avoid
appearing as a gloating conqueror. He spent only five days touring
the South (Schurz's trip had lasted about three months) and visited only those cities along the Eastern Seaboard that had long been
subdued by U.S. Army occupiers. All his conversations were with
whites, not Blacks. The ex-Confederates he met with were cordial

and unequivocal in their Unionism. If there were signs of persistent resentment, Grant missed them—or chose to ignore them. One of his traveling companions noticed that the southern women "who called themselves ladies make faces at the Yankee officers." "They express openly what their husbands and brothers feel but do not show."[23] The observation comported with a phenomenon widespread across the South: elite white women often served as the repositories of Confederate bitterness. A white man from North Carolina bragged to his friend that his wife was teaching their boy "*to hate a Yankee. . . . He cannot but hate them, His bread is buttered with hatred, his milk is sweetened with it, his top spins and his ball bounces with it.*"[24]

Grant's report to President Johnson told a different story, one of harmony rather than rage. It offered the happy news that "the mass of thinking men of the south" accepted submission "in good faith." These men conceded that the divisive questions responsible for the war, "slavery and State rights," had been settled decisively by arms in favor of the Union's position.[25]

The use of the phrase "thinking men" was telling. As his behavior at Appomattox had demonstrated, Grant believed that the bonds of male honor could keep sectional and political divisions at bay. Any flare-ups of insurgency in the South since the Confederate surrenders must not be taken too seriously, Grant assumed, as they were the work of lesser men, non-thinking men, men without honor, and such men could always be held in check by the South's "best men."

Johnson wanted Americans to believe that southern whites accepted not only defeat but also the end of slavery. But dispatches from Schurz and from other northern travelers to the South were filled with accounts of southern whites determined to keep slavery alive. The possibility that slavery still survived raised the obvious question of what, exactly, the war had achieved. The question had a moral dimension—how could whites still allow Black people to be treated as chattel?—but that was not the issue that bothered most northerners, and it certainly troubled President Johnson not at all.

The pressing concern for most northerners was an existential one. If southern whites were willing to go to war over slavery in 1861, what would stop them from doing it again if they thought keeping slavery alive was a viable option? This argument had been crucial in winning reluctant emancipators over to the antislavery amendment when it had been approved by Congress and sent to the states for ratification in early February 1865. Abraham Lincoln and then his successor, Andrew Johnson, had encouraged newly formed legislatures in the South to ratify the measure, but only a few had done so. Lincoln and then Johnson also had demanded that southern state lawmakers prohibit slavery in their new state constitutions. This the southern states did. But it was not enough. So long as southern states stood against the antislavery amendment, they lent credence to fears in the North that the war against slavery would have to be refought. Johnson needed the amendment ratified—and quickly. Otherwise, when Congress came back into session in December 1865, it could use the fact of non-ratification, along with reports like those of Schurz, to bolster their case that slavery and rebellion continued.

By the end of the summer of 1865, most of the southern states and even a few of the northern ones had yet to vote on the amendment. For the amendment to be ratified, it needed approval from at least half a dozen more states.

The exact number of state ratifications needed was a matter of some contention. Some in the North questioned whether the southern states should be included in the tally that required approval of three-quarters of the states for ratification. Also, should the seceded states even be allowed to vote on the measure? Hadn't they declared themselves outside of the Union? Even if they had never left the Union—that is, if secession was unconstitutional in the first place— hadn't their rebellious actions rendered their governments illegitimate? If the national government allowed once-rebellious states to be part of the ratification process, wasn't it effectively declaring the states fully restored? These were all reasonable questions, but President Johnson did not have to worry about them. His predecessor had rendered them moot. Abraham Lincoln had declared in what turned out to be his final speech that the question of whether or not southern states were out of the Union was a "pernicious abstraction." Lincoln insisted that if new, pro-Union, pro-emancipation governments were formed in the once-rebellious states, they should be allowed to vote on the antislavery amendment. To exclude such states from the process, Lincoln said—a position taken by Senator Charles Sumner—would leave the amendment's legitimacy "questionable" in the eyes of later generations. With Lincoln's blessing, Secretary of State Seward, who was in charge of counting votes for ratification, treated reconstructed southern states as "in" so far as the amendment was concerned.[26]

It was Seward whom Johnson turned to in the fall of 1865 to hustle the amendment toward final adoption. The secretary of state, now almost fully recovered from the carriage accident and assassination attempt earlier in the year, was back on his game. He wanted the country to put the war behind it and to take up nationalist policies that he had long supported, such as territorial expansion. Seward was in favor of any strategy that would turn the nation's attention away from the residue of rebellion. Like most members of Andrew Johnson's administration, he found the president personally distasteful. But he shared Johnson's wish to take off the table divisive questions such as whether or not slavery still existed. He told a friend that he "dreaded the settlement of questions resulting from the war more than . . . the war itself."[27] In mid-November 1865, Seward wrote a note to the governor of every state that had yet to ratify the antislavery amendment, urging that a vote be taken "as soon as convenient."[28]

The amendment's enforcement clause, which had given some northern ratifiers pause, was for southern ratifiers a dreadful proposition. A Mississippi lawmaker warned that the clause, which authorized Congress to use "appropriate legislation" to prohibit slavery, "gives to Congress broad, and almost, I may say, unlimited power."[29] Like conservatives in the North, southern whites worried most that the federal government would use the clause to impose Black suffrage on the states.

Seward tried to assuage such fears with lawyerly parsing of the amendment's wording. Any notion that the enforcement clause would lead to Black suffrage was "querulous and unreasonable," he assured white southerners in a public letter. The "appropriate legislation" phrase, Seward said, was "really restraining in its effect, instead of enlarging the powers of Congress."[30] No one knew what Seward meant by the statement—probably Seward least of all. The Radical Republican Benjamin Butler denounced Seward's explanation as "sophistry."[31] The southern legislatures did not buy it, either. Mississippi voted against ratification, pointing to the enforcement clause as the stumbling block. Alabama and South Carolina took a different approach. They voted for ratification but attached declarations saying their approval was predicated on the understanding that Congress had no authority to legislate on the "political status" of the freed people. Was a state allowed to attach a rider to a vote for ratification? What was the national government supposed to do with ratifications that went off script? Such questions might have stalled the ratification process if they had been opened up to public debate. So Seward ignored them. He offered no public statement regarding the qualifying messages made by Alabama and South Carolina. Instead, he simply put both states in the "yes" column.

Using his creative counting method, Seward obtained the requisite number of votes for ratification in early December. Georgia's "yes" vote put the amendment over the top.

President Johnson was thrilled. His annual message to Congress of December 4 invoked the amendment to plead his case once again that the country could consider the war over. The amendment healed "the wound that is still imperfectly closed," Johnson declared.[32]

A healed wound imperfectly closed. That was an elegant metaphor. Too elegant for Johnson: it was almost certainly written by the historian George Bancroft, who ghost-wrote a number of Johnson's early state papers.[33] Had Johnson written it himself, or at least studied it carefully, he might have seen that it fell short of an absolute declaration of war's end. The wound could reopen, after all. Yet Johnson believed that the debate over the war's end or non-end was now finished—and he had won. Two weeks after the address, on December 18, he had Seward release the official proclamation declaring the antislavery amendment part of the Constitution. On the day of Seward's proclamation, Johnson by design released a statement meant to silence for good those who insisted that the country was still at war. The rebellion had been "suppressed," Johnson announced, and "the United States are in possession of every State in which the insurrection existed."[34]

The statement appeared in the president's preface to a set of documents that he issued in response to a request from the Senate. Sumner and like-minded Republicans in the Senate had demanded that Johnson make public the report by Schurz, so that all could see the abolitionist's account of the persistence of hostilities in the

South. Johnson was ready for this. He gave Republicans what they wanted—Schurz's report—but he bookended it between his own statement of the rebellion's suppression on one side and Grant's account of hostilities being "settled forever" on the other. As far as Johnson was concerned, his response to Congress, combined with Seward's proclamation announcing the adoption of the Thirteenth Amendment, closed the debate on whether the war was over.

In fact, the debate was only getting started. The *Chicago Tribune* mocked Johnson for ignoring Schurz's report and saying that "all is quiet on the Potomac!" Sumner thundered on the Senate floor that the president was guilty of "whitewashing" the true state of hostilities in the South. He demanded that the Schurz report be read aloud in its entirety on the Senate floor.[35]

Sumner's Republican colleagues rejected the proposal. For one thing, reciting the extensive document would take days, bringing all other Senate business to a halt. More troubling, it would antagonize the president, and most congressional Republicans still believed that Johnson was their ally—or at least not an enemy. Just before Congress met in December, Representative Schuyler Colfax of Indiana, the Speaker of the House of Representatives, told his colleagues to cooperate with the president, even if that meant taking only small steps toward their larger goals. "Let us make haste rather slowly," he advised.[36] Colfax opened the 39th Congress with words meant to harmonize with the president's assessment of the state of the country: "Congress resumes its legislative authority in these council halls, rejoicing that from shore to shore in our land there is peace."[37]

There *was* peace in the land—some peace, anyway—but the country was not *at* peace, and Colfax knew it. Anyone who had taken the Schurz report seriously knew it. So long as the fate of four million freed people, nearly 10 percent of the nation's population, remained unsettled, the country was in jeopardy. Former slaveholders could rebuild their treasonous oligarchy on the backs of the formerly enslaved. They were already doing so, not only in their day-to-day abuses of Black people but in their creation of local laws that preserved servitude more systematically. Such measures included anti-vagrancy ordinances that authorized whites to arrest

Blacks who had no written proof of employment. Once convicted of vagrancy, Blacks could be delivered to their former masters or leased out as unpaid servants to the highest bidder. In effect, a U.S. officer reported from the South, whites who had fought to preserve slavery sought "to accomplish by state legislation and by covert violation of law what they . . . failed to accomplish by Rebellion."[38] By the end of 1865, all of the legislatures in the South had adopted state-level laws modeled on the oppressive local ordinances. Together, the measures were known as the "Black Codes."

To some whites in the North, the danger facing the nation was less the possible reestablishment of slavery than the onset of a widespread Black uprising. In October 1865, the Black revolt in Morant Bay, Jamaica, convinced U.S. whites that race rebellion would spread to their country. Rumors of a coming "Christmas insurrection" by Black southerners spread across the nation in the last weeks of 1865. "We are preparing for a *war of races*," a South Carolina cotton planter wrote his old friend, a New England textile manufacturer, in December. He predicted "destruction to the women and children of the south and the extermination of the negro."[39] A Black soldier stationed in Mississippi suspected, perhaps correctly, that white leaders had created the Black rebellion hoax as an excuse to further curtail freed people's liberties. With all whites in a panic, he explained, former slaveholders would be able to "reasstablish [*sic*] a kind of secondary slavery."[40]

White leaders in the North were unsure what to make of the rumors. Grant, who still put too much trust in the words of white southerners, decided to assuage their fears. A week before Christmas, Grant recommended to Johnson that all Black soldiers who had been free before the war be mustered out as quickly as possible. He was troubled by reports from southern whites that these soldiers were responsible for the mass exodus of Black laborers from their former masters. As for Black soldiers who had been enslaved before the war, Grant wanted them held in the army but kept in remote areas where they would not antagonize southern whites or imbue any Black civilian with the dangerous notion that "the property of his late master should, by right, belong to him." Also, Grant believed that Black men who had been enslaved could benefit from the discipline that army life instilled. And if they continued to be commanded and surveilled by a mostly white officer class, that would go a long way toward allaying white fears of armed Black insurrections.[41]

For some whites, the danger of a race war was the main reason—even the only reason—for ending slavery. By their warped logic, emancipation was simply a sop to pacify Black men who otherwise would use their newly acquired military skills to destroy the nation.[42]

To be sure, there were plenty of Americans of all races who understood emancipation as a humanitarian imperative, but there were plenty of others—all of them white—who supported Black freedom simply for the sake of national security. These were people who lived in existential dread of the resurgence of war. Maybe the resurgence would be a replay of the proslavery rebellion. Maybe it would take the form of a Black insurrection. The only way to prevent either scenario was to make Black freedom a certainty.

How was this to be done? For Blacks themselves and more progressive white reformers, Blacks, at least the males among them, should become property holders and voters. For Republicans in Congress, the progressive approach was divisive. They had yet to settle on a consensus as to the rights and privileges needed to secure Black freedom. But they were united in the view expressed by Representative James A. Garfield: freedom at the very least had to entail more than "the bare privilege of not being chained."[43] For Andrew Johnson, though, this "bare privilege" was indeed the full extent of Black freedom. The adoption of the new antislavery amendment, Johnson believed, ended the need for further measures. He invested the amendment with near-magical qualities. Its mere presence in the Constitution, without enforcement or explication, put slavery and the war behind the country. It would "efface the sad memory of the past."[44]

When Congress convened in December 1865, most Republicans did not yet know the breadth of the chasm that divided them from the president when it came to attitudes toward Black Americans. They did not appreciate how much he was in thrall to Democrats determined to use progressive issues like Black suffrage to divide the opposition. And they had only begun to get an inkling of the depth of Johnson's racism.

Signs of Johnson's dismal regard of Blacks had been there from the start of his presidency, even earlier. Less than a month after Lincoln's assassination, the man who once had said that he would be Moses to the enslaved told a delegation of Black ministers that their people might end up in "a clime and country suited to you, should it be found that the two races cannot get along together."[45] By October, he was berating freed people publicly for frequenting "low saloons" and displaying general "licentiousness." Prevented by law under slavery from getting married, freed people were now marrying at a stunning rate, but Johnson doubted their readiness for family life. They had yet to appreciate, he chided, "the solemn contract with all the penalties in the association of married life." ("Penalties"? The word opened a window onto the quality of the president's own marriage.)[46] In a conversation with Chief Justice Salmon P. Chase, Johnson walked back his "Moses" speech. He had offered to be the Blacks' Moses, he said, "only if no better one could be found." He was now stepping aside from the role. He could not support Black suffrage, he told Chase, because he had come to believe that it would lead to results that he found unacceptable: "black members of the State Legislatures," or "maybe black Governors," even "a black President." And if Blacks were denied suffrage—which they must be—then they could have no future in the country. "The races must separate," he concluded to Chase.[47] Johnson then made the same statement publicly, in a speech to the 33rd U.S. Colored Troops. Using an awful metaphor, the president asked whether "the digestive powers of the American Government" could absorb the freed people and remain healthy. Johnson thought not. So the freed people most likely would have to depart for other lands. Where would they go? Johnson had no answer. But he had faith that "Providence" would "point out the way, and the mode, and the manner by which these people are to be separated, and to be taken to their lands of inheritance and promise."[48] It was appalling that the president could say such a thing to any group, but to say it to a regiment of Black soldiers, heroes who had proved their worth as Americans willing to die for the Union, revealed an extraordinary bigotry.

Yet whites were largely silent in reaction. The abolitionist Wendell Phillips was one of the exceptions. He called out Johnson for his anti-Black statements, putting the president in the same league as Jefferson Davis. Johnson had "spiked every Northern cannon,"

Phillips declared. He "makes himself three fourths rebel" so that the rebel states "may be one fourth Union."[49]

Frederick Douglass, too, saw Johnson for what he was. At a meeting with the president that Douglass attended with other Black reformers, Johnson again suggested that the "emigration" of Blacks was the only alternative to their "extermination" by whites.[50] Disgusted that an agent of the Slave Power now occupied the White House, Douglass quipped that the man who had begun "as a Moses" was now revealed "as a Pharaoh."[51]

Despite all that had come to light about Johnson's true beliefs, most Republicans in Congress somehow held out hope that that he would work with them—or at least stay out of their way—as they secured the country against the rebellious remnants of the Slave Power. Once they had done that, they would release the South from the grasp of war and join Johnson in declaring peace established.

14

Proclaiming Peace

A s the 39th Congress in early 1866 worked to frame laws that would reconstruct the Union and secure the freedom of the once-enslaved, the proceedings kept getting hung up on the question of if and when the Civil War had ended.

One of the first things Congress had done when it convened in December 1865 was to create the Joint Committee on Reconstruction, which was to set the terms by which states that had seceded could be deemed by Congress to be once again loyal. Once states met those standards, they would be allowed to seat senators and representatives in Congress. By one line of reasoning—the one taken by most Republicans in Congress—until representatives from all the once-rebellious states had been admitted to Congress, the country was not at peace. That approach rejected claims like those made by President Johnson in December 1865 that the country already was at peace—or near to it. It left open to debate, though, whether the absence of peace was the same thing as the presence of war. The question was not new. It had been on the minds of Americans ever since the surrender of Confederate armies in the spring of 1865. It was the question that Richard Henry Dana, Jr., had answered with his "Grasp of War" speech delivered that summer. Dana's theory remained popular, especially among Radical Republicans, but it had never found favor among those who were weary of talk of war and wanted to consign all conflict to the past. By early 1866, the end-of-war question had not been resolved. It still lurked in the shadows.

And sometimes, at moments not always anticipated, it made a grand appearance.

One of those moments came during the debate in Congress over a bill for a new Freedmen's Bureau. The current bureau was about to expire. At least that was the generally held assumption. The act establishing the current bureau had been adopted in early March 1865 and set a time limit for the bureau of one year. When congressmen took up the new bureau bill, they looked back at the language of the original bureau act and found that the expiration date of the current bureau was in fact ambiguous. The first sentence of the act had declared that the bureau would "continue during the present war of rebellion, and for one year thereafter."[1] So the bureau was set to expire not one year after its creation but rather one year after the end of the rebellion. The law had been created when the war was still in full swing. Like most Americans at the time, the law's framers had assumed that the war would eventually end, and that the endpoint would be clear. It would be a discrete moment in time: a day of finality, a day marked on calendars. From the perspective of early 1866, the notion of an obvious, agreed-upon endpoint seemed naïve. But it was a notion that Congress was stuck with. Before taking up the specifics of the new Freedmen's Bureau bill, Congress had to revisit the thorny questions of when and whether the rebellion had ended.

The end-of-war question refused to go away. It was not settled during the debate over the new bill. Indeed, over the course of 1866, and well into 1867, divisions over the question grew sharper. Battle lines were drawn. The fight over whether the war was over became something of a war in itself. To be sure, it was a war of ideas, not armies, but it was nearly as divisive as the shooting war that had begun in 1861. And it threatened to postpone forever the return of peace.

Speeches during the Freedmen's Bill debate in early 1866 laid out the problem. Congressmen were faced with two conflicting bits of evidence. The first was the much-publicized message from President Johnson to the Senate on December 18, 1865, saying that the rebellion had been "suppressed."

The second was the official opinion of the attorney general, James

Speed, issued January 6, 1866, stating that "though active hostilities have ceased, a state of war still exists over the territory in rebellion." Speed had written the opinion in response to a query from the Senate in relation to Jefferson Davis. The former Confederate president was still jailed at Fort Monroe while U.S. authorities tried to figure out whether and how to put him on trial. Although most congressmen had little sympathy with Davis's plight, they wondered, quite reasonably, what authority the U.S. government had to keep him locked up. Speed had provided the answer: "a state of war" still existed. Davis was thus a prisoner of war and might remain one, Speed wrote, "until peace shall come in fact and in law."[2] The Speed opinion was a lawyerly dodge meant to evade the real question, as yet answered, concerning Davis: Would he be tried for treason, and if so, when and where? The unanticipated consequence of the opinion was that it put Speed at odds with his boss, Andrew Johnson, on the rather significant question of whether the Civil War was over.

In the Senate, the Republican Lyman Trumbull of Illinois tried to steer the Freedmen's Bureau bill away from the shoals of the end-of-war conundrum. As chairman of the Senate Judiciary Committee, Trumbull was a crucial figure in shepherding through Congress measures assuring legal freedom and equality for Black Americans. Back in early 1864, his committee had crafted the wording of the bill that eventually became the Thirteenth Amendment abolishing slavery. By early 1866, the growing factionalism among Republicans about rights for the freed people, combined with the president's open hostility to Black equality, was making Trumbull's job harder. But the bookish, unimposing senator—a former Democrat—was a skilled mediator. He was confident that he could carve out common ground among contentious lawmakers and turn a broad set of proposals offered by his colleagues into a single slate of agreed-upon laws.

The nagging question of the war's end or non-end that arose during the Freedmen's Bureau debate was an unexpected glitch for Trumbull. The position of almost all congressional Republicans on the question was the same as that articulated by Attorney General Speed in his January 1866 opinion: a "state of war" still existed. But if that were the case, then no new Freedmen's Bureau was needed. The wording of the 1865 bureau act, combined with the principle that a state of war existed, meant that the first bureau could exist indefinitely—or at least for a year beyond the point at which Congress eventually conceded that the war was over. The problem with that approach was that the first bureau was too ineffective; Republicans wanted a new one.

The new bureau under consideration went much further than the first in granting power to the U.S. Army to ensure that the formerly enslaved were secure in their freedom. For example, the new bureau had broader powers to confiscate land from rebels and rent it to freed people, though these measures were quite limited compared to the land redistribution proposals made by Thaddeus Stevens. The bill also included a long list of rights ensuring freed people's "personal liberty" and "personal security." The U.S. military was authorized to enforce these rights throughout the former Confederacy. Officers could set up military courts to replace civilian courts if they deemed that southern lawmakers were attempting to curtail Black freedom. The bureau could thus negate the effect of the newly adopted "Black Codes" of the South. The codes violated the Thirteenth Amendment, Republicans argued, because even though they did not use the word "slavery," they effectively preserved most aspects of the institution. Trumbull and other congressional Republicans thus invoked the amendment as added justification beyond "war powers" for the new bureau bill.[3]

President Johnson, his allies, and the Democratic Party as a whole refused to put the end-of-war issue aside. Senator Willard Saulsbury called out Trumbull for submitting a bill that signaled an indefinite extension of war powers when everyone knew that the war was over. "What is war but a state of hostilities?" Saulsbury asked. "And if a state of hostilities does not exist how can there be a war?" "Is it a war of words?" the senator quipped. "I thought war meant the meeting in deadly array upon the field of battle; and I never had the idea before that it was possible for a war to exist between two nations or two people when there were in fact no hostilities."[4]

Trumbull knew that he was on shaky ground. He echoed the argument of Attorney General Speed that the government's "war powers" did "not cease with the dispersion of the rebel armies."[5] This was not a radical position, Trumbull maintained, but one that the president himself supported. As evidence of Johnson's support,

Trumbull pointed to the order that General Grant had issued in January 1866—General Order 3—that required U.S. commanders in the South to protect freed people and loyal white citizens, even if that meant intervening against civilian courts. The order assumed that the country was still at war, a position that must have had "the approbation of the Executive," Trumbull declared.[6]

Trumbull's argument flew in the face of the president's statements from December 1865 that the country was at peace, not war. Maybe Trumbull thought that the president was pliable on the end-of-war issue and might genuinely support Grant's General Order 3. In fact, the general had issued the order without Johnson's approval or knowledge. He had been urged to do so by Secretary of War Stanton.[7] Not that the general needed prodding. Although back in midsummer of 1865 he had spoken of a "hope for perpetual peace," the rise in violence against Black and white Unionists in the South since then had convinced Grant that a firm U.S. military presence in the region was still needed.[8] Johnson did not agree. Even Secretary of State Seward was on the fence. Why not just keep the bureau as it was without a new bill? Seward suggested in a memo to Johnson, especially since it turned out that it could stay in operation through at least the spring of 1867.[9]

The bill for the new Freedmen's Bureau easily passed Congress and landed on Johnson's desk on February 13, 1866. Six days later, the president vetoed the measure. The first point he made in his veto message was drawn directly from Seward's memo: a new bureau was not needed because the current bureau was not about to expire and would suffice for some time to come.[10] The logic that Seward had used to arrive at this conclusion—that the nation was still in a state of war—was either lost on Johnson or ignored by him. The president's veto message made clear that he had little patience left for technical arguments about the state of war or non-war. Americans should simply stop asking "whether we are still engaged in war," Johnson said. Raising the question could only "disturb the commerce and credit and industry of the country." Having said that the question should be dropped, the president took it up anyway. "At present there is no part of our country in which the authority of the United States is disputed," he declared. "The country has returned, or is returning, to a state of peace and industry, and the rebellion is in fact at an end."[11] Another hedge by Andrew Johnson. Which was it, "has returned" or "is returning"? A schoolchild could see the possible chasm between those two conditions.

The main reason that Johnson gave for vetoing the bill was that it represented a hostile stance of Congress against the southern states at a time when Congress should be welcoming the states back into the Union. In effect, the president was saying that the problem was not the bill but Congress itself. Senator William Fessenden of Maine, a moderate Republican, worried that this meant that the president would "veto every other bill we pass."[12] Johnson's message suggested that he had not bothered to read the actual bill. The bill said that the bureau was to last for two years; Johnson said that Congress was making the bureau a "permanent branch" of the national government. The message treated the bill as one more extremist scheme hatched by Radical Republicans. The president didn't buy arguments like those of Lyman Trumbull that the bill was moderate. Or, more likely, he didn't care about the arguments. He was focused on the political capital to be gained by calling the measure radical and attacking it as such. The move was part of the long-brewing strategy of Johnson and his inner circle of northern conservatives to reframe the national struggle in wholly new terms: a war against the country continued, but it was a war of politics, not arms, and the enemies were the Radicals, not the Confederates. The Republican journalist Charles H. Ray had warned Trumbull that this was Johnson's game. But even after reading Johnson's blistering message, Trumbull refused to give up. He and a handful of other moderates in Congress still thought that they could find common ground with the president.

Trumbull immediately set to work drafting a response to the veto message that would preserve some kind of working relationship with the president. The senator's tone was nonconfrontational. He went through each provision of the bill, showing how each did something that was already being done. Not one was radical. The senator refused to suggest any bad intent on Johnson's part. The president's characterizations of the bill as radical was simply a misunderstanding, the senator suggested.

But Trumbull had no good answer to the technical problem that Seward had identified and Johnson had exploited: a new bureau should not be needed if the current one would last at least another year. Trumbull said that the new bureau was simply an "amendment" of the old one. He must have known that this semantic adjustment wasn't likely to win over anyone. So he also tried parsing the end-of-war question in a way that explained why the current bureau was in fact about to expire. The "conflict of arms" ceased "when the last rebel army laid down its arms" in May 1865, Trumbull explained. At that point, the clock started to run down on the one year of life left for the current bureau. A new bureau therefore had to be put in place by the spring. Yet even though the "conflict of arms" had ended, Trumbull contended, "the war" had continued. "The war" consisted of both a "conflict of arms" *and* the "consequences" of that conflict. This was a clunky formulation. Even if something could be agreed upon as a consequence of war—for example, the emancipation of more than four million Black Americans—when and how could this consequence be deemed resolved? Trumbull offered no guidance on these matters. He was scrambling, desperate to convince Johnson that moderates in Congress were on his side. It was a futile effort. All he ended up doing was concocting an end-of-war formulation that was as paradoxical as any that Johnson had offered since taking office. Trumbull's boiled down to this: "Peace and harmony are not yet restored, but the war of rebellion is over."[13]

For moderate Republicans like Trumbull, the prospect of salvaging a relationship with the president was slipping away. Radicals in the House of Representatives successfully led the movement to get that chamber to override Johnson's veto. In the Senate, the push for an override came from the Ohio Radical Republican Benjamin Wade. Wade demanded an override vote as soon as the veto message arrived, on February 19, 1866. Trumbull and others were able to put off the vote, arguing that senators needed time to read the document. The next morning, Wade tore into the president. Johnson had revealed his true nature, said Wade: the president who had once blustered about punishing traitors now insisted that traitors be admitted to Congress "unwashed and red with the blood of their countrymen." The senator proposed a constitutional amendment, endorsed by Charles Sumner, that laid out new rules for presidential succession. It stated that if the country had no vice president (the current situation) and the president were no longer in office,

Congress would appoint an interim president to hold office until the next election.[14] The measure was meant as a preliminary step toward impeaching Johnson. Under the current succession rules, if Johnson were removed from office, the Senate president pro tempore became U.S. president. That happened to be Wade. With the proposed amendment, Wade hoped to assure his colleagues that he was not trying to install himself in the White House. The senator's larger purpose—to call for Johnson's impeachment—could not be missed. The Radicals had played right into the president's hands. The one-year anniversary of Lincoln's death was approaching, and Johnson could now cast them as the assassins and himself as the martyr-to-be.

Trumbull sidestepped Wade and tried reason. He delivered the speech that he had prepared explaining to Johnson why his objections were unfounded. Trumbull expected the Senate to override the veto. He was hoping to soften the blow. As it turned out, the Senate failed to muster the two-thirds majority necessary for an override. A few moderate Republicans, though not Trumbull, joined with the Democrats in sustaining Johnson. The veto held. Trumbull and Republican colleagues set to work revising the bill, hoping that a toned-down version might meet with the president's approval. Their optimism that Johnson was open to reason had reached the point of delusion.

Three days after Johnson's veto was February 22, George Washington's birthday. The capital came alive with festivities. Some people made their way to the White House and called on the president to step outside and say a few words. Johnson's allies advised the president to stay indoors. But Johnson could not help himself. He was furious at the rebuke from Congress.

The speech that Johnson gave was a stunner. He vilified the Radicals. With every cheer he heard, he delivered more bile. The Republicans in Congress were nothing more than a cabal, he cried. They cared nothing about the country and its people. Only Johnson cared. The Radicals meant to sow division and then seize power amid the chaos. The leaders of the conspiracy, men such as Thaddeus Stevens, Charles Sumner, and Wendell Phillips (he named them), were worse traitors than Jeff Davis had ever been. They meant to "behead" him.[15]

The more Johnson spoke, the more he believed every fantastical, unscripted word he uttered. Demanding that Congress reseat representatives from the states that had seceded, the president claimed that Lincoln, just before he was assassinated, told him that he hoped a constitutional amendment would be adopted that forced Congress to take back the southern representatives.[16] The story was outlandish. Lincoln had always insisted that Congress take the lead on the issue of readmitting southern representatives. Also, he never confided anything of importance to Johnson. Lincoln had no respect for the man. And now Johnson was showing why. Instead of working with Republican congressmen, he was making demons of them. He ended his Washington's birthday harangue with an apocalyptic vision of his fight with the Radicals. "If the time shall come during the period of my existence when this country is to be destroyed and its Government overturned," Johnson promised, "if you will look out you will find the humble individual who stands before you there with you endeavoring to avert its final destruction."[17]

The performance should have removed all hope from Senator Trumbull's mind that he could find common ground with the president. But he still refused to give up. Perhaps because he was a moderate, and Johnson's speech had named only Radicals, he thought he was safe from the president's ire.

Trumbull had one reason in particular for clinging to hope, and it had nothing to do with the Freedmen's Bureau bill. There was a second piece of legislation concerning Black freedom that was even more important to him, and he wanted the president to support it. This was the Civil Rights bill.

Unlike the Freedmen's Bureau bill, the Civil Rights bill was conceived of as a peacetime measure. Its provisions were permanent. It was authorized not by "war powers," which many found illusory, but rather by an actual constitutional provision, the enforcement clause of the newly adopted Thirteenth Amendment. Support for the amendment had been one of the few consistent positions that President Johnson had taken during his time in office. He and Secretary of State Seward had given the measure its final push toward ratification in late 1865. In all the time that Johnson had backed the measure, he had never expressed concerns about the enforcement clause. By early 1866, it had become clear that Johnson opposed voting rights for Blacks, but that stance had no bearing on his view of either the enforcement clause or the Civil Rights bill, or at least in theory it didn't. During the congressional debates on the amendment and in the ratification debates as well, objections that the enforcement clause would be used to force Black suffrage on the states were met by assurances by Republicans that enforcement could never go that far. At most, they said, the enforcement clause authorized "equality before the law," which meant the prohibition of race discrimination in basic legal matters such as labor agreements, marriage contracts, property holding, and legal proceedings. This legal definition of equality did not include voting rights. The Civil Rights bill, most of which Trumbull had authored, said nothing about the right to vote. That meant there was a chance that Johnson might let it pass.

It was a slim chance. The bill pushed "equality before the law" about as far as it could go—short of equal suffrage. With a couple significant exceptions, it granted citizenship to everyone born on American soil. (The exceptions were Native Americans who had not renounced their tribal allegiance and people born in the United States who were now citizens of other countries.) It attempted to remove every conceivable means of race discrimination by giving all citizens, regardless of color or previous condition of servitude, the "full and equal benefit" of the laws that only "white citizens" currently enjoyed. If passed, the bill would upend laws not only in the former Confederacy but also in states that had remained loyal to the Union. For example, it included a provision that would give Blacks the right to "give evidence." That was a right currently denied to Blacks in Kentucky—at least in cases where the defendants were white. The "full and equal benefit" provision could be used to overturn discriminatory laws in Indiana, including one that prohibited Black immigration to the state.[18] The bill reinstated and bolstered a federal judicial system across the South empowered with protecting Black civil rights. A leading Republican in the House of Representatives, John Bingham of Ohio, approved all aspects of the bill but found that some stretched constitutional authority too far. The measures required a constitutional amendment, he contended. He took the lead in drafting one derived in part from Trumbull's bill.

If Bingham, a champion of equal rights, had reservations about the bill, could it possibly receive the blessing of Andrew Johnson, who thought Blacks would fare best if they "separated" from whites?

Trumbull thought so. He came to this unlikely conclusion after meeting with the president and talking through the bill with him. According to Trumbull, Johnson expressed no objections.[19] Most likely, though, as with the Freedmen's Bureau bill, the president had not read the actual legislation. During their conversation, Trumbull probably put a gloss on the bill that made Johnson abide the measure just for the moment. Perhaps he pointed out to the president that the bill vested him with near-total control over enforcement. The expansive judicial system imposed on the South would be populated with judges appointed by Johnson. Also, as commander in chief, the president would benefit from the enhanced military powers contained within the bill.

The military provisions were crucial. They have been overlooked by historians, yet they contained innovations that would become fixtures in laws regulating the American military. Modern doctrines enabling peacetime forces to act as if war exists can be traced back to the military provisions of the bill that would become the Civil Rights Act of 1866. This peculiar origin story makes perfect sense when one remembers that the bill was crafted when the country was caught between a state of war and a state of peace.

The military provisions were brief. Section 4 of the Civil Rights bill authorized enforcement of civil rights by both civilian judicial agents and members of the armed services, specifically "officers and agents of the Freedmen's Bureau, and every other officer who may be specially empowered by the President of the United States." Section 8 gave the president power to wheel all legal machinery into action in areas where violations of the act "have been or are likely to be committed." Section 9 authorized the president, "or such person as he may empower," to use any part of the U.S. Army, the U.S. Navy, or a local militia "to prevent the violation" of the act.

During the debate on the Civil Rights bill, opponents of the measure battered Trumbull for an explanation of the meaning of these provisions. They could understand the idea that state officials might call for federal military assistance if the local police force could not enforce national laws. That had happened in the North in the era following the passage of the infamous Fugitive Slave Law of 1850. (The Civil Rights bill was actually modeled on that law: it took the clauses that had required federal officials to protect the rights of slaveholders and flipped them around to protect the rights of the formerly enslaved.) The military provisions of the Civil Rights bill not only allowed U.S. forces to be adjuncts to local police; they also authorized the military to be proactive. Troops could act against potential enemies before there had been an overt act of war or a call for assistance from locals. Opponents of Trumbull's bill cried out against such action; today, such action has become commonplace, usually going under the name of preemptive or preventive war.

"What is meant in the bill by the preventive power of the military?" Senator Thomas A. Hendricks demanded to know. How was it, the Indiana Democrat asked, that "before a crime is committed, before a wrong is done under this bill, the president, or any person whom he may appoint, may call in the military power of the Government to prevent a crime." It was an excellent question—one that regularly appears today.

Trumbull was well prepared with an answer. He invoked a statute from 1838 that had been passed in response to an episode known as "the *Caroline* affair." Experts in international law knew about the "affair" and the resulting statute even if most of Trumbull's colleagues didn't. The episode had involved an attack by British forces on Canadian rebels near the Niagara River that had led to the burning of a Canadian ship, the *Caroline,* and the killing of an American citizen. The doctrine that emerged from the short-lived crisis allowed U.S. military forces to act preemptively in self-defense when the threat of an attack was imminent. Such preemptive action did not require a declaration of war and was in itself not to be considered an act of war. The doctrine, today sometimes called "the *Caroline* test," remains a rationale behind policies allowing the U.S. military to act preemptively in times of peace. In defending the military provisions of the Civil Rights bill, Trumbull explained that he was merely building on a well-accepted principle. Democrats like Hendricks could hardly object, Trumbull slyly argued: the 1838 statute that he was using had been adopted by a Democratic administration.[20]

Trumbull then offered a compelling argument based on counterfactual history. He reminded senators that Lincoln had mobilized the U.S. Army only after Confederates had attacked Fort Sumter in April 1861. In retrospect, wouldn't it have been better, Trumbull asked, if the army had intervened in the South *before* the Confederates took the first shot? If U.S. forces had cut down the slavery-loving traitors while they were still conspiring to rebel, rather than waiting for them to strike first, then the Civil War might have been averted. During the secession crisis, Trumbull argued, "if the men who were threatening rebellion ... had been arrested for treason, of which, in my judgment, by setting on foot armed expeditions against the country, they were guilty; and if they had been tried and punished and executed for the crime, I doubt whether this great rebellion would ever have taken place."

By the same logic, Trumbull reasoned, under the proposed Civil Rights bill, the military could act preemptively to prevent a resurgence of rebellion. He offered a hypothetical. "Suppose that the county authorities in Muscogee county, Georgia, combine together to deny civil rights to every colored man in that county. For the purpose of preventing it, before they have done any act, I say the militia may be called out to prevent them from committing an act. We are not required to wait until the act is committed before anything can be done."[21] In this scenario, Trumbull envisioned the president calling up a local militia and making it part of the U.S. Army. Lincoln had made such a move in reaction to the firing on Fort Sumter. But Trumbull's bill also allowed the president to use regular army units in preemptive actions. That promised to be a particularly powerful provision now that Congress had under consideration a proposal—soon to be adopted—that increased the size of the regular army threefold.[22]

If Trumbull thought that the enhancement of U.S. military authority embodied in the Civil Rights bill would appeal to President Johnson, who was effectively being offered unprecedented power as commander in chief, he was mistaken. Johnson had never had much interest in his role as head of the armed forces. He had gladly delegated power over the army to Grant as general in chief and Stanton as secretary of war. He cared even less about the navy and probably did not know the difference between a submarine and a frigate. Gideon Welles, still secretary of the navy, was Johnson's closest friend in the cabinet (though that was not saying much), and the president was fine giving him full control of the country's now much diminished naval forces.

On March 27, 1866, President Johnson vetoed the Civil Rights bill. Few but Trumbull were surprised. From this point on, moderates like Trumbull knew for certain that Johnson was against all congressional Republicans, not just the Radicals. The veto message had many of the same objections as the one that he had written against the Freedmen's Bureau bill. It accused Congress of overreaching its authority by invading the South with a national bureaucracy—in this case, the federal judiciary. It also made outlandish claims about the bill's commitment to equality before the law. The measure did not establish equality, the president argued, because it established "safeguards" for "the colored race" that went "indefinitely beyond any that the General Government has ever provided for the white race." "In fact," he continued, "the distinction of race and color is by the bill made to operate in favor of the colored against the white race." That was simply untrue. Like most white supremacists of his time as well as our own, he had come to think that rights granted to Blacks necessarily weakened rights belonging to whites. As for the military provisions in the bill, Johnson offered the false objection that they made the protection and elevation of Black people the sole objective of the army.

More legitimate was the president's concern about the scale of the "permanent military force" that the Civil Rights bill seemed to endorse. Republicans indeed believed that a large occupying army was needed in the South to oversee the transition from war to peace and from slavery to freedom. Yet the force envisioned by Republicans—perhaps 50,000 to 70,000 men at most—was still tiny compared to the million-man army that the United States had marshalled against the Confederacy.[23]

Johnson accepted that some U.S. garrisons were needed in the South to keep the peace, but he thought the occupying force should be as small as possible. He also believed that southern whites would be more compliant if they believed that he meant to draw down the army presence in the South as quickly as possible. That was one of the reasons why his veto messages harped on his opposition to a large, drawn-out occupation. He wanted southern whites to know that he was against using the military to hold the region in a grasp of war.

At the same time, in his day-to-day role as commander in chief, the president did not stop Stanton and Grant from applying the grasp. He had made no objection to Grant's General Order 3 in January 1866, which sustained the policy of allowing the army to move cases from civilian to military courts. He had vetoed the bill for the new Freedmen's Bureau, but he showed no inclination to shut down the current bureau—though he had the power to do so. Also, at Stanton's behest, he allowed the suspension of habeas corpus to persist across broad swaths of the South. The suspension of habeas was a necessity if the U.S. military was to have meaningful power in the protection of Blacks and loyal whites. It allowed troops to arrest and detain insurgents without having to worry about interference from southern sheriffs and judges, most of whom sympathized with the insurgents. If the suspension were to be lifted, southern civilian judges could free anyone arrested by U.S. troops.

Andrew Johnson was in effect playing two contradictory roles, and, as was becoming clear, he was inept at both of them. As the civilian leader of the nation, he gave lip service to the presence of peace throughout the country and thus opposed any increase in military intervention in the South. As the commander in chief, he knew that the country was still in transition from war to peace. Thus he stayed any impulse he might have had to rein in Stanton or Grant. Johnson was tired of playing both roles at once. In his weariness, he had grabbed hold of the fantasy that the mere passage of time was all that was needed for genuine peace to arrive. But how long would he have to wait?

Secretary of State William Henry Seward also was tired of waiting. He had thought that with the Thirteenth Amendment, which he had steered through ratification, the Union had achieved the crucial goals of the war: the defeat of the rebellion and the prohibition of slavery. He knew that subduing minor insurgencies and resolving thorny questions such as the rights of freed people would take some time, but he had not foreseen that they would postpone for so long the moment when all would agree that peace had arrived. Like Johnson, Seward was impatient for the arrival of that moment.

Seward was as close to Johnson as anyone could be—or could stand to be. The secretary of state was the only member of the cabinet to have earned the unqualified trust of both the president and his predecessor, Abraham Lincoln. Under both he had served as an expert on end-of-war matters, though of course Lincoln had died before he could play that role out to its finish. In the weeks after the assassins killed Lincoln and nearly killed Seward, documents that Seward had drafted for Lincoln in preparation for moving the country away from a state of war, such as a proclamation lifting the blockade, were issued by Johnson. In the weeks just before and after the adoption of the Thirteenth Amendment, Seward had woven messages about the war having ended into Johnson's official communications: his annual address of December 4, 1865 ("our domestic contest, now happily ended"); his report two weeks later on conditions in the South ("the rebellion . . . has been suppressed"); and his veto of the Freedmen's Bureau bill eight weeks after that ("the country has returned, or is returning, to a state of peace . . . and the rebellion is in fact at an end").[24]

Right after the president vetoed the Freedmen's Bureau bill, Seward traveled to New York City. He was the featured speaker at a grand celebration of Washington's birthday on February 22 at the Cooper Institute. Believing that he would be speaking as the representative of the executive branch, he had prepared his comments carefully. He did not know that Johnson would end up delivering an impromptu speech back in Washington on the same night. This was the wild, rambling harangue in which the president attacked his political enemies as traitors and promoted himself as the only true representative of the people. Seward's address in New York was far more measured. But he, too, sniped at Republicans in Congress. They alone were responsible for dragging out the war, Seward said. He took special aim at the Joint Committee on Reconstruction. He was furious that the committee had yet to pass a law explaining what a former state of the Confederacy had to do before its representatives would be accepted in Congress. After more than two months of work, the committee had produced no "plan of reconstruction," Seward carped, only "a plan for indefinite postponement and delay."[25] In fact, Republicans in Congress were on the verge of admitting the delegation from Tennessee, Andrew Johnson's home state. But after the tirade against them that Johnson had delivered at the White House, they scrapped the plan.

Had Seward, during his Cooper Institute address, known what Johnson was saying back in Washington, he would have dropped the part of the speech that praised the president for lacking any "imperial" sense of self-importance.[26] Seward made Johnson out to be conciliatory toward Congress. True, Seward conceded, the president had just vetoed the bill for a new Freedmen's Bureau. But he was just as committed as Republicans in Congress to the principle that "the freedmen and refugees ought not to be abandoned by the nation to persecution and suffering."[27] Anyone who had read what the president said to the Black delegation led by Frederick Douglass earlier that month knew that Seward was painting a false picture of his boss.

Seward, like Johnson, was fine leaving freed people to fend for themselves. He hated slavery and had risen to prominence by denouncing the practice. But the plight of Black people under slavery was not the main source of his hatred. Mostly, he despised the *institution* of slavery. It had skewed national power toward southern white elites. His father, Samuel, had been a slaveholder in western New York. Seward had thus been "born a slaveholder," he would sometimes admit. When New York prohibited slavery in 1827, he would then explain, "my State took away my slaves," though it "did right" to abolish the institution. His father had provided financial support to the people once enslaved by the family. When his father died, Seward was instructed by his father's will to continue to look after the freed people. In an interview that Seward gave soon after his Cooper Institute address of February 1866, he revealed his resentment that he had been required "to support some of them up to this time." "The South must take care of its own negroes as the North did and does," Seward told the journalists. He trusted the "intelligent" whites of the South to protect the "civil rights" of the freed people. If the whites failed in the task, then so be it. "The negroes," he confessed, were not his "concern." "They are God's poor; they always have been and always will be. . . . They must take their level."[28]

Above all—beyond his hatred of the old slavery "system," his devotion to the rule of law, his occasional indifference to Black people—Seward was a pragmatist who wanted Americans to put the war behind them. In his Cooper Institute address, he described how that could be done. Even before Congress fashioned a Reconstruction policy—assuming it ever would—the president or Congress could simply declare the war over with an official announcement of its end. "The existence of the rebellion was legally announced by Executive proclamation in 1861," Seward said—he was referring to Lincoln's April 15, 1861, declaration calling up an army to "suppress" the unlawful "combinations" in the South. In the same way, reasoned Seward, the legal end of the war could be established "if the President or Congress, one or both, officially announces its termination."[29]

This was a novel proposition. Seward surely knew that it had no basis in the established law of war. Lawmaking bodies could proclaim victory, but a legal end of war required some sort of concession by the loser. The argument that this principle was irrelevant to the present circumstances because the conflict was only a rebellion, not a war, could not hold. Yes, the United States had refused to acknowledge the Confederacy as a nation. But ever since the *Prize Cases* of 1863, it had deemed Confederates "belligerents"—lawful combatants—rather than illegitimate insurrectionists. That effectively acknowledged the Confederacy as a nation without giving it that status in law. Seward the pragmatist was ready to put principle aside. Frustrated that the nation was still engulfed in conflict— albeit a war of politics more than a war of arms—he allowed himself to entertain the simplest of solutions: declare the war over.

On the day after the Appomattox surrender, Richard Henry Dana, Jr., had declared that peace could not be "made." It had to "come." Seward was done waiting for peace to come. He had decided that peace *could* be made. All it took was a proclamation saying that it *had* been made. When he returned to Washington after the Cooper Institute address, he floated the idea to President Johnson. Johnson liked it, and the two of them wrote a draft. It was likely sitting on the president's desk when he vetoed the Civil Rights bill on March 27, 1866. The end-of-war proclamation was the perfect follow-up to the veto message, which warned against provisions such as "a permanent military force" that would "resuscitate the spirit of rebellion."[30]

On April 2, six days after the veto message, the president issued the proclamation declaring that "the insurrection . . . is at an end" in all the former Confederate states except Texas. Texas was excluded because voters there had yet to agree to send representatives to Congress or to approve a new state constitution renouncing secession and slavery. A few days before Johnson issued the proclamation, the *New York Herald,* the paper edited by Johnson's confidant James Gordon Bennett, called Texas "the last erring sister to be restored to the family of the Union." Bennett knew about the end-of-war declaration that Johnson was about to deliver, and he hinted at it in his paper, predicting that Texas would return to the "family" if the president were to issue a "proclamation announcing that peace prevails over a restored and firmly reunited country."[31]

Although the proclamation took the form of a legal order, its purpose was purely political. It included a provision implying that the U.S. military presence in the South would now vanish. "Standing armies, military occupation, martial law, military tribunals, and the suspension of the privilege of the writ of habeas corpus"—all of these were to go. A white Mississippian who had once lived near Johnson in Tennessee thanked the president—and God—for the measure. "We are tired of Military," he wrote. "We are tired of War."[32]

Yet for more than a month, nothing actually changed. Right after Johnson issued the proclamation, Stanton and Grant sent orders "with the approval of the President" to officers and Freedmen's Bureau agents that martial law and bureau operations were to continue as before.[33] The heart of the proclamation was a declaration that the Confederate states were now on "like footing" with the rest of the states. But Congress had so far rejected that principle, and Johnson had no power over Congress in the matter. In terms of law, Johnson's assertion that all states were "equals" had no force.

The proclamation was really about changing public opinion. As former attorney general Edward Bates recognized, it was meant to replace "the impudent pretence of the Radicals that the war still continued" with an assurance that "the war is over and peace *does* exist."[34] The current attorney general, James Speed, was swayed. A few months before, he had issued an official opinion saying that the country was still at war. He now yielded to the president. "Our war is over," he wrote to his friend Francis Lieber, though he conceded that "the questions growing out of it have to be settled."[35]

The April 2 proclamation may have had little immediate effect on actual policy, but it sent a chilling message to those Republicans committed to reforming the South. Although Congress controlled the terms by which southern states regained representation in the national legislature, Johnson had the greater power. He controlled the military. If the president made good on the promise of the proclamation and scaled back military occupation, the government would lose its grasp of war over the South. Republicans knew that the laws they were passing for the equal rights of freed people required force behind them if they were to have any effect. In early April, Congress passed the Civil Rights Act over Johnson's veto. Two Black South Carolinians, both future state representatives, had lobbied for the measure as "the Magna Charta [*sic*] of our liberties."[36] In July, Congress adopted a revised bill for the new Freedmen's Bureau—again over a veto. The new version, which borrowed liberally from the Civil Rights Act, included a broad enumeration of rights that the bureau was to enforce. But without continued military occupation, there could be no bureau. There could be no rights. A poignant demonstration of the fact occurred in Norfolk, Virginia. Black residents of the city held a spontaneous celebration in the city when they heard that the Civil Rights Act had been adopted. In the raucousness, a white civilian died, almost certainly by accident. Whites in the city seethed. The commander of the army garrison in Norfolk, certain that a massacre of Black people was about to take place, sent word to his superior for reinforcements. Troops arrived just in time to prevent the murders.[37] Had there been no military presence in the area, an episode that began with a cheer for the Civil Rights Act would have ended with the slaughter of those meant to benefit most from the new law.

Fueling concerns about military power being stripped from the South was a major announcement from the U.S. Supreme Court on April 3, the day after Johnson's proclamation. The Court announced that it had unanimously agreed to order the release from prison of Lambdin P. Milligan and his two accomplices. In 1864 in Indiana, the men had been arrested along with a number of others for subversive activities. They had been tried, convicted, and sentenced by a military commission. Attorneys for the men had filed a habeas corpus petition arguing for their release on the basis that the military never had the authority to try civilians in Indiana, a pro-Union state with perfectly functional civilian courts. In siding with Milligan, the Court signaled that it agreed with the principle that the U.S. military had no judicial authority in areas where pro-Union civilian legal authority had been reestablished. Because functional civilian courts were now operational throughout most of the South, the implication was that the U.S. military could no longer try civilians in the region. Anyone arrested and detained by U.S. soldiers could be released by a civilian judge.

The *Milligan* decision had the potential to undercut U.S. military occupation and Black civil rights in the South. Only military courts, which included all those run by the Freedmen's Bureau, could be relied on to convict whites who terrorized and murdered Blacks. If southern civilian courts now had sole jurisdiction of the region, they could use habeas writs to release violent white insurgents. They could also order the arrest and imprisonment of U.S. soldiers for minor infractions like "disturbing the peace." And all the while, as they claimed to be using their restored powers to keep the peace, southern judges would in fact be sitting idly by as the losers of the Civil War arose in untrammeled insurgencies.

Chief Justice Salmon P. Chase, who was sympathetic to most of the Radicals' agenda, helped stave off this nightmare scenario, at least temporarily. Although the Court was unanimous in deciding to release Milligan, Chase and three other justices believed that military courts still should be allowed to try civilians under certain circumstances in the South (at the very least, they thought, the option of trying Jefferson Davis by a military court needed to be kept open). Chase asked the Court to delay issuing its official opinion until he could write a separate concurring opinion.[38] In fact, Chase was buying time for congressional Republicans, most of whom wanted to keep the nation on a war footing. He hoped that they could quickly come up with a legal justification for military force that could withstand the full counterpunch of the majority's *Milligan* opinion. In the meantime, military courts could continue to exist in the South in a kind of legal limbo.

Seward easily read Chase's play. The two men, longtime political foes who had served together in Lincoln's cabinet, knew each other well. The secretary of state advised the president that he did not have to wait for an official opinion from the Court to start shifting power from U.S. Army occupiers to southern civilian authorities. In May, Johnson announced that civilian courts had exclusive jurisdiction over the South. Stanton and Grant scrambled to preserve what they could of the military's judicial authority. Stanton secretly sent messages to military commanders and Freedmen's Bureau commissioners that they could still arrest and imprison criminals, including those who violated the Civil Rights Act or the new Freedmen's Bureau. Grant went further. Violators *must* be arrested by the military, he ordered his officers, unless civil authorities were willing to prosecute them in earnest. When challenged with the fact that they seemed to be countermanding the president's messages, Stanton and Grant responded that until an actual opinion had been issued in *Milligan,* they were within their rights. But by late summer, army officials knew that an official opinion was coming soon. They were operating on borrowed time.[39]

Also by late summer, Texas, which the president had excluded from his April 2 end-of-war proclamation, voted to approve its new state constitution and send representatives to Congress. To Johnson, that meant that he could issue a revised proclamation declaring that peace truly existed everywhere.

But peace was not everywhere, and even Johnson knew that he would look foolish to say that it was. On July 30, former Confederates in Louisiana determined to take back their state's government converged on New Orleans and attacked a Republican political meeting. They focused their rage on Black attendees, killing more than thirty of them and wounding more than a hundred others. An even more brutal racial massacre had taken place twelve weeks earlier, in Memphis, Tennessee. For three days, white mobs stormed the city. A garrison of U.S. troops was stationed in the city, as was a large office of the Freedmen's Bureau. But there were too few soldiers to beat back the attackers. A Black regiment of occupying soldiers had just been mustered out, an event that helped embolden the racist whites to attack. A local paper printed the lie that the discharged soldiers had committed all the violence.[40] A fairer assessment was offered by the congressional committee that later investigated the massacre. It put the blame on whites and reported that of the forty-eight people killed, forty-six were Black. It also reported that five Black women had been raped; the actual number was almost certainly higher.[41] The New Orleans massacre at the end of July revived memories of what had happened in Memphis. In New Orleans, though, the killings were carried out more systematically. The entire attack had been planned in advance by what one southern reporter called "military organizations" of former Confederates.[42] President Johnson's stance that rebel hearts had been purified now seemed absurd. U.S. Adjutant General Joseph Holt, who had once thought Johnson shared his views of the war's inevitable persistence, now blamed the president for what Holt called "the barbarism of the rebellion in its renaissance."[43]

Incredibly, though, Johnson remained determined to declare that the rebellion and all its vestiges had vanished. Events in New Orleans persuaded him to shelve the new end-of-war declaration that he had prepared. But he did not sit on it for long. On August 20, 1866, only three weeks after the New Orleans massacre, the president issued the proclamation. The "insurrection is at an end," he announced. "Peace, order, tranquillity, and civil authority now exist in and throughout the whole of the United States of America."[44]

15

The Fight for the End

F OR ANDREW JOHNSON, the proclamation of August 20, 1866, was both an end and a beginning. It was the legal end of the country's war of rebellion. It was also the start of a war against Republicans—specifically those among them who denied the existence of peace. Johnson believed that he had achieved the peace that Abraham Lincoln had sought but never settled. Any doubts that Johnson might once have had about his qualifications to succeed Lincoln were gone. In fighting a war to end the war, Johnson saw himself carrying on the work of his predecessor. He even had begun to think that he might be better suited for the task than Lincoln had been. In the speech that he had given back in February on the occasion of Washington's birthday, Johnson had hinted that the "inscrutable Providence" that "saw proper to remove" Lincoln had always intended Johnson to hold his current position.[1]

Of course, there had been rumblings of this new war, strictly a political conflict, for months. But now the fight was out in the open. Johnson had allies, including some prominent moderate Republicans. One was Henry Raymond, the editor of the *New York Times,* which had been the mouthpiece of the Lincoln administration and now backed Johnson against the more radical elements of Raymond's party. Another was Senator James R. Doolittle of Wisconsin. Aside from sharing President Johnson's negative view of Black Americans, Doolittle agreed with the president that the U.S. military needed to be reined in. The senator was in the midst of a fierce feud with the War Department over "Indian Affairs." The army had rejected treaty-making, Doolittle's preferred method of making peace with Native Americans, in favor of a grasp-of-war approach. Across the plains and deserts of the West, U.S. troops were spilling Natives' blood. There must be submission before negotiation, U.S. commanders insisted. Doolittle's protests had no effect. Nor did the series of victories by Native warriors. The army's humiliation only spurred it toward more brutal bloodshed.

Doolittle and Raymond were the featured speakers at the "National Union" Convention, which met in Philadelphia just days before President Johnson issued his August 20, 1866, peace proclamation. The meeting was meant to demonstrate the unity and power of the coalition between Democrats and moderate Republicans that Johnson's handlers had been putting together for well over a year. The convention also was intended to prepare the ground for the president's August 20 proclamation. In the first speech of the meeting, Doolittle declared that "the war is over" and "peace has come, and come to stay."[2] He applauded the piece of theater that had opened the convention: a delegate from Massachusetts had locked arms with one from South Carolina, and the two strode through the center of the throng toward the main stage. The arm-in-arm convention, as it became known, ended with a speech by Henry Raymond. The editor told the delegates "to remember, always and everywhere, that the war is ended, and the nation is again at peace." These delegates were all campaigning for pro-Johnson tickets in the fall elections. Raymond provided lines for their scripts: "The acts of war [have] been discontinued, and the weapons of war laid aside. . . . The state of war no longer exists, and the sentiments, the passions, the relations of war have no longer lawful or rightful place anywhere throughout our broad dominion."[3] Far away in New Orleans, the friends and families of the Black victims massacred by white insurgents only eighteen days earlier must have read Raymond's words with disgust.

After President Johnson issued the August 20 proclamation, he took to the stump. For more than two weeks he traveled across the North, speaking in support of candidates who promised to support his plan of Reconstruction over the Republicans'. The trip became known as "the Swing Around the Circle."

Never before had a sitting president left the White House to take part in barnstorming politicking. The practice would not become common for another sixty-five years. Each oration delivered by Johnson was more rambling and bitter than the one before. Attendees who had long enjoyed the barbs and hyperbole of stump speeches at first roared with laughter and hurrahs at Johnson's performance. Soon, though, some began to question whether such behavior in a president was appropriate. Lincoln had loved entertaining audiences at rallies on the campaign circuit prior to becoming president, but once he entered the White House, he gave all that up. As president, the only political address that he had given outside of Washington was the short, solemn address at Gettysburg in November 1863. Andrew Johnson was pushing the populist orator routine too far.

A turning point came in Cleveland, on September 3. When someone in the audience yelled out, "Hang Jeff Davis"—still a popular refrain in the fall of 1866—the president shot back: "Why not hang Thad Stevens and Wendell Phillips?"[4] He thought he was being funny, and indeed some people laughed—nervously. Every speech started out with reason and devolved into vitriol. By the time he arrived in St. Louis on September 9, his handlers had learned to shuffle him offstage to a waiting carriage or train car as soon as they saw his temper kick in. In St. Louis, it was a heckler, not Johnson, who won the day. Hours into his standard diatribe portraying himself as the victim of the insidious Radicals, his fury made its inevitable appearance. His enemies accused him of "offenses," he bellowed. Tell me "what offenses I have committed," he asked rhetorically. "Plenty, here, to-night" came the heckler's reply.[5]

Johnson's advisors were irate. By making the speeches entirely about himself, the president had deviated disastrously from the strategy of keeping listeners focused on the two issues immediately at hand. First, he was supposed to build support for the peace proclamation that he had just issued. Second, he was supposed to whip up opposition to the new proposed constitutional amendment, which Congress had sent to the states for ratification three months earlier.

This was the amendment that Representative John Bingham had set out to craft in early 1866 after deciding that the Civil Rights Act exceeded what the current Constitution allowed. The measure had bounced back and forth between the Joint Committee on Reconstruction and the two houses of Congress for five months, receiving constant revision and picking up new provisions along the way. The final, five-section version was a hodgepodge of Bingham's original language, some bits from the Civil Rights Act, and whole passages devoted to seemingly mundane matters like the war debt amassed by the Confederacy.

Yet within the convoluted language were passages representing the most far-reaching changes ever to be proposed to the U.S. Constitution. These included provisions similar to those in the Civil Rights Act meant to secure equality before the law for Black Americans. The amendment granted citizenship to anyone born in the United States and guaranteed "privileges and immunities," "equal protection," and "due process of law," though the exact meaning of these phrases was not spelled out in detail. Arguably its most radical phrase was "the right to vote," which appeared in the amendment's second section. However, it took at least a few readings of that section to begin to understand what if anything the new amendment did to change the laws of suffrage in the country. The provision left full power over suffrage to the states. However, it offered to the states a strong inducement to grant voting rights to male citizens who were at least twenty-one years old. States that banned members of this group from voting would have their representation in the House of Representatives reduced in proportion to the percentage banned. The complicated formula amounted to this: states would do well to grant voting rights to adult Black men, but they would gain nothing by granting such rights to women of any age or color. Advocates of women's suffrage made a heroic effort to keep the word "male" out of the provision, but the male lawmakers were near united in their opposition. They were not ready to relinquish the age-old principle that women's interests were fully represented by men, who always knew what was best for the "weaker" sex. A handful of Republicans in Congress supported female suffrage, but they worried about making the amendment seem *too* radical. Maybe they calculated right. Then again, any measure that endorsed suffrage for Black men was certain to be criticized by opponents as ultra-radical no matter what it said about women.[6]

The centrists who supported Andrew Johnson and packed him off on his speaking tour in the fall of 1866 expected the proposed amendment to be the single most important issue in the coming elections. They were right. The president was supposed to play to racist fears by warning that the amendment put centralized power into the hands of despotic Republican congressmen who were determined to destroy the "white man's government." At every stop on the "Swing Around the Circle," the president said what he had been told to say, but then he went off script. He buried the amendment beneath his bile and buffoonery. By the time he returned to the capital, his embarrassing behavior had lost him the support of crucial allies like the Democratic editor James Gordon Bennett, who no longer believed that a new party could be fashioned around such a fool. As Bennett and like-minded centrists feared, the fall elections went resoundingly in favor of the Republicans. Those elected would not begin their terms until December 1867, when the 40th Congress convened. But when that moment came, Republicans would control well over two-thirds of the seats of each house. They would be able to override any presidential veto.

Indeed, Republicans might already have the numbers they needed in the current Congress, the 39th, which was to begin its second session in December. Johnson's antics had alienated moderate Republicans, who were now open to voting with the main body of their party, the Radicals. If Republicans controlled the national government, they could control the messaging on the end-of-war issue. Congressional Republicans still held firm to the position that the war continued. Representative Thaddeus Stevens announced the fact on December 2, 1866, the day before Congress convened, in a speech delivered in Washington to volunteers who had mustered out of the army. "Citizen-soldiers and fellow citizens," he declared, "the war of blood has been suspended—I wish I could say ended. But the war is not over."[7]

Johnson had lost his advantage on the end-of-war issue. But his August 20, 1866, proclamation remained in place. Congress had no authority to revoke it. And he was still president. That meant he could use his powers as commander in chief to end the military occupation of the South. If Congress wanted to say that the war still existed in theory, so be it. Johnson could stop the war from existing in fact—as long as he controlled the army.

—

Theory and fact. The tension between the two turned out to be at play in the matter of who controlled the army. In theory, it was President Johnson. In fact, it was Secretary of War Edwin M. Stanton.

From the moment that Johnson took office, he deferred to Stanton in the management of military affairs. Unlike Lincoln, Johnson had no interest in running the army. In the first year of his presidency, most of the declarations that he made concerning the army were written by Stanton. Even when he authored the proclamations, he rarely bothered to check that they were carried out. For this reason, Stanton in the summer of 1866 had been able to sustain the power of the occupying forces over civilian affairs in the South even after President Johnson issued his first end-of-war proclamation on April 2 and began revoking the suspension of habeas corpus in May.

Secretary of the Navy Gideon Welles, who *was* on Johnson's side, had repeatedly told the president that Stanton was not. The war secretary was a wolf in the fold, the Radicals' man in the cabinet, Welles insisted. But Welles's warnings had been easy for Johnson to dismiss. Welles had always held a personal grudge against Stanton and frequently ranted about the man's intention to rule the country as a military despot.

In reality, though Welles had overestimated Stanton's despotic ambitions, he was right about his radical sympathies. Stanton had long been disgusted by Johnson's leniency toward former Confederates and his laissez-faire attitude toward the freed people. The war secretary sided with the Radicals on these issues and also agreed with them that a state of war still existed. At the urging of his allies in Congress, Stanton decided not to openly break with Johnson but rather to hold on to his post for as long as he could. He knew that he could help carry out the Republicans' agenda from within the cabinet better than from without.

By the fall of 1866, President Johnson had come to believe that he had enemies hiding in every corner, but for some reason, his suspicions had yet to turn on Stanton. Whether the president acted from misplaced trust or willful ignorance is impossible to know. Whatever the reason, Stanton's game was almost up. When Johnson resolved at the end of 1866 to take a firm hand over military affairs in order to end the war by action, not just by proclamation, he unwittingly put himself on a collision course with Stanton.

Caught in the middle of these two men was General in Chief Ulysses S. Grant. After the surrender at Appomattox, the general, who had staked his reputation on the agreement that he had made with Lee, initially rebuffed assertions that the war had persisted beyond the Confederate surrenders. When friction emerged between Johnson and congressional Republicans on the end-of-war question at the end of 1865, he took the president's side. His December 18, 1865, report to Congress announced that the issues that had divided the country had been "settled forever." But the general was distraught by how the president manipulated that statement to make exaggerated claims about the absence of hostilities in the South. Realizing that he had been used by Johnson, Grant told friends that he had "regrets for what he has done."[8]

Almost immediately Grant decided to begin collecting information that would give him a fuller picture of the situation in the South. He telegraphed the U.S. generals stationed in the region and asked them to report "all known outrages" that had occurred under their command during the period after the major Confederate surrenders.[9]

For help in his fact-finding endeavor, Grant relied in particular on Major General Oliver O. Howard, the head of the Freedmen's Bureau.[10] Howard and Grant still had a close relationship, though Howard's feelings for Secretary of War Stanton had soured of late. After the Freedmen's Bureau had been renewed in mid-1866 by the congressional override of President Johnson's veto, Stanton had slowly whittled away at Howard's authority. The bureau had technically been part of the War Department almost from its inception, but Howard and his agents had enjoyed a fair amount of autonomy during the bureau's first year. That changed in the latter half of 1866, as Stanton took a firmer grip of the bureau's operations and its budget. Still, Howard did not allow this unwelcome encroachment to dampen his determination to help the freed people in their ongoing fight against ex-Confederates. He gladly agreed to supply Grant with information that would put the lie to President Johnson's claim that the South was now free of hostilities. Howard harbored an eternal grudge against Johnson for forcing him in late 1865 to rescind the government's promise of land to the newly free families along the southeast coast. Delivering the news to Black families in the lowcountry that they had to give their land back to former Confederates had been the low point of Howard's tenure at the bureau. He relished the chance to embarrass the peace-proclaiming president with evidence that ex-Confederates were as warlike as ever. Howard ended up with plenty of material to draw from. In December 1866, for example, two Freedmen's Bureau agents in Mississippi were assassinated. The perpetrators were never identified. Howard could find no volunteers willing to replace the dead men.[11]

The file that General Grant kept on "outrages" in the South had grown thick by the end of 1866. Typical was an episode from Grimes County, Texas, about sixty miles northwest of Houston. A Black man there named Dick Perkins had left his home in the county when he heard that his former master, a man named Darwin, meant to kill him. Eventually Perkins returned home. A U.S. officer had assured him that he would be safe. When Perkins was at a local store one day in December, Darwin entered with a pistol. The store owner hustled to the door and threw the lock, trapping Perkins inside. Perkins drew his gun and got off a few shots before the two white men closed on him. He managed to get both men briefly in a hammerlock before Darwin finally shot him. The wound was nearly fatal, but some U.S. soldiers managed to get Perkins to a hospital in Houston, where a doctor saved him. The Grimes County sheriff showed up at the hospital, arrested Perkins for attempted murder, and hauled him back to the county jail. There, Perkins shared a cell with a U.S. soldier, who had been arrested by the sheriff on some trumped-up charge. What exactly had been won in the Civil War, the two men must have wondered.[12]

Incidents like this made General Grant wonder the same thing. When a newspaper interviewer a couple months after the Grimes County affair congratulated him for work "well done" in putting down the rebellion, he replied: "No, the work is not all done." The clash of armies was over, "the fighting is finished," he said. But attacks on loyal civilians and U.S. soldiers continued. Anyone expressing pro-Union sentiments in the South risked being shot, Grant told the interviewer, and any such shooting "would probably be passed off as justifiable homicide, if the murderer was arrested at all."[13]

Grant had accurately described circumstances in the South that would be permanent if President Johnson's peace proclamation was accepted as the law of the land. The U.S. occupying force would be rendered powerless, with soldiers and loyal civilians—Blacks in particular—arrested and imprisoned by local authorities who only a year before had been fighting for the Confederacy.

To prevent such a disaster, Grant had relied on General Orders that he had issued in the first half of 1866 that declared the legal supremacy of U.S. forces in the South over local law enforcement. First came General Order 3, issued in January 1866, which authorized U.S. troops to operate in the South without interference. Then, after President Johnson's first peace proclamation, on April 2, 1866, Grant countered with General Order 44. The new order authorized military arrests of anyone who threatened or attacked U.S. military personnel or southern civilians, Black or white.[14]

President Johnson's final peace proclamation of August 20, 1866, threatened to render Grant's General Orders inoperative. Grant found himself in an impossible position. How could he continue to enforce a policy that kept the South in a grasp of war while serving a president who proclaimed that the grasp had been released? Resignation was not an option. He had given everything to the causes of the war—reunion and emancipation—and would not yield now. Also, he knew that he was the most beloved American in the country—in the North, anyway—and that if he broke with the president, the political fallout would be disastrous. What was he to do, then, when Johnson asked Grant to join him on his celebratory "Swing Around the Circle," which followed the issuing of the August 20 peace proclamation? The president knew what he was doing. Having Grant at his side would add credibility to his claims that peace was real, jeopardized only by the Radical Republicans. The general thought it was crucial to maintain the appearance of harmony in the national government as the country reeled from the reports of the New Orleans massacre. He agreed to go on the trip with the president—and regretted every moment of it. He told his wife, Julia, that Johnson's tirades were "a national disgrace."[15]

Through the end of 1866, Grant and Stanton were able to keep the occupying forces functional, despite Johnson's August 20 peace proclamation. This was no easy feat, as some whites in the South interpreted the proclamation as saying that U.S. military authority in the region had come to an end.

In North Carolina, for example, Governor Jonathan Worth decided that Johnson's decree invalidated military orders in the state that were meant to end the vestiges of slavery. Worth received reports late in 1866 that U.S. officers were still preventing the enforcement of old state laws that allowed civilian authorities to whip Black people and to force them into coercive apprenticeships. On the basis of Johnson's August 20 proclamation, the governor informed civilian authorities that they could resume the whippings and the apprenticeships. White sheriffs whipped at least one Black man and re-enslaved two young Black women as "apprentices."[16]

Stories of the reappearance of slavery in the wake of the August 20 proclamation became national news. The artist Thomas Nast put a newspaper excerpt describing the whipping in North Carolina into a sketch he published in *Harper's Weekly* titled "(?) Slavery is Dead (?)" Nast's sketch also featured a story from Maryland about Black convicts being sold as a "punishment for crime," a practice allowed under Maryland state law. Enslavement—or at least "servitude"—as a "punishment for crime" was also allowed under the Thirteenth Amendment, though it would be a few years before whites began to exploit the amendment's clause systematically. As for the state and local laws allowing enslavement that had been on the books since before the war and had yet to be overturned, those were a different matter. Southern whites, as Nast had reminded Americans in a visual way, were ready to put the measures back into force immediately. In the wake of Johnson's August 20 proclamation, the onetime Confederates revealed how undefeated they truly were, especially when it came to emancipation. The message conveyed by Johnson's decree, that peace reigned across the old Slave South—even in faraway Texas—was clearly false. The "peace was all on one side," a loyal, pro-emancipation judge in Texas wrote: the side of the white diehards. In his state, he explained, things were as "peaceable as the volcano smothered up until it got air."[17]

In response to incidents of whites openly treating Blacks as slaves following Johnson's August 20 proclamation, General in Chief Grant assured his commanders that their authority to ban such practices was intact. His long-standing order, that soldiers protect the "law-abiding against the acts of the lawless," must still be followed.[18]

A Thomas Nast illustration titled "(?) Slavery is Dead (?),"
from *Harper's Weekly*. Nast sought to convey the resurrection
of slavery that ensued because of President Andrew Johnson's end-of-war proclamation of August 20, 1866. On the
left, Black convicts are sold into servitude. On the right, a
Black man is whipped. Below each image is a newspaper
excerpt from late 1866 describing the scene depicted. The
episodes made a mockery of Lincoln's Emancipation Proclamation of 1863 and the Civil Rights Act of 1866, both of
which appear in the middle of the image.

While Grant attended to the effects of Johnson's August 20 proclamation in the field, some of which were disastrous, Stanton dealt
with the thicket of legal and political problems in Washington. On
December 3, 1866, Congress convened for a session scheduled to last
for four months. Stanton knew that it would take many weeks for
Republicans to pass some kind of act that would supersede Johnson's
August 20 proclamation and give sure legal footing to the continued
use of the military in the South. To justify military occupation in
the meantime, Stanton had to do the best he could with the laws
that Congress had already passed. The most important of these was
the new Freedmen's Bureau Act, which authorized military arrests
and military courts to protect Blacks in the South. Although the
president had lifted the suspension of habeas corpus, Stanton contended that bureau courts still could block habeas petitions issued by
civilian courts. To put things in non-legalese: the U.S. Army could
continue its war to ensure freedom for the once-enslaved.

Or maybe not. On December 12, 1866, the U.S. Supreme Court delivered its full opinion in the *Milligan* case. Chief Justice Salmon P. Chase had held off on the release for as long as he could. The opinion declared in unqualified terms that the military had no authority in any state where civilian courts were operative. There was no wiggle room as far as the states of the former Confederacy were concerned. The opinion applied equally to all states where civilian courts were operative. The president's August 20 proclamation had declared that civilian courts were operative in the southern states. Thus the Supreme Court in an instant stripped away the army's authority in the South. Stanton told a reporter that the opinion "overthrows the Freedmen's Bureau, and renders the army utterly powerless in the South." All restraints on racial violence were removed. As Stanton put it to the interviewer, the effect of the opinion would be to "turn the negroes over to the tender mercies of the rebel legislatures and courts in the South."[19]

The secretary of war was determined not to cede to white masters what had been wrested from them by Black and white U.S. soldiers over the past five years. One reason that he had given an interview about the Court's *Milligan* opinion was to make sure that northerners understood the stakes of treating the war as at an end. He needed them to see that letting go of the grasp of war now would lead inevitably to a collapse of all that had been achieved. The country would find itself right back where it had been at the start of secession, ruled by the same slaveholding oligarchs who had started the war.

The best way for Stanton to make his case would be to present the country with a full accounting of all the violence against Blacks committed by whites in the South during the past year and a half. Northerners knew something of the seismic massacres at Memphis and New Orleans, but they knew next to nothing of the day-to-day barbarities suffered by Black southerners. Stanton knew that Grant had been keeping a file of reports from his commanders that detailed the violence. This record of "murders and outrages," as it would become known, offered Stanton proof that he could take to the American people to show them that the president's peace proclamation and the Court's *Milligan* opinion had been issued prematurely. But there was a problem. The secretary of war could not simply release the information on his own. Such an undercutting of the president would rightly be regarded as an act of disobedience. Worse, the information that he wanted disseminated was sure to be lost amid sensational stories of Stanton's treachery. A release of the report would also jeopardize Grant's standing. The general was sure to be asked embarrassing questions. Why had he been collecting the information—to humiliate his superior, Andrew Johnson? Or: If he thought the accounts important, why hadn't he released them earlier? Secretary of War Stanton faced a challenge of a sort that would confound politicians in the years to come. He knew the truth about a phenomenon—in this instance, the recent racial violence in the South—but he had no sure way to deliver this truth in a manner guaranteed to make everyone believe it.[20]

The details of what happened next remain unclear, but almost certainly, Stanton worked behind the scenes with Republicans in the U.S. Senate to have the record of "murders and outrages" released in a way that did the greatest possible political harm to Andrew Johnson. Stanton's good friend Senator Henry Wilson, chair of the Senate Military Affairs Committee, was an important ally. Eventually, Stanton would leak the record of "murders and outrages" to the Massachusetts senator. Early on, though, it was Senator George H. Williams of Oregon whose maneuverings proved decisive in ensuring that Stanton prevailed in the political joust with Johnson.

Williams was a brilliant lawmaker who had spent most of his life in the East before settling in Portland, Oregon. He would eventually become U.S. attorney general and then be nominated to the U.S. Supreme Court, though the nomination was ultimately withdrawn. Unlike fellow Radical Republicans in the Senate like Charles Sumner and Benjamin Wade, Williams did not go in for fiery speeches and grand gestures. He was a committee man. He liked to have a hand in the drafting of actual legislation. He was one of the members of the Joint Committee on Reconstruction, the body that was primarily responsible for drafting the monumental constitutional amendment now before the states for ratification—the measure that would become the Fourteenth Amendment. He was the author of the two bills that had become the most important and controversial laws of the current congressional session: the Tenure of Office Act and the Reconstruction Act (sometimes called the Military Reconstruction Act). These laws proved to be the most effective challenge to President Johnson's authority that Congress would ever pass. Maybe Stanton sought out Williams directly. Maybe he approached him through intermediaries. However Stanton did it, Williams agreed to play a part in Stanton's scheme.

Stanton's plan hinged on the Civil Rights Act of 1866, specifically its military provisions. The ninth clause of the act declared that "it shall be lawful" for the president or "such person as he may empower" to use all available military forces "to prevent the violation" of the act and to "enforce the due execution of this act." The phrase "it shall be lawful" left room for interpretation. Did it mean that the president was merely authorized to use the military for the purposes described, or that he was *required* to use it? Stanton and the Republicans in Congress opted for the second meaning. If they could show that Black civil rights were being violated, then the president must prevent further violations by authorizing the army's presence in the South. If the president did nothing, Stanton would still be in his rights, as once "empowered" by the president, to act on his own to keep the army and its powers in place in case it needed to take preemptive action to sustain civil rights. In the wake of the *Milligan* opinion and the president's peace proclamation, the Civil Rights Act had become the only tool left to sustain the power of the U.S. Army in the South. Because the legal authority for the act came not from open-ended "war powers" but from the second clause of the Thirteenth Amendment, a measure meant for times of peace as well as war, the act could withstand the nullifying power of *Milligan*, which applied only to legislation passed specifically to prosecute a war.

In early January 1867, Stanton's plan went into motion. On January 8, Senator Williams issued a resolution that called on the president to supply "information" relating to violations of the Civil Rights Act. It carried easily. The president intended to respond with a token report. He wanted to preserve the myth that all was well and peaceful in the South. He ordered his cabinet members to supply him with any evidence they had of civil rights infractions, but he made it clear that the shorter their accounts, the better. Minimal reports, some effectively blank, came to Johnson from all of his cabinet members—except Stanton. The secretary of war had been sitting on Grant's record of "murders and outrages" long before President Johnson received the request for "information" from the Senate. Once the request arrived, Stanton turned to Grant and Major General Howard for news of any further episodes of white violence against Blacks. By February 15, Stanton's record of "murders and outrages" was massive. On that day, Johnson convened the cabinet to discuss the response that he had to give to the Senate. No one seemed to have much to say except Attorney General Henry Stanbery, who had reported to the president a handful of cases that federal attorneys had prosecuted in the South. They showed no worrisome pattern, Stanbery said, no evidence of the absence of peace.

Then Stanton dropped his report on the table with a thud. The effect was immediate, and devastating. The secretary of war had put the president face-to-face with a mountain of evidence showing that the peace he had proclaimed simply did not exist.[21]

Johnson had two choices. He could either suppress the report, thus deceiving Congress, or he could send it and suffer a sure rebuke from his Republican critics, who would use the material to mock his peace proclamations.

Johnson opted for deceit. He would not forward Stanton's material to Congress, he told his cabinet. At least a few cabinet members were fine with that. They told the president that he could send just a few parts of the report, or none of it, if that was his inclination.

Then Stanton dropped the final bomb. Keeping the report from Congress was not an option, he announced. "There was little doubt," said Stanton, that some members of the Senate already had the full report. Actually, there was no doubt. Stanton had leaked the report to his allies in the Senate. That had been his plan from the start. Everyone at the cabinet meeting saw what the war secretary had done. From this point on, no one in the Johnson administration, least of all Johnson himself, would trust Stanton.

Having backed the president into a corner, the secretary of war now presented him with a way out. All the president had to do, Stanton explained, was to issue a proclamation ordering U.S. officers in the South to enforce the Civil Rights Act. Yes, this would concede that southern whites were not abiding by their promises to uphold the law, but it need not concede that the nation was still at war. Johnson could save face by announcing that he was merely enforcing *peacetime* civil rights. Stanton had already composed the proclamation that the president could issue. He had taken a piece of War Department stationery, crossed out "War Department" and wrote in "Executive Mansion," and then pasted onto it the provision from the Civil Rights Act granting the president the power to use the army to protect civil rights. Then Stanton had written that this section of the act had effectively become part of military law by General Order 50. That order, issued back in mid-1866, did nothing more than inform commanders of the text of the Civil Rights Act. The order contained no instructions and thus was seen as trivial compared to General Orders 3 and 44, which were the basis of military rule in the South until they were annulled by the *Milligan* decision. Stanton's draft proclamation enabled military authority in the South to survive *Milligan*. It did so by taking an ostensibly peacetime measure, the Civil Rights Act, and exploiting a vague provision within it to keep the nation at war.[22]

President Johnson did not issue the order. His report to the Senate responding to its request for information included only a small part of what Stanton had wanted. The text of the Civil Rights Act was included, as were the relevant General Orders, and also a handful of recent incidents involving civil rights violations—a fraction of the detailed record of "murders and outrages."[23]

Republicans in the Senate were not satisfied with this meager offering, of course. They had seen Stanton's full report. They spoke publicly of its contents and of the fact that the president had suppressed it.

Johnson was certain that he would be impeached. He feared that congressional Republicans might even skip the formalities and simply arrest and "depose" him.[24] As always, Johnson assumed that there was a treasonous plot against him. This time, it turned out that he was close to the mark. His secretary of war was now in open opposition and had joined forces with the president's enemies in Congress. But Johnson had no intention of being deposed quietly. He would fire Stanton first.

For the moment, Stanton's job was safe. Congress was about to pass the Tenure of Office Act, one of the measures drafted by Senator Williams. The act prohibited the president from firing certain high-ranking officials, including the secretary of war, without the "advise and consent" of the Senate (the language of presidential dismissal was borrowed from the Constitution's language of presidential appointment). Keeping Stanton in charge of the army had always been the main purpose of the act. The senators who had worked in secret with Stanton to make public the "murders and outrages" report knew that the secretary's position would be in jeopardy once he made his opposition to Johnson public. They wanted Stanton to stay in his post because they needed the army to enforce congressional legislation.

The Tenure of Office Act was sure to pass. It had more than enough support from congressional Republicans to override a veto. Johnson was tempted to fire Stanton before the act took effect. He decided to wait. If he fired Stanton after the act was in place, then once the Senate blocked the removal, he could bring the act before the Supreme Court. He assumed that the Court would rule it unconstitutional.

Republicans in Congress looked forward to the moment when Johnson tried to fire Stanton. Once he did that, they could claim that he had violated the Tenure of Office Act and then use that violation as the basis of impeachment proceedings. Impeachment of Johnson was clearly on the mind of Senator Charles Sumner when he spoke in favor of the Tenure of Office Act. Although he did not invoke impeachment explicitly, Sumner implied that removing the president was a necessity in the still-ongoing war against southern rebels. What other choice was there? Johnson was "fomenting the rebel spirit and awakening anew the dying fires of the rebellion."[25]

The strategy of passing the Tenure of Office Act as a preliminary to presidential impeachment had been hatched by Johnson's severest critics in December 1866. In that month, the president crossed the line from being incompetent to being impeachable—at least in the view of the more radical congressional Republicans.

The decisive moment came when Johnson vetoed the bill granting voting rights to Black men in Washington, D.C. Most Republicans could live with the argument that Congress lacked the constitutional authority to impose Black suffrage on the states. But the District of Columbia was under exclusive federal jurisdiction. The president's veto removed any doubt as to why he opposed Black suffrage. The reason was racism, and racism alone. No one should have been surprised. For months Johnson had been expressing his skepticism about the nation being able to "absorb" Blacks into the body politic. By December 1866, the majority of white Republicans supported Black suffrage. Some saw it as the logical fulfillment of the promise of freedom. Others regarded it from a political standpoint only: in the South, Black votes were needed to counter the votes of white ex-Confederates if Republicans were going to hold on to power and keep the former Confederacy in a grasp of war. The author of the "Grasp of War" speech, Richard Henry Dana, Jr., had from the start identified Black voting rights as one of the concessions that must be secured from the southern states in order to guarantee the safety of the nation and its citizens.

When President Johnson vetoed the D.C. suffrage bill, he unwittingly nudged wavering Republicans into the camp of those who favored impeachment. As a first step in that direction, Republicans rallied behind the Tenure of Office Act.[26] They also voted to override Johnson's veto of the suffrage bill. By early 1867, Black men in the District had the right to vote.

With Secretary of War Stanton safely in place because of the forthcoming Tenure of Office Act, Congress could now start working openly and directly with him to manage military affairs. But Johnson was still commander in chief and could countermand any order that Stanton gave. Congressional Republicans and Stanton devised a solution. The secretary of war acknowledged the supreme military authority of the president but asked him to direct all of his orders to General Grant, who would implement them. In this way, because of Stanton's close working relationship with Grant, the secretary of war could monitor the president's orders. He and Grant would modify or withhold any they found objectionable. Johnson had no choice but to agree to the arrangement. To refuse was to imply that Grant was too unqualified or too untrustworthy to act as a conduit for the president's commands. If news got out that Johnson had put his own military abilities over those of Grant, he would be doomed. No president could disrespect the credentials of the nation's greatest military hero and expect to survive the political backlash.

Through Stanton and Grant, Congress now possessed more power than the president over the army. At no time before or since has the legislative branch so successfully usurped control over the army from the executive, the branch that was explicitly put in command of the armed forces by the Constitution. The president could take back some of that power by firing Stanton and replacing him with an ally. Once the Tenure of Office Act passed in early March, Washington insiders expected the firing to happen at any moment. It ended up taking Johnson nearly a year to remove Stanton, though not for want of trying. He was bedeviled by impediments. He could not fire Stanton until he had someone to fill the position. But no one wanted it. For months Grant was pressured by the president into taking the post. Eventually came the day when Johnson said that Grant had told him he would step in; Grant denied saying such a thing. The president reacted with fury, and a rift with the general ensued. No one took Johnson's side. Then there were the episodes of Johnson finding someone to take the job on an interim basis but Stanton refusing to make way for his replacement. At one point, Stanton barricaded himself in his office for days. His wife brought him his meals. During the whole months-long sequence of events, Congress was able to maintain command over the occupying forces in the South through its relationship with Stanton and Grant.

But power of command over the army meant nothing if the army had no power. The legal foundation of the military's authority in the South remained precarious. Stanton's proposed solution, which rested on a military provision of the Civil Rights Act, offered a temporary fix at best. It was a clever work-around of the obstacle presented by the Supreme Court's *Milligan* decision, but the Court might rule it unconstitutional. Indeed, the Court had yet to rule on the constitutionality of the Civil Rights Act as a whole, and it seemed likely that the Court would have to do so soon (as it turned out, the act was never ruled on by the Court; it was one of the only pieces of civil rights legislation of the era to survive the Court's counterattack on civil rights in the late nineteenth and early twentieth centuries). Military occupation of the South needed a firmer legal foundation if the army was going to be an effective, reliable tool for Congress to use in its war to finish off the Slave Power. Congress created the solution as part of its Reconstruction Act, adopted in March 1867.

The Reconstruction Act superimposed five military districts over all the states of the former Confederacy but Tennessee. Tennessee was exempted because its pro-Union government had already ratified the Fourteenth Amendment, leading Republicans in Congress to accept the state's delegation. Each of the military districts created by the Reconstruction Act had a commander, a command structure, and a set of military garrisons. The army in each district had superior authority to all civil authorities. Between the power that the act gave the occupying army and the informal command of the army that Congress possessed, Republicans in Congress now ruled the South—by force.

The contentious debate in Congress over the act began in December 1866, but the story of Congress trying to create *any* Reconstruction Act went back to December 1863. At that time, no one expected that it would take more than three years for Congress to adopt a measure that set the terms by which former Confederate states could be restored to the Union. Lincoln was alive in December 1863, of course, and he assumed that he would live long enough to sign a congressional bill for Reconstruction into law. The president's annual message of December 1863 included a statement of his own views of Reconstruction as well as a proclamation, intended to be temporary in effect, that set the terms by which rebel states could resume what he called their "practical relations" to the Union. It was up to Congress, Lincoln said, to write a permanent law that established guidelines for restoring the Union. Congress then began its debate about a Reconstruction bill. In July 1864, at the end of the congressional session, Congress adopted a measure known as the Wade-Davis bill and sent it to the president. Lincoln refused to sign it. The bill was thus rejected by "pocket veto." When Congress reconvened later that year, it failed to reach consensus on a new bill. Indeed, it would not agree on a new bill until it passed the Reconstruction Act of 1867.

Compared to the Reconstruction Act of 1867, the Wade-Davis bill proposed by Congress three years earlier seemed incredibly lenient, and Lincoln's objections to the measure seemed trivial. His ostensible reason for rejecting it was that it prohibited slavery in the southern states, something he said could only be done by a constitutional amendment. But this rationale was somewhat disingenuous. The president knew that the slavery would be abolished by constitutional amendment eventually—certainly within the next eighteen months or so—and he could simply have asked Congress to remove that one clause on this basis. (Asking Congress to modify the wording of a bill before he signed it was something that Lincoln had done before—for example, with the Second Confiscation Act of 1862). The real reason that Lincoln had pocket-vetoed the Wade-Davis bill was that he thought it treated Confederates too harshly. It excluded them from the processes of writing new state constitutions and voting for new state governments.

Yet much of the 1864 Wade-Davis bill had been perfectly acceptable to the president. The bill allowed states to deny voting rights to Blacks. That was fine by Lincoln. Not until April 1865 did he publicly endorse Black suffrage—and then only for Black veterans and the "most intelligent" of the race. The Wade-Davis bill also met with Lincoln's approval in the way it justified its constitutionality. The bill did not use "war powers" to authorize Congress to dictate how states would reconstruct their governments. Instead, it relied on the "guarantee clause" of the Constitution. This clause guaranteed that every state would have a "republican form of government." By the common reasoning of 1864, the states of the Confederacy were un-republican—they allowed slavery, and they supported secession—so Congress had the power to make them republican. New state constitutions would have to prohibit slavery and renounce secession. For Lincoln in particular, the use of the guarantee clause instead of "war powers" to authorize Reconstruction was crucial. He had crafted and tried to implement his Reconstruction policy at the height of the war, but he had expected most of Reconstruction to take place in a time of peace. Once the United States was victorious and peace was made, he reasoned, the "war powers" would disappear. Reconstruction therefore had to rest on a constitutional principle like the guarantee clause that was operational in peacetime.

The Reconstruction Act of 1867, adopted less than two years after Lincoln's death, would have seemed alien to him. It stipulated that if former Confederate states wanted representation in Congress, they first had to ratify the Fourteenth Amendment, a measure that Lincoln had never anticipated and parts of which he surely would have found objectionable—most notably the clause denying the right to hold government office to thousands of ordinary whites who had supported the Confederacy. Lincoln also might have balked at the provision in the Reconstruction Act of 1867 that required states to allow *all* adult Black men to vote, not just veterans and the "most intelligent." But by far the most troubling aspect of the act for Lincoln would have been its position in regard to peace. The act left no doubt that the country was in a state of war. In seeking constitutional justification for the measure, lawmakers in Congress had turned away from the guarantee clause and relied solely on Richard Henry Dana's "grasp of war" theory. Representative James Garfield made the connection between Dana's theory and the new law explicit: "We must lay the heavy hand of military authority upon these rebel communities, and hold them in its grasp till their madness is passed."[27] The U.S. armies had been victorious; the Confederate armies had signed surrenders. Where was the peace that Lincoln had expected?

It would be a mistake to assume, however, that Lincoln would have disapproved of the steps taken by Republican lawmakers over the past two years, or that his presence, had he not been assassinated, would have kept lawmakers from taking them. Events had a logic of their own, the slain president had understood. He could not control events, he liked to say; they controlled him. Or, to put it in the religious terms that he had used in his Second Inaugural: "The Almighty has His own purposes."

Not all of the Republicans who backed the Reconstruction Act of 1867 believed that the United States was still in a state of war. The measure had much support from a group described by the historian Gregory Downs as "peacetime Republicans"—lawmakers who insisted that peace existed so far as the initial rebellion was concerned, but that residual "war powers" remained, allowing for the passage of legislation like the Reconstruction Act. Yet there was no clear factional split between the "peacetime" and "wartime" Republicans in Congress. Each lawmaker seemed to have his own theory as to where to draw the line between war and peace. Some acknowledged that there might be no obvious point where war ended and peace began, that instead there was something of a spectrum ranging from one state to the other. But even these lawmakers could not find consensus. Each put the country on a different point on the war-to-peace spectrum.[28]

Regardless of what any single person's view was on the end-of-war question, all could see that if the country was still at war, the war was different now than it had once been. Americans looked for language to capture the difference—before was a war of arms, now was a war of ideas; before was a rebellion, now was an occupation—but the perfect words eluded them.

The Reconstruction Act did not settle all or even most of the end-of-war questions, but it did provide clear answers to two of the questions at least. First, it resolved who was in charge of the war: Congress, not the president. Second, it specified when the war would be over. It would happen on the day that all of the former states of the Confederacy were represented in Congress. In other words, when all of the once-rebellious states had met the conditions imposed on them by the Reconstruction Act, the war would end. Congress had done precisely what Richard Henry Dana had recommended in the summer of 1865, though it had taken them nearly two years to get there. It had resolved to hold the South in a grasp of war until it received from the South far-reaching concessions that would assure the security of the country.

Naturally, Dana was thrilled by the Reconstruction Act. He saw that it contained "the principle" at the heart of his "Grasp of War" speech of June 1865. The nation needed a new foundation, he told his friend Charles Francis Adams, and the act went "down to the *hard pan*. It builds up upon the rock." Until now, he told Adams, the victors had simply been "drifting." They had been too "trifling" with the vanquished, "annoying and guerrilla-ing the South, to little purpose."[29] Only now, Dana believed, had the war to end the war begun in earnest.

At some point in lawmakers' deliberations about the Reconstruction Act, they discovered a small, important detail in the congressional record. In late February 1867, only days before the final vote on the Reconstruction Act took place, Congress had approved a measure establishing new pay rates for the army. Within the bill was a phrase that all had overlooked. It affirmed August 20, 1866, the day of President Johnson's peace proclamation, as the day the war ended. Now *that* was a potential snarl, Republicans in Congress agreed. If they took seriously what they had done, then they must relinquish the argument that the war still continued. But that would kick the supports out from under their Reconstruction bill. Senator James

Dixon of Connecticut, a Republican who had been ready to vote for the Reconstruction bill, now said that he could not. He had voted for an end date of August 20, 1866, he declared. True, he had not known at the time that he was approving that date, but no matter. He could not now vote for a measure—the Reconstruction bill—that denied the date.[30] Yet Dixon was the only Republican who opted for principle, or at least *a* principle, the principle of consistency. The rest decided that a higher principle was served by ignoring the apparent obstacle and pressing on with the Reconstruction bill.

At the various moments after 1867 when the U.S. Supreme Court took up the question of when the Civil War ended, the Court returned more than once to the moment in February 1867 when Congress unwittingly accepted August 20, 1866, as the end date. In 1869, Justice David Davis dismissed what had happened as insignificant. He declared that the war could be "considered as suppressed for one purpose and not for another." In legalistic parsing of a sort that had occurred often during the debate over the Reconstruction Act—indeed, that had occurred often in the whole period from Appomattox to the passage of that act and beyond— Justice Davis argued that there was a difference between the "actual termination of the war" and "the political question of the continuance of the rights of war, after the termination in fact of hostilities." A year after Davis made his argument, the Court put an end to the parsing. In a little-noted decision of 1871, the Court ruled that when Congress affirmed the August 20, 1866, end date, even if it did so unwittingly, it made that date a fact. Or at least a fact of law.[31] The Court's 1871 decision held. From that point forward, the Supreme Court treated August 20, 1866, as the end of the Civil War. So it turned out that when Congress adopted the Reconstruction Act on March 2, 1867, the war was already over after all. And, of course, it wasn't.

The Reconstruction Act itself was never overturned by the Supreme Court. It stayed in effect until February 1, 1871. On that day, the last member of Georgia's congressional delegation was seated by Congress. All of the former states of the Confederacy were now represented in the national legislature. By its own terms, the Reconstruction Act ceased to be in effect. The war was over—again.

George P. A. Healy, *The Peacemakers* (1868)

The Peacemakers

. . . the end of all our exploring
Will be to arrive where we started
And know the place for the first time.

T. S. Eliot, "Little Gidding" (1942), *Four Quartets*[1]

ABRAHAM LINCOLN'S VOYAGE to Virginia in the spring
of 1865, undertaken to end the Civil War, was immortalized
in *The Peacemakers,* the 1868 painting by George P. A. Healy. Healy
tried to capture the moment when Lincoln advised his commanders
to be merciful to their onetime enemies. The painting shows storm
clouds giving way to sunshine outside the ship. Lincoln is bathed
in light, his head haloed by a distant rainbow. The scene evokes the
passing of war, the coming of peace: an ending.

There is no hint in the painting of the disappointment that Lincoln felt when his venture on the James River came to an end with
no peace in hand. Nothing in the painting suggests the reality of
months of warring that followed the historic meeting. Instead, the
painting delivers a message of hope: Even the nation's bloodiest
conflict could be brought to a peaceful end.

The message was compelling. It shaped the history of the Civil
War, as well as the war's memory in American culture. It also became
one of the tenets underpinning notions of American exceptionalism: the United States knows how to end its wars.

—

Until recently, histories of the Civil War ended at Appomattox Court House, the site of the most famous surrender in American history. Lincoln was not present at the surrender. That was likely the reason that Healy chose for his painting an event that took place two weeks before Appomattox. He needed a place where Lincoln, quite literally, was in the picture. American historians, though, opted for the Appomattox ending. Bruce Catton's multivolume centennial history of the war ends with Grant trotting up the road toward the McLean house to see Lee.[2] In his four-volume history of the war, Allan Nevins follows the description of the Appomattox surrender with the statement that "the collapse and surrender of other Confederate pockets may be briefly dismissed."[3] He does not mention the battles of Columbus, Georgia, or Palmito Ranch, Texas, by name. They cannot be found in Shelby Foote's multivolume saga of the war, nor in James M. McPherson's *Battle Cry of Freedom,* the bestselling single-volume history of the war. All of these authors mention the surrenders that followed Appomattox, but all seem content to treat Appomattox as the final battle.

Columbus and Palmito Ranch have not gone missing, though. Regional and local historians, antiquarians, history buffs, bloggers, and trivia fanatics of all sorts have kept their stories alive. Books about Palmito Ranch describe it as the last battle of the Civil War.[4] But the historian Charles A. Misulia says no: Columbus was the last. The title of his book conveys his argument: *Columbus, Georgia, 1865: The Last True Battle of the Civil War.* The battle at Columbus preceded Palmito Ranch by more than a month, so Misulia devotes much of the book to explaining why the engagement in Texas did not count as an actual battle. A long appendix at the end of the book provides standards for what counts as a battle and what counts as a mere skirmish. Columbus had the numbers of soldiers and casualties to qualify it as a battle, Misulia claims, but Palmito Ranch failed to make the cut; it ranked only as a "skirmish."[5] Misulia may be onto something. Back on August 10, 1865, the officer who commanded U.S. troops at Palmito Ranch wrote the official report of what happened there. He called it an "engagement," not a battle. But he did say that it was the "last" engagement. Indeed, he called it "the last actual conflict between hostile forces in the great rebellion."[6]

Do the words really matter? It is important to get history right, and the writers who draw attention to the battles (or skirmishes or engagements) that took place after Appomattox should be applauded for their commitment to accuracy. Yet all of them are perpetuating a fiction: that the Civil War necessarily had a battle that was final.

The approach contains another fallacy as well: that the war must be considered separately from the conflicts associated with "postwar" Reconstruction or the wars of the same period that were fought by the United States against Native Americans. Glory does not shine on these other conflicts the way that it does on the Civil War. In keeping the Civil War insulated from these other conflicts, historians help maintain its reputation as a good war, a noble war, the truest American war.

Consider the impact—for good or for bad—if a battle typically kept out of the Civil War frame were brought into focus. Take, for example, the Battle of Platte Bridge Station, July 26, 1865, in present-day Wyoming. It is another battle that comes in under the wire before President Johnson gave his August 20, 1866, proclamation ending the Civil War. In this engagement, a coalition of Lakota Sioux and Cheyenne successfully attacked a bridge guarded by U.S. troops. Almost forty soldiers died, most of them white Federals. The battle was in many ways a culmination of a much longer struggle between the Lakota and the U.S. government, the most infamous incident of which was the Sand Creek massacre of December 1864. But how can Platte Bridge be counted as a *Civil War* battle? the skeptic asks. This was not a conflict between troops of the Confederate army and the U.S. Army. Yet that requirement for a legitimate battle is rather arbitrary. Plenty of Civil War engagements later counted as battles involved unaffiliated guerrilla groups. Moreover, members of many indigenous tribes and nations, including the Sioux and Cheyenne, affiliated with Confederate or U.S. units during various points of the war. So why can't a conflict previously relegated to the category of "Indian War" be brought into the constellation of Civil War battles?

Here is another candidate for the "last battle," this one coming long after President Johnson's peace proclamation: the Battle of Ellenton, South Carolina, September 18–19, 1876. The combatants numbered in the thousands and included U.S. troops, southern white paramilitary groups, and a well-trained Black militia unit.

Participants called it a battle—or a war—and when the two days of fighting were over, as many as fifty soldiers lay dead, almost all of them African Americans. It was one of the last victories of the white armed forces of South Carolina. Seven months later, on April 11, 1877, more than ten years after Appomattox, Wade Hampton, who had been elected governor by southern whites who opposed the U.S. occupying forces in the state, surrendered to Daniel Chamberlain, the governor recognized by the U.S. government. As one historian would later describe the moment, "the Civil War, one chapter in a great American struggle, had finally come to a close."[7]

The movement to rethink the temporal and spatial boundaries of the Civil War is gaining ground. One line of attack contends that the multiple instances of racial violence during Reconstruction leading to the "redemption" of the white South should be counted as Civil War battles. That is the message of *Redemption: The Last Battle of the Civil War* (2006), Nicolas Lemann's riveting account of how the Civil War continued unabated in Mississippi, where in the 1870s U.S. troops, white "terrorists," and once-enslaved Blacks fought over the same causes that had animated the war in the prior decade. Most historians are reluctant to treat the period from 1861 to 1877 as one long Civil War. But they get pretty close to this position. The more common tendency these days is to treat the violence following Confederate surrender as a new phase of war rather than a continuation of the same war. Still, there is little consensus on what this phase should rightly be called—a war of Reconstruction? a war against insurgency? a war of occupation?—or how long it lasted. It is no coincidence that the debates echo those over the proper names and dates of the recent U.S. wars in Iraq and Afghanistan.[8] As always, the present shapes the past. So will the future. We are not done asking the question: When was the Civil War over?

As for *where* the Civil War was, a question that necessarily affects the *when* of its endpoint, that, too, is unresolved. In the period between when I began writing this book and when I completed it, at least a dozen books were published that weave into the war people and regions that are normally cut out: European imperialists in Mexico; Irish radicals in English Canada; and Native Americans in the deserts and plains of the U.S. West. Bringing these actors into the drama of the Civil War makes it even harder to know when to drop the curtain. In mid-1867, after Napoleon III removed his troops from Mexico, Maximilian's republican opponents seized control of the country and executed the interloping emperor. The U.S. need for an "Army of Observation" at the Mexican border was gone. That was an ending of sorts, wasn't it? In the same year, Great Britain passed the act consolidating all of its holdings north of the United States into a single province: Canada. North America was now clearly divided into three stable sovereign spaces: Canada, the United States, and Mexico.[9] By one line of reasoning, 1867 was an endpoint to a Civil War that was, among other things, a conflict about sectionalism.

But that date doesn't work when one factors in the indigenous population living in North America. By 1867, the United States had signed new treaties with the Five Civilized Tribes, restoring their semi-sovereign status and their pre–Civil War borders. All the tribes were required to prohibit slavery. The Cherokee, who had had the longest dalliance with the Confederacy, paid an extra price: they were required to extend tribal citizenship to freed people in their territory.[10] Not until 1868 did the U.S. government settle an agreement with the Sioux—the Fort Laramie Treaty, which the U.S. Army immediately began to violate. In 1871, the U.S. government declared that it would make no further treaties with tribes, a policy that the U.S. Army had been advocating for more than a decade. That was the same year that Congress declared that the Civil War was over because it had admitted the last representatives from the formerly seceded states. The United States was united once again—and could find common cause in fighting Native Americans. There were defeats in that fight, the Battle of Little Bighorn in 1876 most famously, but by the end of 1877, the same year that the United States removed the last troops from the former Confederacy, the army had subdued all the major tribes of the West.[11]

During the period when the U.S. Army withdrew from the former Confederacy and threw its full force against Native Americans, two men had held ranks above all others. One was William T. Sherman, now a full general and commander of the army. The other was the commander in chief, which is to say the president: Ulysses S. Grant. The two men were still fighting for peace, the peace that was

supposed to have arrived soon after their meeting with Abraham
Lincoln aboard the *River Queen* in March 1865.

Each officer depicted in *The Peacemakers* represented a distinct theater of war: Ulysses S. Grant, the general of the eastern armies (and of
course the general in chief as well); William T. Sherman, the general
of the West; and David Dixon Porter, the admiral of the oceans. One
can imagine these as simple spheres with clear boundaries. Grant
will soon make peace with Lee: peace will ensue in the East. Then
Sherman will make peace with Johnston: that will end the war in
the West. Porter through all this will help oversee the lifting of the
naval blockade and the recall of U.S. warships.

   The painting offers no hints of the actual geographical messiness
of the war or the chaos that would follow the meeting on board the
River Queen. Grant would have to deal not only with Confederate
diehards in the East but also guerrillas in the West. Sherman would
attempt to make a peace that would mar the U.S. general's reputation
forever. Porter, along with the rest of the high command of the U.S.
Navy, failed to prevent the devastation wrought by the *Shenandoah*.
The painting tells of only one war, the Union conflict with the Confederacy, and of only one time, 1861 to 1865. We take in the scene
without having to think of the wars west of the Mississippi and
beyond the temporal boundary of 1865. The "West" is not the West
where Lakota Sioux control the Great Plains and Navajo struggle
to break free from the Bosque Redondo. The "West" stops at the
Mississippi, the boundary of Sherman's theater. As for the imagined
war to come with Maximilian's Mexico, or the real wars with Native
Americans already underway and unceasing, or the endless bloody
feuding in Texas—all these are left invisible. But they all turned out
to be crucial when investigators of one sort or another tried to hunt
down the true end of the Civil War.

   Recall Lewis Grant, one of those investigators. Grant, a lawyer for
the U.S. War Department in the last years of the nineteenth century,
struggled to find the end of the Civil War long before historians of
the recent era set out on a similar quest. What set him on his path
was a pension dispute. The claimant said his military service was
wartime service. A pension agent said that the soldier had fought at

the wrong time and in the wrong place to be considered a Civil War veteran. Grant ended up with a different answer.

It matters quite a bit that the question that flummoxed the investigators turned on the issue of violent conflicts between whites and Native Americans. Was it right to count such episodes as part of the Civil War? By the time that Lewis Grant took up the question, the history of the U.S. Civil War and the history of the "Indian Wars," stories once entangled, had been unwoven into separate strands.

The untangling, which created a history at once simpler and less accurate, had been done with the help of U.S. lawmakers. The first law establishing pensions for U.S. soldiers in the Civil War was adopted in 1862. It granted pensions only to veterans who were visibly disabled. A widow or an orphan could claim the pension if the soldier had died. The law said nothing about where the soldier had served or whom he had been fighting. To receive the pension, he only needed to have been "in the service of the United States, and in the line of duty."[12] A U.S. soldier who lost a leg fighting Dakotas in Minnesota in the fall of 1862 would receive the same pension as a soldier who suffered the same injury during the same period at the hands of Confederates in Virginia. By the 1880s, however, policy had changed. Pension officers by then, like most Americans, had bought into the myth that the Civil War was a conflict between only two sides—Unionists versus Confederates—and it had ended neatly in the spring of 1865. In this compartmentalization of time and of war, there was no way to make easy sense of U.S. soldiers who had enlisted to fight Confederates in the South but instead had been dispatched to contend with Native Americans in the West. Such was the story of John Barleyoung, the soldier of the 13th New York Infantry whose case would eventually cross the desk of Lewis Grant, launching the War Department official on his quest to find the endpoint of the Civil War.

A decade before Grant took up the case of Barleyoung, a different but related sort of puzzle had arrived at the pension office. Eight veterans of the 1st Michigan Cavalry applied for Civil War pensions in 1880. Their unit had served in the East for most of the war, been present at Lee's surrender at Appomattox, and then been assigned to the Bosque Redondo to quell uprisings there among the Navajo and Mescalero Apache. Eventually the unit joined the Powder River Expedition in midsummer 1865. The pension applicants had left their unit and gone home as soon as orders arrived sending them to the Bosque. Like others in their situation, they had assumed that they had fulfilled their duty: they had signed up to fight "during the war," and the war was over once the last of the Confederate armies surrendered in mid-1865. Now, fifteen years later, they were taking the logical step of requesting a Civil War pension. The pension agent was stymied. On the one hand, he agreed with the applicants that the Civil War had ended by mid-1865, and therefore the men had fulfilled their terms. On the other hand, he could see that the men had left their unit without being officially discharged, and that their regiment had not mustered out until March 1866—so they were deserters and thus were disqualified to receive pensions. The pension officer took the question to his superiors, but they could provide no answer. The Pension Bureau then asked the U.S. attorney general, Charles Devens, for a ruling.

Devens himself had been in the war, commanding a Massachusetts regiment and eventually being promoted to brevet major general. All of his service had been in Virginia. It was natural, then, that his first instinct was to assume that the war had indeed ended at Appomattox—that's where it had ended for him—and that the Michigan soldiers had been justified in leaving their unit. But how, then, to explain the soldiers' unit not mustering out until March 1866, almost a year after Appomattox? He worried that the War Department had broken some law by requiring the volunteers to serve for a year beyond the end of the war. Devens took the matter to his colleague, Secretary of War Alexander Ramsey.

Ramsey assured Devens that no law had been broken. "The war," he explained to the attorney general, encompassed more than the U.S. fight against the Confederacy and lasted well beyond mid-1865. Ramsey's thinking was shaped by his own experience of the war, which had been quite different from that of Devens. He had been the governor of Minnesota during the Dakota uprising in 1862. He had pleaded successfully with the War Department at the time to send troops to his state to end the uprising and, if possible, to drive all the Sioux from Minnesota. It had not mattered to Ramsey at the time if the volunteers dispatched to Minnesota thought that "the war" they had signed up to fight was restricted to battles with Confederates. In his mind, war was war, regardless of the enemy of the moment. He applied this same logic to the case of the Michigan men now applying for Civil War pensions. Ramsey may well have thought that the "Indian War" was not exactly the same as the "Confederate War," but any difference was irrelevant. Men who had committed to fighting "the war" were on the hook for *all* wars. The Michigan men were thus deserters, Ramsey decided. Attorney General Devens deferred to his colleague, no doubt relieved that he could avoid accusing the War Department of breaking the law. As for the Michigan veterans, they would not be receiving pensions. But they also would not be going to prison for desertion. Civil War deserters had been granted amnesty many years earlier.[13]

As the back-and-forth between Devens and Ramsey revealed, pension law through at least 1880 allowed for a version of history in which the Civil War lasted into 1866, maybe longer, and involved U.S. soldiers fighting Native Americans as well as Confederates. That version of history did not survive to the turn of the twentieth century. In a new pension law of 1890, applicants were required to have served at least ninety days "during the late war of the rebellion."[14] The new law made clear that service in a war against "Indians" did not count as service in "the late war of the rebellion." During the debate over the law, some congressmen pointed out that wars against "Indians" and wars against Confederates had overlapped. The chairman of the Senate Committee on Pensions, Cushman K. Davis of Minnesota, responded that veterans who had served only in "Indian wars" deserved their own pension law, and that he would soon propose one (he didn't). At the same time, he insisted that men who had fought Native Americans were not *Civil War* veterans. "Indian wars were very different" from the Civil War, Davis explained. "Very often they sprang up and were suppressed by people who were not mustered into the service of the United States."[15] Davis had grown up in Wisconsin, served in the Civil War, mostly in Arkansas, and moved in 1865 to St. Paul, Minnesota, where he launched his political career. Just before he arrived in Minnesota, thirty-eight Dakota Sioux had been hanged and the rest driven from the state, all by soldiers "mustered into the service of the United States" to fight the Civil War. Even in 1865 and afterward, Davis must have heard reports of the continued fighting just to the west between Civil War soldiers and the Dakotas and their allies. Somehow, though, between 1865 and 1890, he had filed that history in a separate compartment of his memory from the history of the Civil War.

U.S. soldiers who had fought only Native Americans during the Civil War eventually got pensions—but not Civil War pensions. In 1892, two years after it adopted the new Civil War pension law, Congress passed its first law granting pensions to veterans of "Indian Wars," though only those conflicts fought before 1842. Not until 1927 did Congress pass an act allowing pensions for U.S. soldiers who had served against Native Americans—and *only* against Native Americans—during the era of the Civil War. These veterans would receive only half as much as those who had fought against the Confederacy. From the perspective of lawmakers—and, eventually, of history as well—these men were not Civil War heroes but soldiers of an inferior class: "Indian fighters." It was no longer possible, no longer conceivable, that they could have been both.[16]

Returning again to Healy's *Peacemakers,* one must state the obvious: all the subjects pictured are white. There are no Black soldiers in the painting, though many were stationed at City Point at the time. When the four men met on the *River Queen,* the wharves surrounding them were likely teeming with Black stevedores. It is simply impossible to read anything about race or slavery into the painting. Healy carefully constructed a contrast between shadows and light. But these are not the shadows of slavery. This is not the light of freedom.

Putting the end of slavery into the story of the end of the Civil War has rarely if ever been done well. The two endings, so obviously connected, are kept in different frames. Maybe mere chronology is to blame. Military victory over the Confederacy came first. Destruction of slavery, the Confederacy's cornerstone, came later. Yet the sequence does not in itself explain why only the first event, and almost never the second, is typically counted as the end of the Civil War.

The centennial celebration at Appomattox, held on April 9, 1965, offers a clue (by 1965, the town of Appomattox Court House had been renamed simply Appomattox). The National Park Service, which planned the event, decided to keep it low-key. Resentment among white southerners ran high. Civil rights activists had been active across the South in the past year, making sure that anti-segregation policy enacted by the Civil Rights Act the year before was being upheld. In Mississippi the previous summer, hundreds of northerners had bused into the state to enroll Black voters and ensure that they were able to cast their ballots. Whites in Appomattox thought that the South was suffering a second Yankee invasion. They were less than eager to commemorate the defeat they had suffered in the first. The Park Service, reading well the landscape of public opinion, decided to focus on the theme of reconciliation instead of defeat. There was no reenactment of the failure of Lee's troops to break free of the Federals' cordon—though the decision not to reenact Lee's defeat was as much about public health as political propriety. The Park Service had been wary of incorporating battle reenactments into centennial events ever since the debacle at Manassas (Bull Run), Virginia, four years earlier, when scores of wool-clad reenactors had fainted in the summer heat. Observers had mocked the "pagan" pretend fighting of the "pseudo-soldiers." At Appomattox four years later, organizers kept the affair subdued. The only reenactment was the friendly meeting between Grant and Lee at the McLean house. A speaker then introduced General Lee's great-grandson to the onlookers, and the U.S. Marine Corps Band played "Dixie."[17] The featured speech of the day, delivered by the historian Bruce Catton, acknowledged the "Lost Cause" tradition that romanticized Lee and his men. "The story of the Lost Cause," Catton declared, was "a positive asset to the united country." It was a story with a central truth essential to American greatness: Lee's noble men had accepted defeat over "unending rancor," and in doing so had "helped the country to put itself together again."[18]

One of the journalists who attended the Appomattox centennial was Tania Long, who had earned much fame as one of the only female reporters to report from London during the bombing raids of World War II. Sympathetic to the cause of civil rights, Long, a white woman, decided to investigate the attitudes of Black residents of Appomattox. She found that almost all lived in a small working-class community cut off from the main town by a highway. "The two races never mingle socially," Long learned; "the Negroes go to their own church and leave community affairs to the whites." Almost all of them worked for a local foundry, which had given them no time off to attend the centennial events. Their employer demanded that they work an eight-hour shift every day of the week, including Sundays. When Long asked the oldest Black resident of the town, Scott Palmer, whose parents had been enslaved, how things had changed over the past hundred years, Palmer replied, "Oh, they's about the same, about the same. Human nature don't change."[19]

In Appomattox County today, the story of emancipation is still eclipsed by a story of reunion laced with Lost Cause mythology. A small sign put up just before the centennial declaring Appomattox County the place "where our country reunited" has been replaced by a larger sign with the exact same message. Monuments to Confederate heroes have come down in the state capital of Richmond a hundred miles to the east. But the main road through Appomattox is still called "Confederate Boulevard." "I don't see any Emancipation Boulevard," a Black pastor in the town recently remarked to a reporter.[20]

While in most of Appomattox County today, the theme of sectional reconciliation overshadows that of Black freedom, at Appomattox Court House National Historical Park, the centrality of the African American experience in the Civil War cannot be missed. Displays draw attention to Black Virginians who lived in the area when the legendary meeting between Grant and Lee took place. One notable panel tells the story of Hannah Reynolds, an enslaved Black woman in Appomattox Court House who was the only civilian killed in the area during the fighting that ended with Lee's surrender. The integration of African American history into the National Historical Park began in about 2010, when National Park Service historians saw the coming 150th anniversary in 2015 as an opportunity to remind visitors that the Civil War, including its ending, was part of a greater struggle for Black freedom. At the visitors center, guests are invited to examine a list of Black people enslaved in Appomattox County at the time of Lee's surrender and then to write the name of one of these people on a small bag. Park staff convert the bags into luminaries, which are lit and displayed in an evening ceremony every year on the anniversary of the surrender. The yearly commemoration, once known simply as Surrender Day, is now called Surrender and Freedom Day. Prominently displayed in the park's bookstore is Elizabeth R. Varon's *Appomattox: Victory, Defeat, and Freedom at the End of the Civil War*. Varon's prizewinning book, published in 2014, helped transform the history of the site. It emphasized the role played by Black soldiers in the battles leading up to the surrender and reminded readers that African Americans in Virginia in the late 1800s regularly celebrated April 9 as a Freedom Day.[21]

On the 150th anniversary of the surrender, in 2015, many of the changes to the park had yet to be implemented, and Varon's book had only recently hit the shelves. It was nearly impossible to get to the commemoration without passing one of the road signs at the county border that celebrated a "country reunited." The historian David Blight, who spoke at the park during the anniversary, hit a sour but appropriate note when he declared that "the great issues of the war"—meaning Black freedom and racial justice—"were not resolved on that April morning at Appomattox." "In this sense," he reflected, "not only is the Civil War not over; it can still be lost."[22] He was echoing the historian Barbara Fields, the only commentator in Ken Burns's 1990 popular documentary of the Civil War to question what, if anything, the war had really resolved (Fields also happened to be the only Black historian featured in the documentary). If the Civil War was a "struggle to make something higher and better out of the country," said Fields, then "the Civil War is not over." "If some citizens live in houses and others live in the street, the Civil War is still going on. . . . It's still to be fought, and regrettably it can still be lost."[23]

Alas, such high aspirations of what Americans can achieve with their wars, coupled with the dizzying complexity attending the end of any war, leaves the seeker of a just, moral end to the Civil War in a fog. Is it any wonder that so many choose the simple, safe haven of Appomattox? Blessed are the peacemakers. Woe to those who would dim their sacred glow.

In George Healy's 1868 painting, the peacemakers shine. The message of *The Peacemakers*—that the Civil War had an ideal and final endpoint—was so compelling that American presidents kept the painting hanging in the White House for more than a hundred years. As the United States entered each new war, *The Peacemakers* stirred nostalgia for a noble war-ending and gave faith that every war ended. Appropriately, it hung in the Treaty Room for most of its years in the White House. It was there in 1898 when the Treaty Room got its name with the signing of the peace treaty with Spain in 1898. That "end" of war was followed by four more years of U.S. military intervention in the Philippines. Richard Nixon was standing before *The Peacemakers* in 1973 when he announced that peace with Vietnam had been settled, though the United States continued fighting there for two more years. In 1990, after George H. W. Bush ordered the invasion of Iraq, he gave two separate speeches declaring his affection for the painting. His son, George W. Bush, used the painting as a backdrop on October 7, 2001, when he announced that U.S. troops had invaded Afghanistan.

Soon after taking office in 2021, President Joe Biden announced that the U.S. war in Afghanistan would come to an end on September 11 of that year. The date was carefully chosen: the twentieth anniversary of the terrorist attacks that set the United States on the road to its longest war ever. Biden was not the first president to promise an end to American involvement in Afghanistan. This time, though, the promise was kept. A few commentators contrasted the retreat with the Union's victory in the Civil War. One wrote that a failure of resolve such as Biden had shown would have been anathema to Ulysses S. Grant, who "hammered away" at Robert E. Lee until decisive and complete victory was attained.[24] Former president Donald Trump, who had his own ideas about who had come out on top at Appomattox, declared: "If only we had Robert E. Lee to command our troops in Afghanistan, that disaster would have ended in a complete and total victory many years ago."[25] The historian Dillon Carroll offered an entirely different perspective, suggesting that the end of the Civil War had not been that different from the end of the war in Afghanistan. "The lenient peace process that allowed most Confederates to go unpunished and enabled white supremacy to descend anew on the South left many Northern veterans bitter, anguished and frustrated," Carroll wrote. The withdrawal from Afghanistan was not the first time that those who had fought for the United States wondered "whether their sacrifices were worth making."[26] The comparison was incisive but bordered on heresy. Who dared suggest that the ending of the American Civil War was anything but perfect?

The American war in Afghanistan ended poorly. A few thousand U.S. military personnel were left in Afghanistan after the official troop withdrawal. The skeletal American force could not stop the Taliban from surging back into power. Many of the advances that had been made in the country during twenty years of U.S. occupation, especially the increased freedom and opportunity for Afghani women, were lost in a matter of weeks.

George Healy's painting of the end of the Civil War—or rather, *an* end—no longer hangs in one of the highly visible spaces of the White House. At some point soon after President Biden took office in 2021, his staff moved *The Peacemakers* out of its place next to the Oval Office and into an undisclosed private location. There are no plans to bring it back into public view.[27]

Acknowledgments

The seeds of this book were planted at a conference held at Dickinson College in 2005 on war powers and the laws of war. Matt Pinsker, the organizer of the conference, thus deserves much credit or blame. Either way, I am grateful to him for the wisdom that he has shared with me during a friendship that goes back thirty-five years to a legendary seminar that we took together on Abraham Lincoln.

At Brown University, I have had the good fortune to work with learned, generous colleagues whose work and advice helped me at every stage of the book's creation. When I contemplated the risky move of taking up the end-of-war topic in earnest, which meant putting on hold a book that was well underway, three colleagues gave crucial encouragement (alas, two have since left Brown). They may not remember, but I certainly do. So thank you to Jim Campbell, Karl Jacoby, and Robert Self. Karl also nudged me in the right direction as I began looking for an agent and a publisher. As I worked on the book, scholars at Brown provided important feedback as well as suggestions for broadening my perspective. Most of these people I know as fellow members of the history department. Others I have met through my involvement with the Simmons Center for the Study of Slavery and Justice, the Cogut Institute for the Humanities, and the Pembroke Center for Teaching and Research on Women. They include Faiz Ahmed, Omer Bartov, Tony Bogues, Jonathan Conant, Lin Fisher, Phil Gould, Chris Grasso, Françoise Hamlin, Bonnie Honig, Rebecca Nedostup, Emily Owens, Seth

Rockman, Naoko Shibusawa, Kerry Smith, Michael Steinberg, and Suzanne Stewart-Steinberg. The staff of the history department—Julissa Bautista, Mary Beth Bryson, and Cherrie Guerzon—deserve medals. Every day they deal with salvos fired at them from the high ground, and they refuse to surrender.

Archivists and librarians at Brown and elsewhere have facilitated the research process and introduced me to sources that I otherwise would never have found. At Brown's John Hay Library, Tom Horrocks, Mary-Jo Kline, and Holly Snyder were generous and helpful beyond belief. Similar kindness and assistance were provided by David Mihaly and Olga Tsapina at the Huntington Library in San Marino, California, as well as Peter Drummond and Kate Viens at the Massachusetts Historical Society in Boston. My greatest good fortune, archivally speaking, was meeting Mike Musick of the National Archives before he retired. Mike patiently explained to me the arcane organizational structure of Civil War–era legal and military records at the archives. On a whim, he brought me some dusty boxes that only he seemed to know about containing the mysterious Frech Files (yes, the word is "Frech," not "French"). One of those files opened my eyes to the topic that became the subject of this book.

Grants from the National Endowment for the Humanities enabled me to be part of vibrant academic communities centered at the Massachusetts Historical Society and the Newberry Library. Fellows and visiting scholars at these institutions provided advice, guidance, and camaraderie during the early stages of my work. They included Christopher Cameron, Leon Fink, Danny Greene, Jon Grinspan, Toby Higbie, Ellie Shermer, Nancy Shoemaker, Susan Sleeper-Smith, and Scott Manning Stevens. In Chicago, former Brown colleagues Deborah Cohen and Elliott Gorn made my stay in the city particularly rewarding. Deborah was a great host and, as usual, taught me a hundred things that I never would have known otherwise. Whether in Chicago, Los Angeles, or Providence, Elliott has always been a welcome friend without benefits. He is indispensable, like a toilet plunger. Tom Silfen, fellow film enthusiast, kept me from being alone in the dark.

In 2018–19, I was the Ray Allen Billington Visiting Professor in U.S. History at Occidental College. This position made me a member of two fantastic groups: the faculty of Occidental's history department and the community of fellows and visiting scholars at the Huntington Library. Marla Stone, the chair of the Occidental history department, was a warm and welcoming colleague, as were Erica Ball, Sharla Fett, Jane Hong, and Alexandra Puerto. At the Huntington, the cohort of specialists in nineteenth-century North America was stellar. These luminaries, patient in answering my questions and generous in providing advice, included Kate Adams, Gary Gallagher, Marjoleine Kars, Greg Nobles, Martha Sandweiss, Rachel St. John, and Louis Warren.

During the past decade, I have had the opportunity to present work in progress that audiences have helped me to reshape into parts of this book. I owe much to the organizers of these conferences, lectures, and workshops: Mary Bilder, Corey Brooks, Paul Finkelman, Harold Holzer, Daniel Immerwahr, Mark Peterson, Christopher Samito, Patricia Sullivan, David Tanenhaus, and Frank Towers. The attendees at these events, who offered valuable ideas and leads, included Catherine Clinton, Brian Dirck, Don Doyle, Carole Emberton, Amy Greenberg, Patrick J. Kelly, Randall Kennedy, Tom Laqueur, Bruce Levine, Caleb McDaniel, Robbie Nelson, Dylan Penningroth, Chris Phillips, James Gray Pope, John Quist, Andrés Reséndez, Heather Cox Richardson, Adam Rothman, Anne Sarah Rubin, George Rutherglen, Lucy Salyer, Samantha Seeley, Rachel Shelden, Andrew Slap, Yael Sternhell, Elizabeth Varon, Peter Wallenstein, Jonathan W. White, and Rebecca Zietlow. I have done my best to attend to these scholars' suggestions, but I know that I have often fallen short. Still, without their input, this book would be a far weaker piece of work.

On specific topics covered in the book, a number of historians have kindly responded to my queries, providing essential information to help me puzzle out problems. Again, I wish that the book did justice to their expertise, and they should be absolved of the fact that I have left many puzzles unsolved. Caroline Janney and Chandra Manning shared their thoughts and leads on what happened after the surrenders of 1865 to enslaved Black people impressed by the Confederate armies. On the disconnect between the end of the Civil War and the end of slavery, I benefited from the insights of Mary Frances Berry, David Blight, Eric Foner, Annette Gordon-Reed,

Edna Greene Medford, James Oakes, Hannah Rosen, and John Stauffer. Mary Dudziak and John F. Witt enhanced my understanding of the role of law in simultaneously delimiting and expanding the temporality of war. On the conflicting meanings of surrender, I learned much from Joan Waugh and from David Silkenat, who generously shared with me in draft form the book that became *Raising the White Flag*.

Old friends in the historical profession have offered counsel, encouragement, and patience as I have plodded along. Of these people, no one was closer to me and more helpful in all my endeavors than Jeff Moran. His death in 2024 broke my heart. Other long-time acquaintances to whom I am indebted but have yet to mention include Thomas J. Brown, Michael S. Green, Kate Masur, Megan Kate Nelson, Tom Underwood, and Ted Widmer.

Former students at Brown at both the graduate and undergraduate levels have produced stellar scholarship that has enriched my knowledge and influenced my thinking on a number of topics covered in this book. Christopher Jones, Glenn LaFantasie, and Jonathan Lande in particular taught me more than I could ever have taught them. The superb senior theses by Katherine Jessiman-Ketcham and Samantha Miller were works that I consulted frequently.

Research assistants have contributed significantly to the project. Katie Alberts, fellow lover of libraries, searched out materials to help me understand French attitudes toward North America during the latter stages of the American Civil War. Occidental College students Milo Goodell and Spencer Raub helped me make sense of court-martial records in the post-Appomattox period. At Brown, I have benefited from the labor and insights of some truly impressive researchers. Early on, the detailed memos by Hilary Lynd, now a daunting scholar of history across three continents, provided me an education in the theories, premodern and modern, of how to end a war. Dan Meyer and Jonah Newman found rich material across vast archives relating to Americans' complex attitudes after April 1865 toward the Civil War's supposed end. Their work was continued by other skilled researchers from Brown: Kellan Barr, Greer Christensen-Gibbons, Sarah Novicoff, Sam Rosen, and Gwenyth Winship. Naya Lee Chang, Gerritt Self, and Luke Patusky were my go-to experts on the prisoners at Fort Jefferson, Dry Tortugas, from

1865 to 1869. Toward the end of the project, Evelyn Daigneault was vital in providing last-minute research and editing.

Scholars working outside the walls of academia have awed me with their knowledge, generosity, and commitment to public history. National Park Service historians currently or previously stationed at Appomattox Court House National Historical Park—Jim Bailey, Beth Parnicza, Ernie Price, and Robin Snyder—provided me with a detailed account of their admirable work to integrate African American history into the park site. Patrick Schroeder, a current park historian, sent me research, supplied an important photograph for the book, explained every detail of the McLean house, and indulged me in all my odd questions. At the Everglades Research and Education Center, the National Park Service historian Jim Williams filled in gaps in the complicated history of Key West and the Dry Tortugas during the Civil War and Reconstruction. He made the archives at the center readily accessible, and he shared with me the vast data that he and his staff had compiled. Jim has left for a different National Park Service site, but the work that he began continues under the direction of Bonnie Ciolino, who also helped in transmitting information to me. At Bennett Place in North Carolina, the historian Fred Brems gave a wonderful tour and spent much time afterward discussing facts and imponderables related to the surrender of Confederate forces in North Carolina and the rest of the Confederate Southeast. The artist Dennis Parker, whose painting of the surrender of Stand Watie appears in the book, spent hours on the phone with me providing details and leads about that poorly documented event.

My greatest scholarly debt is to the historians who generously agreed to read and comment on all or part of the first draft of the book: Bill Blair, Bob Bonner, Greg Downs, Laura Edwards, Martha Hodes, and Ari Kelman. Their thorough readings saved me from errors, alerted me to lacunae, and improved the writing. I can never repay them for their time and insights. The flaws that are now in the book slipped in only after the manuscript left their keen eyes and are entirely of my creation.

I could never have navigated the ever-shifting landscape of publishing without the guidance of some extraordinary experts in the field. At Writers House, Geri Thoma agreed to take on the project.

She read and reread countless drafts of the book proposal, offering much-needed assurances along the way. After Geri retired, Lisa DiMona took over, steering the book through the final stages of production. At a pivotal moment, when all could have been lost, Lisa saved the ship. I am fortunate to have such a skilled and attentive agent. At Alfred A. Knopf, Andrew Miller made the initial commitment to publish the book and offered helpful critiques of an early draft. When Andrew left Knopf, Todd Portnowitz did the heavy lifting of turning the submitted manuscript into a final book. A superb editor, Todd has also been a much-needed calming influence. Others at Knopf deserve special thanks: the publisher, Jordan Pavlin; the production editor Kathleen Cook; the production manager Felecia O'Connell; and the marketer Ellen Whitaker. I am grateful for the artistic work of the text designer Michael Collica and the jacket designer Jared Bartman. Elora Weil, the senior publicist, has worked tirelessly to ensure that the book actually gets read.

A complete list of friends and family members who cheered me along could fill the pages of another book. A few deserve special mention. Brucie Harvey and Kara Provost read and improved early versions of the book proposal. Arik Levinson and Susan Ullman provided room and board in the D.C. area, came to my talks, and always seemed more interested in my work than even I was. Pete Hare ribbed me for taking longer to finish the book than it took to finish the Civil War. But he also provided me an idyllic summer residence along Lake Dunmore, where he helped me to write a separate book. Peter B. Rosenthal deserves thanks, though I'm not sure why. He kept me amused, I suppose, but he also slowed the progress on the work, took too much pleasure in my morose moments, and pressed me to include bawdy cryo-EM images and untranslatable puns. As for the Vorenberg/Troubh cuzzies and their spouses, they are the best. With them, I was always cared for, entertained and well fed, and only slightly bruised by interrogation. Barnaby Jackson must be singled out as grill master and photographer extraordinaire. Maggie Philbrick, the most saintly family member I have (alas, the bar is low), is more eager to see the book than anyone. I only wish that Gerald Sacks could be at her side when her copy arrives. Lauren Bates, along with her fabulous family, has brought much love and joy to the Vorenbergs. She is a wonder. I refused to let her design the cover, however. She knows why. My brothers, Dan and Tom, have been there for me always and in all ways. Tom read the earliest chapter drafts and boosted my morale with his comments and excitement. Dan made sure that I maintained my sanity and, most of all, that I enjoyed myself, even at the risk of putting my mortal soul in jeopardy.

Ethan Pollock defies easy categorization. He has been a colleague, a friend, and, most relevantly, a writing partner. Without the partnership, this book would never have existed. He kept me moving forward, read and reread chapters, offered brilliant ideas for revisions, and pulled me out of the writer's mire on more occasions than I care to remember.

I have dedicated this book to my wife, Katie, and our daughter, Emma. They deserve so much more than a dedication. I thank them for their love, their companionship, their humor, their patience, and their rainbow sleeves, which I'll hang on to forever.

A Note on Language

Historians must always perform a delicate balancing act when it comes to language. On one side are the words from the past that have no place in the present, either because their meaning is opaque or because their message is offensive and perhaps always has been. On the other side are words from the present that would be unfamiliar to those in the past. In the middle are words that are recognizable to all, past and present, but have gained either more or less acceptability over time. In choosing words for this book, I have tried to balance respect for the past and the present while keeping the language intelligible to a broad readership.

In historical scholarship, the conventions of racial language are constantly in flux. Labels and capitalizations change with the shifting currents of awareness, circumstance, and politics. The choices I have made—to capitalize "Black," for example—are consistent with current convention.[1] Although "white" and "Black" are adjectives, the nouns "whites" and "Blacks" appear sometimes in the book as shorthand for groups of political actors. I recognize that these terms have both a usefulness in describing a racialized society as well as an imprecision in flattening the personal subjectivities of the men and women at the heart of my study. When quoting or paraphrasing from past documents or speakers, the book allows the language of the time. As a result, terms from the past appear that can be offensive, such as "colored" or "Negro," even though these terms were not always used in a pejorative way at the time. Other terms for Black people that are offensive today were just as offensive in the past.

Repeating these terms risks replicating the violence that these terms were meant to inflict, so I have either avoided them or used ellipses in their place.

Writers for some time have been trying to figure out what to do about the terms "slave" and "slave owner." The terms were common in the period covered in this book, but using them now as if they are unproblematic risks legitimizing the dehumanization at the core of enslavement. Thus many writers have opted for the phrase "enslaved persons" in favor of "slaves," and "enslavers" in favor of "slave owners." One result of this shift in usage is that researchers investigating the subject of enslavement are sometimes frustrated and confused when they cannot find the term "slave," "slave owner," or even "slavery" in the indexes of books that provide valuable information about these subjects. Reasonable people who care deeply about their fellow human beings have not reached a consensus on which set of terms is most accurate or most ethical. No system of usage for these terms is perfect.[2]

In making choices as to which words to use to describe the Black people who were enslaved and the white people who held them as slaves, I have considered the arguments on all sides and have ended up with the following necessarily imperfect conventions. I use "enslaved people" instead of "slaves," though I use the latter term if I am quoting from or paraphrasing past speakers or writers who used that term. To describe whites who claimed Blacks as "their slaves," I use the term "slaveholders." This term is more accurate and (I hope) less offensive than "slave owners." The term "slaveholder" avoids the implication that people can be "owned" but acknowledges that some whites forcibly held Blacks in a condition of bondage generally considered lawful at the time. "Enslaver" is a term that I avoid. A reader who sees a person described as an "enslaver" might understandably assume that the person was singularly responsible for forcing a free person into a condition of enslavement. Few of the slaveholders and former slaveholders mentioned in this book played this direct role. "Enslaver" also tends to suggest a time period earlier than the one covered in this book. Like the similar word "slaver," "enslaver" is and was most commonly used to describe people who captured and sold Blacks during the transatlantic slave trade of the seventeenth and eighteenth centuries. The term seems out of place to me in a book that takes place in the middle decades of the nineteenth century, when most of the commerce in enslaved people in the United States occurred domestically.

Perhaps the most controversial choice I have made is to use "master" sometimes to describe a white person who held or once held a Black person in a condition of enslavement. I do not accept "master" as a legitimate status, and I recognize the harm and trauma of enslavement that the term can evoke. But the term was common in the period covered in this book, used regularly by Blacks and whites alike. More to the point of this book: the term "master" represented continuity, or at least potential continuity, between the period when slavery was legal in the United States and the period when it was outlawed. U.S. officials as well as formerly enslaved people regularly described white former slaveholders as "masters" even after the Thirteenth Amendment prohibiting slavery was adopted in December 1865. The fact that the usage continued is crucial to this book, as it indicates that people of the time understood the precarity and instability of Black freedom. Black people in particular rightly worried that "masters" would continue to be allowed to claim them as slaves, thus necessitating the continuation of the war for Black freedom. The very existence of the term "master" in the months and years after Confederate armies surrendered was seen by some as evidence that the Civil War was not over.

When referring to indigenous populations of North America, I follow the convention of using the English-language terms used today to describe specific Native peoples. I acknowledge that many Native peoples prefer the names that they call themselves—Diné instead of Navajo, for example—but for the sake of standardization and ease of recognition for the greatest number of readers, I have used the English-language names. When the book is referring to multiple Native peoples as a collective, I use "Native Americans," "Natives," "Native peoples," and "indigenous Americans" interchangeably, as these terms are all in common usage today.[3] The book uses the terms "Indian" and "Indians" only when paraphrasing or quoting from original sources that used these terms.

The term "Reconstruction" can be confusing because it is commonly used to refer both to a time period and to a process. As a time period, the dates most often associated with Reconstruction are 1863 to 1877. These are the dates given in the best-known and most highly regarded book about Reconstruction, which was published by the historian Eric Foner in 1988 and reissued in 2014.[4] Reconstruction as a *process,* however, necessarily began before 1863. As soon as southern states began seceding from the Union in 1860 and '61, and certainly after the Civil War began in the spring of 1861, it was clear that for the Union to continue to exist, some sort of reconstruction would be necessary. Furthermore, the processes of reconstruction that began at this time—reestablishing the supremacy of the national government over the states; reintegrating into the United States the states that had made war against it; ending slavery and establishing the formerly enslaved as equal members of the American polity; and redefining rights and citizenship for all Americans—were not complete by 1877 (some reasonably argue that they are still not complete). This book engages with Reconstruction as a process without becoming overly concerned, as some books do, with the precise dates of Reconstruction.[5] This choice reflects the argument of the book. It is natural to assume that the start date of Reconstruction is either the end date of the Civil War or the end date of slavery in the United States. Yet this book argues that no end date for the Civil War or for slavery can be definitive. Thus, at least for this book, "Reconstruction" as a term referring to a discrete, tangible time period cannot work. Nor do other temporal terms involving Reconstruction and the end of the war. Readers will not find "wartime Reconstruction" and "postwar Reconstruction" in these pages. Yet the term "Reconstruction" does appear—as a word describing a process with an indefinite start date and end date.

Notes

Key to Abbreviations

AJ   Andrew Johnson

AL   Abraham Lincoln

CG   *Congressional Globe*

CWAL   Roy P. Basler, et al., eds., *Collected Works of Abraham Lincoln* (New Brunswick, NJ: Rutgers University Press, 1954–1955)

FDHE   Ira Berlin, et al., eds., *Freedom: A Documentary History of Emancipation, 1861–1867* (Cambridge: Cambridge University Press, 1982–1993; Chapel Hill, NC: University of North Carolina Press, 2008–)

HEH   Henry E. Huntington Library, San Marino, CA

MDLC   Manuscript Division, Library of Congress, Washington, D.C.

MHS   Massachusetts Historical Society, Boston

NA   National Archives, Washington, D.C.

OR, Armies *The War of the Rebellion: A Compilation of the Official Records of the War of the Union and Confederate Armies* (Washington, D.C.: Government Printing Office, 1880–1901)

OR, Navies *Official Records of the Union and Confederate Navies in the War of the Rebellion* (Washington, D.C.: Government Printing Office, 1894–1922)

PAJ   LeRoy P. Graf, et al., eds., *The Papers of Andrew Johnson* (Knoxville: University of Tennessee Press, 1967–2000)

PUSG   John Y. Simon, et al., eds., *The Papers of Ulysses S. Grant* (Carbondale: Southern Illinois University Press, 1967–2009)

RG   Record Group

USG   Ulysses S. Grant

Prologue: Endings and Beginnings

1. T. S. Eliot, "Little Gidding," V, lines 215–16, in T. S. Eliot, *Four Quartets,* rev. ed. (New York: Harcourt Brace Jovanovich, 1971), 58.

2. *New York Herald,* Apr. 10, 1865, p. 1.

3. Headquarters of the Army, Adjutant General's Office, Washington, D.C., Oct. 29, 1890, General Orders, No. 128, p. 3, in *General Orders and Circulars, Adjutant General's Office. 1890* (Washington, D.C.: Government Printing Office, 1891).

4. Lewis A. Grant to Redfield Proctor, Jan. 2, 1891, approved by Redfield Proctor, Jan. 5, 1891, Adjutant General Office, Decisions of the Secretary of War, Jan. 5, 1891, 14754 *A.G.O.* 1890, transcribed in Administrative Precedent File ("Frech File"), RG 94, box 16, file E8A9F(3), "Documents on the Termination Date of the Civil War," NA. See Ida M. Tarbell, "Close of the War" (subsection titled "Remarkable Pension Case"), Washington (D.C.) *Evening Star,* Aug. 14, 1897, p. 15.

5. "Report of Lieutenant-General U.S. Grant, of the United States Armies— 1864–'65," July 22, 1865, in *Personal Memoirs of U.S. Grant* (New York: Charles L. Webster & Company, 1886), 2:555–632 (quotation at 632).

6. Lewis A. Grant to Redfield Proctor, Jan. 2, 1891, approved by Redfield Proctor, Jan. 5, 1891, Adjutant General Office, Decisions of the Secretary of War, Jan. 5, 1891, 14754 *A.G.O.* 1890, transcribed in Administrative Precedent File ("Frech File"), RG 94, box 16, file E8A9F(3), "Documents on the Termination Date of the Civil War," NA.

7. AJ, "Proclamation 157—Declaring That Peace, Order, Tranquillity, and Civil Authority Now Exists in and Throughout the Whole of the United States of America," https://www.presidency.ucsb.edu/documents/proclamation-157 -declaring-that-peace-order-tranquillity-and-civil-authority-now-exists; William O. Stoddard, *Abraham Lincoln and Andrew Johnson* (New York: Frederick A. Stokes and Brother, 1888), 46.

8. "Correlates of War," https://correlatesofwar.org. The project provides data, including start dates and end dates, on wars throughout the world beginning in 1816. Wars are divided into four categories: "Inter-State Wars," "Intra-State Wars," "Extra-State Wars," and "Non-State Wars." The U.S. Civil War is categorized as an "Intra-State War" that began on April 10, 1861, and ended on April 9, 1865. The U.S.-Iraq war falls into two categories. It is categorized as an "Inter-State War" between the United States and Iraq that began on March 19, 2003, and ended on May 2, 2003; then it is categorized as an "Extra-State War" between the United States and "al-Qaeda and Iraqi resistance" that began on May 3, 2003, and had not ended as of Dec. 31, 2007.

9. James A. Garfield, Inaugural Address, Mar. 4, 1881, https://millercenter.org /the-presidency/presidential-speeches/march-4-1881-inaugural-address.

10. "Remarks by the President in Address to the Nation on the End of Combat Operations in Iraq," Aug. 31, 2010, https://obamawhitehouse.archives.gov /the-press-office/2010/08/31/remarks-president-address-nation-end-combat -operations-iraq.

11. Col. Matthew Moten, *Between War and Peace: How America Ends Its Wars* (New York: Free Press, 2011), x.

12. "Remarks by the President in Address to the Nation on the End of Combat Operations in Iraq," Aug. 31, 2010.

13. Mary L. Dudziak, *War Time: An Idea, Its History, Its Consequences* (New York: Oxford University Press, 2012).

14. Avery C. Rasmussen and Saikrishna Bangalore Prakash, "The Peace Powers: How to End a War," *University of Pennsylvania Law Review* 170 (2022): 717–82.

15. Rachel Maddow, "Overcommitted" (review of Andrew J. Bacevich, *Breach of Trust: How Americans Failed Their Soldiers and Their Country*), *New York Times*, Sep. 5, 2013, Book Review, p. 15.

16. See Dexter Filkins, *The Forever War* (New York: Knopf, 2008), a book that did much to increase the currency of the "forever war" phrase.

17. "How Does the War in Ukraine End?," *Foreign Affairs*, July 17, 2023, https://www.foreignaffairs.com.

18. Samuel Charap, "An Unwinnable War: Washington Needs an Endgame in Ukraine," *Foreign Affairs* 102 (July/August 2023): 22–35.

19. Margaret MacMillan, "How Wars Don't End: Ukraine, Russia, and the Lessons of World War I," *Foreign Affairs* 102 (July/August 2023): 52–65.

20. James Speed to Francis Lieber, May 26, 1866, Francis Lieber Papers, box 62, folder LI-3213, HEH.

21. Ambrose Bierce, *The Devil's Dictionary* (Project Gutenberg edition).

22. Edward L. Ayers, "Exporting Reconstruction," in Ayers, ed., *What Caused the Civil War* (New York: Norton, 2005), 145–66; Bertram Wyatt-Brown, "The Changing Faces of Honor in National Crises: Civil War, Vietnam, Iraq, and the Southern Factor," paper presented at the Johns Hopkins History Seminar, Fall 2005.

23. John Patrick Daly, *The War After the War: A New History of Reconstruction* (Athens: University of Georgia Press, 2022); Douglas R. Egerton, *The Wars of Reconstruction: The Brief, Violent History of America's Most Progressive Era* (New York: Bloomsbury, 2013).

24. See, for example, Jeremi Suri, *Civil War by Other Means: America's Long and Unfinished Fight for Democracy* (New York: PublicAffairs, 2022). For a thoughtful review and critique of the "one long war" argument, see Gary W. Gallagher, "Did the War End in 1865?," in Gallagher, ed., *The Enduring Civil War: Reflections on the Great American Crisis* (Baton Rouge: Louisiana State University Press, 2020), 129–32.

25. See Don H. Doyle, "Toward an International History of Reconstruction," in Adam H. Domby and Simon Lewis, eds., *Freedoms Gained and Lost: Reconstruction and Its Meanings 150 Years Later* (New York: Fordham University Press, 2022), 181–205.

26. Lewis A. Grant to Redfield Proctor, Jan. 2, 1891 (see note 5 above for the full citation for Grant's memo); for the enlistment record of the soldier in question, John Barleyoung, see *US, Registers of Enlistments in the United States Army, 1798–1914*, NA, microfilm M233, reel 31, p. 53.

27. For persuasive studies that treat the "Indian Wars" of the 1860s as part of the Civil War, see Megan Kate Nelson, *The Three-Cornered War: The Union, the Confederacy, and Native Peoples in the Fight for the West* (New York: Scribner, 2020); and Ari Kelman, *A Misplaced Massacre: Struggling over the Memory of Sand Creek* (Cambridge, MA: Harvard University Press, 2013). For the counterargument, that the Civil War and the "Indian Wars" were separate conflicts, see Gary W. Gallagher, "One War or Two? The United States Versus Confederates and Indians, 1861–1865," in Gallagher, ed., *The Enduring Civil War*, 27–34.

28. The phrase "Greater Reconstruction" comes from Elliott West, "Reconstructing Race," *The Western Historical Quarterly* 34 (Spring 2003). Since the publication of that article, works too numerous to list here have been published that amplify, interrogate, and expand upon West's argument. See, for example, Heather Cox Richardson, *West from Appomattox: The Reconstruction of America After the Civil War* (New Haven, CT: Yale University Press, 2008); Claudio Saunt, "The Paradox of Freedom: Tribal Sovereignty and Emancipation During the Reconstruction of Indian Territory," *Journal of Southern History* 70 (Feb. 2004): 63–94; Rachel Purvis, "Maintaining Intact Our Homogeneousness: Race, Citizenship, and Reconstructing Cherokee" (PhD diss., University of Mississippi, 2012); Stacey L. Smith, *Freedom's Frontier: California and the Struggle over Unfree Labor, Emancipation, and Reconstruction* (Chapel Hill: University of North Carolina Press, 2013); Steven Hahn, *A Nation Without Borders: The United States and Its World in an Age of Civil Wars, 1830–1910* (New York: Viking, 2016); Andrés Reséndez, *The Other Slavery: The Uncovered Story of Indian Enslavement in America* (Boston: Houghton Mifflin Harcourt, 2016), esp. 295–316; and Gregory P. Downs, *The Second American Revolution: The Civil War–Era Struggle over Cuba and the Rebirth of the American Republic* (Chapel Hill: University of North Carolina Press, 2019).

29. AL, "Last Public Address," Apr. 11, 1865, *CWAL*, vol. 8, 399.

30. Michael Vorenberg, "Spielberg's *Lincoln*: The Great Emancipator Returns," *Journal of the Civil War Era* 3 (Dec. 2013), 549–72, esp. 569–70.

31. See "AHR Roundtable: Ending Civil Wars," *American Historical Review* 120 (Dec. 2015): 1682–837, esp. William A. Blair, "Finding the Ending of America's Civil War," 1753–66; on the conflicting statuses of the Confederacy, see Cynthia Nicoletti, *Secession on Trial: The Treason Prosecution of Jefferson Davis* (Cambridge: Cambridge University Press, 2017).

32. Gregory P. Downs, *After Appomattox: Military Occupation and the Ends of War* (Cambridge, MA: Harvard University Press, 2015), 236.

33. Giuliana Perrone, *Nothing More Than Freedom: The Failure of Abolition in American Law* (Cambridge, MA: Cambridge University Press, 2023).

34. Annette Gordon-Reed, "Growing Up with Juneteenth," June 19, 2020, *The New Yorker*.

35. Michael Vorenberg, *Final Freedom: The Civil War, the Abolition of Slavery, and the Thirteenth Amendment* (Cambridge: Cambridge University Press, 2001),

232–42. Works about the persistence or reemergence of racialized slavery after the Thirteenth Amendment are plentiful. See, for example, Andrés Reséndez, *The Other Slavery: The Uncovered Story of Indian Enslavement in America* (Boston: Houghton Mifflin Harcourt, 2016), 295–314; Douglas A. Blackmon, *Slavery by Another Name: The Re-Enslavement of Black Americans from the Civil War to World War II* (New York: Doubleday, 2008); and the essays in Alexander Tsesis, ed., *The Promises of Liberty: The History and Contemporary Relevance of the Thirteenth Amendment* (New York: Columbia University Press, 2010).

36. David W. Blight, "The Civil War Isn't Over," *The Atlantic,* Apr. 8, 2015.

37. In the wake of the U.S. war in Vietnam, U.S. "Operational Law" became a model not only for the United States but for other countries in providing legal justification for wars without end; see Craig Jones, "Operationalizing International Law: From Vietnam to Gaza," in Brian Cuddy and Victor Kattan, eds., *Making Endless War: The Vietnam and Arab-Israeli Conflicts in the History of International Law* (Ann Arbor: University of Michigan Press, 2023), 212–15.

38. Howells quoted in David W. Blight, *Race and Reunion: The Civil War in American Memory* (Cambridge, MA: Harvard University Press, 2001), 1.

39. *Address by Bruce Catton at Appomattox Court House, April 9, 1965, The Centennial Anniversary of the Surrender of General Robert E. Lee of the Army of Northern Virginia* (Richmond: Virginia Civil War Commission, 1965), 13.

40. Allan Nevins, *The War for the Union,* vol. 4, *The Organized War to Victory, 1864–1865* (New York: Charles Scribner's Sons, 1971), 370.

41. Noah Andre Trudeau, *Out of the Storm: The End of the Civil War, April–June 1865* (Boston: Little, Brown, 1994), 419.

42. Richard Zuczek, "The Last Campaign of the Civil War: South Carolina and the Revolution of 1876," *Civil War History* 42 (Mar. 1996): 31; on southern redemption as a tragic success, see Nicholas Lemann, *Redemption: The Last Battle of the Civil War* (New York: Farrar, Straus and Giroux, 2006).

43. Brian Matthew Johnson, *Marching Home: Union Veterans and Their Unending Civil War* (New York: Liveright, 2015), 203.

44. Douglas MacArthur, "Speech to Veterans of the Forty-Second Infantry Division," Washington, D.C., July 14, 1935, in William M. Leary, ed., *MacArthur and the American Century: A Reader* (Lincoln: University of Nebraska Press, 2001), 7. MacArthur wrongly attributed the adage to Plato; it most likely comes from George Santayana. See Elizabeth Knowles, *And I Quote: A History of Using Other People's Words* (New York: Oxford University Press, 2018), 197–99.

45. David Kennedy, *Of Law and War* (Princeton, NJ: Princeton University Press, 2006), 121.

46. Michael Vorenberg, "'The Deformed Child': Slavery and the Election of 1864," *Civil War History* 47 (Sep. 2001): 240–57.

47. C. V. Wedgwood, *William the Silent: William of Nassau, Prince of Orange, 1533–1584* (New Haven, CT: Yale University Press, 1944), 35.

Part I: Peace Was Not Made

1. "The Meeting in Winthrop Square," article in undated, unidentified newspaper, in RHD, Scrapbooks, vol. 175.12, Dana Family Papers, MHS.

1: The Peacemaker

1. Wayne C. Temple, *Lincoln's Travels on the* River Queen (Mahomet, IL: Mayhaven Publishing, 2007), 9–14.
2. Michael Vorenberg, *Final Freedom: The Civil War, the Abolition of Slavery, and the Thirteenth Amendment* (Cambridge: Cambridge University Press, 2001), 223–24.
3. AL to William Dennison, Feb. 28, 1865, *CWAL,* vol. 8, 323.
4. USG to Robert E. Lee, Mar. 4, 1865, in John Y. Simon, ed., *PUSG,* vol. 14, 98–99; Edwin M. Stanton to USG, Mar. 3, 1865, *CWAL,* vol. 8, 330–31.
5. AL, Second Inaugural Address, Mar. 4, 1865, *CWAL,* vol. 8, 332–33.
6. AL, Second Inaugural Address, Mar. 4, 1865, *CWAL,* vol. 8, 333.
7. AL, Speech to One Hundred Fortieth Indiana Regiment, Mar. 17, 1865, *CWAL,* vol. 8, 361–62.
8. See AL to John Pope, Mar. 19, *CWAL,* col. 8, 365–66, n. 1.
9. Albert Alexander Woldman, *Lincoln and the Russians* (Cleveland: World Publishing Company, 1952), 253.
10. William H. Seward to Frances A. Seward, Mar. 13, 1865, in Frederick W. Seward, ed., *William H. Seward* (New York: Derby and Miller, 1891), vol. 3, 266.
11. David Dixon Porter, *Incidents and Anecdotes of the Civil War* (New York: D. Appleton and Company, 1886), 285.
12. John Sanford Barnes, "With Lincoln from Washington to Richmond in 1865," *Appleton's Magazine* 9 (May 1907): 522.
13. For all details given here about the Mar. 28, 1865, meeting on board the *River Queen,* see Noah Andre Trudeau, *Lincoln's Greatest Journey: Sixteen Days That Changed a Presidency, March 24–April 8, 1865* (El Dorado Hills, CA: Savas Beatie, 2016), 82–86.
14. Doris Kearns Goodwin, *Team of Rivals: The Political Genius of Abraham Lincoln* (New York: Simon and Schuster, 2005), 339–44.
15. Porter, *Incidents and Anecdotes,* 285.
16. AL to Edwin M. Stanton, Mar. 30, 1865, *CWAL,* vol. 8, 377.
17. Porter, *Incidents and Anecdotes,* 294.
18. William H. Crook, *Through Five Administrations* (New York: Harper and Brothers, 1910), 48.
19. Jefferson Davis, "Address of the President," Danville, VA, Apr. 4, 1865, https://www.loc.gov/item/rbpe.24502300.
20. Mark Wahlgren Summers, *A Dangerous Stir: Fear, Paranoia, and the Making of Reconstruction* (Chapel Hill: University of North Carolina Press, 2009), 50.
21. John F. Marszalek, ed., *The Personal Memoirs of Ulysses S. Grant: The Complete Annotated Edition* (Cambridge, MA: Harvard University Press, 2017), 702–4.

22. AL to Edwin M. Stanton, Apr. 3, 1865, *CWAL*. Details here are drawn from Richard Wightman Fox, "Lincoln's Greatest Escapade: Walking Through Richmond on April 4, 1865," in Harold Holzer and Sara Vaughn Gabbard, eds., *1865: America Makes War and Peace in Lincoln's Final Year* (Carbondale: Southern Illinois University Press, 2015), 66–80; and Michael D. Gorman, "A Conqueror or a Peacemaker? Abraham Lincoln in Richmond," *Virginia Magazine of History and Biography* 123 (2015): 2–88.

23. "Agate" (Whitelaw Reid), dispatch of Apr. 5, 1865, in James G. Smart, ed., *A Radical View: The "Agate" Dispatches of Whitelaw Reid, 1861–1865* (Memphis, TN: Memphis University Press, 1976), 2:202–3.

24. Godfrey Weitzel, *Richmond Occupied: Entry of the United States Forces into Richmond, Va., April 3, 1865,* ed. Louis H. Manarin (Richmond, VA: Richmond Civil War Centennial Committee, 1965), 50.

25. John A. Campbell, *Recollections of the Evacuation of Richmond* (Baltimore: John Murphy, 1880), 5–8.

26. Gorman, "A Conqueror or a Peacemaker?," 44, 49.

27. AL to John A. Campbell, Apr. 5, 1865, *CWAL,* vol. 8, 386.

28. Everyone but Lincoln who was present at the meeting on the *Malvern* on Apr. 5, 1865, eventually wrote recollections of what happened there; their stories differ from one another in a number of details. See Trudeau, *Lincoln's Greatest Journey,* 203–5; and Gorman, "A Conqueror or a Peacemaker?," 60–63.

29. The story that Lincoln told Sherman and Grant to accept Confederate state legislatures as legitimate became a source of much controversy in mid-1865 and afterward. See David Herbert Donald, *Lincoln* (New York: Simon and Schuster, 1995), 579, 682.

30. AL to Seward, Apr. 5, 1865, *CWAL,* vol. 8, 387, n. 1.

31. AL to USG, Apr. 6, 1865, *CWAL,* vol. 8, 388.

32. AL to Seward, Apr. 5, 1865, *CWAL,* vol. 8, 387.

33. Charles Francis Adams to William Henry Seward, Mar. 17, 1865, in H. Ex. Doc. 1, "Message of the President of the United States," 39th Cong., 1st Sess., 250–51.

34. John Baldwin and Ron Powers, *Last Flag Down: The Epic Journey of the Last Confederate Warship* (New York: Crown, 2007), 198–205.

35. Lew Wallace to USG, Feb. 22, 1865, *OR, Armies,* ser. 1, vol. 48, pt. 1, 937. See James W. Daddysman, *The Matamoros Trade: Confederate Commerce, Diplomacy, and Intrigue* (Newark: University of Delaware Press, 1984).

36. Frederick W. Seward, *Seward at Washington as Senator and Secretary of State* (New York: Derby and Miller, 1891), 270.

37. *CWAL,* vol. 8, 388, n. 1.

38. *CWAL,* vol. 8, 388, n. 1.

39. Benjamin P. Thomas and Harold M. Hyman, *Stanton: The Life and Times of Lincoln's Secretary of War* (New York: Knopf, 1962), 355.

40. AL to USG, Apr. 7, 1865, *CWAL,* vol. 8, 392.

41. Trudeau, *Lincoln's Greatest Journey,* 237.

42. AJ, "Remarks on the Fall of Richmond," Apr. 3, 1865, *PAJ,* vol. 7, 544–45;

Carl J. Guarneri, *Lincoln's Informer: Charles A. Dana and the Inside Story of the Union War* (Lawrence: University Press of Kansas, 2019), 356.

43. Trudeau, *Lincoln's Greatest Journey*, 241.

44. Trudeau, *Lincoln's Greatest Journey*, 250–51.

45. Frederick Seward, *Reminiscences of a War-Time Statesman and Diplomat, 1830–1915* (New York: G. P. Putnam's Sons, 1916), 253; Donald, *Lincoln*, 581.

2: A Big Country

1. USG to Robert E. Lee, Mar. 4, 1865, *PUSG*, vol. 14, 98–99; Edwin M. Stanton to USG, Mar. 3, 1865, *CWAL*, vol. 8, 330–31.

2. Elizabeth R. Varon, *Appomattox: Victory, Defeat, and Freedom at the End of the Civil War* (New York: Oxford University Press, 2014), 42; David Silkenat, *Raising the White Flag: How Surrender Defined the American Civil War* (Chapel Hill: University of North Carolina Press, 2019), 199.

3. James M. McPherson, *Battle Cry of Freedom: The Civil War Era* (New York: Oxford University Press, 1988), 848.

4. Varon, *Appomattox*, 43–44.

5. Joshua Lawrence Chamberlain, *The Passing of the Armies* (1915; repr., Lincoln: University of Nebraska Press, 1998), 240.

6. H. B. Scott, "The Surrender of General Lee and the Army of Northern Virginia at Appomattox, Virginia, Apr. 9, 1865," paper read at a meeting of surviving officers of the Second Massachusetts Infantry, Boston, Aug. 9, 1916, p. 2.

7. John F. Marszalek, ed., *The Personal Memoirs of Ulysses S. Grant: The Complete Annotated Edition* (Cambridge, MA: Harvard University Press, 2017), 720, 725.

8. Frederick Maurice, ed., *An Aide-de-Camp of Lee: Being the Papers of Colonel Charles Marshall . . .* (Boston: Little, Brown, and Company, 1927), 268–74.

9. Joan Waugh, "'I Only Knew What Was in My Mind': Ulysses S. Grant and the Meaning of Appomattox," *Journal of the Civil War Era* 2 (Sep. 2012): 307–36.

10. Marszalek, ed., *The Personal Memoirs of Ulysses S. Grant*, 724. The phrasing here about Grant saying this might be "the last battle" comes from Grant's *Memoirs*; the historian Elizabeth Varon, also relying on the *Memoirs*, has Grant going further, saying that "he hoped and believed that this would be the close of the war." Varon, *Appomattox*, 58.

11. E. A. Paul to *New York Times*, Apr. 25, 1865, in *New York Times*, Apr. 30, 1865, p. 2.

12. Munford, Special Orders No. 6, Apr. 21, 1865, *OR, Armies*, ser. 1, vol. 46, pt. 3, 1395.

13. USG to George G. Meade, Apr. 9, 1865, *OR, Armies*, ser. 1, vol. 46, pt. 3, 668.

14. *OR, Armies*, ser. 1, vol. 46, pt. 1, 1267.

15. Caroline E. Janney, "We Were Not Paroled: The Surrenders of Lee's Men Beyond Appomattox Court House," in Janney, ed., *Petersburg to Virginia: The*

End of the War in Virginia (Chapel Hill: University of North Carolina Press, 2018), 193.

16. Elizabeth R. Varon, "Lee Surrendered, but His Lieutenants Kept Fighting," *New York Times* ("Disunion" series), Apr. 9, 2015 (quoting Edward Porter Alexander).

17. Diary of Henry S. Thacher, Apr. 10, 1865, Thacher Family Papers, MHS.

18. USG to Stanton, June 16, 1865, in *PUSG*, 15:149–51.

19. J. C. Pemberton to USG, July 3, 1863, *OR, Armies,* ser. 1, vol. 24, pt. 1, 115; USG to Pemberton, July 4, 1863, ibid., 116.

20. John Gibbon to USG, April 13, 1865, *PUSG*, vol. 14, 384.

21. William H. Harrison, interviewed by Irene Robertson, *Born in Slavery: Slave Narratives from the Federal Writers' Project, 1936–1938,* vol. 2, Arkansas, pt. 3, 186, https://www.loc.gov/collections/slave-narratives-from-the-federal -writers-project-1936-to-1938/about-this-collection.

22. Caroline E. Janney, *Ends of War: The Unfinished Fight of Lee's Army After Appomattox* (Chapel Hill: University of North Carolina Press, 2021), 77–79; Varon, *Appomattox,* 93–101.

23. See, for example, *New York Times,* Apr. 14, 1865, p. 8 (correspondence from Jetersville, Virginia, Apr. 5, 1865, reporting capture of a Confederate wagon train and "several hundred negroes").

24. Jaime Amanda Martinez, *Confederate Slave Impressment in the Upper South* (Chapel Hill: University of North Carolina Press, 2013), 140–41, and appendices at 165–85.

25. Andrew R. Linscott to "Dear Sister," Apr. 24, 1865, Andrew R. Linscott Papers, MHS.

26. Thavolia Glymph, "'This Species of Property': Female Slave Contrabands in the Civil War," in John D. Fowler, ed., *The Confederate Experience Reader: Selected Documents and Essays* (New York: Routledge, 2008), 293–301.

27. R. A. Brock, ed., "Paroles of the Army of Northern Virginia . . . ," *Southern Historical Society Papers,* vol. 15 (Richmond, VA: Southern Historical Society, 1887), p. 45; "Black Soldiers on the Appomattox Campaign," Appomattox Court House, National Park Service, https://www.nps.gov/apco/learn /historyculture/parole-passes-a.htm (see bottom of page, describing "thirty-nine enslaved African Americans or free Black people impressed . . . into labor service with the army").

28. Janney, *Ends of War,* 77.

29. E. A. Paul to *New York Times,* Apr. 25, 1865, in *New York Times,* Apr. 30, 1865, p. 2.

30. Janney, *Ends of War,* 76.

31. John W. Hoopes, "The Confederate Memoir of William M. Abernathy," *Confederate Veteran* 3 (2003): 17.

32. Burke Davis, *To Appomattox: Nine April Days, 1865* (New York: Rinehart, 1959), 344.

33. Thomas S. Gaines, *Buried Alive (Behind Prison Walls) for a Quarter of a Century: Life of William Walker* (Saginaw, MI: Friedman and Hynan, 1892), 208. Elizabeth R. Varon, "The Last Hour of the Slaveholders' Rebellion: African

American Discourse on Lee's Surrender," in Caroline E. Janney, ed., *Petersburg to Appomattox: The End of the War in Virginia* (Chapel Hill: University of North Carolina Press, 2018).

34. William Marvel, *A Place Called Appomattox: Community at the Crossroads of History*, rev. ed. (Chapel Hill: University of North Carolina Press, 2016), 271.

35. *Chicago Tribune*, Apr. 10, 1865, p. 1.

36. AL, "Response to Serenade," Apr. 10, 1865, *CWAL*, vol. 8, 394.

37. AL, "Response to Serenade," Apr. 10, 1865, *CWAL*, vol. 8, 393.

38. "The Meeting in Winthrop Square," article in undated, unidentified newspaper, in RHD, Scrapbooks, vol. 175.12, Dana Family Papers, MHS.

39. Marszalek, ed., *The Personal Memoirs of Ulysses S. Grant*, 726–27. One of Lee's officers, Charles Marshall, wrote an account of the April 10, 1865, meeting that added an unlikely detail: Grant suggesting to Lee that he travel with him to Washington, D.C., and meet with Lincoln. See Maurice, ed., *An Aide-de-Camp of Lee*, 274–75. Marshall told the story decades after the surrender, and he conceded that he was not present. It is highly unlikely Grant would have made such a suggestion to Lee, as Grant well understood that military personnel were not supposed to negotiate with civilian leaders.

3: Righteous Peace, Fearful Retribution

1. Joshua Lawrence Chamberlain, *The Passing of the Armies* (1915; repr., Lincoln: University of Nebraska Press, 1998), 260.

2. Chamberlain, *The Passing of the Armies*, 267–68; on the identification of the speaker as Henry Wise, see Brooks Simpson introduction to this edition, xiiix–iv.

3. Michael R. Ridderbusch, ed., "The Lincoln Reminiscence Manuscript in the Francis Harrison Pierpont Papers," *West Virginia History* 1 (Spring 2007): 86–89.

4. Gideon Welles, *Diary of Gideon Welles* (Boston: Houghton Mifflin, 1911), vol. 2, 280.

5. *CWAL*, vol. 8, 396–98.

6. "The Union Victories and the Draft," *Baltimore Sun*, Apr. 13, 1865, p. 1.

7. Washington, D.C., *Daily National Republican*, Apr. 12, 1865, p. 2; Caroline E. Janney, *Remembering the Civil War: Reunion and the Limits of Reconciliation* (Chapel Hill: University of North Carolina Press, 2013), 49.

8. All quotations from the address of Apr. 11, 1865, are from AL, "Last Public Address," Apr. 11, 1865, *CWAL*, vol. 8, 399–405.

9. Allan Nevins and Milton Halsey Thomas, eds., *The Diary of George Templeton Strong: The Civil War, 1860–1865* (New York: Macmillan, 1952), vol. 3, 581.

10. Matthew 7:1. See Charles Sumner to Salmon P. Chase, Apr. 10, 1865, in Beverly Wilson Palmer, ed., *The Selected Letters of Charles Sumner* (Boston: Northeastern University Press, 1990), 2:282.

11. Louis P. Masur, *Lincoln's Last Speech: Wartime Reconstruction and the Crisis of Reunion* (New York: Oxford University Press, 2015), 6–7.

12. David Herbert Donald, *Lincoln* (New York: Simon and Schuster, 1995), 577–79.

13. David Donald, *Charles Sumner and the Rights of Man* (New York: Knopf, 1970), 215.

14. Harlan Hoyt Horner, *Lincoln and Greeley* (Urbana: University of Illinois Press, 1953), 380.

15. Masur, *Lincoln's Last Speech,* 166–67.

16. Martha Hodes, *Mourning Lincoln* (New Haven, CT: Yale University Press, 2015), 38; Michael Burlingame, *Abraham Lincoln: A Life* (Baltimore: Johns Hopkins University Press, 2008), 2:803; Donald, *Lincoln,* 581.

17. Hodes, *Mourning Lincoln,* 23.

18. This number, of more than 100,000 Confederate soldiers still in the field after Lee's surrender, is a conservative estimate. In the Southeast, there were as many as 90,000 troops. See Stephen Cushman, "Surrender According to Johnston and Sherman," in Gary W. Gallagher and Stephen Cushman, eds., *Civil War Writing: New Perspectives on Iconic Texts* (Baton Rouge: Louisiana State University Press, 2019), 82. In the Trans-Mississippi West at this time, according to the Confederate commander Edmund Kirby Smith, there were as many as 50,000 troops, though this was a generous estimate. See Edmund Kirby Smith, "Memorandum for Col. Sprague," *OR, Armies,* ser. 1, vol. 48, pt. 1, 186–94.

19. Stephen M. Mallory, "Last Days of the Confederate Government," *McClure's Magazine* 16 (Jan. 1901): 239.

20. Mallory, "Last Days of the Confederate Government," 240.

21. J. E. Johnston to W. T. Sherman, Apr. 14, 1865, *OR, Armies,* ser. 1, vol. 47, pt. 3, 206–7.

22. Mark L. Bradley, *This Astounding Close: The Road to Bennett Place* (Chapel Hill: University of North Carolina Press, 2000), 105.

23. Bradley, *This Astounding Close,* 144–45.

24. William T. Sherman to Joe Johnston, Apr. 14, 1865, *OR, Armies,* ser. 1, vol. 1, pt. 3, 207.

25. Welles, *Diary of Gideon Welles,* vol. 2, 282–3.

26. On the planning and execution of the ceremony at Fort Sumter, see *CWAL,* vol. 8, 375 (AL to USG, Mar. 26, 1865; with annotation of USG to AL, Mar. 25, 1865); William T. Sherman, *Memoirs of General W. T. Sherman* (New York: Literary Classics of the United States, 1990), 839; E. D. Townsend, *Anecdotes of the Civil War in the United States* (New York: D. Appleton and Company, 1884), 210–20; and Welles, *Diary of Gideon Welles,* vol. 2, 267 (Monday, March 27). Welles records that Stanton originally planned to attend the event; it is not clear why he ended up not going.

27. David Brion Davis, *Inhuman Bondage: The Rise and Fall of Slavery in the New World* (New York: Oxford University Press, 2006), 263.

28. John L. Thomas, *The Liberator: William Lloyd Garrison* (Boston: Little, Brown, 1963), 430–31.

29. David W. Blight, *Frederick Douglass: Prophet of Freedom* (New York: Simon and Schuster, 2018), 271–73; Leonard L. Richards, *The Slave Power: The Free North and Southern Domination, 1780–1860* (Baton Rouge: Louisiana State University Press, 2000).

30. Beecher to AL, Feb. 4, 1865, *CWAL,* vol. 8, 318 n. 1.

31. Henry Ward Beecher, *Oration at the Raising of the "Old Flag" at Sumter; and Sermon on the Death of Abraham Lincoln, President of the United States* (Manchester, UK: Alexander Ireland, 1865), 24–25.

32. Hodes, *Mourning Lincoln,* 25.

33. George B. Todd to Henry P. Todd, Apr. 15, 1865, John Hay Library, Brown University, Providence, RI.

34. On the question of what exactly Stanton said, see Donald, *Lincoln,* 579, 686; and Adam Gopnik, *Angels and Ages: A Short Book About Darwin, Lincoln, and Modern Life* (New York: Alfred A. Knopf, 2009), 13. (Gopnik is more open than most to the possibility that Stanton said "Now he belongs to the angels.")

35. Mary Lincoln to Francis Bicknell Carpenter, Nov. 15, 1865, in Justin G. Turner and Linda Levitt Turner, eds., *Mary Todd Lincoln: Her Life and Letters* (New York: Knopf, 1972), 285.

36. Edward Burgess Peirce to "Dear Father" (John N. Peirce), Apr. 18, 1865, Edward Burgess Peirce letters, MHS; Peirce to "Dear Mother" (Mary Miller Peirce), Apr. 20, 1865, ibid.

37. Samuel Miller Quincy to Mary Quincy, Apr. 19, 1865, Samuel Quincy Papers, MHS.

38. Samuel Quincy to Mary Quincy, May 10, 1865, Samuel Quincy Papers, MHS.

39. Louis A. Bringier to "Shel" Bringier, Apr. 23, 1865, Louis A. Bringier and Family Papers, Special Collections, Hill Memorial Library, Louisiana State University.

40. Emma LeConte, *Diary, 1864–1865,* transcribed by Jordan Davis, "Documenting the American South," University of North Carolina, Academic Affairs Library (1998), pp. 65–66, http://docsouth.unc.edu/fpn/leconteemma/leconte .html.

41. "The Assassination and the Rebellion," *New York Times,* Apr. 20, 1865, p. 4.

42. Hodes, *Mourning Lincoln,* 118.

43. Elizabeth D. Leonard, *Lincoln's Avengers: Justice, Revenge, and Reunion After the Civil War* (New York: Norton, 2004), 10–12.

44. Noah Brooks, letter of Apr. 16, 1865, in P. J. Staudenraus, *Mr. Lincoln's Washington: Selections from the Writings of Noah Brooks, Civil War Correspondent* (South Brunswick, NJ: Thomas Yoseloff, 1967), 450.

45. AJ, "Speech to Indiana Delegation," Apr. 21, 1865, *PAJ,* vol. 7, 612.

46. AJ, "Speech to Indiana Delegation," Apr. 21, 1865, *PAJ,* vol. 7, 612.

47. Sherman, "Testimony Before the Committee on the Conduct of the War," *New York Times,* June 1, 1865, p. 2.

48. Bradley, *This Astounding Close,* 163.

49. Hodes, *Mourning Lincoln,* 121.

50. Jacob Dolson Cox, *Military Reminiscences of the Civil War* (New York: Charles Scribner, 1900), 2:465.

51. Bradley, *This Astounding Close,* 163–64.

52. William T. Sherman, Special Field Order No. 50, Apr. 17, 1865, reprinted in *Memoirs of General W. T. Sherman,* 839.

4: The War to Cease

1. R. E. Lee to Jefferson Davis, Apr. 20, 1865, in Aaron Sheehan-Dean, ed., *The Civil War: The Final Year Told by Those Who Lived It* (New York: Library of America, 2014), 704. See Elizabeth R. Varon, *Appomattox: Victory, Defeat, and Freedom at the End of the Civil War* (New York: Oxford University Press, 2014), 20–22.
2. *New York Herald,* April 29, 1865, p. 5.
3. Varon, *Appomattox,* 144 (quoting Reverend Gilbert Haven of Boston).
4. Stephen R. Mallory, "Last Days of the Confederate Government," *McClure's Magazine* 16, no. 3 (Jan. 1901): 244.
5. *OR, Armies,* ser. 1, vol. 47, pt. 3, 806–7.
6. David Silkenat, *Raising the White Flag: How Surrender Defined the American Civil War* (Chapel Hill: University of North Carolina Press, 2019), 230.
7. *New York Times,* Apr. 27, 1865.
8. *New York Times,* Apr. 27, 1865.
9. *OR, Armies,* ser. 1, vol. 47, pt. 3, 243–44.
10. Jason Phillips, *Diehard Rebels: The Confederate Culture of Invincibility* (Athens: University of Georgia Press, 2007), 172.
11. J. Cutler Andrews, "The Southern Telegraph Company, 1861–1865: A Chapter in the History of Wartime Communication," *Journal of Southern History* 30 (Aug. 1964): 341–43.
12. Charles A. Misulia, *Columbus, Georgia, 1865: The Last True Battle of the Civil War* (Tuscaloosa: University of Alabama Press, 2010), 174.
13. Misulia, *Columbus, Georgia, 1865,* 176.
14. Misulia, *Columbus, Georgia, 1865,* 196.
15. Misulia, *Columbus, Georgia, 1865,* 211.
16. William T. Sherman to Joseph E. Johnston, April 21, 1865, *OR, Armies,* ser. 1, vol. 47, pt. 3, 265–66.
17. William T. Sherman to Joseph E. Johnston, April 20, 1865, *OR, Armies,* ser. 1, vol. 47, pt. 3, 257.
18. Jefferson Davis to Varina Davis, Apr. 23, 1865, in Sheehan-Dean, ed., *The Civil War: The Final Year,* 706–7.
19. Silkenat, *Raising the White Flag,* 233.
20. *New York Times,* Apr. 23, 1865, p. 1.
21. "The Murderer of Mr. Lincoln," *New York Times,* Apr. 21, 1865, p. 3.
22. Henry S. Thacher diary, Apr. 24, 1865, Thacher Family Papers, MHS.
23. *New York Times,* Apr. 27, 1865, p. 4.
24. William T. Sherman to Joseph E. Johnston, April 21, 1865, *OR, Armies,* ser. 1, vol. 47, pt. 3, 266.
25. *New York Times,* Apr. 23, 1865, p. 1.
26. Mark Grimsley, "Wars for the American South: The First and Second Reconstructions Considered as Insurgencies," *Civil War History* 58 (2012): 6–36.
27. Silkenat, *Raising the White Flag,* 234; Mark Grimsley, "Learning to Say 'Enough': Southern Generals and the Final Weeks of the Confederacy," in

Mark Grimsley and Brooks D. Simpson, eds., *The Collapse of the Confederacy* (Lincoln: University of Nebraska Press, 2001), 74.

28. Sydney Nathans, *To Free a Family: The Journey of Mary Walker* (Cambridge, MA: Harvard University Press, 2012), 222.

29. See Gary W. Gallagher and Stephen Cushman, eds., *Civil War Writing: New Perspectives on Iconic Texts* (Baton Rouge: Louisiana State University Press, 2019), 81–82.

30. Basil W. Duke, "Last Days of the Confederacy," in Robert U. Johnson and Clarence C. Buel, eds., *Battles and Leaders of the Civil War* (New York: The Century Co., 1888), vol. 4, 765. See James Elliott Walmsley, "The Last Meeting of the Confederate Cabinet," *Mississippi Valley Historical Review* 6 (Dec. 1919): 344–46.

31. Aiken never actually said the words. See Stephen M. Walt, "'Declare Victory and Get Out'?," *Foreign Policy*, Dec. 19, 2012; Rory O'Connor, "Declaring Victory, Going Home," *HuffPost*, Aug. 31, 2009.

32. AJ, "Order Restoring Virginia," May 9, 1865, *PAJ*, vol. 8, 53.

33. Benjamin P. Thomas and Harold M. Hyman, *Stanton: The Life and Times of Lincoln's Secretary of War* (New York: Alfred A. Knopf, 1962), 404.

34. AJ, "Proclamation 132—Ordering the Arrest of Insurgent Cruisers," May 10, 1865, https://www.presidency.ucsb.edu/documents/proclamation -132-ordering-the-arrest-insurgent-cruisers.

35. Howard K. Beale, ed., *Diary of Gideon Welles, Secretary of the Navy Under Lincoln and Johnson* (W. W. Norton, 1960), vol. 2, 309–10.

36. *New York Herald*, May 12, 1865, p. 4.

37. *Chicago Tribune*, May 11, 1865, p. 2.

38. Butler to AJ, Apr. 25, 1865, *PAJ*, vol. 7, 637.

39. Chase to Stanley Matthews, Apr. 14, 1865, in Annie A. Nunns, ed. "Some Letters of Salmon P. Chase," *American Historical Review* 34 (Apr. 1929): 554.

5: Currents Convulsive

1. David Silkenat, *Raising the White Flag: How Surrender Defined the American Civil War* (Chapel Hill: University of North Carolina Press, 2019), 248.

2. Nathan Bedford Forrest to "Soldiers," Gainesville, Alabama, May 9, 1865, in John Milton Hubbard, *Notes of a Private* (St. Louis: Nixon-Jones Printing Co., 1911), 202.

3. William J. Cooper, Jr., *Jefferson Davis, American* (New York: Alfred A. Knopf, 2000), 574–75. See Nina Silber, "Intemperate Men, Spiteful Women, and Jefferson Davis," in Catherine Clinton and Nina Silber, eds., *Divided Houses: Gender and the Civil War* (New York: Oxford University Press, 1992), 283–305; and Chester D. Bradley, "Was Jefferson Davis Disguised as a Woman When Captured?," *Journal of Mississippi History* 36 (Aug. 1974): 243–68.

4. Ebenezer Nelson Gilpin, *The Last Campaign: A Cavalryman's Journal* (Leavenworth, KS: Ketcheson, 1908), 58–59.

5. Diary of Lydia Lyman Paine, vol. 1, in Robert Treat Paine III Papers, box 15, ms. N-642, MHS.

6. Henry Clay Dickinson, *Diary of Capt. Henry C. Dickinson, C.S.A. Morris Island, 1864–1865* (Denver, CO: Williamson-Haffner, 1910), 189.

7. Cooper, *Jefferson Davis, American,* 536.

8. Oliver Wilcox Norton to "Sister L.," May 16, 1865, in Oliver Wilcox Norton, *Army Letters, 1861–1865* (Chicago: O. L. Deming, 1903), 260.

9. On the decision to have a review of troops on May 23–24, see *PUSG,* vol. 5, 73–75.

10. C. A. Dana to James S. Pike, May 10, 1865, James S. Pike Papers, Calais Free Library, Calais, Maine.

11. *New York Times,* May 11, 1865, p. 4.

12. General Order 90, *OR, Armies,* ser. 1, vol. 46, pt. 3, 1134.

13. Silkenat, *Raising the White Flag,* 232.

14. The *Howard Union* (Glasgow, MO), July 20, 1865, p. 1. See Wheeling (WV) *Daily Register,* May 16, 1865, p. 3.

15. Gallipolis (WV) *Journal,* reprinted in *West Virginia Journal,* July 19, 1865, p. 3.

16. Colonel John W. Brown, Accounts book and Civil War diary, May 31, 1865, Arkansas Historical Commission, Little Rock, AR.

17. Winthrop Rutherfurd, "The Partisan Ranger Act: The Confederacy and the Laws of War," *Louisiana Law Review* 79 (Spring 2019): 807–37.

18. John Fabian Witt, *Lincoln's Code: The Laws of War in American History* (New York: The Free Press, 2012), 195–96.

19. Gallipolis (WV) *Journal,* reprinted in *West Virginia Journal,* July 19, 1865, p. 3.

20. J. W. Barnes to W. T. Clarke, May 10, 1865, *OR, Armies,* vol. 48, pt. 2 (1896), 388.

21. For Robert E. Lee, the Confederacy, and the issue of guerrilla warfare, see Mark E. Neely, Jr., "Guerrilla Warfare, Slavery, and the Hopes of the Confederacy," *Journal of the Civil War Era* 6 (Sep. 2016): 4376–412.

22. The story is retold in Winik, *April 1865: The Month That Saved America,* 315.

23. Caroline E. Janney, "Guerrillas, Vengeance, and Mercy After Appomattox: The Trial of John W. McCue," in Caroline E. Janney, Peter S. Carmichael, and Aaron Sheehan-Dean, eds., *The War That Made America: Essays Inspired by the Scholarship of Gary W. Gallagher* (Chapel Hill: University of North Carolina Press, 2024), 126–27.

24. *Lynchburg Republican,* June 14, 1865, reprinted in *Washington Evening Star,* June 21, 1865, p. 1. See *New York Herald,* June 23, 1865, p. 4, and June 29, 1865, p. 5.

25. W. H. Emory, to C. H. Morgan, Apr. 25, 1865, and C. H. Morgan to W. H. Emory, Apr. 25, 1865, *OR, Armies,* ser. 1, vol. 46, pt. 3, 951.

26. General Order 90; Daniel E. Sutherland, *A Savage Conflict: The Decisive Role of Guerrillas in the American Civil War* (Chapel Hill: University of North Carolina Press, 2009), 274.

27. Caroline E. Janney, "We Were Not Paroled: The Surrenders of Lee's Men Beyond Appomattox," in Janney, ed., *Petersburg to Appomattox: The End of the War in Virginia* (Chapel Hill: University of North Carolina Press, 2018), 211.

28. The military operations described here and on the pages that follow are typically grouped together and called "The Battle of Palmito Ranch" or "The Battle of Palmetto Ranch." I use the term "Palmito Ranch," as it is most

common, and except where noted, I rely on two books for the details of the engagements: Jeffrey W. Hunt, *The Last Battle of the Civil War: Palmetto Ranch* (Austin: University of Texas Press, 2002); and Phillip Thomas Tucker, *The Final Fury: Palmito Ranch, The Last Battle of the Civil War* (Mechanics-burg, PA: Stackpole Books, 2001).

29. James Marten, "For the Army, the People, and Abraham Lincoln: A Yankee Newspaper in Occupied Texas," *Civil War History* 39 (June 1993): 126–47.

30. Ida M. Tarbell, "Close of the War," Washington, D.C., *Evening Star,* Aug. 14, 1897, p. 15.

31. J. E. Slaughter to Lyman G. Aldrich, May 13, 1865, *Galveston Daily News,* June 1, 1865, reprinted in Janet B. Hewett, Noah Andre Trudeau, and Bryce A. Suderow, eds., *Supplement to the Official Records of the Union and Confederate Armies* (Wilmington, NC: Broadfoot Publishing, 1997), 905–6. See Robert L. Kerby, *Kirby Smith's Confederacy: The Trans-Mississippi South, 1863–1865* (Tuscaloosa: University of Alabama Press, 1991), 365–71.

32. *OR, Armies,* ser. 1, vol. 48, pt. 1, 265.

33. *Chicago Tribune,* May 30, 1865, p. 2.

34. USG to Sheridan, May 17, 1865, in *Personal Memoirs of P. H. Sheridan* (New York: Charles L. Webster and Company, 1888), 2:208–9.

35. Charles Royster, *The Destructive War: William Tecumseh Sherman, Stonewall Jackson, and the Americans* (New York: Vintage, 1993), 416.

36. Benjamin Brown French, *Witness to the Young Republic: A Yankee's Journal, 1828–1870,* eds. Donald B. Cole and John J. McDonough (Hanover, NH: University Press of New England, 1989), 478–79. The quotation is "Speak ye comfortably to Jerusalem, and cry unto her, that her warfare is accomplished, that her iniquity is pardoned . . ." (Isaiah 40:2).

37. Carl Schurz, *The Reminiscences of Carl Schurz* (New York: McClure, 1908), vol. 3, 137.

38. Brian Matthew Jordan, *Marching Home: Union Veterans and Their Unending Civil War* (New York: Liveright, 2014), 15.

39. French, *Witness to the Young Republic,* 479.

40. Thomas M. Vincent to J. A. Wilcox, May 18, 1865, *OR, Armies,* ser. 3, vol. 5, 25. See John C. Sparrow, *History of Personnel Demobilization in the United States Army* (Department of the Army Pamphlet 20-210) (Washington, D.C.: Department of the Army, 1965), p. 6.

41. Schurz, *The Reminiscences of Carl Schurz,* vol. 3, 137.

42. *Chicago Tribune,* May 24, 1865, p. 2 (col. 2, news item under "Illinois").

43. "The Sultana Disaster," *Chicago Tribune,* May 24, 1865, p. 2. See Gene Salecker, *Disaster on the Mississippi: The Sultana Explosion, April 27, 1865* (Annapolis, MD: Naval Institute Press, 2015), 192–97.

44. Clayton R. Newell and Charles R. Shrader, *Of Duty Well and Faithfully Done: A History of the Regular Army in the Civil War* (Lincoln: University of Nebraska Press, 2011), 42 (table 9: "Present for Duty Strength of the Regular Army, 1861–1865").

45. AL, "Memorandum Respecting Reduction of the Regular Army," *CWAL,* vol. 8, 409.

46. William D. Guernsey to Emeline Donaldson Guernsey, June 1, 1865, Guernsey Family Papers, box 3, HEH.

47. Chapin Warner to "Father and Mother," May 31, 1865, June 4, June 7, 1865, Chapin Warner Papers, MHS.

48. Diary of Moses Cleveland, May 23, 1865, MHS.

49. Walt Whitman, "Spirit Whose Work Is Done" (1865), *Leaves of Grass* (Project Gutenberg eBook release date: Aug. 24, 2008; updated Nov. 5, 2012 [(eBook #1322]).

50. "our fallen fortunes"; "brighter hues than its parent"; "the Trans-Mississippi will save us": all from Yael Sternhell, *Routes of War: The World of Movement in the Confederate South* (Cambridge, MA: Harvard University Press, 2012), 188–89.

51. Eliza Frances Andrews, *The Wartime Journal of a Georgia Girl, 1864–1865* (New York: D. Appleton and Company, 1908), 198.

52. Elizabeth B. Custer, *Tenting on the Plains* (New York: Charles L. Webster, 1887), 21.

53. Silkenat, *Raising the White Flag,* 261.

54. "The Situation and Future Prospects of the War," *Galveston Tri-Weekly News,* Apr. 19, 1865, p. 2.

55. *Galveston Tri-Weekly News,* May 19, 1865, p. 3.

56. Thomas W. Cutrer, *Theater of a Separate War: The Civil War West of the Mississippi River, 1861–1865* (Chapel Hill: University of North Carolina Press, 2017), 432.

57. *Personal Memoirs of P. H. Sheridan* (New York: Charles L. Webster and Company, 1888), 2:209–10.

58. William E. Hardy, "South of the Border: Ulysses S. Grant and the French Intervention," *Civil War History* 54 (Mar. 2008): 68–75; Robert Ryal Miller, "Lew Wallace and French Intervention in Mexico," *Indiana Magazine of History* 59 (Mar. 1963): 31–50.

59. Adam Badeau, *Grant in Peace: From Appomattox to Mount McGregor* (Hartford, CT: S. S. Scranton and Company, 1887), 180. See Don H. Doyle, "Toward an International History of Reconstruction," in Adam H. Domby and Simon Lewis, eds., *Freedoms Gained and Lost: Reconstruction and Its Meanings 150 Years Later* (New York: Fordham University Press, 2022), 188–89.

60. Jason Phillips, *Diehard Rebels: The Confederate Culture of Invincibility* (Athens: University of Georgia Press, 2007), 172.

61. *Wisconsin Pinery,* April 7, 1865, p. 2.

6: Almost an End

1. Kate Stone, *Brokenburn: The Journal of Kate Stone, 1861–1868,* ed. John Q. Anderson (Baton Rouge: Louisiana State University Press, 1955), 34.

2. Stone, *Brokenburn,* 7.

3. Stone, *Brokenburn,* 340.

4. Stone, *Brokenburn,* 340–41.

5. Eric H. Walther, *The Fire-Eaters* (Baton Rouge: Louisiana State University Press, 1992), 230.

6. Joseph T. Durkin, ed., *John Dooley, Confederate Soldier: His War Journal* (Washington, D.C.: Georgetown University Press, 1945), 185. On white women's resistance to loyalty oaths, see Anne Sarah Rubin, *A Shattered Nation: The Rise and Fall of the Confederacy, 1861–1868* (Chapel Hill: University of North Carolina, 2005), 97–99.

7. Stone, *Brokenburn*, 349.

8. Stone, *Brokenburn*, 341.

9. James Slaughter to Kirby Smith, May 17, 1865, Kirby Smith Papers, Southern Historical Collection, University of North Carolina, Chapel Hill, NC.

10. Arndt M. Stickles, *Simon Bolivar Buckner: Borderland Knight* (Chapel Hill: University of North Carolina Press, 1940), 277.

11. David Silkenat, *Raising the White Flag: How Surrender Defined the American Civil War* (Chapel Hill: University of North Carolina Press, 2019), 262–64; Rodman L. Underwood, *Waters of Discord: The Union Blockade of Texas During the Civil War* (Jefferson, NC: McFarland and Company, 2003), 144.

12. Allan Nevins and Milton Halsey Thomas, eds., *The Diary of George Templeton Strong: The Civil War, 1860–1865* (New York: Macmillan, 1952), vol. 3, 601.

13. General Order 108, *OR, Armies,* ser. 1, vol. 46, pt. 3, 1248.

14. William B. Holbertson, *Homeward Bound: The Demobilization of the Union and Confederate Armies, 1865–66* (Mechanicsburg, PA: Stackpole Books, 2001), 103–4.

15. John McElroy, *Andersonville: A Story of Rebel Military Prisons* (Washington, D.C.: The National Tribune, 1879), vol. 2, 493.

16. Fred T. Wilson, *Laws, Rulings, and Decisions Governing the Military Crime of Desertion* (Washington, D.C.: Government Printing Office, 1882), 46.

17. AL, "Order Commuting Sentence of Deserters," *CWAL,* vol. 7, 208.

18. General Order 98, *OR, Armies,* ser. 2, vol. 8, 580.

19. *New York Herald,* May 28, 1865, p. 4.

20. For examples of imprisoned U.S. soldiers with term-of-enlistment sentences who were still being held long after May 1865, see the relevant records of John Morgan, 18th N.Y. Independent Battery Light Artillery; and William H. Smith, 14th R.I. Heavy Artillery. Both men were released on Feb. 5, 1866, by Special Orders No. 49, War Department, Adjutant General's Office. For Morgan, see *U.S. v. John Morgan,* RG 153, Records of the Office of the Judge Advocate General (Army), 1792–2010, Court Martial Case Files, file nn2967, NA; and "Morgan, John," *New York Civil War Muster Roll Abstracts, 1861–1890,* Record #249, fold3 database, www.fold3.com. For Smith, see *U.S. v. William H. Smith,* RG 153, Court Martial Case Files, file ll1891; and "Smith, W. H.," line 918, Prisoner Record Book, Fort Jefferson, Dry Tortugas, RG 94, NA.

21. George M. Neese, *Three Years in the Confederate Horse Artillery* (New York: The Neale Publishing Co., 1911), 353.

22. Paul H. Bergeron, *Andrew Johnson's Civil War and Reconstruction* (Knoxville: University of Tennessee Press, 2011), 76.

23. Caroline E. Janney, "Guerrillas, Vengeance, and Mercy After Appomattox: The Trial of John W. McCue," in Caroline E. Janney, Peter S. Carmichael,

and Aaron Sheehan-Dean, eds., *The War That Made America: Essays Inspired by the Scholarship of Gary W. Gallagher* (Chapel Hill: University of North Carolina Press, 2024), 130.

24. Gregory P. Downs, *After Appomattox: Military Occupation and the Ends of War* (Cambridge, MA: Harvard University Press, 2015), 71–72.

25. *U.S. v. McCarty,* 26 Fed. Cases 1049 (1865) (U.S. App. LEXIS 429).

26. "Important Decision," St. Paul (MN) *Pioneer and Democrat,* June 30, 1865, p. 10.

27. *Army and Navy Journal,* June 3, 1865, p. 648.

28. *Army and Navy Journal,* June 3, 1865, p. 649 (the article misspelled the name of the valley as "Shanandoah").

29. *Army and Navy Journal,* June 3, 1865, p. 649.

30. *Army and Navy Journal,* Feb. 25, 1865, p. 422.

31. William T. Sherman to John A. Spooner, July 30, 1864, in *Army and Navy Journal,* Aug. 27, 1864, p. 7.

32. *Army and Navy Journal,* May 6, 1865, p. 580.

33. *Army and Navy Journal,* June 3, 1865, p. 650.

34. On contemporaneous and later commentary on the absence of African Americans at the Grand Review, see Gary W. Gallagher, *The Union War* (Cambridge, MA: Harvard University Press, 2011), 9–10, 19–21, 28–31 (20–21 describes William Lloyd Garrison's position).

35. H. Ex. Doc. 1, "Report of the Secretary of War," 39th Cong., 1st Sess., 30–31; Sparrow, *History of Personnel Demobilization in the United States Army,* 5; Lorenzo Thomas, Orders No. 6, *OR, Armies,* ser. 3, vol. 5, 3; James B. Fry to W. H. Sidell, May 8, 1865, *OR, Armies,* ser. 3, vol. 5, 13; James B. Fry to Rufus Saxton, June 1, 1865, *OR, Armies,* ser. 3, vol. 5, 48.

36. *New York Times,* June 9, 1865, p. 1.

37. Downs, *After Appomattox,* 108–9.

38. R. J. M. Blackett, ed., *Thomas Morris Chester, Black Civil War Correspondent: His Dispatches from the Virginia Home Front* (Baton Rouge: Louisiana State University Press, 1989), 353.

39. Charles D. Spurlin, "The World Turned Upside Down? The Military Occupation of Victoria and Calhoun Counties," in Kenneth W. Howell, ed., *Still the Arena of Civil War: Violence and Turmoil in Reconstruction Texas, 1865–1874* (Denton: University of North Texas Press, 2012), 116.

40. Report of George W. Cole, June 1865, and unsigned letter to "Sir," Dec. 1865, both in *FDHE,* ser. 2, 725–27. See Michael E. DeGruccio, "Unmade: American Manhood in the Civil War Era" (PhD diss., University of Notre Dame, 2007), 222–25.

41. *Galveston Tri-Weekly News,* May 15, p. 3.

42. William L. Richter, "'It Is Best to Go In Strong-Handed': Army Occupation of Texas, 1865–1866," *Arizona and the West* 27 (Summer 1985): 114.

43. Silkenat, *Raising the White Flag,* 265; Joseph Howard Parks, *General Edmund Kirby Smith, C.S.A.* (Baton Rouge: Louisiana State University Press, 1954), 481–82. The details given here of the journey of Shelby's band to and beyond the Rio Grande are drawn from Todd W. Wahlstrom, *The Southern Exodus to*

Mexico: Migration Across the Borderlands After the American Civil War (Lincoln: University of Nebraska Press, 2015), 58–61; and Anthony Arthur, *General Jo Shelby's March* (New York: Random House, 2010), 74–86.

44. See, for example, *Galveston Tri-Weekly News,* May 22, 1865, p. 2.
45. Wahlstrom, *The Southern Exodus to Mexico,* 16–17; John Baldwin and Ron Powers, *Last Flag Down: The Epic Journey of the Last Confederate Warship* (New York: Crown, 2007), 84.

7: Juneteenths

1. John W. McCarty, "Lessons from the Life and Death of a Good Ruler. A Discourse Delivered on the Day of National Mourning, June 1, 1865" (Cincinnati: Joseph B. Boyd, 1865), 5, 16–17. See Martha Hodes, *Mourning Lincoln* (New Haven, CT: Yale University Press, 2015), 245–47.
2. Affidavit of Mary Wilson, June 17, 1865, *FDHE,* ser. 1, vol. 1, 623–24. See Chandra Manning, *Troubled Refuge: Struggling for Freedom in the Civil War* (New York: Alfred A. Knopf, 2016), 253.
3. *CWAL,* vol. 5, 317–18. See James Oakes, *Freedom National: The Destruction of Slavery in the United States, 1861–1865* (New York: W. W. Norton, 2014).
4. Amy Dru Stanley, "Instead of Waiting for the Thirteenth Amendment: The War Power, Slave Marriage, and Inviolate Human Rights," *American Historical Review* 115 (June 2010): 732–65.
5. John M. Palmer to AJ, July 29, 1865, *PAJ,* vol. 8, 489. See Charles Roxborough et al. to AJ, undated (late June 1865), *FDHE,* ser. 1, vol. 1, 624–25; Gregory P. Downs, *After Appomattox: Military Occupation and the Ends of War* (Cambridge, MA: Harvard University Press, 2015), 42; and Oakes, *Freedom National,* 486–87. On the number of African Americans still enslaved in Kentucky in July 1865, see John M. Palmer to AJ, July 29, 1865, *PAJ,* vol. 8, 489.
6. Gregory P. Downs, "Force, Freedom, and the Making of Emancipation," in William A. Link and James J. Broomall, eds., *Rethinking American Emancipation: Legacies of Slavery and the Quest for Black Freedom* (Cambridge: Cambridge University Press, 2016), 49–50; Stephen V. Ash, *A Year in the South: 1865* (2002; repr., New York: Perennial, 2004), 124.
7. Downs, *After Appomattox,* 42.
8. *Galveston Tri-Weekly News,* May 15, 1865, p. 3.
9. Mary Elizabeth (Buckner) Tooke to Simon B. Buckner, June 17, 1865, Buckner Family Papers, HEH.
10. Downs, *After Appomattox,* 43. See Leon F. Litwack, *Been in the Storm So Long: The Aftermath of Slavery* (New York: Alfred A. Knopf, 1979), 184–85.
11. E. A. Paul, "From Petersburgh," *New York Times,* Apr. 30, 1865, p. 2.
12. Michael Perman, *Reunion Without Compromise* (Cambridge: Cambridge University Press, 1973), 87.
13. Carl Schurz to Frederick Althaus, July 30, 1865, in Joseph Schafer, ed., *Intimate Letters of Carl Schurz, 1841–1869* (Madison: State Historical Society of Wisconsin, 1928), 341.

14. "Speech of Wendell Phillips," *The Liberator,* May 20, 1864, p. 1.
15. "Lee's Surrender," *New York Anglo-African,* Apr. 15, 1865, p. 1.
16. J. J. Wright, "Reconstruction," *Christian Recorder,* July 8, 1865, p. 1.
17. "Dinah Allen, interview by Kate Barrett," in George P. Rawick, ed., *The American Slave: A Composite Autobiography,* vol. 6, *Mississippi Narratives, Part 1* (Westport, CT: Greenwood Press, 1977), 50.
18. "Annie Coley, interview by Mrs. C. E. Wells," ser. 0436, Mississippi Department of Archives and History, Jackson, MS, https://da.mdah.ms.gov/series /federal/harrison/436/coley-annie/detail/32943.
19. Rawick, ed., *The American Slave,* vol. 1, *From Sundown to Sunup: The Making of the Black Community* (Westport, CT: Greenwood Press, 1972), 175.
20. Emphasis added. John W. Blassingame, *Slave Testimony: Two Centuries of Letters, Speeches, Interviews, and Autobiographies* (Baton Rouge: Louisiana State University Press, 1977), 739.
21. Ta-Nehisi Coates, "The Unromantic Slaughter of the Civil War," *The Atlantic,* June 20, 2013; and Coates, "Talk to Me Like I'm Stupid: Locke's State of Slavery and War," *The Atlantic,* Apr. 27, 2011.
22. AL, "Last Public Address," Apr. 11, 1865, *CWAL,* vol. 8, 404.
23. Oakes, *Freedom National,* 437–45; Michael Vorenberg, *Final Freedom: The Civil War, the Abolition of Slavery, and the Thirteenth Amendment* (Cambridge: Cambridge University Press, 2001), 99–107, 127–36, 185–97.
24. *CG,* 38th Cong., 1st Sess., 1465.
25. *CG,* 38th Cong., 1st Sess., 2989.
26. Sumner to George William Curtis, Apr. 13, 1864, in Beverly Wilson Palmer, ed., *The Selected Letters of Charles Sumner* (Boston: Northeastern University Press, 1990), 2:233. See Vorenberg, *Final Freedom,* 51–3, 55–60, 106–7.
27. Smith to Robert Hamilton, in *Weekly Anglo-African,* Aug. 27, 1864, in C. Peter Ripley, ed., *The Black Abolitionist Papers* (Chapel Hill: University of North Carolina Press, 1992), vol. 5, 300–301.
28. "Junius" to the *Christian Recorder,* Feb. 13, 1864, p. 2.
29. *Weekly Anglo-African,* Sep. 26, 1863, in Ripley, ed., *Black Abolitionist Papers,* vol. 5, 256.
30. Garrison to Lydia Maria Child, July 10, 1865, in Walter M. Merrill, *The Letters of William Lloyd Garrison,* vol. 5, *Let the Oppressed Go Free, 1861–1867* (Cambridge, MA: Harvard University Press, 1979), 282.
31. James M. McPherson, *The Struggle for Equality: Abolitionists and the Negro in the Civil War and Reconstruction* (Princeton, NJ: Princeton University Press, 1964), 304.
32. McPherson, *Struggle for Equality,* 304.
33. Frank J. Cirillo, *The Abolitionist Civil War: Immediatists and the Struggle to Transform the Union* (Baton Rouge: Louisiana State University Press, 2023), 252–63.
34. James A. Hawley to Col. Samuel Thomas, July 4, 1865, *FDHE,* ser. 3, vol. 1, 119.
35. AJ, "Reply to Delegation of Black Ministers," May 11, 1865, *PAJ,* vol. 8, 61–63.

36. Lydia Maria Child to *The Liberator,* May 6, 1865, in *The Liberator,* May 26, 1865, p. 84.

37. Salmon P. Chase to AJ, May 17, 1865, in Brooks D. Simpson et al., *Advice After Appomattox: Letters to Andrew Johnson, 1865–1866* (Knoxville: University of Tennessee Press, 1987), 29.

38. David W. Blight, *Frederick Douglass: Prophet of Freedom* (New York: Simon and Schuster, 2018), 472–73.

39. Frederick Douglass, "In What New Skin Will the Old Snake Come Forth? An Address Delivered in New York, New York, on May 10, 1865," https:// frederickdouglasspapersproject.com/s/digitaledition/item/17945; Blight, *Frederick Douglass,* 472–73.

40. *Army and Navy Journal,* Sep. 2, 1865, p. 25.

41. AJ, "Interview with South Carolina Delegation," June 24, 1865, *PAJ,* vol. 8, 283.

42. "Agate" (Whitelaw Reid), Aug. 8, 1865, in Whitelaw Reid Papers, MDLC, Washington, D.C.

43. Amy Murrell Taylor, *Embattled Freedom: Journeys Through the Civil War's Slave Refugee Camps* (Chapel Hill: University of North Carolina Press, 2018), 223.

44. Douglas R. Egerton, *Thunder at the Gates: The Black Civil War Regiments That Redeemed America* (New York: Basic Books, 2016), 295–96; Donald G. Nieman, *To Set the Law in Motion: The Freedmen's Bureau and the Legal Rights of Blacks, 1865–1868* (Millwood, NY: KTO Press, 1979), 38.

45. "Address from the Colored Citizens of Norfolk, Va., to the People of the United States," June 26, 1865, in Ripley, ed., *Black Abolitionist Papers,* vol. 5, 336. In much of the South through the spring of 1865, white civilians also relied on U.S. Army–issued passes. See, for example, Ben F. Cheney to Stuart Eldridge, Apr. 21, 1865, *FDHE,* ser. 1, vol. 3, 886–87.

46. Oliver O. Howard, "Bureau of Refugees, Freedmen and Abandoned Lands, Circular No. 2," https://www.virginiamemory.com/online-exhibitions/items /show/509.

47. See William A. Blair, *The Record of Murders and Outrages: Racial Violence and the Fight over Truth at the Dawn of Reconstruction* (Chapel Hill: University of North Carolina Press, 2021), esp. 31–37; and Paul A. Cimbala, *Under the Guardianship of the Nation: The Freedmen's Bureau and the Reconstruction of Georgia, 1865–1870* (Athens: University of Georgia Press, 1997). For a different perspective, one that gives Black civilians equal if not greater credit over armed occupiers for resisting violence and attaining freedom and equality, see Kidada E. Williams, *I Saw Death Coming: A History of Terror and Survival in the War Against Reconstruction* (New York: Bloomsbury, 2023).

48. E. T. Wright to H. B. Clitz, Oct. 6, 1865, *FDHE,* ser. 3, vol. 1, 557.

49. Harry W. Pfanz, "Soldiering in the South During the Reconstruction Period, 1865–1877" (PhD diss., Ohio State University, 1958), 178.

50. Murray Davis to James A. Hardie, May 13, 1865, *FDHE,* ser. 1, vol. 2, 701.

51. *New York Tribune,* June 12, 1865, reprinted in *The Liberator,* June 16, 1865, p. 94.

52. Bill Homer interview (interviewer unknown), *Born in Slavery: Slave Nar-*

ratives from the Federal Writers' Project, 1936–1938, https://www.loc.gov
/collections/slave-narratives-from-the-federal-writers-project-1936-to-1938
/about-this-collection, vol. 16, Texas, pt. 2, p. 156.

53. Booker T. Washington, *Up from Slavery: An Autobiography* (New York: Dou-
    bleday, Page, 1901), 20–21.
54. Major General M. H. Williams to E. M. McCook, May 16, 1865, *OR, Armies,*
    ser. 1, vol. 49, pt. 2, 801. See McCook to E. B. Beaumont, May 13, 1865, ibid.,
    747. Also see Edward Baptist, *Creating an Old South: Middle Florida's Planta-
    tion Frontier Before the Civil War* (Chapel Hill: University of North Carolina
    Press, 2002), 279–80; Joe M. Richardson, *African Americans in the Reconstruc-
    tion of Florida, 1865–1877,* 8–9; and William Watson Davison, *The Civil War
    and Reconstruction in Florida* (New York: Longmans, Green, 1913), 340–42.
55. John M. Schofield to Henry Halleck, May 7, 1865, *OR, Armies,* ser. 1, vol. 47,
    pt. 3, 431; H. W. Halleck to John M. Schofield, May 5, 1865, *OR, Armies,* ser.
    1, vol. 47, pt. 3, 404.
56. C. C. Andrews to the Freedmen of Selma and Vicinity, May 9, 1865, *OR,
    Armies,* ser. 1, vol. 49, pt. 2, 728–29. A similar sentiment about masters' respon-
    sibility to the needy was expressed in the emancipation order of Major Gen-
    eral James H. Wilson in Macon, Georgia, on July 5, 1865. See *OR, Armies,*
    ser. 1, vol. 49, pt. 2, 1068.
57. Carole Emberton, "The Freedwoman's Tale: Reconstruction Remembered in
    the Federal Writers' Project Ex-Slave Narratives," in Carole Emberton and
    Bruce E. Baker, eds., *Remembering Reconstruction: Struggles Over the Mean-
    ing of America's Most Turbulent Era* (Baton Rouge: Louisiana State University
    Press, 2017), 114.
58. Ambrose Douglass, interviewed by Martin Richardson, *Born in Slavery: Slave
    Narratives from the Federal Writers' Project, 1936–1938,* https://www.loc.gov
    /collections/slave-narratives-from-the-federal-writers-project-1936-to-1938
    /about-this-collection, vol. 3, Florida, 103. See Joseph P. Reidy, *Illusions of
    Emancipation: The Pursuit of Freedom and Equality in the Twilight of Slavery*
    (Chapel Hill: University of North Carolina Press, 2019), 115–17.
59. Mitch Kachun, *Festivals of Freedom: Memory and Meaning in African American
    Celebrations, 1808–1915* (Amherst: University of Massachusetts Press, 2003),
    186. Prior to the twenty-first century, as Annette Gordon-Reed observes,
    whites generally ignored Juneteenth. Annette Gordon-Reed, *On Juneteenth*
    (New York: Liveright, 2021), 122–36.
60. Edward T. Cotham, Jr., *Juneteenth: The Story Behind the Celebration* (Kerrville,
    TX: State House Press, 2021), 193.
61. Cotham, *Juneteenth,* 193–94.
62. "The Negro Question in Texas," *New York Times,* July 9, 1865, p. 4.
63. Downs, *After Appomattox,* 40.

8: A Short Time in Peace

1. For competing later versions of the story, both of which provide information
   regarding the relevant original sources, see William H. Armstrong, *Warrior*

in Two Camps: Ely S. Parker, Union General and Seneca Chief (Syracuse, NY: Syracuse University Press, 1978), 109–11; and Arthur C. Parker, *The Life of Ely S. Parker: Last Grand Sachem of the Iroquois and General Grant's Military Secretary* (Buffalo, NY: Buffalo Historical Society, 1919). For an example of the story being used to conclude the history of the Civil War in a common U.S. history textbook, see Joyce Appleby et al., *The American Vision* (New York: McGraw Hill, 2010), 349.

2. Kevin Waite, "War in Indian Country," in Aaron Sheehan-Dean, ed., *The Cambridge History of the American Civil War*, vol. 1, *Military Affairs* (Cambridge: Cambridge University Press, 2019), 576–600.

3. Robert Gould Shaw to "My dear Father," June 5, 1863, in Russell Duncan, ed., *Blue-Eyed Child of Fortune: The Civil War Letters of Colonel Robert Gould Shaw* (Athens: University of Georgia Press, 1992), 339.

4. William Whiting, "Citizenship and Enlistment of Indians," June 1863, RG 107, Records of the Office of the Secretary of War, vol. 2, Opinion 465, NA.

5. Alaina E. Roberts, *I've Been Here All the While: Black Freedom on Native Land* (Philadelphia: University of Pennsylvania Press, 2021), 16–21.

6. Claudio Saunt, *Unworthy Republic: The Dispossession of Native Americans and the Road to Indian Territory* (New York: W. W. Norton, 2020), 22–24, 124–36, 162–68, 268–81.

7. Ned Blackhawk, *The Rediscovery of America: Native Peoples and the Unmaking of U.S. History* (New Haven, CT: Yale University Press, 2023), 308–14; W. Dale Weeks, *Cherokee Civil Warrior: Chief John Ross and the Struggle for Tribal Sovereignty* (Norman: University of Oklahoma Press, 2023), 58–66; Roberts, *I've Been Here All the While*, 31–35; Clarissa W. Confer, *The Cherokee Nation in the Civil War* (Norman: University of Oklahoma Press, 2007), 42–51.

8. Gerald Thompson, *The Army and the Navajo* (Tucson: University of Arizona Press, 1976), 6–7.

9. Steven Hahn, "Slave Emancipation, Indian Peoples, and the Projects of a New American Nation-State," *Journal of the Civil War Era* 3 (Sep. 2013): 308.

10. Pekka Hämäläinen, "Reconstructing the Great Plains: The Long Struggle for Sovereignty and Dominance in the Heart of the Continent," *Journal of the Civil War Era* 4 (Dec. 2016): 496–500. On western tribes that seized and enslaved enemy captives, see Andrés Reséndez, *The Other Slavery: The Uncovered Story of Indian Slavery in America* (Boston: Houghton Mifflin, 2016), 277–84, which focuses on the Navajo in particular.

11. William A. Blair, "Protecting Their Self-Interest: Native American Governance in the Confederacy," in Caroline E. Janney, Peter S. Carmichael, and Aaron Sheehan-Dean, eds., *The War That Made America: Essays Inspired by the Scholarship of Garry W. Gallagher* (Chapel Hill: University of North Carolina Press, 2024), 20–24; Weeks, *Cherokee Civil Warrior*, 66–72.

12. Roberts, *I've Been Here All the While*, 24–25; Fay A. Yarbrough, *Choctaw Confederates: The American Civil War in Indian Country* (Chapel Hill: University of North Carolina Press, 2021), 89–91.

13. Patrick N. Minges, *Slavery in the Cherokee Nation: The Keetoowah Society and the Defining of a People* (New York: Routledge, 2003), 95–114.

14. "Declaration by the people of the Cherokee Nation . . . ," Oct. 28, 1861, *OR, Armies,* ser. 1, vol. 13, 504.

15. William G. McLoughlin, *After the Trail of Tears: The Cherokees' Struggle for Sovereignty, 1839–1880* (Chapel Hill: University of North Carolina Press, 1993), 176–97.

16. Alvin M. Josephy, Jr., *The Civil War in the American West* (New York: Alfred A Knopf, 1991), 319–32.

17. Sarah C. Watie to Stand Watie, June 12, 1864, in Edward Everett Dale and Gaston Litton, eds., *Cherokee Cavaliers: Forty Years of Cherokee History as Told in the Correspondence of the Ridge-Watie-Boudinot Family* (Norman: University of Oklahoma Press, 1939), 189.

18. James Carleton to Christopher Carson, Oct. 12, 1862, *OR, Armies,* ser. 1, vol. 15, 579. See James Carleton to Joseph R. West, Oct. 11, 1862, ibid., 580–81.

19. James Carleton to Lorenzo Thomas, Sep. 6, 1863, in *Condition of the Indian Tribes: Report of the Joint Special Committee, appointed under resolution of March 3, 1865* (Washington, D.C.: Government Printing Office, 1867), p. 134.

20. Blackhawk, *The Rediscovery of America,* 321–23.

21. Ari Kelman, "From Manassas to Mankato: How the Civil War Bled into the Indian Wars," in Kent Blansett, Cathleen D. Cahill, and Andrew Needham, eds., *Indian Cities: Histories of Indigenous Urbanization* (Norman: University of Oklahoma Press, 2022), 75–94. See Blackhawk, *The Rediscovery of America,* 293–95; and Pekka Hämäläinen, *Lakota America: A New History of Indigenous Power* (New Haven, CT: Yale University Press, 2019), 248–63.

22. John Pope to Henry Sibley, Sep. 28, 1862, *OR, Armies,* ser. 1, vol. 13, 686.

23. Pope's 1865 plan was the same as his similarly ambitious and futile plans of the summers of 1863 and 1864. See Michael Clodfelter, *The Dakota War: The United States Army Versus the Sioux, 1862–1865* (Jefferson, NC: McFarland, 1998), 202–20.

24. Edmund Kirby Smith to D. H. Cooper, Apr. 8, 1865, *OR, Armies,* ser. 1, vol. 48, pt. 2, 1271.

25. Edmund Kirby Smith to Albert Pike, Apr. 8, 1865, *OR, Armies,* ser. 1, vol. 48, pt. 2, 1266.

26. Edmund Kirby Smith to Albert Pike, Apr. 8, 1865, *OR, Armies,* ser. 1, vol. 48, pt. 2, 1266–69; Edmund Kirby Smith to D. H. Cooper, Apr. 8, 1865 (2 letters), *OR, Armies,* ser. 1, vol. 48, pt. 2, 1270–71; Kirby Smith to James W. Throckmorton, Apr. 8, 1865, *OR, Armies,* ser. 1, vol. 48, pt. 2, 1271–72. See Jeffrey Lee Fortney, Jr., "Robert M. Jones and the Choctaw Nation: Indigenous Nationalism in the American South, 1820–1877" (PhD diss., University of Oklahoma, 2014), 248–49.

27. Stand Watie to Tuckabatcho Micco, Mar. 19, 1865, in Edward E. Dale, "Additional Letters of General Stand Watie," *Chronicles of Oklahoma* 1 (Oct. 1921): 43–44.

28. Muriel H. Wright, "General Douglas H. Cooper, C.S.A.," *Chronicles of Oklahoma* 32 (Spring 1954): 142–84.

29. D. H. Cooper to T. M. Scott, May 10, 1865, *OR, Armies,* ser. 1, vol. 48, pt. 2, 1297.

30. D. H. Cooper to S. S. Anderson, May 15, 1865, *OR, Armies,* ser. 1, vol. 48, pt. 2, 1306.
31. *OR, Armies,* ser. 1, vol. 48, pt. 2, 1103.
32. D. H. Cooper to Tandy Walker, May 24, 1865, *OR, Armies,* ser. 1, vol. 48, pt. 2, 1318.
33. D. H. Cooper to Stand Watie, May 22, 1865, *OR, Armies,* ser. 1, vol. 48, pt. 2, 1318.
34. D. H. Cooper to S. S. Anderson, May 25, 1865, *OR, Armies,* ser. 1, vol. 48, pt. 2, 1319.
35. D. H. Cooper to George Weissenger, June 16, 1865, *OR, Armies,* ser. 1, vol. 48, pt. 2, 1323.
36. James C. Veatch to D. H. Cooper, July 15, 1865, *OR, Armies,* ser. 1, vol. 48, pt. 2, 1107.
37. Annie Heloise Abel, *The American Indian Under Reconstruction* (Cleveland, OH: Arthur H. Clark, 1925), 140–43.
38. Wilfred Knight, *Red Fox: Stand Watie and the Confederate Indian Nations During the Civil War Years in Indian Territory* (Glendale, CA: Arthur C. Clark, 1988), 274.
39. Fortney, "Robert M. Jones and the Choctaw Nation," 253.
40. Fortney, "Robert M. Jones and the Choctaw Nation," 253.
41. *OR, Armies,* ser. 1, vol. 48, pt. 2, 1100–1101.
42. Weeks, *Cherokee Civil Warrior,* 66–67, 127–28.
43. A. C. Mathews to Winchester Colbert, June 23, 1865, *OR, Armies,* ser. 1, vol. 48, pt. 2, 1105.
44. *OR, Armies,* ser. 1, vol. 48, pt. 2, 1100–1101.

Part II: The Grasp of War

1. RHD, "'Grasp of War' Speech," June 21, 1865, delivered in Faneuil Hall, Boston, Massachusetts, Richard H. Dana III, ed., *Richard Henry Dana, Jr., Speeches in Stirring Times and Letters to a Son* (Boston: Houghton Mifflin Company, 1910), 246.

9: Complete and Perfect Freedom

1. AL, "Annual Message to Congress," Dec. 6, 1865, *CWAL,* vol. 8, 151–52.
2. RHD, *Two Years Before the Mast* (Boston: Houghton Mifflin, 1911), 294–96.
3. RHD, *Two Years Before the Mast,* 122–25.
4. "The Blacks and the Ballot," *Christian Recorder,* May 27, 1865, p. 3.
5. RHD, "'Grasp of War' Speech," June 21, 1865, delivered in Faneuil Hall, Boston, Massachusetts, Richard H. Dana III, ed., *Richard Henry Dana, Jr., Speeches in Stirring Times and Letters to a Son* (Boston: Houghton Mifflin Company, 1910), 248.
6. Jeffrey L. Amestoy, *Slavish Shore: The Odyssey of Richard Henry Dana, Jr.* (Cambridge, MA: Harvard University Press, 2015), 195–98.

7. Amestoy, *Slavish Shore,* 210.
8. "The Two Roads to Peace!" (broadside) (New York: Astor House, undated).
9. Edward Kent to RHD, Apr. 14, 1865, Dana Family Papers, Dana Family I, box 17, folder Apr. 1865, MHS.
10. RHD to "Dear Bryant," Apr. 22, 1865, Dana Family Papers, Dana Family I, box 17, folder Apr. 1865, MHS.
11. RHD to Richard Henry Dana III, May 28, 1865, Dana Family Papers, Dana Family I, box 17, folder May 1865, MHS.
12. RHD to Charles Francis Adams, Sr., June 3, 1865, Dana Family Papers, Dana Family I, box 17, folder June 1865, MHS.
13. RHD to Charles Francis Adams, Sr., June 3, 1865, Dana Family Papers, Dana Family I, box 17, folder June 1865, MHS.
14. Hugo Grotius, *The Law of War and Peace,* trans. Francis W. Kelsey (New York: Bobbs-Merrill, 1925), 832.
15. Grotius, *The Law of War and Peace,* 828.
16. Charles Sumner, "Our Domestic Relations; Or, How to Treat the Rebel States," *Atlantic Monthly* 12 (Oct. 1863): 507–29 (see esp. 521–22).
17. RHD to Charles Francis Adams, Sr., June 3, 1865, Dana Family Papers, Dana Family I, box 17, folder June 1865, MHS.
18. Emmerich de Vattel, *Law of Nations,* ed. Joseph Chitty (Philadelphia: Johnson and Co., 1866), 431.
19. RHD to Charles Francis Adams, Sr., June 3, 1865, Dana Family Papers, Dana Family I, box 17, folder June 1865, MHS.
20. Carl von Clausewitz, *On War,* eds. Michael Howard and Peter Paret (1976; repr., New York: Alfred A. Knopf, 1993), 85.
21. Clausewitz, *On War,* 83–84.
22. RHD, "'Grasp of War' Speech," June 21, 1865, 258.
23. RHD to Charles Francis Adams, Sr., June 3, 1865, Dana Family Papers, Dana Family I, box 17, folder June 1865, MHS.
24. Amestoy, *Slavish Shore,* 254.
25. RHD, "'Grasp of War' Speech," June 21, 1865, 246.
26. RHD, "'Grasp of War' Speech," June 21, 1865, 248.
27. RHD, "'Grasp of War' Speech," June 21, 1865, 250.
28. David W. Blight, *Frederick Douglass: Prophet of Freedom* (New York: Simon and Schuster, 2018), 416–17; James M. McPherson, *The Struggle for Equality: Abolitionists and the Negro in the Civil War and Reconstruction* (Princeton, NJ: Princeton University Press, 1964), 305.
29. "On Death of A. Lincoln," undated (speech given at Cooper Union, New York City, June 1, 1865), Frederick Douglass Papers, microfilm reel 14, LC.
30. RHD, "'Grasp of War' Speech," June 21, 1865, 246, 248–53.
31. Francis Lieber, New York City, to RHD, July 11, 1865, Dana Family Papers, Dana Family I, box 17, folder July 1865, MHS.
32. John Bigelow to RHD, Aug. 8, 1865, Dana Family Papers, Dana Family I, box 17, folder Aug. 1865, MHS.
33. John L. Motley to RHD, Aug. 28, 1865, Dana Family Papers, Dana Family I, box 17, folder Aug. 1865, MHS.

34. Charles F. Adams, Sr., to RHD, Oct. 11, 1865, Dana Family Papers, Dana Family I, box 17, folder Oct. 1865, MHS.
35. Charles F. Adams, Sr., to RHD, Oct. 11, 1865, Dana Family Papers, Dana Family I, box 17, folder Oct. 1865, MHS.
36. Charles F. Adams, Sr., to RHD, Oct. 11, 1865, Dana Family Papers, Dana Family I, box 17, folder Oct. 1865, MHS.
37. Francis Lieber to RHD, July 11, 1865, Dana Family Papers, Dana Family I, box 17, folder July 1865, MHS.
38. Francis Lieber, "Amendments of the Constitution," in Lieber, *Contributions to Political Science* (Philadelphia: J. B. Lippincott, 1880), 137–79 (quotations at 152).
39. John Murray Forbes to N. M. Beckwith, June 25, 1865, in Sarah Forbes, ed., *Letters and Recollections of John Murray Forbes* (Boston: Houghton, Mifflin, 1899), 2:110.
40. *Chicago Tribune*, July 13, 1865, pp. 2–3.
41. Henry Winter Davis to Joseph Medill, July 18, 1865, Joseph Medill Papers, Cantigny Park Museum, Wheaton, IL, box 1, folder 1.
42. AJ, "Interview with South Carolina Delegation," *PAJ*, vol. 8, 280–85.
43. *Albany (NY) Argus*, reprinted in "President Johnson and the South Carolina Delegation—Opinions of the Democratic Press," *Detroit Free Press*, June 28, 1865, p. 2.
44. RHD to Charles Francis Adams, Sr., Dec. 18, 1865, Adams Family Papers, microfilm reel 577, MHS.
45. John Murray Forbes to N. M. Beckwith, June 25, 1865, in Sarah Forbes, ed., *Letters and Recollections of John Murray Forbes* (Boston: Houghton, Mifflin, 1899), 2:110.
46. Francis Lieber, New York City, to RHD, July 11, 1865, Dana Family Papers, Dana Family I, box 17, folder July 1865, MHS.
47. "The President's Advice," *Chicago Tribune*, June 29, 1865, p. 1.
48. William E. Gienapp and Erica L. Gienapp, eds., *The Civil War Diary of Gideon Welles, Lincoln's Secretary of the Navy* (Urbana: University of Illinois Press, 2014), 521–22 (Oct. 1, 1864).
49. Gregory P. Downs, *After Appomattox: Military Occupation and the Ends of War* (Cambridge, MA: Harvard University Press, 2015), 45, 65, 69; Chandra Manning, *Troubled Refuge: Struggling for Freedom in the Civil War* (New York: Alfred A. Knopf, 2016), 262–70; Benjamin P. Thomas and Harold M. Hyman, *Stanton: The Life and Times of Lincoln's Secretary of War* (New York: Alfred A. Knopf, 1962), 306–7.
50. William Marvel, *Lincoln's Autocrat: The Life of Edwin Stanton* (Chapel Hill: University of North Carolina Press, 2015), 367–68; Thomas and Hyman, *Stanton*, 357–58.
51. Thomas and Hyman, *Stanton*, 445.
52. James E. Sefton, *The United States Army and Reconstruction, 1865–1877* (Baton Rouge: Louisiana State University Press, 1967), 16–17.
53. Just before his death, Lincoln drafted a plan for a regular army that would

have one soldier per 1,000 civilians—roughly 35,000 troops in total. *CWAL*, vol. 8, 408–9.

54. L. D. Ingersoll, *A History of the War Department of the United States* (Washington, D.C.: Francis B. Mohun, 1880), 368–70.

55. Howard K. Beale, ed., *Diary of Gideon Welles, Secretary of the Navy Under Lincoln and Johnson* (New York: W. W. Norton, 1960), vol. 2, 352.

56. Beale, ed., *Diary of Gideon Welles*, vol. 2, 328.

57. "The Negro Question in Texas," *New York Times*, July 9, 1865, p. 4.

58. William L. Richter, *Overreached on All Sides: The Freedmen's Bureau Administrators in Texas, 1865–1868* (College Station: Texas A&M University Press, 1991), 8–10; F. W. Emery to John H. Kelly, June 28, 1865, *OR, Armies*, ser. 1, vol. 48, pt. 2, 1017–18 (source of quotation of "abuse" by Blacks of their rights).

59. Sefton, *The United States Army and Reconstruction*, 44.

60. Downs, *After Appomattox*, 257–60 (Appendixes 1–4).

61. Donald G. Nieman, *To Set the Law in Motion: The Freedmen's Bureau and the Legal Rights of Blacks, 1865–1868* (Millwood, NY: KTO Press, 1979), 6.

62. Congress in 1864 had already passed a law allowing Black testimony against whites in courts-martial and military commissions. *U.S. Statutes at Large*, 38th Cong., 1st Sess., Chap. 210, Sec. 3, 351. On Indiana's Black testimony law, see Kate Masur, *Until Justice Be Done: America's First Civil Rights Movement, from the Revolution to Reconstruction* (New York: W. W. Norton, 2021), 327–28.

63. John T. O'Brien, "Reconstruction in Richmond: White Restoration and Black Protest, April-June 1865," *Virginia Magazine of History and Biography*, 89 (July 1981), 279–80; Nieman, *To Set the Law in Motion*, 6.

64. Arney R. Childs, ed., *The Private Journal of Henry William Ravenel, 1859–1887* (Columbia: University of South Carolina Press, 1947), 246.

65. David L. Swain to William A. Graham, July 7, 1865, in Max R. Williams, ed., *The Papers of William Alexander Graham* (Raleigh: North Carolina Division of Archives and History, 1976), vol. 6, 324.

66. *Celebration by the Colored People's Educational Monument Association in Memory of Abraham Lincoln on the Fourth of July, 1865* (Washington, D.C.: McGill and Witherow, 1865), 5.

67. *Celebration by the Colored People's Educational Monument Association*, 30–31.

68. *Celebration by the Colored People's Educational Monument Association*, 30.

69. Shannon M. Smith, "'They Mustered a Whole Company of Kuklux as Militia': State Violence and Black Freedom in Kentucky's Readjustment," in Adam H. Domby and Simon Lewis, eds., *Freedoms Gained and Lost: Reconstruction and Its Meanings 150 Years Later* (New York: Fordham University Press, 2022), 96–120.

70. Clinton B. Fisk to O. O. Howard, July 20, 1865, *FDHE*, ser. 1, vol. 2, 706.

71. *FDHE*, ser. 1, vol. 1, 619–21; ibid., Ser 1., vol. 2, 703–4; John M. Palmer to AJ, July 29, 1865, *PAJ*, vol. 8, 487–90.

72. *FDHE*, ser. 1, vol. 2, 702–3; General Order 43, *OR, Armies*, ser. 1, vol. 49, 1012.

73. All quotations come from John M. Palmer, *Personal Recollections of John M. Palmer: The Story of an Earnest Life* (Cincinnati: Robert Clarke, 1901), 240–

42. See Clinton B. Fisk to O. O. Howard, July 6, 1865; and H. M. Spofford to R. W. Johnson, July 10, 1865, both in *FDHE*, ser. 3, vol. 1, 128–31. For more on Palmer's emancipation declaration in Kentucky, see Bridget Ford, *Bonds of Union: Religion, Race, and Politics in a Civil War Borderland* (Chapel Hill: University of North Carolina Press, 2016), 297–302; and Downs, *After Appomattox*, 59–60.

74. Palmer, *Personal Recollections*, 243–45. By the time Palmer was tried, in December 1865, the Thirteenth Amendment abolishing slavery had been ratified. Palmer's lawyer successfully argued that because slavery was now outlawed in Kentucky as well as all other states, no one could be convicted of helping slaves to escape. The judge refused to quash the indictment, though, reasoning that to do so would be the same as allowing a horse thief to go free simply because the horse had died at some point before the indictment. See Palmer, *Personal Recollections*, 247.

10: Armies of Observation

1. *Detroit Free Press*, June 6, 1865, p. 1.
2. John Pope to Senator James R. Doolittle, undated (1865), in *Condition of the Indian Tribes: Report of the Joint Special Committee, appointed under resolution of March 3, 1865* (Washington, D.C.: Government Printing Office, 1867), 426.
3. Patrick Edward Connor to Grenville Dodge, July 3, 1865, *OR, Armies*, ser. 1, vol. 48, pt. 2, 1045.
4. Patrick Edward Connor to C. H. Potter, July 3, 1865, *OR, Armies*, ser. 1, vol. 48, pt. 2, 1045. The order by Connor to Potter related only to male "Indians" found near the "mail route." But at least one of Connor's underlings interpreted this to mean the entire vast area north of the South Platte River in Colorado Territory. See testimony of Colonel C. H. Potter, *Condition of the Indian Tribes*, Appendix, 71.
5. Report of G. M. Dodge, June 18, 1865, *OR, Armies*, ser. 1, vol. 48, pt. 1, 332.
6. *CG*, 38th Cong., 2nd Sess., 250–51.
7. James Harlan to William P. Dole, June 22, 1865, RG 75, Records of the Bureau of Indian Affairs, NA.
8. AJ to James Harlan, June 22, 1865, *PAJ*, vol. 8, 270–71.
9. James R. Doolittle to James Harlan, May 31, 1865, *OR, Armies*, ser. 1, vol. 48, pt. 2, 868–69.
10. James H. Carleton to Erastus W. Wood, Apr. 24, 1865, *Condition of the Indian Tribes*, Appendix, 224–25.
11. James H. Carleton to William McCleave, June 17, 1865, *OR, Armies*, ser. 1, vol. 48, pt. 2, 914–15.
12. James H. Carleton to William H. Lewis, June 19, 1865, and Ben C. Cutler to William H. Lewis, June 25, 1865, in *Condition of the Indian Tribes*, Appendix, 227–29; Thompson, *The Army and the Navajo*, 87–89.
13. *Condition of the Indian Tribes*, 4.
14. Gerald Thompson, *The Army and the Navajo* (Tucson: University of Arizona Press, 1976), 121–26.

15. Harry Kelsey, "The Doolittle Report of 1867: Its Preparation and Shortcomings," *Arizona and the West* 17 (Summer 1975): 107–20.
16. Annie Heloise Abel, *The American Indian Under Reconstruction* (Cleveland, OH: Arthur H. Clark, 1925), 177, 219–26.
17. Wilfred Knight, *Red Fox: Stand Watie and the Confederate Indian Nations During the Civil War Years in Indian Territory* (Glendale, CA: Arthur C. Clark, 1988), 277–83; Abel, *The American Indian Under Reconstruction,* 181–218.
18. Grenville M. Dodge to James Harlan, June 22, 1865, *OR, Armies,* ser. 1, vol. 48, pt. 2, 974.
19. David E. Wagner, *Patrick Connor's War: The 1865 Powder River Indian Expedition* (Norman, OK: Arthur H. Clark, 2010), 66–67.
20. Wagner, *Patrick Connor's War,* 67–68.
21. Patrick E. Connor to Grenville Dodge, July 21, 1865, *OR, Armies,* ser. 1, vol. 48, pt. 2, 1112.
22. Richard N. Ellis, "Volunteer Soldiers in the West, 1865," *Military Affairs* 34 (Apr. 1970): 54.
23. Grenville Dodge to William T. Sherman, Aug. 15, 1865, *OR, Armies,* ser. 1, vol. 48, pt. 2, 1183–84.
24. Howard K. Beale, ed., *Diary of Gideon Welles, Secretary of the Navy Under Lincoln and Johnson* (W. W. Norton, 1960), vol. 2, 360–61; USG to Sherman, Aug. 21, 1865, *OR, Armies,* ser. 1., vol. 48, pt. 2, 1199; Walter Stahr, *Stanton: Lincoln's War Secretary* (New York: Simon and Schuster, 2017), 456.
25. John Pope to Grenville Dodge, Aug. 11. 1865, *OR, Armies,* ser. 1, vol. 48, pt. 1, 353; Pope to Dodge, July 31, 1865, ibid., 350. See Peter Cozzens, *General John Pope: A Life for the Nation* (Urbana: University of Illinois Press, 2000), 265–67; and Cozzens, *The Earth Is Weeping: The Epic Story of the Indian Wars for the American West* (New York: Alfred A. Knopf, 2016), 28–29.
26. P. H. Sheridan to USG, Nov. 27, 1865, RG 94, Letters Received by the U.S. Adjutant General, file 1071G1865, RG 94, NA. See Don H. Doyle, "Reconstruction and Anti-imperialism: The United States and Mexico," in William A. Link, ed., *United States Reconstruction Across the Americas* (Gainesville: University Press of Florida, 2019), 47–80; Alfred Jackson Hanna and Kathryn Abbey Hanna, *Napoleon III and Mexico: American Triumph over Monarchy* (Chapel Hill: University of North Carolina Press, 1971), 232; and Todd W. Wahlstrom, *The Southern Exodus to Mexico: Migration Across the Borderlands After the American Civil War* (Lincoln: University of Nebraska Press, 2015), 23–24.
27. Elizabeth R. Varon, *Appomattox: Victory, Defeat, and Freedom at the End of the Civil War* (New York: Oxford University Press, 2014), 45–46; Paul Andrew Hutton, *Phil Sheridan and His Army* (Lincoln: University of Nebraska Press, 1986), 32.
28. Elizabeth B. Custer, *Tenting on the Plains* (New York: Charles L. Webster, 1889), 218.
29. *Pulaski (TN) Citizen,* May 4, 1866, p. 2.
30. Beale, ed., *Diary of Gideon Welles,* vol. 2, 317. See Patrick Kelly, "The Lost Continent of Abraham Lincoln," *Journal of the Civil War Era* 9 (June 2019): 223–48.

31. USG to AJ, July 15, 1865, *PAJ,* vol. 8, 410.
32. "Report of Lieutenant-General U.S. Grant, of the United States Armies— 1864–'65," July 22, 1865, in *Personal Memoirs of U.S. Grant* (New York: Charles L. Webster & Company, 1886), 2:632.
33. Beale, ed., *Diary of Gideon Welles,* vol. 2, 348.
34. Joseph Howard Parks, *General Edmund Kirby Smith, C.S.A.* (Baton Rouge: Louisiana State University Press, 1954), 483.
35. *New York Herald,* June 29, 1865, p. 1; William C. Davis, *Breckinridge: Statesman, Soldier, Symbol* (Baton Rouge: Louisiana State University Press, 1974), 549.
36. Quoted in Charles C. Osborne, *Jubal: The Life and Times of General Jubal A. Early* (Chapel Hill, NC: Algonquin Books, 1992), 402.
37. Christopher L. Jones, "Deserting Dixie: A History of Emigres, Exiles, and Dissenters from the American South, 1866–1925" (PhD diss., Brown University, 2009), 23–25.
38. Hanna and Hanna, *Napoleon III and Mexico,* 224–27.
39. "Passports for Paroled Prisoners" (reprint of Executive Order of Aug. 22, 1865), *New York Herald,* Aug. 27, 1865, p. 5; Philp H. Sheridan, *Personal Memoirs of P.H. Sheridan* (New York: C. L. Webster and Company, 1888), 2:218–19; Anthony Arthur, *General Jo Shelby's March* (New York: Random House, 2010), 170–71.
40. "Report of Maj. Gen. Philip H. Sheridan," Nov. 14, 1866, *OR, Armies,* ser. 1, vol. 48, pt. 1, 300.
41. "Report of Maj. Gen. Philip H. Sheridan," Nov. 14, 1866, *OR, Armies,* ser. 1, vol. 48, pt. 1, 300.
42. Custer, *Tenting on the Plains,* 260–61.
43. RHD, "'Grasp of War' Speech," June 21, 1865, delivered in Faneuil Hall, Boston, Massachusetts. Reprinted in Richard H. Dana III, ed., *Richard Henry Dana, Jr., Speeches in Stirring Times and Letters to a Son* (Boston: Houghton Mifflin Company, 1910), 246.
44. William L. Richter, "'It Is Best to Go In Strong-Handed': Army Occupation of Texas, 1865–1866," *Arizona and the West* 27 (Summer 1985): 123.
45. Charles T. Clark, *Opdycke Tigers: 125th O. V. I.* (Columbus, OH: Spahr and Glenn, 1895), 400.
46. *FDHE,* ser. 2, 465–71; Prisoner Record Book, Fort Jefferson, Dry Tortugas, RG 94, NA.; Detlev F. Vagts, "Military Commissions: A Concise History," *American Journal of International Law* 101 (Jan. 2007): 240.
47. Richter, "'It Is Best to Go In Strong-Handed,'" 131.
48. William A. Blair, *The Record of Murders and Outrages: Racial Violence and the Fight over Truth at the Dawn of Reconstruction* (Chapel Hill: University of North Carolina Press, 2021), 113.
49. "Rufus," July 15, 1865, in Edwin S. Redkey, ed., *A Grand Army of Black Men: Letters from African-American Soldiers in the Union Army, 1861–1865* (Cambridge: Cambridge University Press, 1992), 198.
50. Joseph T. Glatthaar, *Forged in Battle: The Civil War Alliance of Black Soldiers and White Officers* (New York: The Free Press, 1990), 219.
51. "Rufus," July 15, 1865, in Redkey, ed., *A Grand Army of Black Men,* 198.

52. Jonathan Lande, "Disciplining Freedom: U.S. Army Slave Rebels and Emancipation in the Civil War" (PhD diss., Brown University, 2018), 247–324; Noah Andre Trudeau, *Like Men of War: Black Troops in the Civil War, 1862–1865* (Boston: Little, Brown, 1999), 455–63; Brooks D. Simpson, "Quandaries of Command: Ulysses S. Grant and Black Soldiers," in David W. Blight and Brooks D. Simpson, eds., *Union and Emancipation: Essays on Politics and Race in the Civil War Era* (Kent, OH: Kent State University Press, 1997), 141–42; Glatthaar, *Forged in Battle,* 209–10; Mary F. Berry, *Toward Freedom and Civil Rights for the Freedmen: Military Policy Origins of the Thirteenth Amendment and the Civil Rights Act of 1866* (Department of History, Howard University, 1975), 13–17.

53. Richter, "'It Is Best to Go In Strong-Handed,'" 134.

54. Glatthaar, *Forged in Battle,* 223–24.

55. Harry Willcox Pfanz, "Soldiering in the South During the Reconstruction Period, 1865–1877" (PhD diss., Ohio State University, 1958), 187–88.

56. Sheridan to John A. Rawlins, Oct. 29, 1865, Ulysses S. Grant Papers, MDLC, Washington, D.C. See Simpson, "Quandaries of Command," 141–42; Richter, "'It Is Best to Go In Strong-Handed,'" 130–34. On the differing responses among white commanders about whether to allow discharged African American soldiers to buy their rifles, see Gregory P. Downs, *After Appomattox: Military Occupation and the Ends of War* (Cambridge, MA: Harvard University Press, 2015), 111; Berry, *Toward Freedom and Civil Rights for the Freedmen,* 16–17; and James E. Sefton, *The United States Army and Reconstruction* (Baton Rouge: Louisiana State University Press, 1967), 42–43.

57. Edward B. Rugemer, "Jamaica's Morant Bay Rebellion and the Making of Radical Reconstruction," in William A. Link, ed., *United States Reconstruction Across the Americas* (Gainesville: University Press of Florida, 2019), 100. See Carole Emberton, *Beyond Redemption: Race, Violence, and the American South After the Civil War* (Chicago: University of Chicago Press, 2013), 33–34.

58. *FDHE,* ser. 2, 725–26. See Michael E. DeGruccio, "Unmade: American Manhood in the Civil War Era" (PhD diss., University of Notre Dame, 2007), 220–29.

11: Demons Incarnate

1. Martha Hodes, *Mourning Lincoln* (New Haven, CT: Yale University Press, 2015), 236.

2. John R. Kelso, "Speech Delivered at Walnut Grove, Missouri, Sep. 19, 1865," in Christopher Grasso, ed., *Bloody Engagements: John R. Kelso's Civil War* (New Haven, CT: Yale University Press, 2017), 191.

3. Kelso, "Speech Delivered at Walnut Grove," 190–92.

4. Kelso, "Speech Delivered at Walnut Grove," 190.

5. William A. Blair, *Why Didn't the North Hang Some Rebels? The Postwar Debate over Punishment for Treason* (Milwaukee: Marquette University Press, 2004), 8–9.

6. Charles A. Dana to James S. Pike, May 10, 1865, James S. Pike Papers, Calais Free Library, Calais, ME.

7. Howard K. Beale, ed., *Diary of Gideon Welles* (W. W. Norton, 1960), vol. 2, 338–39.

8. Francis Lieber, *Amendments to the Constitution, Submitted to the Consideration of the American People* (New York: Loyal Publication Society, 1865), 36–38. See Michael Vorenberg, "Emancipating the Constitution: Francis Lieber and the Theory of Amendment," in Charles R. Mack and Henry H. Lesesne, eds., *Francis Lieber and the Culture of the Mind* (Columbia: University of South Carolina Press, 2005), 23–32; Cynthia Nicoletti, *Secession on Trial: The Treason Prosecution of Jefferson Davis* (Cambridge: Cambridge University Press, 2017), 256–57; and John Fabian Witt, *Lincoln's Code: The Laws of War in American History* (New York: The Free Press, 2012), 287.

9. Howard K. Beale, ed., *The Diary of Edward Bates, 1859–1866* (Washington, D.C.: Government Printing Office, 1933), 477.

10. Robert Saunders, *John Archibald Campbell: Southern Moderate, 1811–1889* (Tuscaloosa: University of Alabama Press, 1997), 187.

11. Terry Alford, *Fortune's Fool: The Life of John Wilkes Booth* (New York: Oxford University Press, 2015), 320–23.

12. "The Week," *The Nation*, 1 (July 13, 1865), 34.

13. William Marvel, *Lincoln's Autocrat: The Life of Edwin Stanton* (Chapel Hill: University of North Carolina Press, 2015), 376.

14. Beale, ed., *Diary of Gideon Welles*, vol. 2, 362–63.

15. James Speed, *Opinion of the Constitutional Power of the Military to Try and Execute the Assassins of the President* (Washington, D.C.: Government Printing Office, 1865), 16. On the manipulation of Speed by Holt and Stanton, see Beale, ed., *The Diary of Edward Bates*, 483; Elizabeth D. Leonard, *Lincoln's Avengers: Justice, Revenge, and Reunion After the Civil War* (New York: Norton, 2004), 67–68; Marvel, *Lincoln's Autocrat*, 376–78; and Witt, *Lincoln's Code*, 293.

16. Speed, *Opinion of the Constitutional Power*, 16.

17. Beale, ed., *The Diary of Edward Bates*, 483.

18. *New York Times*, July 8, 1865, p. 1.

19. James Speed, "Surrender of the Rebel Army of Northern Virginia," Apr. 22, 1865, *Opinions of the Attorney General* 11:208–9.

20. General Order 2, reprinted in *Weekly Panola (MS) Star*, Aug. 5, 1865, 3.

21. James Ramage, *Gray Ghost: The Life of Col. John Singleton Mosby* (Lexington: University Press of Kentucky, 1999), 268–70.

22. *Wheeling (WV) Daily Intelligencer*, Oct. 9, 1865, p. 4.

23. General Order 70, reprinted in *Daily Richmond Whig*, June 12, 1865, p. 2; "Scenes in the Reconstructed South," *The Independent*, Jan. 25, 1866, p. 1; Richmond *Daily Dispatch*, Aug. 31, 1866, p. 1 (commenting on Charles Howard).

24. Shae Smith Cox, *The Fabric of Civil War Society: Uniforms, Badges, and Flags, 1859–1939* (Baton Rouge: Louisiana State University Press, 2024), 112–20.

25. *Howard (MO) Union*, June 22, 1865, p. 3.

26. Daniel E. Sutherland, *A Savage Conflict: The Decisive Role of Guerrillas in the American Civil War* (Chapel Hill: University of North Carolina Press, 2009), 274–76 (quotation at 276).

27. Thomas Goodrich, *Black Flag: Guerrilla Warfare on the Western Border, 1861–1865* (Bloomington: Indiana University Press, 1995), 163–64.

28. R. H. Milroy to George H. Thomas, May 12, 1865, *OR, Armies,* ser. 1, vol. 49, pt. 2, 737; Sutherland, *A Savage Conflict,* 274.

29. For examples of Holt agreeing to commute guerrillas' death sentences because of their youth, see *U.S. v. Willis Berry,* RG 153, Records of the Office of the Judge Advocate General (Army), 1792–2010, Court Martial Case Files, file mm2835, NA; and *U.S. v. James Harvey Wells,* ibid., file mm3406. On Wells, see Sutherland, *A Savage Conflict,* 275 and 354, n. 25.

30. For an example of President Johnson's commutation of a guerrilla's death sentence against the recommendation of Holt, see *U.S. v. Samuel "One Arm" Berry,* RG 153, Records of the Office of the Judge Advocate General (Army), 1792–2010, Court Martial Case Files file mm3127. For other examples of Johnson's interventions against execution of guerrillas, see *U.S. v. Joseph Morgan,* ibid., file mm3127 (convicted of attempted murder of General Canby); and *U.S. v. Omer Boudreaux,* ibid., file mm2802 (convicted of the rape of a civilian woman and the killing of a U.S. soldier).

31. *U.S. v. Jerome Clarke,* ibid., file mm1732; *U.S. v. Henry Magruder,* ibid., file mm2958; Henry C. Magruder, *Three Years in the Saddle: The Life and Confession of Henry C. Magruder, the Original "Sue Munday," the Scourge of Kentucky, Written by Himself* (Louisville, KY: Maj. Cyrus J. Wilson, 1865).

32. *Nashville Union,* Oct. 21, 1865, reprinted in *New York Herald,* Oct. 29, 1865, p. 2. See Aaron Astor, *The Civil War Along Tennessee's Cumberland Plateau* (Charleston, SC: The History Press, 2015), 113–33, 159–79; and Witt, *Lincoln's Code,* 297–98.

33. Sutherland, *A Savage Conflict,* 275–77.

34. W. T. Clarke to J. H. Baker, June 3, 1865, *OR, Armies,* ser. 1, vol. 46, pt. 3, 760. For a full accounting of the fate of guerrillas arrested and tried by military commissions between April and October 1865, see Caroline E. Janney, "Guerrillas, Vengeance, and Mercy After Appomattox: The Trial of John W. McCue," in Caroline E. Janney, Peter S. Carmichael, and Aaron Sheehan-Dean, eds., *The War That Made America: Essays Inspired by the Scholarship of Gary W. Gallagher* (Chapel Hill: University of North Carolina Press, 2024), 130.

35. Earl J. Hess, "Civil War Guerrillas in a Global, Comparative Context," in Brian D. McKnight and Barton A. Myers, eds., *The Guerrilla Hunters: Irregular Conflicts During the Civil War* (Baton Rouge: Louisiana State University Press, 2017), 345.

36. Andrew F. Lang, "Challenging the Union Citizen-Soldier Ideal," in McKnight and Myers, eds., *The Guerrilla Hunters,* 305–34.

37. Marley Brant, *The Outlaw Youngers: A Confederacy Brotherhood* (Lanham, MD: Madison Books, 1992), 72–75; Goodrich, *Black Flag,* 163–64.

38. James M. Smallwood, Barry A. Crouch, and Larry Peacock, *Murder and Mayhem: The War of Reconstruction in Texas* (College Station: Texas A&M University Press, 2003), 49; Elaine Frantz Parsons, *Ku-Klux: The Birth of the Klan During Reconstruction* (Chapel Hill: University of North Carolina Press, 2016), 27–34.

39. William A. Blair, *The Record of Murders and Outrages: Racial Violence and the Fight over Truth at the Dawn of Reconstruction* (Chapel Hill: University of North Carolina Press, 2021), 48; Mark Grimsley, "Wars for the American South: The First and Second Reconstructions Considered as Insurgencies," *Civil War History* 58 (Mar. 2012): 6–36.

40. Kidada E. Williams, *I Saw Death Coming: A History of Terror and Survival in the War Against Reconstruction* (New York: Bloomsbury, 2023), 41–47.

41. J. J. Cornwell to S. P. Lee, June 20, 1865, *OR, Navies,* ser. 1, vol. 27, 276; S. P. Lee to Gideon Welles, June 27, 1865, ibid., ser. 1, vol. 27, 282–83; James P. Foster to S. P. Lee, July 10, 1865, ibid., ser. 1, vol. 27, 294–95; S. P. Lee to Gideon Welles, July 18, 1865, ibid., ser. 1, vol. 27, 294; Beale, ed., *Diary of Gideon Welles,* vol. 2, 347.

42. Brainerd Dyer, "Confederate Naval and Privateering Activities in the Pacific," *Pacific Historical Review* 3 (Dec. 1934): 440–42; Benjamin Franklin Gilbert, "The Salvador Pirates," *Civil War History* 5 (1959): 294–307.

43. William C. Whittle, Jr., *The Voyage of the CSS* Shenandoah: *A Memorable Cruise,* eds. D. Alan Harris and Anne B. Harris (Tuscaloosa: University of Alabama Press, 2005), 84 (Dec. 6, 1864).

44. The *Shenandoah* took on four African Americans: Williams; Charles Hopkins, who, like Williams, was a free African American from the North ordered by Waddell to serve in the galley; Edward Weeks, who came aboard as the slave of a southern white man, George Canning, in early 1865; and Joseph Stevenson, a free Black sailor of whom little is known except that he was part of the crew of a U.S. vessel captured in April 1865 near Ascension (now Pohnpei), a tiny Pacific island roughly 1,000 miles north of the Solomon Islands. Of the sailors who refused to ship aboard the *Shenandoah* and were ultimately sent from the ship, none was reported by crew members as being Black. See Tom Chaffin, *Sea of Gray: The Around-the-World Odyssey of the Confederate Raider* Shenandoah (New York: Hill and Wang, 2006), 99–100, 107, 210, 340–43, 360.

45. Chaffin, *Sea of Gray,* 99–100, 160–61; John Baldwin and Ron Powers, *Last Flag Down: The Epic Journey of the Last Confederate Warship* (New York: Crown, 2007), 123, 146, 151, 172–73.

46. Whittle, *The Voyage of the CSS* Shenandoah, 124 (Mar. 14, 1865).

47. Whittle, *The Voyage of the CSS* Shenandoah, 170 (June 27, 1865); Baldwin and Powers, *Last Flag Down,* 208, 244–45; *Army and Navy Journal,* Aug. 12, 1865, p. 814.

48. Whittle, *The Voyage of the CSS* Shenandoah, 171 (June 28, 1865).

49. James D. Bulloch to James I. Waddell, June 19, 1865, *OR, Navies,* ser. 1, vol. 3, 776–77.

50. *Army and Navy Journal,* Apr. 15, 1865, p. 533; and ibid., May 6, 1865, p. 581.

51. Welles to George F. Pearson, Aug. 3, 1865, *OR, Navies,* ser. 1, vol. 27, 576. Because Welles had always followed the official U.S. line that the Confederacy was not a legitimate nation, he had regularly called Confederate cruisers "rebel pirates" even before the *Shenandoah* set sail.

52. Whittle, *The Voyage of the CSS* Shenandoah, 182 (Aug. 2, 1865); Chaffin, *Sea of Gray,* 301–4.
53. Chaffin, *Sea of Gray,* 350.
54. Waddell to Lord Earl Russell, Nov. 5, 1865, reprinted in *Army and Navy Journal,* Nov. 25, 1865, p. 212.
55. "The Salvador Pirates," *San Francisco Bulletin,* reprinted in *New York Times,* Aug. 12, 1865, p. 2; Dyer, "Confederate Naval and Privateering Activities in the Pacific," 442; Gilbert, "The Salvador Pirates," *Civil War History* 5 (1959): 302–6.
56. Beale, ed., *Diary of Gideon Welles,* vol. 2, 404.
57. "New Bedford" to the *Boston Daily Advertiser,* Feb. 7, 1866.
58. *Albany (NY) Journal,* reprinted in *Milwaukee Daily Sentinel,* Nov. 28, 1865.

12: The Final Trial

1. *Chicago Tribune,* Nov. 11, p. 1.
2. Article 148, General Order 100, https://avalon.law.yale.edu/19th_century /lieber.asp.
3. Article 56, General Order 100.
4. William Marvel, *Lincoln's Autocrat: The Life of Edwin Stanton* (Chapel Hill: University of North Carolina Press, 2015), 387–89.
5. Joan E. Cashin, *First Lady of the Confederacy: Varina Davis's Civil War* (Cambridge, MA: Harvard University Press, 2009), 174–75.
6. *PAJ,* vol. 9, 350–51.
7. William A. Blair, *With Malice Toward Some: Treason and Loyalty in the Civil War Era* (Chapel Hill: University of North Carolina Press, 2014), 1–3, 36–38, 239–41.
8. Cynthia Nicoletti, "The American Civil War as a Trial by Battle," *Law and History Review* 28 (Feb. 2010): 71–110.
9. Cynthia Nicoletti, *Secession on Trial: The Treason Prosecution of Jefferson Davis* (Cambridge: Cambridge University Press, 2017), 186. Although Davis never had a full civilian trial, a grand jury indicted him and a petit jury was assembled; both juries included African American men. See Nicoletti, *Secession on Trial,* 270–73.
10. Howard K. Beale, ed., *Diary of Gideon Welles* (W. W. Norton, 1960), vol. 2, 335–36; Cynthia Nicoletti, "Did Secession Really Die at Appomattox? The Strange Case of *U.S. v. Jefferson Davis*," *University of Toledo Law Review* 41 (Spring 2010): 595–96.
11. James Speed to Francis Lieber, June 27, 1865, box 62, folder LI 3211, Francis Lieber Papers, HEH.
12. Thomas E. Schott, *Alexander H. Stephens of Georgia: A Biography* (Baton Rouge: Louisiana State University Press, 1988), 454.
13. Lieut. Col. Stewart L. Woodford to Maj. Genl. John G. Foster, Aug. 17, 1864, reprinted in "Exchange of Prisoners," H. Ex. Doc. 32, 38th Cong., 2nd Sess., 85–86.
14. *Frank Leslie's Illustrated,* vol. 18, no. 455 (June 18, 1864), 193, 199 (quotation at

199); John Stauffer, "The 'Terrible Reality' of the First Living-Room Wars," in Anne Wilkes Tucker and Will Michels with Natalie Zelt, eds., *War/Photography: Images of Armed Conflict and Its Aftermath* (Houston: Museum of Fine Arts, Houston, 2012), 86–87; Vicki Goldberg, *The Power of Photography: How Photographs Changed Our Lives* (New York: Abbeville Press, 1991), 20–24.

15. Lucretia Bancroft Farnum to George Bancroft, San Francisco, June 30, 1865, George Bancroft Papers, MHS.

16. Martha Hodes, *Mourning Lincoln* (New Haven, CT: Yale University Press, 2015), 257.

17. Letter of G. W. McElres, Camp Fisk, Apr. 12, 1865, *Tipton (IA) Advertiser,* Apr. 27, 1865, p. 3.

18. Unless otherwise noted, the source for biographical information on Wirz is R. Fred Ruhlman, *Captain Henry Wirz and Andersonville Prison* (Knoxville: University of Tennessee Press, 2006).

19. William Marvel, *Andersonville: The Last Depot* (Chapel Hill: University of North Carolina Press, 1994), 35–38; *The Demon of Andersonville; or, the Trial of Wirz, for the Cruel Treatment and Brutal Murder of Helpless Union Prisoners in His Hands . . .* (Philadelphia: Barclay & Co., Publishers, 1865), 118.

20. *Haunted by Atrocity: Civil War Prisons in American Memory* (Baton Rouge: Louisiana State University Press, 2010), 27.

21. Ruhlman, *Captain Henry Wirz and Andersonville Prison,* 170.

22. Marvel, *Lincoln's Autocrat,* 388–89.

23. Susan Wallace to "My dear Brother," Sep. 30, 1865, Lew Wallace Papers, Indiana Historical Society, Indianapolis.

24. Robert Scott Davis, *Ghosts and Shadows of Andersonville: Essays on the Secret Social Histories of America's Deadliest Prison* (Macon, GA: Mercer University Press, 2006), 196–97.

25. Marouf Hasian, Jr., *In the Name of Necessity: Military Tribunals and the Loss of American Civil Liberties* (Tuscaloosa: University of Alabama Press, 2005), 129.

26. Report of the Judge Advocate General, "Trial of Henry Wirz," 814.

27. Charges and Specifications, "Trial of Henry Wirz," H. Ex. Doc. 23, 40th Cong., 2d Sess., 3–8. On the topic of "war crimes," see John Fabian Witt, *Lincoln's Code: The Laws of War in American History* (New York: The Free Press, 2012), 297, 323. In describing the trial and execution of Champ Ferguson in the summer of 1865, Witt writes that Ferguson was charged with "war crimes." That phrase does not appear in any of the proceedings against Ferguson. Witt rightly points out that Francis Lieber was the first to use the term "war-crime," and that he did so in a memo most likely intended for Secretary of War Stanton that is undated but probably was written in 1865. Lieber did not define "war-crime" in the memo. In the same document, Lieber used the phrase "military crime," which he defined as "a crime at the common law of war." The context of the memo is important. Lieber was not commenting on the Wirz trial. Rather, as Witt writes, he was offering advice on how best to prosecute Jefferson Davis. See Francis Lieber, Memorandum, box 2, folder 33, Joseph Holt Papers, MDLC.

28. "Trial of Henry Wirz," 5.

29. Walter Johnson, *River of Dark Dreams: Slavery and Empire in the Cotton King-dom* (Cambridge, MA: Harvard University Press, 2013), 234–40 (the phrase "weaponized dogs" appears on 235). See Bill L. Smith, "'Open Jaws of this Monster-Tyranny': Abolitionism, Resistance, and Slave-Hunting Canines," *American Nineteenth Century History* 23 (May 2022): 61–92.

30. *Narrative of the Life of Frederick Douglass* (1845), chapter 10 (Project Guten-berg edition).

31. Thomas Gossett, *Uncle Tom's Cabin and American Culture* (Dallas: Southern Methodist University Press, 1985), 268; John W. Frick, *Uncle Tom's Cabin on the American Stage and Screen* (New York: Palgrave, 2012), 123–25. As Frick explains, prior to the Civil War, the dogs were represented by offstage howling and whistles. Only about ten years after the war did actual dogs begin to be used in stage shows.

32. Testimony of John A. Cain, "Trial of Henry Wirz," 401.

33. Testimony of Samuel M. Riker, "Trial of Henry Wirz," 371.

34. Testimony of Lewis Dyer, "Trial of Henry Wirz," 408.

35. Testimony of William Henry Jennings, "Trial of Henry Wirz," 187 (whipped with thirty lashes and put into the stocks); John Fisher, ibid., 280–81 ("bucked and gagged, and whipped with thirty-nine lashes," and seeing three other African American soldiers with stripes on their backs from whipping at the prison); Lewis Dyer, ibid., 408 (not whipped himself but knew of one or two men who were whipped, at least one who received 250 lashes of the 500 sup-posedly ordered by Wirz—the extraordinarily high number, a fatal sentence, throws some doubt on the testimony's reliability).

36. Testimony of F. G. Castlen, "Trial of Henry Wirz," 109; testimony of Oli-ver B. Fairbanks, ibid., 154–55; testimony of Joseph R. Achuff, ibid., 167; tes-timony of W. W. Crandall, ibid., 259; testimony of Charles E. Tibbles, ibid., 295.

37. Testimony of Frederick Guscetti, "Trial of Henry Wirz," 519, 527.

38. Testimony of Calvin Huneycutt, "Trial of Henry Wirz," 129; testimony of Frank Maddox, ibid., 177; testimony of Vincenzio Bardo, ibid., 512 (Bardo claimed that he was the white man in question).

39. Testimony of F. G. Castlen, "Trial of Henry Wirz," 113–14; testimony of Rob-ert Merton, ibid., 174.

40. Karen Halttunen, "Humanitarianism and the Pornography of Pain in Anglo-American Culture," *American Historical Review* 100 (Apr. 1995): 303–34; Elizabeth B. Clark, "'The Sacred Rights of the Weak': Pain, Sympathy, and the Culture of Individual Rights in Antebellum America," *Journal of American History* 82 (Sep. 1995): 463–93.

41. Testimony of Calvin Huneycutt, "Trial of Henry Wirz," 129.

42. Kristin Hoganson, "Garrisonian Abolitionists and the Rhetoric of Gender, 1850–1860," *American Quarterly* 45 (Dec. 1993): 558–95.

43. Caroline E. Janney, *Remembering the Civil War: Reunion and the Limits of Rec-onciliation* (Chapel Hill: University of North Carolina Press, 2013), 50.

44. "Trial of Henry Wirz," 772.

45. "Trial of Henry Wirz," 758–62.

46. "Report of the Judge Advocate General," Nov. 13, 1865, in *Annual Report of the Secretary of War, 1865,* 39th Cong., 1st Sess., H. Exec. Doc. 1, pt. 2, 1005.

47. "Trial of Henry Wirz," 706.

48. Ruhlman, *Captain Henry Wirz and Andersonville Prison,* 207–8; Tony Horwitz, *Confederates in the Attic: Dispatches from the Unfinished Civil War* (New York: Pantheon, 1998), 318–25.

49. AJ, "Proclamation 134—Granting Amnesty to Participants in the Rebellion, with Certain Exceptions," May 29, 1865, Art. VI, https://www.presidency .ucsb.edu/documents/proclamation-134-granting-amnesty-participants-the -rebellion-with-certain-exceptions.

50. "Trial of Henry Wirz," 813.

51. "Trial of Henry Wirz," 10.

52. "Trial of Henry Wirz," 3.

53. "Trial of Henry Wirz," 723–24.

54. "Perley" [Benjamin Perley Poore] to the *Boston Journal,* Nov. 10, 1865, reprinted in the *Orleans Independent Standard* (Irasburgh, VT), Nov. 17, 1865, p. 2.

55. Ruhlman, *Captain Henry Wirz and Andersonville Prison,* 230–31.

13: Imperfectly Closed

1. Frederick Douglass, "Abraham Lincoln, a Speech," undated manuscript, MDLC, Washington, D.C., https://rememberinglincoln.fords.org/node/812. On the date of the draft of the speech, see Theodore Hamm, "'The Clouds That Lower at This Time on the Political Sky': When Frederick Douglass Spoke at BAM," *Village Voice,* Jan. 18, 2017.

2. George W. Julian, *Dangers and Duties . . .* (speech delivered in the hall of the House of Representatives, Indianapolis, Ind., Nov. 17, 1865) (Cincinnati: Gazette Steam Print, 1865), 15, 6. Dana's views at this time can be found in his letters to Charles F. Adams, Sr., Sep. 14, 1865, and Dec. 18, 1865, both in Adams Family Papers, microfilm reel 577, MHS. Dana was much more restrictive in his views on Black suffrage than Douglass was; Dana told Adams that Black suffrage should not be a requirement of new southern state constitutions but only that "there *ought* to be a suffrage attainable by intelligent and respectable people of color." RHD to Adams, Dec. 18, 1865, ibid.

3. C. Comstock to Manton Marble, Apr. 21, 1865, Manton M. Marble Papers, MDLC, Washington, D.C.

4. Michael Vorenberg, *Final Freedom: The Civil War, the Abolition of Slavery, and the Thirteenth Amendment* (New York: Cambridge University Press, 2001), 232.

5. Clinton B. Fisk to O. O. Howard, July 20, 1865, *FDHE,* ser. 1, vol. 2, 706.

6. John M. Palmer, *Personal Recollections of John M. Palmer: The Story of an Earnest Life* (Cincinnati: The Robert Clarke Company, 1901), 242–43; *FDHE,* ser. 1, vol. 1, 516–18; John M. Palmer to AJ, July 27, 1865, reprinted in *Boston Daily Advertiser,* Aug. 10, 1865, p. 3; Charles J. Meng to AJ, Oct. 3, 1865,

Andrew Johnson Papers, MDLC, Washington, D.C.; John M. Palmer to Joseph S. Fowler, Sep. 4, 1865, and Sep. 7, 1865, both in John M. Palmer letter books, Illinois State Library, Springfield, IL.

7. Donald G. Nieman, *To Set the Law in Motion: The Freedmen's Bureau and the Legal Rights of Blacks, 1865–1868* (Millwood, NY: KTO Press, 1979), 43–44.

8. "The Insurgent States," *Army and Navy Journal,* Sep. 9, 1865, p. 40.

9. Thad Sitton and James H. Conrad, *Freedom Colonies: Independent Black Texans in the Time of Jim Crow* (Austin: University of Texas Press, 2005), 13.

10. Sitton and Conrad, *Freedom Colonies,* 11.

11. Sidney Andrews, *The South Since the War* (Boston: Ticknor and Fields, 1866), 21.

12. Garrett Epps, "The Undiscovered Country: Northern Views of the Defeated South and the Political Background of the Fourteenth Amendment," *Temple Political and Civil Rights Law Review* 13 (2004): 411–28.

13. Carl Schurz to AJ, Aug. 29, 1865, in Brooks D. Simpson et al., *Advice After Appomattox: Letters to Andrew Johnson, 1865–1866* (Knoxville: University of Tennessee Press, 1987), 114.

14. Vorenberg, *Final Freedom,* 183–84. See LaWanda Cox and John H. Cox, *Politics, Principle, and Prejudice, 1865–1866: Dilemma of Reconstruction America* (New York: The Free Press, 1963), 50–67, 88–95.

15. Cox and Cox, *Politics, Principle, and Prejudice,* 103.

16. "Report of Carl Schurz . . . ," in "Message of the President of the United States," 39th Cong., 1st Sess., Sen. Ex. Doc. 2, 28.

17. Hans L. Trefousse, *Carl Schurz: A Biography,* 2nd ed. (New York: Fordham University Press, 1998), 155.

18. "Report of Carl Schurz . . . ," 21.

19. "Report of Carl Schurz . . . ," 45.

20. Elizabeth R. Varon, *Appomattox: Victory, Defeat, and Freedom at the End of the Civil War* (New York: Oxford University Press, 2014), 238–39.

21. Fergus M. Bordewich, *Klan War: Ulysses S. Grant and the Battle to Save Reconstruction* (New York: Alfred A. Knopf, 2023), 232–39.

22. Brooks D. Simpson, *Let Us Have Peace: Ulysses S. Grant and the Politics of War and Reconstruction, 1861–1868* (Chapel Hill: University of North Carolina Press, 1991), 112–13.

23. Simpson, *Let Us Have Peace,* 119.

24. W. D. Gale to "Meck" [William Mecklenburg Polk], Aug. 26, 1865, Southern Historical Collection, University of North Carolina, Chapel Hill.

25. "Letter of General Grant Concerning Affairs at the South," Dec. 18, 1865, in "Message of the President of the United States," 39th Cong. 1st Sess., Sen. Ex. Doc. 2, 106.

26. Vorenberg, *Final Freedom,* 224–29.

27. Joshua Speed to James Speed, Sep. 15, 1865, in James Speed, *James Speed: A Personality* (Louisville, KY: John P. Morton, 1914), 66–67.

28. Vorenberg, *Final Freedom,* 232.

29. Howard Devon Hamilton, "The Legislative and Judicial History of the Thirteenth Amendment" (PhD diss., University of Illinois, 1950), 29.

30. "Message of the President of the United States," 39th Cong., 1st Sess., Sen. Ex. Doc. 26, 254, 198.

31. Benjamin Butler to Thaddeus Stevens, Nov. 20, 1865, Thaddeus Stevens Papers, MDLC, Washington, D.C.

32. AJ, "Annual Message to Congress," Dec. 4, 1865, *PAJ*, vol. 9, 472.

33. John H. and LaWanda Cox, "Andrew Johnson and His Ghost Writers: An Analysis of the Freedmen's Bureau and Civil Rights Veto Messages," *Mississippi Valley Historical Review* 48 (Dec. 1961): 460–61.

34. "Message of the President of the United States," 39th Cong., 1st Sess., Sen. Ex. Doc. 2, 1.

35. Trefousse, *Carl Schurz*, 159–60.

36. A. Y. Moore, *The Life of Schuyler Colfax* (Philadelphia: T. B. Peterson and Brothers, 1868), 324.

37. *CG*, 39th Cong., 1st Sess., 5.

38. William A. Dobak, *Freedom by the Sword: The U.S. Colored Troops, 1862–1867* (Washington, D.C.: U.S. Army Center of Military History, 2011), 469.

39. R. B. Habersham to Isaac P. Hazard, Dec. 10, 1865, Isaac P. Hazard Papers, Rhode Island Historical Society, Providence, RI.

40. Calvin Holly to O. O. Howard, Dec. 16, 1865, *FDHE*, ser. 2, 756.

41. "Letter of General Grant Concerning Affairs at the South," Dec. 18, 1865, in "Message of the President of the United States," 39th Cong., 1st Sess., Sen. Ex. Doc. 2, 106–7; Brooks D. Simpson, "Quandaries of Command: Ulysses S. Grant and Black Soldiers," in David Blight and Brooks D. Simpson, eds., *Union and Emancipation: Essays on Politics and Race in the Civil War Era* (Kent, OH: Kent State University Press, 1997), 141–42.

42. Mary F. Berry, *Toward Freedom and Civil Rights for the Freedmen: Military Policy Origins of the Thirteenth Amendment and the Civil Rights Act of 1866* (Department of History, Howard University, 1975), 13–17.

43. James Garfield, "Oration delivered at Ravenna, Ohio, July 4, 1865," in Burke A. Hinsdale, ed., *The Works of James Abram Garfield* (Boston: J. R. Osgood and Company, 1882), vol. 1, 86.

44. AJ, "Annual Message to Congress," Dec. 4, 1865, *PAJ*, vol. 9, 472.

45. *PAJ*, vol. 8, 63.

46. *PAJ*, vol. 9, 221–22.

47. Salmon P. Chase to William Sprague, Sep. 6, 1865, Salmon P. Chase Papers, 2nd series, MDLC, Washington, D.C.

48. *PAJ*, vol. 9, 223. The newspaper report of the meeting identified the regiment as the 1st District of Columbia Colored Regiment, but the designation of this unit had been changed in April 1864 to the 33rd U.S. Colored Troops.

49. James Brewer Stewart, *Wendell Phillips: Liberty's Hero* (Baton Rouge: Louisiana State University Press, 1896), 268–69.

50. *PAJ*, vol. 10, 41–48.

51. Robert S. Levine, *The Failed Promise: Reconstruction, Frederick Douglass, and the Impeachment of Andrew Johnson* (New York: W. W. Norton, 2021), 102.

14: Proclaiming Peace

1. Ch. XC, *U.S., Statutes at Large,* 13:507.
2. "Case of Jefferson Davis," Jan. 6, 1866, *Official Opinions of the Attorneys General of the United States* (Washington, D.C.: W. H. and O. H. Morrison, 1869), 11:411.
3. Ch. CC, Ch. XC, *U.S., Statutes at Large,* 14:173–77; Mark A. Graber, "The Second Freedmen's Bureau Bill's Constitution," *Texas Law Review* 94 (2016): 1361–1402.
4. *CG,* 39th Cong., 1st Sess., 363.
5. *CG,* 39th Cong., 1st Sess., 320.
6. *CG,* 39th Cong., 1st Sess., 320.
7. Benjamin P. Thomas and Harold M. Hyman, *Stanton: The Life and Times of Lincoln's Secretary of War* (New York: Alfred A. Knopf, 1962), 476.
8. Brooks D. Simpson, *Let Us Have Peace: Ulysses S. Grant and the Politics of War and Reconstruction, 1861–1868* (Chapel Hill: University of North Carolina Press, 1991), 127–28.
9. John H. and LaWanda Cox, "Andrew Johnson and His Ghost Writers, An Analysis of the Freedmen's Bureau and Civil Rights Veto Messages," *Mississippi Valley Historical Review* 48 (Dec. 1961): 464. Seward expounded on the point about the first Freedmen's Bureau being allowed to exist for another year or so in a speech delivered a few days after writing the memo to Johnson. See William H. Seward, *Restoration of Union* (Washington, D.C., 1866) (speech at Cooper Institute, New York City, Feb. 22, 1866), 14.
10. *PAJ,* vol. 10, 120.
11. *PAJ,* vol. 10, 122.
12. *CG,* 39th Cong., 1st Sess., 986.
13. *CG,* 39th Cong., 1st Sess., 937, 939.
14. *CG,* 39th Cong., 1st Sess., 931–32.
15. AJ, "Washington's Birthday Address," Feb. 22, 1866, *PAJ,* vol. 10, 150–51.
16. AJ, "Washington's Birthday Address," Feb. 22, 1866, *PAJ,* vol. 10, 153.
17. AJ, "Washington's Birthday Address," Feb. 22, 1866, *PAJ,* vol. 10, 157.
18. Kate Masur, *Until Justice Be Done: America's First Civil Rights Movement, from the Revolution to Reconstruction* (New York: W. W. Norton, 2021), 327–28.
19. *CG,* 39th Cong., 1st Sess., 1755.
20. Michael Vorenberg, "The 1866 Civil Rights Act and the Beginning of Military Reconstruction," in Christian Samito, ed., *The Greatest and the Grandest Act: The Civil Rights Act of 1866 from Reconstruction to Today* (Carbondale: Southern Illinois University Press, 2018), 62–67, 75–84.
21. For Trumbull's remarks on the military provisions of the Civil Rights bill, as well as the objections of Hendricks, see *CG,* 39th Cong., 1st Sess., 602–6. Also see ibid., 1760.
22. "An Act to Increase and Fix the Military Peace Establishment of the United States," *U.S. Statutes at Large,* 39th Cong., 1st Sess., Chap. 14, 332–38. The regular army prior to the Civil War consisted of roughly 16,000 men. The 1866 law increased that number to about 54,000. The number ultimately would be reduced to about 37,000 in 1869 and then to about 27,500 in 1876.

See Marvin A. Kreidberg and Merton G. Henry, *History of Military Mobilization in the United States Army, 1775–1945* (Washington, D.C.: U.S. Department of the Army, 1955), 141.

23. AJ, "Veto of Civil Rights Bill," Mar. 27, 1866, *PAJ*, vol. 10, 312–20; Gregory P. Downs, *After Appomattox: Military Occupation and the Ends of War* (Cambridge, MA: Harvard University Press, 2015), 132–33.

24. *PAJ*, vol. 9, 481; "Message of the President of the United States," 39th Cong., 1st Sess., Sen. Ex. Doc. 2, 1; *PAJ*, vol. 10, 122.

25. Seward, *Restoration of Union*, 9.

26. Seward, *Restoration of Union*, 8.

27. Seward, *Restoration of Union*, 13.

28. "An Interview with Secretary Seward," New York *Evening Post*, Mar. 24, 1888, p. 14.

29. Seward, *Restoration of Union*, 14; for Lincoln's 1861 Proclamation, see *CWAL*, vol. 4, 331–33.

30. AJ, "Veto of Civil Rights Bill," Mar. 27, 1866, *PAJ*, vol. 10, 319–20.

31. *New York Herald*, Mar. 26, 1866, p. 4.

32. G. W. Williams to AJ, Apr. 12, 1866, *PAJ*, vol. 10, 409–10.

33. Downs, *After Appomattox*, 146–47.

34. Howard K. Beale, ed., *The Diary of Edward Bates, 1859–1866* (Washington, D.C.: Government Printing Office, 1933), 556.

35. James Speed to Francis Lieber, May 26, 1866 (LI 3213), Francis Lieber Papers, HEH.

36. Douglas R. Egerton, *The Wars of Reconstruction: The Brief, Violent History of America's Most Progressive Era* (New York: Bloomsbury, 2013), 202.

37. Harry W. Pfanz, "Soldiering in the South During the Reconstruction Period, 1865–1877" (PhD diss., Ohio State University, 1958), 508–9.

38. *Chicago Tribune*, Apr. 4, 1866, p. 1.

39. Vorenberg, "The 1866 Civil Rights Act and the Beginning of Military Reconstruction," 70–72; Downs, *After Appomattox*, 147.

40. "The Late Riots," Memphis, TN, *Public Ledger*, May 3, 1866, p. 2.

41. Hannah Rosen, *Terror in the Heart of Freedom: Citizenship, Sexual Violence, and the Meaning of Race in the Postemancipation South* (Chapel Hill: University of North Carolina Press, 2009), 63–73.

42. "From New Orleans: Military Report on the New Orleans Riot," Nashville, TN, *Republican Banner*, Sep. 7, 1866, p. 3.

43. Joseph Holt to Henry C. Warmoth, Aug. 1, 1866, Henry Clay Warmoth Papers, Special Collections, University of North Carolina, Chapel Hill.

44. AJ, "Proclamation *re* End of Insurrection," *PAJ*, vol. 11, 103.

15: The Fight for the End

1. AJ, "Washington's Birthday Address," Feb. 22, 1866, *PAJ*, vol. 10, 156.

2. Speech of James R. Doolittle, Aug. 14, 1866, in *The Proceedings of the National Union Convention, Held at Philadelphia, August 14, 1866* (np, 1866), 9.

3. Speech of Henry Raymond, Aug. 16, 1866, in *The Proceedings of the National Union Convention*, 18.

4. Eric Foner, *Reconstruction: America's Unfinished Revolution, 1863–1877* (New York: Harper and Row, 1988), 265.

5. Eric L. McKitrick, *Andrew Johnson and Reconstruction* (Chicago: University of Chicago Press, 1960), 434–36.

6. Eric Foner, *The Second Founding: How the Civil War and Reconstruction Remade the Constitution* (New York: W. W. Norton, 2019), 55–88.

7. Thaddeus Stevens, "Speech to Soldiers and Citizens of Washington, December 2, 1866," in Beverly Wilson Palmer, ed., *The Selected Papers of Thaddeus Stevens* (Pittsburgh: University of Pittsburgh Press, 1998), 2:207.

8. William A. Blair, *The Record of Murders and Outrages: Racial Violence and the Fight over Truth at the Dawn of Reconstruction* (Chapel Hill: University of North Carolina Press, 2021), 18.

9. Blair, *The Record of Murders and Outrages*, 18.

10. *PUSG*, vol. 17, 50–51.

11. William S. McFeely, *Yankee Stepfather: General O. O. Howard and the Freedmen* (New York: W. W. Norton, 1968), 291–94.

12. "Message of the President of the United States," 39th Cong., 2nd Sess., Sen. Ex. Doc. 29, vol. 2, 37–43.

13. *PUSG*, vol. 17, 51–52.

14. Blair, *The Record of Murders and Outrages*, 22.

15. William S. McFeely, *Grant: A Biography* (New York: W. W. Norton, 1981), 252. See Joan Waugh, *U. S. Grant: American Hero, American Myth* (Chapel Hill: University of North Carolina Press, 2013), 115.

16. *Weekly North-Carolina Standard*, Dec. 25, 1866, p. 1; Mark L. Bradley, *Bluecoats and Tarheels: Soldiers and Civilians in Reconstruction North Carolina* (Lexington: University Press of Kentucky, 2009), 125–26.

17. Richard B. McCaslin, "William Longworth, Republican Villain," in Kenneth W. Howell, ed., *Still the Arena of Civil War: Violence and Turmoil in Reconstruction Texas, 1865–1874* (Denton: University of North Texas Press, 2012), 138.

18. Downs, *After Appomattox*, 152.

19. *Chicago Tribune*, Dec. 28, 1866, p. 2.

20. The divisive politics of truth-telling during this period and afterward are the subjects of Blair, *The Record of Murders and Outrages*; and Mark Wahlgren Summers, *A Dangerous Stir: Fear, Paranoia, and the Making of Reconstruction* (Chapel Hill: University of North Carolina Press, 2014).

21. James G. Randall, ed., *The Diary of Orville Hickman Browning* (Springfield: Illinois State Historical Library, 1933), vol. 2, 130.

22. Draft proclamation in Stanton's hand, Feb. 9, 1867, #14468, Edwin M. Stanton Papers, MDLC, Washington, D.C.

23. 39th Cong., 2nd Sess., Sen. Ex. Doc. 29, 12–43.

24. Randall, ed., *The Diary of Orville Hickman Browning*, vol. 2, 131.

25. *CG*, 39th Cong., 2nd Sess., 542.

26. Brenda Wineapple, *The Impeachers: The Trial of Andrew Johnson and the Dream of a Just Nation* (New York: Random House, 2019), 185.

27. Downs, *After Appomattox,* 168. See *CG,* 39th Cong., 2nd Sess., 1076; and Harold M. Hyman, *A More Perfect Union: The Impact of the Civil War and Reconstruction on the Constitution* (New York: Alfred A. Knopf, 1973), 499, n. 15.

28. Downs, *After Appomattox,* 167–78.

29. RHD to Charles F. Adams, Sr., Apr. 14, 1867, in Charles Francis Adams, *Richard Henry Dana: A Biography* (Boston: Houghton, Mifflin and Company, 1890), 2:334.

30. *CG,* 39th Cong., 2nd Sess., 1974.

31. Downs, *After Appomattox,* 150–51; *The Protector,* 79 U.S. 700 (U.S. Supreme Court Opinion, 1871).

Epilogue: The Peacemakers

1. T. S. Eliot, "Little Gidding," V, lines 240–42, in T. S. Eliot, *Four Quartets,* rev. ed. (New York: Harcourt Brace Jovanovich, 1971), 59.

2. Bruce Catton, *A Stillness at Appomattox* (Garden City, NY: Doubleday, 1954), 379–80.

3. Allan Nevins, *The War for the Union,* vol. 4, *The Organized War to Victory, 1864–1865* (New York: Charles Scribner's Sons, 1971), 359.

4. Jeffrey W. Hunt, *The Last Battle of the Civil War: Palmetto Ranch* (Austin: University of Texas Press, 2002); Phillip Thomas Tucker, *The Final Fury: Palmito Ranch, The Last Battle of the Civil War* (Mechanicsburg, PA: Stackpole Books, 2001).

5. Charles A. Misulia, *Columbus, Georgia, 1865: The Last True Battle of the Civil War* (Tuscaloosa: University of Alabama Press, 2010), 233–47.

6. "Report of Col. Theodore H. Barrett, Sixty-second U.S. Colored Troops," *OR, Armies,* ser. 1, vol. 48, pt. 1, 265–67.

7. Richard Zuczek, "The Last Campaign of the Civil War: South Carolina and the Revolution of 1876," *Civil War History* 42 (Mar. 1996): 31; for the events at Ellenton, SC, see ibid., 25.

8. Gregory P. Downs, "A Palace That Will Fall upon Them: Reconstruction as a Problem of Occupation," *Reviews in American History* 39 (Mar. 2011): 118–26.

9. Alan Taylor, *American Civil Wars: A Continental History, 1850–1873* (New York: W. W. Norton, 2024); Jewel L. Spangler and Frank Towers, eds. *Remaking North American Sovereignty: State Transformation in the 1860s* (New York: Fordham University Press, 2020), 1–79.

10. Rachel Purvis, "Maintaining Intact Our Homogeneousness: Race, Citizenship, and Reconstructing Cherokee" (PhD diss., University of Mississippi, 2012); Claudio Saunt, "The Paradox of Freedom: Tribal Sovereignty and Emancipation During the Reconstruction of Indian Territory," *Journal of Southern History* 70 (Feb. 2004): 63–94.

11. Ned Blackhawk, *The Rediscovery of America: Native Peoples and the Unmaking of U.S. History* (New Haven, CT: Yale University Press, 2023), 339–53; Pekka Hämäläinen, *Lakota America: A New History of Indigenous Power* (New Haven,

CT: Yale University Press, 2019), 267–373; Elliott West, *The Last Indian War: The Nez Perce Story* (New York: Oxford University Press, 2009), 123–282.

12. *U.S. Statutes at Large*, 37th Cong., 2nd Sess., Chap. 166, 566.

13. Transcriptions of the relevant correspondence involving Ramsey and Devens, including the transcription of a May 6, 1880, letter from U.S. Solicitor General S. F. Phillips to Ramsey, approved by Ramsey, that declared the retention of the 1st Michigan Cavalry beyond mid-1865 lawful and the soldiers in question "deserters," may be found in Administrative Precedent File ("Frech File"), RG 94, box 16, file E8A9F(3), "Documents on the Termination Date of the Civil War," NA. Pension files of one of the soldiers, Edward Corselius, affirm that he was classified as a deserter, though they also suggest that he ultimately received a pension after new pension acts were passed in the early twentieth century (only the pension index cards for Corselius and his fellow deserters are available; the actual pension files have been lost). See "Corselius, Edward," Jan. 3, 1934, U.S. Civil War Pensions Index, 1861–1900, RG 15, NA; and "Corselius, Edward," Sep. 26, 1913, RG 15, U.S. Veterans Administration Pension Payment Cards, NA.

14. William H. Glasson, *Federal Military Pensions in the United States*, ed. David Kinley (New York: Oxford University Press, 1918), 234.

15. *Congressional Record*, 51st Cong., 1st Sess., 840–42 (quotation by Davis at 842).

16. "Service in and Close of War of Rebellion . . . ," *Decisions of the Department of the Interior in Appealed Pension and Bounty-Land Claims* (Washington, D.C.: Government Printing Office, 1895), vol. 7, 532–34; Glasson, *Federal Military Pensions in the United States*, 114–15; Sen. Rep. 1613, "Granting Pensions to Certain Soldiers Who Served in the Indian Wars from 1859–1898, and for Other Purposes," 69th Cong., 2nd Sess., 1–3. On the difference in pension amounts received by "Indian-war veterans" and "Civil War veterans," see 74th Cong., 2nd Sess., House of Representatives, *Pensions-Indian Wars: Hearing Before the Committee on Pensions*, Apr. 7, 1936 (Washington, D.C.: Government Printing Office, 1936), 2.

17. William Chapman, "Appomattox Centennial Rites Subdued," *Washington Post*, Apr. 10, 1965, p. 1965, p. A3.

18. *Address by Bruce Catton at Appomattox Court House, April 9, 1965, The Centennial Anniversary of the Surrender of General Robert E. Lee of the Army of Northern Virginia* (Richmond: Virginia Civil War Commission, 1965), 12–13.

19. Tania Long, "Centennial Today at Appomattox," *New York Times*, Apr. 9, 1965, p. 35.

20. Brad Kutner, "The Year That Drove Old Dixie Down," Courthouse News Service, Apr. 11, 2021.

21. Elizabeth R. Varon, *Appomattox: Victory, Defeat, and Freedom at the End of the Civil War* (New York: Oxford University Press, 2014). See "Annual Commemoration of Surrender and Freedom Day," Appomattox Court House, National Historic Park, Virginia, National Park Service (https://www.nps .gov). I am grateful to James C. Bailey, Elizabeth Parnicza, Ernie Price, Patrick Schroeder, and Robin F. Snyder, all National Park Service historians who have relayed to me the changes involving African American history made to

the Appomattox Court House National Park; I have been able to detail only some of these changes here.

22. David W. Blight, "The Civil War Isn't Over," *The Atlantic,* Apr. 8, 2015.
23. "The Civil War; Interviews with Barbara Fields," transcript, American Archive of Public Broadcasting, Apr. 13, 1988, https://americanarchive.org /catalog/cpb-aacip_509-2r3nv99t98.
24. Shmuley Boteach, "Can Biden Overcome His Afghanistan Mistake?" *Jerusalem Post* (online edition), Aug. 30, 2021.
25. A. J. McDougall, "Trump Suggests Robert E. Lee Would Have Won in Afghanistan," *Daily Beast,* Sep. 8, 2021.
26. Dillon Carroll, "The Future in Afghanistan May Be Key to the Well-Being of America's Soldiers," *Washington Post,* May 6, 2021.
27. Laura Rozen, "In W.H., Are Pictures Telling a Story?" *Politico,* Nov. 15, 2009; email of Alexandra C. Lane to Michael Vorenberg, May 19, 2021.

A Note on Language

1. "Black and White: A Matter of Capitalization," CMOS Shop Talk, June 22, 2020, https://cmosshoptalk.com/2020/06/22/black-and-white-a-matter-of -capitalization.
2. James Robert Burns, "'Slaves' and 'Slave Owners' or 'Enslaved People' and 'Enslavers'?," *Transactions of the Royal Historical Society* (2023): 1–18.
3. Bryan C. Rindfleisch, "What We Say Matters: The Power of Words in American and Indigenous History," *American Historian* 11 (Feb. 2017): 23–27.
4. Eric Foner, *Reconstruction: America's Unfinished Revolution, 1863–1877,* updated edition (New York: HarperPerennial, 2014).
5. A number of excellent works use the phrase "long Reconstruction" to signal an argument that Reconstruction extended beyond the temporal bounds of 1863 to 1877. For a recent book that makes a compelling case for expanding the dates of Reconstruction, see Manisha Sinha, *The Rise and Fall of the Second American Republic: Reconstruction, 1860–1920* (New York: Liveright, 2024).

List of Illustrations

Interior

Insert

Index

Page numbers in *italics* refer to illustrations.

Juaristas, 127–8, 213–15, 223
  See also Juárez, Benito
Julian, George W., 277
Juneteenth, xxvi–xxvii, xxx, 152–3, 193,
  280, 393n59, *insert 8*

Kansas, xxiii, 94, 234–5
Keetoowah Society, 162, 163, 164
Kelso, John R., 225–6
Kent, Edward, 182
Kentucky
  Black testimonial rights in, 195
  emancipation and enslavement in,
    197–200, 399–400nn73–74
  guerrilla fighting in, 94, 235, 237
  slaveholders move of enslaved people
    from, 134–5
  slavery survival in, 129–30, 131–3,
    197–200, 278–80, 390n5
Kidd, James Harvey, 210
Kirby Smith, Cassie, 216
Kirby Smith, Edmund, 56, 92–3, 98,
    104–5, 381n18
  alliance with Maximilian, 106–7, 108,
    109, 127–8, 213–16, 217–19
  alliance with Native Americans,
    168–74
  emigration to Mexico and Cuba of,
    114, 126, 213, 216–17
  surrender of, xvi, 100, 111–15, 124, 126,
    171–2, 211, 213
  surrender of as end of the war, 113–15,
    114, 117, 120
  See also Trans-Mississippi region
Knights of the White Camellia, 240
Ku Klux Klan, 89, 240–1, 285

Lakota Sioux, 160, 165, 167–8, 345, 348
Langston, John Mercer, 199
LeConte, Emma, 64
Lee, Fitzhugh "Fitz," 31, 39
Lee, Henry "Light-Horse Harry," 33
Lee, Robert E.
  Davis relationship with, 68–9, 75
  delaying tactics before surrender of,
    29–32

farewell speech to Army of Northern
  Virginia by, 39–40
fighting at Appomattox Court House
  under, 31–2, 33–4, 38
guerrilla warfare rejected by, 32–3, 96
parole given to, 69, 261–2
peace discussions with Grant, 1, 47–9,
  49, 56, 68–9, 380n39
plan to join with Johnston's forces, 6,
  9, 13, 15–16, 31
Richmond defense by, 8, 13–14
trial and execution of, calls for, 40–1,
  52–3, 69, 258, 261–2
  See also Appomattox Court House,
  surrender
Lee, Sydney Smith, Jr., 245, 248, 254
Lemann, Nicolas, 346
Liberator, 61
Lieber, Francis, 95, 187–9, 227–9, 239,
  258–9, 263, 272, 314, 408n27
Lincoln (film), xxv
Lincoln, Abraham
  Black Americans, attitudes toward,
    xxvi–xxvii, xxx, 53–4, 55, 86, 129–31,
    138
  City Point visit by, 3–4, 7–12, *8*,
    26–8
  compared to Johnson, 318
  day of mourning for, 129
  death of, 63
  end of slavery and, xxx, 53–4, 138
  funeral train of, 77
  Hampton Roads meeting, 4, 6, 11–12,
    16, 107, 229
  kidnapping of, plans for, 55
  last speech of, 51–5, 84
  naval blockade, lifting of by, 51–2, 84
  Reconstruction Proclamation (1863),
    79, 131–2
  reelection campaign platform of, xxx,
    131
  relationship with Johnson of, 27
  relationship with Seward of,
    10–11, 28
  relationship with Sherman of, 9
  Richmond visit by, 14–20, *insert 1*

A Note About the Author

Michael Vorenberg is a professor of history at Brown University, in Providence, Rhode Island. He is the author of *Final Freedom: The Civil War, the Abolition of Slavery, and the Thirteenth Amendment,* which was a finalist for the Lincoln Prize and a key source for Steven Spielberg's 2012 film, *Lincoln.* He is also the author of *The Emancipation Proclamation: A Brief History with Documents,* as well as a number of essays on slavery, emancipation, and the U.S. Constitution. His writings have appeared in the *Chicago Tribune, The New York Times, Politico,* and *The Washington Post.*

A Note on the Type

This book was set in a modern adaptation of a type designed by the first William Caslon (1692–1766). The Caslon face, an artistic, easily read type, has enjoyed more than two centuries of popularity in our own country. It is of interest to note that the first copies of the Declaration of Independence and the first paper currency distributed to the citizens of the newborn nation were printed in this typeface.

Composed by North Market Street Graphics,
Lancaster, Pennsylvania

Designed by Michael Collica